Contents

KU-788-721

Preface viii
Acknowledgements xi
Guided tour xiv

CONTEXT

Chapter 1: Introduction to Electronic Commerce 3
The background to electronic commerce 3
Understanding commerce 6
E-commerce so far 10
Some e-commerce companies 12

Chapter 2: The Internet and the World Wide Web for E-Commerce 18
The origins of the Internet 18
The World Wide Web 20
Information infrastructure 21
Global information infrastructure – some examples 25
The Internet revolution 28
The concept of the virtual organisation and cyberspace 29
The Internet as a business environment 31
Business processes in the electronic age 34
Business process re-engineering (BPR) 35
Supply chain 35
Procurement 36
The benefits of Internet-based business 36

Chapter 3: Information in Organisations 43
Understanding organisations 43
Different views of an organisation 46
The information society 47
New perspectives on information 49
Information management and the modern organisation 53
IT strategies in the information age 55

Chapter 4: The Intelligent Organisation 61
Organisational behaviour in cyberspace 61
The knowledge economy and the intelligent organisation 63
Technical and business concepts underpinning the knowledge economy 66

Sharing knowledge in the Internet age 67
The concept of knowledge management 69
A framework for knowledge management 75
The technological infrastructure of knowledge management 78
Business-to-consumer (B2C) communication 78
Business-to-business (B2B) communication 81
Intra-organisational communication 82
Communication for competitive advantage 82

CONCEPTS

Chapter 5: Communications Infrastructure for E-Commerce 91
The concept of a computer system 92
Hardware 92
Software 96
Inter-computer communications 98
Communication channels 98
Network devices 99
Protocols 100
The relationship between computers in a network 102
IT strategies for e-commerce systems 105
The principles behind technology infrastructure 106
Communications technologies – an overview 106
Communications technologies – the choices 108
Networking options 108
Wired connections 109
Wireless communication 114
Access to the Internet 119
The technologies of security 121
Encryption 122
Password control 125
Firewall 126
Virtual private networks 127

Chapter 6: Information Management Infrastructure for E-Commerce 132
The framework for an information management infrastructure 132
Creating an information management infrastructure 135
Identification of the sources of information and knowledge 135
Capturing information for easy access 135
Retrieval of knowledge 139
Systems for knowledge management 141
Enterprise resource planning 142
Directory services 142
Middleware 143
Customer relationship management 144
Data warehousing and mining 145
Customer interface 148
Intranets 149
Groupware 152
Extranets 154

Interface development for knowledge management 155
The technologies for interface building 155
HTML 157
DHTML 158
VRML 158
XML and XSL 158
Java 159
Scripting languages 159
CGI 160
An effective user interface 161

Chapter 7: Operational Infrastructure for E-Commerce 168
Challenges for organisations in the global market 168
Business models in the digital economy 170
The operational infrastructure 171
Supply-chain management 171
Procurement 174
Payment infrastructure 176
Distribution channels and logistics 181
Legal aspects of e-commerce 182
Marketing 188
Market research 189
Advertising 189
Branding 191
Building customer relationships 193
Understanding customer behaviour 195
Management issues 196

CONSEQUENCES

Chapter 8: Strategic Implementation of E-Commerce 205
Defining business strategy in the Internet era 205
Approaches to strategy formulation 208
The strategic potential of e-commerce 218
SWOT analysis 218
The value chain 219
Critical success factors 220
Return on investment 221
Preparing for e-commerce 221
Implementation of e-commerce 224
Infrastructure building 225
Developing e-commerce initiatives 228
Step-wise implementation 229
Managing change 230

Chapter 9: Creating Trust in E-Commerce 236
The importance of trust in cyberspace 236
Problems with trust building 239
The nature of the security risks in e-commerce 240
Taking action to enhance security 242
The defence programme 242

Privacy in e-commerce 246
The moves made to create public confidence in e-commerce 247

Chapter 10: E-Commerce and Society in the Twenty-first Century 257
The four waves of industry 257
The emerging issues – the two sides of the coin 259
Buyers and sellers 259
Large and small companies 260
Employers and employees 261
Old and new generations 262
Rich and poor 263
Developed and developing countries 264
Global and local 265
Isolation and community building 267
Control and freedom 269
Women and men 273
Old and new forms of learning 275
Autocracy and democracy 275
The role of a government in e-commerce 278
Predictions for the twenty-first century 280

Glossary 286
Index of Case Studies 298
Subject Index 299

N. Bandyo-padhyay is a Senior Lecturer in the Department of Innovation Studies at the University of East London, and the co-ordinator of the IT Combined Studies courses in the department.

Originally a physicist, N. Bandyo-padhyay started in computing as a programmer at Unilever and received training in systems analysis before starting a career teaching computing at Southgate Technical College. After completing an MSc in Computer Science at University College London, the author was subsequently promoted to Head of Computing/Computer Manager for the college.

In addition to this text, the author has previously written the book *Computing for Non Specialists*. Current research interests include the influence of IT on developing countries.

Preface

THE RATIONALE BEHIND THE BOOK

The widespread use of Internet technologies is remoulding classic business paradigms and prompting organisations to offer their services electronically and, in the process, completely rethink their attitudes and goals. New models of commercial interaction are developing as businesses and consumers participate in the new, electronic, marketplace. This has had a profound effect on the global trade in products and services for all concerned, from suppliers to distributors, marketers and consumers. As a result, there is a growing need for graduates with expertise in information and communications technologies relevant to the modern business world. They are required to have a clear understanding of how technology can play a part in business processes and how businesses can make the best use of technology. Students therefore need to understand the technical and organisational *context* within which today's businesses function; the technical *concepts* underlying electronic communication as well as the business concepts driving technical ventures; and the issues an organisation needs to address in order to understand the *consequences* of the implemented system and ensure that it can provide a productive, prosperous and secure solution to the organisation's strategic plans. This book is designed to serve these needs.

THE AIMS

Electronic commerce (e-commerce) is a new and fast-growing area, yet there are very few books on the market which are appropriate for use alongside a taught course. Those which are available do not take the interdisciplinary approach, which is a common goal for most of today's courses. The purpose of this book is to give students the technical as well as the business information which would prepare them for taking part in decision making in today's enterprises. It is based on how much students 'need to know' in order to become prospective managers of technology in the electronic marketplace, bearing in mind that a company's decisions on technology should be driven by its overall business needs. The main aims of the author are to:

1. Give students a clear and unambiguous introduction to e-commerce.
2. Present the debates and issues underpinning e-commerce within a conceptual framework.
3. Explain the technologies behind e-commerce within the above framework.
4. Explain the business concepts behind e-commerce with the same perspective.
5. Discuss the issues surrounding successful implementation and utilisation of e-commerce locally and globally.
6. Perform the above tasks using a language that is clear but not simplistic.

THE CONTENT

The content of the book is based on explicating the above aims. Special attention is paid throughout to clarity of explanation by avoiding unnecessary and uncommon jargon. On the other hand attempts have been made to maintain a high intellectual level by presenting the material within a theoretical context appropriate for degree level students, before technical and organisational details are introduced. The structure of the book represents this approach and is reflected in the title. The *context* section sets the scene and provides the background for the concepts related to e-commerce. It describes the 'what', and although at some points it may give a hint of the 'how' in an attempt to indicate the issues surrounding the existence of e-commerce, it does not discuss them at length. The purpose of the section is to describe the debates, the phenomena and the concepts which underpin the emergence and existence of e-commerce. Thus, having introduced readers to e-commerce it moves on to discuss the role of the Internet, the resulting emergence of the information society and its role in creating a knowledge economy. The *concepts* section discusses the technical and organisational concepts which help to build an infrastructure for e-commerce. Here, the chapters are about how things work: factual details of the technology and business processes supporting e-commerce. We discuss the contribution of suitable infrastructures for communication, information and operation to a framework for business in cyberspace. Finally, the *consequences* section addresses the issues surrounding the successful implementation of e-commerce. It discusses the importance of a strategic view in the implementation process, explores the issues organisations need to address in order to create trust in the industry and the consequences of e-commerce we might have to deal with, in local as well as a global context, in the twenty-first century.

The book is targeted at second or third year undergraduate students doing an e-commerce module in a non-specialist information technology (IT) or information systems (IS) degree who want to learn about the role of computers in organisations without going into too much detail about the technology itself. This could be a combined Honours degree which is a common offering in many 'new' universities where students study IT/IS as a major, joint or minor part of a degree in combination with another, often unrelated, subject. Those doing a combined studies degree in business studies and IT should benefit especially from the book. Students reading this book are expected to have completed introductory information technology units and to have a basic understanding of the concept of a computer system: what it is, how it works, how it is used, implemented and maintained, and so on. However, a brief introduction to the relevant technical concepts are included and the glossary at the end of the book describes all technical terms used. No background in business studies is assumed; starting at an elementary level, business/organisational matters are covered with non-specialists in mind, keeping the discussion within the framework of the Internet and electronic communications. Most of today's courses, especially in the new universities, teach their IT modules with social and organisational perspectives, thus preparing students to see a computer as a tool used to meet business needs rather than an object to be studied in detail. This book is designed to take them further in this direction, this time focusing on the use of technology for electronic communication in both B2B and B2C contexts. It should be able to serve as the text for a 12-week module and it is likely that the theoretical concepts covered in the book will be supplemented by some computer-based practical sessions on matters such as web design or object-oriented programming in order to give students an idea of the practicalities involved in the implementation of e-commerce.

Each chapter includes a list of objectives, an introduction, a brief summary of each section of the text in the margins, a chapter summary and a bibliography which indicates valuable material for further reading. Short case studies are used throughout the book. These are summaries of detailed studies done by researchers in various fields and students are strongly advised to read the original sources for fuller information. Each chapter is accompanied by a list of 'revision questions' intended to test readers' understanding of the text; 'further investigation questions' are inserted in appropriate places in the text in order to encourage students to get deeper into the topics in hand and find answers by independent research; and discussion questions are set to provide scope for readers to integrate the material covered and perform critical analysis. Additionally, case studies used are accompanied with questions designed to provoke critical thinking around the issues raised. A glossary of key technical terms is included at the end of the book.

A SPECIAL NOTE ON THE STRUCTURE

The structure of the book follows the 'context, concepts and consequences' theme. Thus, the same topic often appears in different sections with a different focus. For example, customer relationship management is mentioned in the context section in order to explain its role in e-commerce, the techniques available to establish it are discussed in the concepts section, while the consequences section is used to explore how it can be implemented in a way that benefits an enterprise and is acceptable to its users. This is done in order to present each topic within an appropriate context rather than describe all aspects of it in one place in its entirety. It is hoped that this will help readers to understand how different components of e-commerce relate to each other.

SUPPLEMENTARY MATERIAL

A website accompanying the book provides up-to-date information on the subject. It includes new case studies, additional material where appropriate, additional discussion questions, links to other useful on-line sources, Powerpoint slides for lecturers and so on. Attempts will be made to update the website at regular intervals and keep it as 'live' as possible in order to make it a valuable source of relevant information. Comments and discussions raised through the website will be an invaluable resource for improvements to be incorporated in future editions of the book, which are expected to be published every three years. It is hoped that eventually this book will fill an important gap in the market and establish itself as a major text in e-commerce.

N. Bandyo-padhyay

Acknowledgements

The book could not possibly achieve the intended standard without the attention of my daughter Bidisha. Using her skill in writing and her talent for absorbing new material, she edited each chapter thoroughly and made numerous suggestions which raised the calibre of the book to a different level. I am also enormously grateful to my cousin Dr Sumantra Ghoshal and his colleagues, especially Dr Aya Chacar, at the London Business School for introducing me to a wealth of material on the subject. I am very thankful to my brother Deb for encouraging me throughout and providing me with valuable material on the subject.

I could not have completed the book on time without the support of all my colleagues in the Department of Innovation Studies at the University of East London. I am indebted to Dr Gavin Poynter, the head of the department, for allowing me the time and the space I needed for the project. Special mention must also be made of Eva Turner, Graham Thomas, Miriam Mukasa and Dr Josephine Stein for the practical help and encouragement I received. I am also incredibly grateful to Maurice Moore for his expert comments on legal aspects of e-commerce.

My sincere thanks go the staff at McGraw-Hill for their co-operation during the project. I thank Jackie Harbor for her unshaken belief in me, Andy Goss for presenting the idea to me, accepting my proposal with great enthusiasm and providing guidance and help at the initial stage of the project, Julian Partridge for his support and understanding, Judith Spencer for her help with copyright permissions and Nikki Wimpory for her prompt and ongoing help.

Finally, as always, thanks to my mother for everything.

I am grateful to the following for permission to use copyright material for case studies:

Reed Business Information Ltd. for:

1 Beckett, H., One year on . . . , Interview on hmv.com:, *e-business review*, May, 2000, p. 21.
2 Bicknell, D., The IT department of tomorrow, *e.business review*, July/August, 2000, p. 13, Unilever.
3 Campbell, A., Sabre Group: WAP or scrap? *e.business review*, December, 2000, p. 66.
4 Classe, A., E-skills on the up and up, *Computer Weekly*, 29 March, 2001, p. 58, NSPCC.
5 Classe, A., Tomorrow the world . . . , *Computer Weekly*, 26 October, 2000, p. 80, Dulux Paints.
6 Dudman, J., A measure for measures, *Computer Weekly*, 29 March 2001, p. 62, Lloyds TSB Commercial Finance.
7 Goodwin, B., Anderson-Charnley, Financial firm blazes a trail to go live with PKI Web solution, *Computer Weekly*, 16 November, 2000, p. 16.
8 Harvey, F., Angel guides the customers, *Computer Weekly*, 14 December, 2000, Net Angel.
9 Hunter, P., Doing the knowledge, *Computer Weekly*, 26 October, 2000, p. 58, British Gas.
10 Hunter, P., Knowledge sharing to tickle those tastebuds, *Computer Weekly*, 1 March, 2001, p. 28, Recipe for Success.

11 Nicolle, L., 'Bricks' lead brand backlash, *Computer Weekly*, 22 March, 2001, p.53, Urbia.co.uk.
12 Paston, T., How Freeserve plans to create the Uberportal, *e-business review*, June, 2000, p. 18.
13 Warren, L., Handle with care, *Computer Weekly*, 8 March, 2001, p. 8, Wedgewood.
14 Warren, L., Size doesn't matter; just the ticket from Nottinghamshire County Cricket Club, *Computer Weekly*, 18 May, 2000, p. 54.
15 Warren, L., Turning e-dash into e-cash, *Computer Weekly*, 26 October, 2000, p. 62, Hanson Construction.
16 Warren, L., Electronic makeover, *Computer Weekly*, 8 February, 2001, p. 27, Watford Electronics.

Harvard Business School for:
1 Akers, C., Edmunds.com, *Harvard Business Review*, September, 2000.
2 Applegate, L., Frito-Lay, Inc.: A strategic transition, *Harvard Business Review*, February, 1993.
3 Applegate, M, Paving the Information Superhighway, Harvard Business School, July, 1996, Hyatt Hotels + San Jose Mercury News.
4 Dickson L. L., First Direct, *Harvard Business Review*, 9 April, 1998.
5 Eisenhardt, M. K. and Sull, D. N., Strategy as Simple Rules, *Harvard Business Review*, 2001, pp. 105–116, Autodesk.
6 Escalle, C. X. and Cotteleer, M. J., Enterprise Resource Planning, *Harvard Business Review*, February, 1999, Cisco.
7 Ghosh, S., Making Business Sense of the Internet, *Harvard Business Review*, March–April, 1998, pp. 125–135, Staples
8 Gladstone, J. A., KPMG Peat Marwick: The shadow partner, *Harvard Business Review*, 5 October, 1995.
9 Iansiti, M., Lucent Technologies: Optical Networking Group, *Harvard Business Review*, 12 November, 1999.
10 Knoop, C., Valor, J. and Sasser, W. E., Information at The World Bank: In search of a technology solution, *Harvard Business Review*, 17 September, 1997.
11 Ovans, A., E-Procurement at Schlumberger: A conversation with Alian-Michael Diamant-Berger, *Harvard Business Review*, 2000.
12 Quinn, J. B., Anderson, P. and Finkelstein, S., Managing professional intellect: making the most of the best, *Harvard Business Review*, March–April, 1996, Merrill Lynch.

Burrows, R., Nettleton, S., Pleace, N., Loader, B. and Muncer, S. for: Virtual community care? Social policy and the emergence of computer mediated social support, *Information, Communication and Society*, 3(1), 2000, pp. 95–121, UK Home Repossession Page.

Butler, C. and Ghoshal, S. for: Kao Corporation: A Learning Organisation, INSEAD EURO–ASIA CENTRE, 1992.

Cap Gemini Ernst & Young LLC for: *Electronic Commerce: A Need to Change Perspective*, 2000 Special Report on the Financial Services Industry, 2000, Charles Schwab.

Computing for: Samuels, M. and Phillips, T., Retail goes e-tail – and more besides, *Computing*, 26 October, 2000, p.37, Sainsbury's

E-Commerce Times & NewsFactor Network for: Greenberg, P. A., Ernst & Young Debuts E-Commerce Trust Community, 4 November, 1999.

Graham, I., Spinardi, G., and Williams, R. for: Diversity in the emergence of electronic commerce, *Journal of Information Technology*, 1996, Ford.

KPL for: Hills, T., A recipe for success: Mansfield Motors, *E-business – Best practice for SMEs and PLCs*, published by KPL in association with e-centre^{UK}, 1999, p. 49.

Madon, S. and Sahay, S. for: Democracy and information: A case atudy of new local governance structures in Bangalore, *Information, Communication and Society*, 3(2), 2000, pp. 173–191, Citizens' Webpage in Bangalore.

Stanford University for: Charlet, J., Firefly Network; Graduate School of Business, March, 1998.

The Newham Online for: Art of Change; Infinity Story, Newham Online Report, 1999.

VNU Business Publications for:

1 Lee, C., Booker selects PKI encryption to secure online share trading, *IT Week*, 16 April, 2001.
2 Middleton, J., Provident connects offices worldwide; *Network News*, 4 July, 2000, Friends Provident.

A number of other publications also gave permission to use their material in the text; acknowledgement of these are inserted in the appropriate places. I am very thankful to all of them.

The author and the publishing team would also like to thank the following university experts who took the time and effort to take part in the market research. They have added enormously to the development of this text:

Regina Connolly	Dublin City University
Brid Lane	Portobello College
Debbie Gilliland	Staffordshire University
Lisa Harris	Brunel University
Ritchie Macefield	University of Wolverhampton
Ulf Hoglind	Orebro University
Ifan Shepherd	Middlesex University
Richard Hollywood	Manchester City College
Teemu Ylikoski	University of Helsinki
Elizabeth Williamson	Glasgow Caledonian University
Kevin Edwards	Nottingham Trent University
Dave Chaffey	Derby University
Mathias Klang	University of Gothenburg
Barbara Bardzki	Glasgow Caledonian University
John Hassal	University of Wolverhampton
Barbara Armstrong	University of Central England
Fiona Miekle	Leeds Metropolitan University
Glenn Behenna	University of Wales, Swansea
John McNulty	University College Cork
Stephen Tagg	University of Strathclyde.

Guided Tour

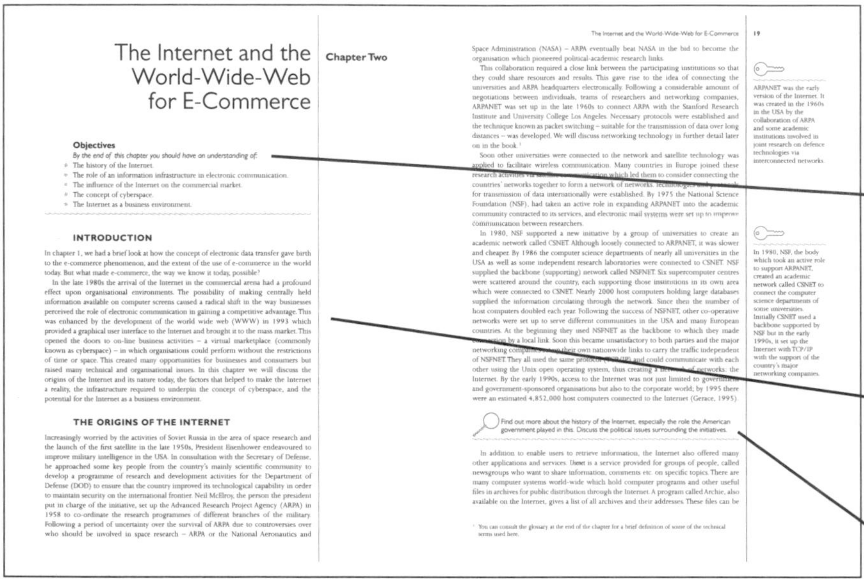

Learning objectives identify the topics covered and the abilities and skills the student should be able to demonstrate after reading the chapter.

Chapter introductions give a brief overview of the coverage and purpose of the topics in the coming chapter.

Further investigation questions test student knowledge, encouraging them to apply what they have learnt and research further around the subject.

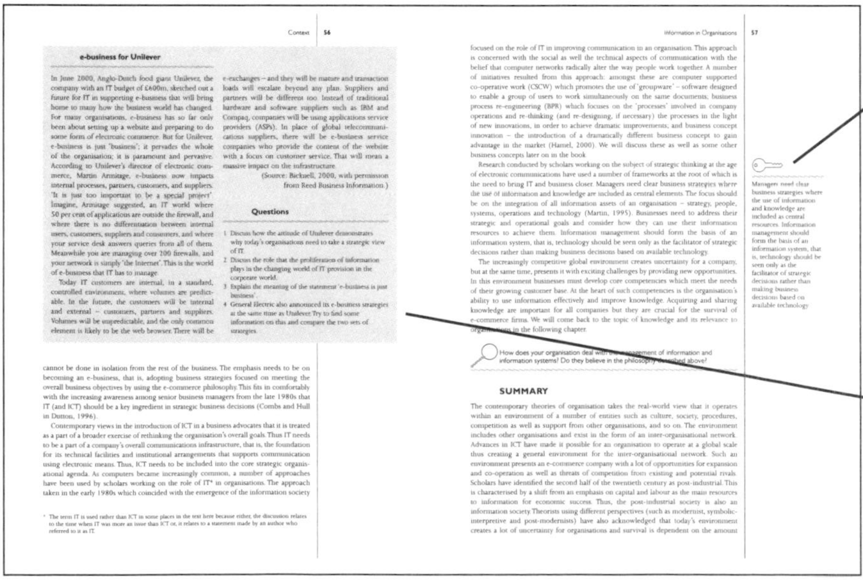

Key concepts and margin definitions draw attention to core concepts or techniques and summarise critical aspects of the text. Margin definitions help put the concept into context and offer an accessible method of revision.

Integrated mini cases and questions encourage students to apply what they have covered in each chapter to real-life situations; the questions help to test their understanding and put into practice what they have learnt.

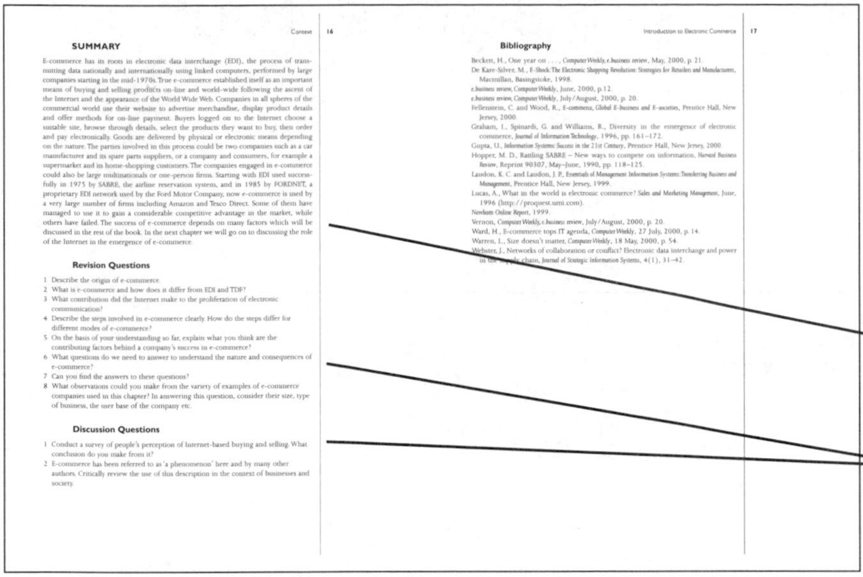

Context 16

SUMMARY

E-commerce has its roots in electronic data interchange (EDI), the process of transmitting data nationally and internationally using linked computers, performed by large companies starting in the mid-1970s. True e-commerce established itself as an important means of buying and selling products on-line and world-wide following the ascent of the Internet and the appearance of the World Wide Web. Companies in all spheres of the commercial world use their website to advertise merchandise, display product details and offer methods for on-line payment. Buyers logged on to the Internet choose a suitable site, browse through details, select the products they want to buy, then order and pay electronically. Goods are delivered by physical or electronic means depending on the nature. The parties involved in this process could be two companies such as a car manufacturer and its spare parts suppliers, or a company and consumers, for example a supermarket and its home-shopping customers. The companies engaged in e-commerce could also be large multinationals or one-person firms. Starting with EDI used successfully in 1975 by SABRE, the airline reservation system, and in 1985 by FORDNET, a proprietary EDI network used by the Ford Motor Company, now e-commerce is used by a very large number of firms including Amazon and Tesco Direct. Some of them have managed to use it to gain a considerable competitive advantage in the market, while others have failed. The success of e-commerce depends on many factors which will be discussed in the rest of the book. In the next chapter we will go on to discussing the role of the Internet in the emergence of e-commerce.

Revision Questions

1 Describe the origin of e-commerce.
2 What is e-commerce and how does it differ from EDI and TDF?
3 What contribution did the Internet make to the proliferation of electronic communication?
4 Describe the steps involved in e-commerce clearly. How do the steps differ for different modes of e-commerce?
5 On the basis of your understanding so far, explain what you think are the contributing factors behind a company's success in e-commerce?
6 What questions do we need to answer to understand the nature and consequences of e-commerce?
7 Can you find the answers to these questions?
8 What observations could you make from the variety of examples of e-commerce companies used in this chapter? In answering this question, consider their size, type of business, the user base of the company etc.

Discussion Questions

1 Conduct a survey of people's perception of Internet-based buying and selling. What conclusion do you make from it?
2 E-commerce has been referred to as 'a phenomenon' here and by many other authors. Critically review the use of this description in the context of businesses and society.

Introduction to Electronic Commerce 17

Bibliography

Beckett, H., One year on . . . , *Computer Weekly, e.business review*, May, 2000, p. 21.

De Kare-Silver, M., *E-Shock: The Electronic Shopping Revolution: Strategies for Retailers and Manufacturers*, Macmillan, Basingstoke, 1998.

e.business review, Computer Weekly, June, 2000, p.12.

e.business review, Computer Weekly, July/August, 2000, p. 20.

Fellenstein, C. and Wood, R., *E-commerce, Global E-business and E-societies*, Prentice Hall, New Jersey, 2000.

Graham, I., Spinardi, G. and Williams, R., Diversity in the emergence of electronic commerce, *Journal of Information Technology*, 1996, pp. 161–172.

Gupta, U., *Information Systems: Success in the 21st Century*, Prentice Hall, New Jersey, 2000.

Hopper, M. D., Rattling SABRE – New ways to compete on information, *Harvard Business Review*, Reprint 90307, May–June, 1990, pp. 118–125.

Laudon, K. C. and Laudon, J. P., *Essentials of Management Information Systems: Transferring Business and Management*, Prentice Hall, New Jersey, 1999.

Lucas, A., What in the world is electronic commerce? *Sales and Marketing Management*, June, 1996 (http://proquest.umi.com).

Newham Online Report, 1999.

Vernon, *Computer Weekly, e.business review*, July/August, 2000, p. 20.

Ward, H., E-commerce tops IT agenda, *Computer Weekly*, 27 July, 2000, p. 14.

Warren, L., Size doesn't matter, *Computer Weekly*, 18 May, 2000, p. 54.

Webster, J., Networks of collaboration or conflict? Electronic data interchange and power in the supply chain, *Journal of Strategic Information Systems*, 4(1), 31–42.

Chapter summaries briefly review and reinforce topics students have covered in the chapter, tying all aspects together.

Revision and discussion questions help reinforce students' understanding of the chapter, either individually or in a group.

Teaching and learning resources

The accompanying website to the book provides up-to-date information on the subject and can be visited at www.mcgraw-hill.co.uk/textbooks/bandyo. It contains an extensive range of teaching and learning resources for both lecturers and students.

Accessible to students:

1 100 self testing MCQs.
2 'Exploring the topic further' – snippets of articles from leading publications exploring further the topics in the text.
3 'Hot off the press' – links to recent articles with commentary and questions.
4 Case studies.

Accessible to lecturers only:

1 PowerPoint slides to aid lecturing.
2 Module Handbook with a plan of week by week suggested lecture plans and seminar/tutorial activities.

Context

Part One

Introduction to Electronic Commerce

Chapter One

Objectives

By the end of this chapter you should have an understanding of:

- The history of electronic commerce.
- The basic concept behind electronic commerce.
- The extent to which electronic commerce has established itself in the business world.

INTRODUCTION

Electronic commerce (known commonly and referred to from here onwards as e-commerce) has revolutionised nearly every industry in the world. It is a buzzword that appeared in the early to the middle of the 1990s and fast became a common term in the commercial and academic world. Other related terms that emerged over the next few years are e-cash, e-business, e-procurement, e-market, e-tail and so on. What do they all mean? How do they influence the way organisations run their business? How do they affect countries, societies, communities, governments and individuals? What role does technology play in this new milieu? These are only some of the questions that need to be answered in order for us to have an understanding of the concept of e-commerce and its consequences for the modern world.

Taken literally, e-commerce means 'doing business electronically' – that is, trading goods, services and expertise using computers linked to each other. However, this definition is rather inadequate as it does not take account of the influence e-commerce has on every aspect of a business nor does it reflect the complexity of the technical and organisational infrastructure that is required to support the existence of e-commerce. Other terms such as e-business and e-enterprise have been introduced in order to incorporate these factors. We will look how scholars have distinguished between them later on in the book. In this chapter we are going to give you an overview of the nature of e-commerce, the factors which contributed to its birth and what effect it has had in the business world. Many of the issues addressed here will be covered in further depth in later chapters.

THE BACKGROUND TO ELECTRONIC COMMERCE

Two images which forecast a wholly technologised society more than 20 years ago – the paperless office and cashless transactions – have not materialised for various reasons. However, e-commerce is the phenomenon that has brought us closest to those concepts. The rapid evolution of computer and communications technology has enabled organisations to store vast amounts of information and transfer it via telecommunications lines. In the early 1990s many major companies were using the existing infrastructure of national and international computer networks to communicate with each other.

Transborder data flow (TDF), a term used to mean electronic movement of data internationally, has been in use widely among multinational organisations for nearly two decades. Another related term frequently used in the business community is electronic data interchange (EDI) – the exchange of information between computers. Using an agreed standard, EDI enables businesses to exchange data on customers and products, send orders and invoices on-line, and settle finances electronically with minimum human intervention. Early examples of the commercial sectors that made significant use of electronic data transmission (TDF and/or EDI) are airlines reservation systems to enable travel agents to keep up-to-date information on flight reservations and offer bookings to customers accordingly, the automobile industry to set up electronic links between suppliers, manufacturers and dealers in order to gain an advantage in the market, and financial institutions to transfer funds across national and international borders.

Have you ever used a credit card abroad? Find out how the transaction works.

The above functions informed the foundation of e-commerce as companies involved in EDI or TDF used computer networks to transfer some of their business processes to electronic forms. By creating and utilising links with the computer systems of their trading partners, organisations communicated electronically to achieve fast, inexpensive and reliable business transactions. However, the term e-commerce appeared in the scene widely[1] in the early 1990s hand in hand with the introduction of the Internet and the world wide web (WWW). Before the days of the WWW, electronic communication involved text-based interface and using a computer system required technical knowledge and specialist training. Computing was therefore the territory of IT experts; it was a 'closed' industry and computer systems were built to provide large centralised applications such as inventory (stock) control and accounting. This meant that companies intending to transfer data electronically had to employ technically qualified personnel to handle the applications. This reliance on specialist skill, combined with the necessity to support such workers prevented them from being able to use these applications to replace day-to-day paper-based transactions. In addition to this, there was the serious problem of the incompatibility of computer systems. No agreed standards existed between hardware manufacturers, software developers and policy-making bodies: computers and other devices built by different companies followed their own (proprietary) system of communication and used their own network operating systems to transmit data. Transaction succeeded only if the receiver of the messages used the same brand of hardware and software as the sender. In the absence of standardisation and a communications infrastructure, data sent by one network to an incompatible system had to be translated before the receiving network could accept it. This need for conversion made electronic communication slow, cumbersome and expensive. The WWW changed all this and enabled true electronic commerce by facilitating fast and easy communication between users. Thus, we could say that while EDI enabled companies to simply transfer data between each other electronically, e-commerce enabled them to conduct business fully over a world-wide network called the Internet. This involves the sharing of business information electronically by using electronic messaging services such as email, the WWW, electronic bulletin boards, smart cards, and EDI (Fellenstein and Wood, 2000).

EDI and TDF are the processes by which data is transferred electronically via linked computers. Thus they are the precursors of e-commerce, and were used by many large companies since the middle of the 1970s.

The origin of the Internet lies in a US-based network called the ARPANET (Advanced Research Project Agency) set up in 1969. It was initially designed to co-ordinate the

[1] The term e-commerce has been used by academics and business researchers since the middle of 1980s.

research and development (R&D) activities of different sections of the Department of Defense (DoD). ARPANET provided the means for the DOD to share research findings with the academics working on their projects. At the beginning it included a number of universities who were commissioned by the DoD to carry out R&D work. The popularity of the service amongst its users gave rise to the concept of sharing information with institutions world-wide by connecting large networks in different countries to each other, ultimately to create a 'superhighway' for data communication. By the early 1990s much of this had been achieved and the infrastructure was set up to enable users to access information from any part of this global network. This attracted an enormous amount of interest from academics and business organisations. Certain necessary protocols[2] (TCP/IP) were established to allow users anywhere on the network to use the service effectively. Software developers also augmented the range of options provided by such a global network by introducing a large number of applications such as email, remote file transfer facilities and applications software designed to search the large databases of information available on the network.

Electronic communication is expensive and inefficient without an effective infrastructure and agreed protocols between communicating systems. Widespread communication was only made possible following the establishment of the Internet and the WWW, as well as necessary standards to be followed by user groups.

In the early days of the Internet era, users had to enter text-based commands to gain access to the Internet. It was rather like using an application program such as a word-processor, without Windows. The introduction in 1993 of the world wide web (WWW), a graphical user interface for the Internet, was one of the most important stages in the popularisation of the service. By using text, sound, graphics and animation, the WWW creates an 'environment' in which users can access various available facilities without specialist training. The existence of easy-to-use interfaces and a standard protocol encouraged companies to make use of the web for business purposes. For the first time companies had a well-established world-wide network that they could connect to cheaply and efficiently and many endeavoured to use the WWW to offer a number of their services over the network. Some small and medium sized companies also utilised the facility for parts of their functions; even companies without their own local area network could access the services of the Internet via a modem[3] and a personal computer. Early users of this service includes Dell who extended their telephone-based operations to the Internet for marketing and selling their PCs in the mid 1990s, First Direct offered a telephone banking service in the UK in the early 1990s and adopted the Internet as soon as it became viable and Amazon.com set up an e-commerce site to sell books in 1995 thus challenging the existing large physical bookstores. Many other companies used the Internet initially to advertise their goods but later on they adopted full e-commerce. The potential of the WWW for running a business encouraged many entrepreneurial individuals to start small firms that offered a variety of products and services on-line. Electronic commerce became a new paradigm for the business world. We will come back to the subject of the history of the Internet and its contribution to businesses in the next chapter.

The phenomenon of e-commerce has given rise to an entirely new vocabulary: we now know of e-business, e-procurement, and the e-market. As more and more business activities are performed electronically, e-commerce has ceased to remain within the limits of buying and selling of consumer goods. It has forced senior managers to rethink the way a business uses technology. The WWW has questioned the meaning and value of information and technology, and led to an examination of the relationship between the two. For example, businesses can find it advantageous to trade information as in the case of priceline.com (as described later in the chapter) or access to information, for

[2] A protocol is a set of rules or conventions which govern the way a message is transmitted from the sender to the receiver passing through a number of steps and via a number of network elements. TCP/IP (Transmission Control Protocol/Internet Protocol) is the protocol used by the Internet.

[3] A device that enables data to move via a telephone line.

example, the Internet service providers such as America On Line (AOL). Although some jargon has appeared as a result of frivolous use of newly coined terminology, some important new concepts have entered the business community as a result of the new mode of trading. We will discuss those in later chapters.

UNDERSTANDING E-COMMERCE

In its most basic form e-commerce represents transactions which are handled electronically rather than on paper, for example, sending product orders and invoices through a network. It includes, but is not limited to, buying on the Internet (Lucas, 1996). However, as explained above, it is the Internet which encouraged the whole concept of e-commerce to emerge by taking EDI into a new level of accessibility. Now e-commerce is visualised as a virtual meeting place for buyers and sellers. The meeting could be between two or more businesses, between a business and its customers, or between one-person companies and individual buyers. The products on sale can also be almost anything: information, goods and services. E-commerce is a form of on-line business relationships which can exist through the whole process of buying and selling: first advertising, then the first contact between the buyer and the seller, the conduction of the sale, the delivery of the product, payment, and, finally, after-sale service. For some businesses, for example those selling software, all of these stages can be done on-line while for others, such as companies selling spare parts for a computer, physical delivery of the goods is required at some stage.

E-commerce is the process of conducting business activities over the Internet. It includes, but is not limited to, buying on the Internet. It is a philosophy which utilises the features of the Internet to transform business processes in order to gain a competitive advantage.

So, how does e-commerce work? E-commerce is the result of the application of computer and telecommunications technologies to business processes. A meaningful discussion of how it works should be preceded by an in-depth discussion of the business context within which e-commerce is situated as well as a thorough understanding of the technologies involved in its working. We will go into those in later chapters. For an initial understanding, Fig. 1.1 gives a user's eye view of how e-commerce works, especially in relation to an individual performing a purchase on-line. The steps mentioned in the diagram are explained below.

What qualities do you expect from a website when you buy on-line?

- *Step* 1. A customer logs on to the Internet and either uses known URLs (addresses for sites) or a search engine to find on-line sellers of the product he or she is interested in. Thus the customer 'enters' a virtual market looking for a product. The companies who have an established customer base – either because they have managed to build it by providing good service for a period of time or because they have a monopoly in the market – have a distinct advantage in that a customer would in most cases go straight on to their websites rather than look for a company. For these customers step 2 is not necessary. The others would either go by recommendation or search for companies using step 2.
- *Step* 2. The customer examines a number of sites and selects one that he or she wants to use for the purchase. When sellers are in competition in this way, the quality of the interface customers are presented with when they access the site (normally the homepage, that is, the interface used as the entry point to a company's website) is very important. If a customer dislikes the homepage either because the layout is poor, the design is off-putting or the site does not

give an indication of the variety and nature of products available, they will move on to another site. It is rather like the window of a shop; if customers do not like the look of it, they will not enter it.

- *Step* 3. Having chosen a site to look into, the buyer searches for the goods required using the interface provided. The website should have a good keyword search facility which is easy to use and should be imaginatively laid out, with links to different product categories and services clearly visible. Electronic shopping follows the same marketing philosophy as high-street shopping: if a customer is not satisfied with the look of the product or the service, he or she will go somewhere else. The electronic catalogue replaces the products on the physical shop floor and customers have to be taken through the available goods comfortably and quickly.
- *Step* 4. E-commerce sites would normally have the facility for choosing (marking) a number of products to order – the same way we collect items in a basket in a shop. As the customer chooses each product the system would normally respond with delivery details such as availability, time taken to deliver and so on. The interface would also enable the customer to indicate when all the items have been chosen. Usually, this would be easy to use with intuitive captions and icons on screen.
- *Step* 5. At this stage the customer is normally presented with an electronic form to enter personal (name, address etc.) and financial (credit/debit card number) details. Either at this stage or before, security statements are made to remind the customer of the possible risk involved in sending personal data

People buying on-line follow the electronic equivalent of the steps involved in physical (off-line) shopping. The philosophy of making a physical shop front and the internal layout attractive and easy to use and the process of buying quick and easy, need to be transformed into their electronic equivalent via a website.

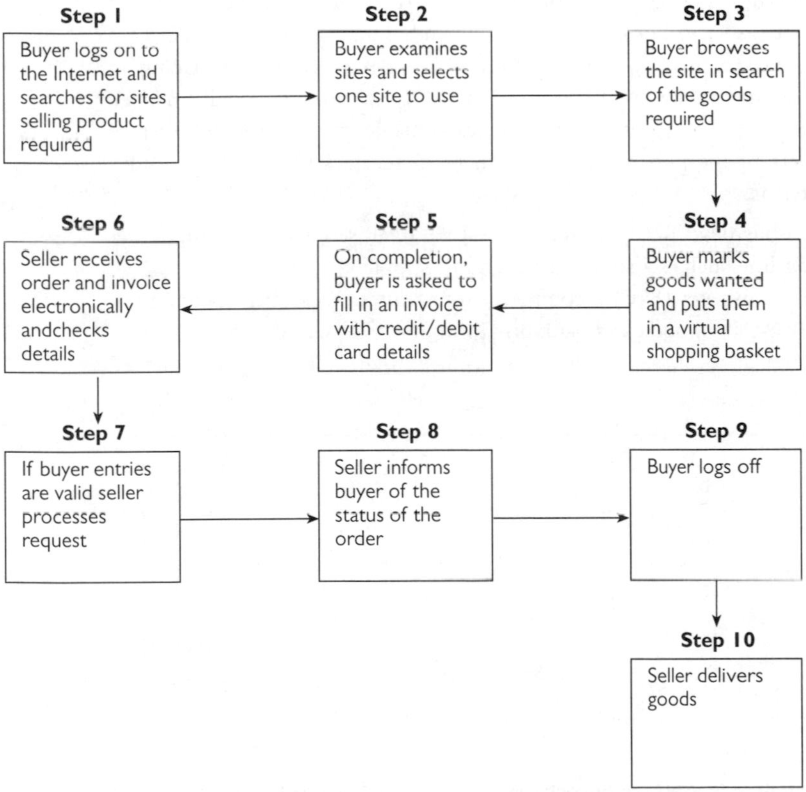

Fig. 1.1 Buying on-line

electronically and the customer is given the opportunity either to continue or withdraw.

- *Step* 6. The details are checked for validity, credit worthiness etc. by the seller on-line following which the system responds with a statement of either acceptance or rejection.
- *Step* 7. If the order is accepted, the seller then processes it by sending it through to the appropriate department.
- *Step* 8. If the order is sent successfully, the customer is presented with a message confirming this and with information on when the delivery should be expected. However, for products which can be delivered on-line, such as, a train seat reservation or the membership of a club, the delivery is often made at the same time.
- *Step* 9. The user can now log off. If the experience was satisfactory and enjoyable, he or she is likely to come back to the same supplier for future use, thus becoming a potential long-term customer of the company.
- *Step* 10. For goods not suitable for delivery on-line, the first off-line activity takes place when it is delivered by physical means. For a large majority of e-commerce sites, this is the normal mode of supply.

Have you got any experience of buying on-line? How does your experience compare with the above scenario? Draw an alternative diagram if appropriate.

A few points need to be noted at this stage. Although the scenario just sketched out is based on an individual buying physical items on-line, the principle is the same for any form of e-commerce. The model could be applied equally (although some details will be different for different cases) to books ordered by an individual from a publisher or a dealer, a large supermarket ordering its stock from its suppliers, a car dealer placing an order to the manufacturer following a specification from a customer, or full financial services such as savings, mortgages, insurance etc. available on-line from a finance company to members of the public. Such differences in services have given rise to a number of related terms:

- Business-to-business (B2B) e-commerce – two organisations conducting business on-line such as a supermarket and its suppliers.
- Business-to-consumer (B2C) e-commerce – organisations selling on-line to individual customers such as a bank providing financial services to its members.

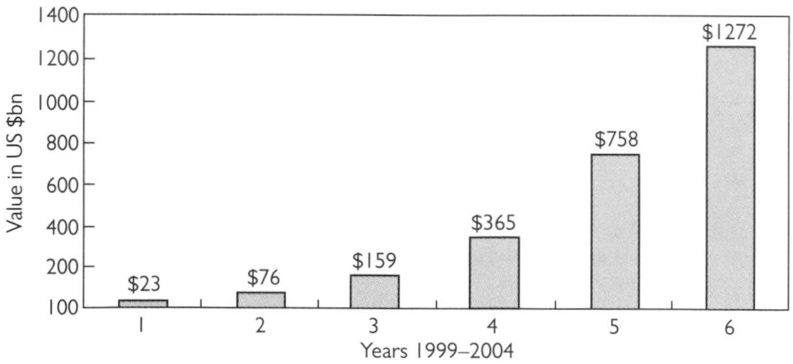

Fig. 1.2 B2B e-commerce in Western Europe (values in billions) (Source: *Computer Weekly, e-business review*, April, 2000, p. 10)

- Consumer-to-consumer (C2C) – involves business transaction between individuals such as teenagers exchanging CDs or a courseware (teaching aids) developer selling to teachers on-line.
- Consumer-to-business (C2B) – individuals selling to businesses for example, a web designer offering her services to e-commerce companies.

In this book we will concentrate mainly on B2B and B2C with the expectation that readers will be able to extend their knowledge to the other categories. Figs 1.2 and 1.3 give some statistics related to the extent of the adoption of e-commerce in the arena of B2B and B2C in the Western world.

The scenario described in Fig. 1.1 (a B2C operation) also raises the following questions:

- What are the driving forces behind the acceptance of e-commerce?
- What makes a customer choose a company to do business with?
- What makes a good website?
- Why does an organisation need e-commerce? Could we not run a business as we have done in the past?
- How do consumers benefit?
- How does the Internet influence and or facilitate e-commerce?
- What must companies do to make e-commerce work for them?
- What are the risks involved for the buyer and the seller?

E-commerce has the potential to revolutionise the way a business is run and thereby redefine the concept of work, home, marketplace and society. In order to understand the impact e-commerce can have in the modern world, we need to comprehend the philosophy behind an organisation, the role of information and its communication for an organisation, the technologies that underpin communication in business, the technical and organisational issues which need to be dealt with to make e-commerce work, and the consequences of e-commerce now and in future. In this chapter we are only able to lay the foundations for some of those; we will come back to them and many other issues in the rest of the book. In the rest of this chapter we will take a look at the extent to which e-commerce has been used so far.

Many organisational, technical, political and ethical issues need to be addressed in order to make e-commerce a successful activity. A thorough investigation of all those issues are required to understand the full potential of e-commerce.

Try to browse through an e-commerce site and write a review of your experience as a shopper.

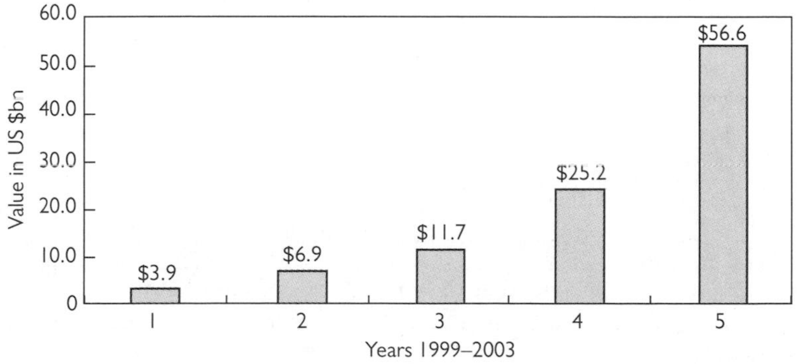

Fig. 1.3 B2C e-commerce in Western Europe (values in billions) (Source: *Computer Weekly, e-business review*, May, 2000, p. 14)

E-COMMERCE SO FAR

In an article written in 1996 (Lucas), a company vice president was quoted as saying that by the year 2000, e-commerce would reach 15 per cent to 25 per cent of typical bankcard[4] transactions. According to a survey published in 2000, 29 per cent of the companies surveyed use the Internet for trading (Ward, 2000). While not using the Internet for full trading, many more companies are using it for advertising and communication with trading partners and consumers. Figure 1.4 shows some relevant statistics from another survey.

Out of a sample of 390 respondents:

22 per cent (86) are actively using e-commerce for trade.
35 per cent (134) are using e-commerce for advertising and communication.
24 per cent (95) have e-commerce under development – expected to be operational in 12 months.
16 per cent (64) still examining routes to achieve this.
2.5 per cent (10) have no current plans to implement e-commerce.
0.25 per cent (1) did not make comments.

The term electronic commerce began to appear in academic literature in the middle to late 1980s. This was the time when telecommunications technologies were developed well enough to enable companies to use EDI to gain certain competitive advantages in business. Companies such as McKesson – dealing in pharmaceutical distribution, American Hospital Supply (AHSC) – delivering medical supplies to hospitals in the USA, and SABRE – American Airlines' computerised reservation system – were some of the pioneers in this field (Graham *et al.*, 1996). They established electronic links with customers; firstly, by removing other means of purchase and secondly, by establishing a monopoly in their market. These were large, lone corporations which established electronic partnerships with a small group of selected suppliers and dealers – their so-called trading partners. They used proprietary systems (technology standards supported within the selected community) to lock in the trading partners to create a monopoly. For example, SABRE was initially set up by American Airlines (AA) in the early 1960s as a computerised inventory control system, and was expanded to a full decision support system by the mid-1970s (Hopper, 1990). It was used by American Airlines and its authorised travel agents for the distribution and management of flight reservation for its passengers. SABRE and Apollo, the equivalent system for United Airlines, controlled 75 per cent of the American air travel market (Laudon and Laudon, 1999). In 1985, Ford Motor Company developed Fordnet, a corporate (proprietary) EDI system encompassing their European counterparts and selected trading partners. They established their own standards and ensured that their partners abided by them by supplying willing associates with the requisite software and ensuring that they had the necessary hardware to join Fordnet. At this stage, e-commerce was limited to businesses and their suppliers, and not available to customers.

In the 1980s organisations began to use telecommunications technologies to gain a competitive advantage. American Airlines attempted to do this via EDI with SABRE, their fully computerised reservation system, in the early 1960s which allowed the whole process of seat reservation to be performed on-line. The company gained major business advantage through this pioneering project and began the trend for e-commerce.

Why do you think certain types of company adopted EDI at an early stage while some others did not?

In the late 1980s, the market began to be opened up to larger number of suppliers and, more importantly, to consumers, with the intention of gaining a large on-line customer

[4] To mean a transaction using an electronic payment system which is a part and parcel of e-commerce.

base by providing a unique service. This forced them to adopt the accepted global standard supported by the majority of companies, including competitors. An example of a company that used this model was Kwik-Fit. They used a proprietary system with some of their suppliers in 1982; in 1990 they joined Fleetnet, a joint EDI venture between some car leasing companies and their suppliers. Fleetnet used a generic telecommunications standard to create a more realistic electronic market consisting of buyers, sellers and competitors. Direct Line, an insurance company set up in the mid-1980s in the UK was the first to establish the philosophy of full virtual selling directly to customers. They used TV and the print media to advertise their services to get customers to phone or fax them directly. They arranged insurance over the phone, thus avoiding the middle agents (brokers and distributors) and saving time and other resources. It quickly became popular with customers for the time advantage it offered. At the same time, it enabled Direct Line to build up the infrastructure for on-line business which made it easy for them to set up Internet-based e-commerce when the service became available.

A number of companies, for example, Kwik-Fit and Ford used EDI in the early 1980s with proprietary systems to lock in their business partners. Although it worked for a while, soon they had to conform to more widely accepted EDI standards in order to maintain their customer base.

In the early 1990s, when the Internet and the WWW became regular features on desktop computers, many companies decided to establish their presence in the cyberworld by introducing a webpage. As explained already, this is the time when the scope for electronic buying and selling became a viable option for almost any firm and e-commerce became common in business terminology. Many companies jumped on the bandwagon by apparently offering their services on-line, but in reality most of the websites at that stage essentially provided information on the products they sold. Some critics used the term brochureware to describe those sites because they did nothing more than advertise their stock on-line.

If you were an entrepreneur, what would you like to sell on-line and why?

On the other hand some companies saw the true potential of the Internet and invested in creating web-based e-commerce sites to take advantage of electronic trading for the full range of business activities. The following is a list of only a few of the very large

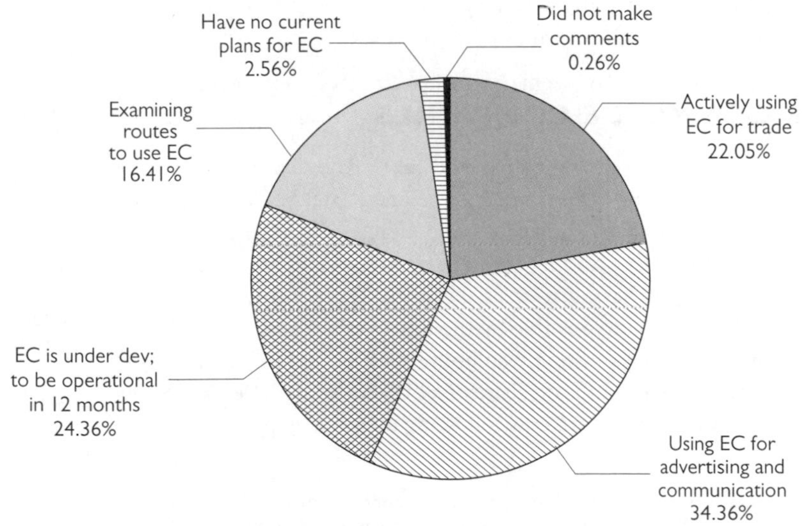

Fig. 1.4 E-commerce in the year 2000 (Source: *Computer Weekly*, 27 July, 2000)

Ford Motor Company

In 1985 Ford established Fordnet, a proprietary network covering all their European sites and including links with their most significant trading partners, including main dealerships and key suppliers. The inter-organisational links in Fordnet allowed Ford to gain competitive edge by integrating their systems with their customers and by encouraging their more significant suppliers to switch to EDI. Ford adapted the German automotive industry's standards for electronic messages because it was available at the time. Initially they joined ODETTE, the EDI project established by the European automotive industry association, but later withdrew because they sought to gain an advantage by introducing electronic trading ahead of their competitors without waiting for sector-wide standards to become available. Ford developed standard systems for use by their trading partners, to minimise the difficulties of trading electronically for their partners. Ford's strategy caused problems for at least one of their largest suppliers, who were themselves developing electronic trading, when the supplier tried to integrate Ford's system directly into their mainframe systems. When the ODETTE message standards were implemented by other manufacturers, Ford's policy forced them to maintain parallel systems for Ford. Large car dealerships also needed internal systems capable of linking to both Ford and other manufacturers to avoid the danger of being bound to Ford by non-standard systems.

Ford's policy was challenged as EDI became widely adopted by other manufacturers using standards developed by the European collaborative community, ODETTE. As the costs for suppliers of dealing with two incompatible standards became apparent, Ford agreed in principle to migrate to the EDIFACT (EDI for Administration, Commerce and Transport), an international standard for EDI use, when it becomes adopted in the US. Thus, the erosion of the competitive advantage of Ford's early proprietary systems forced them to co-operate in the more diverse community.

(Source: Graham, Spinardi and Williams, 1996. Adapted with permission.)

Questions

1 What do you think are the advantages and disadvantages of proprietary systems?
2 On the basis of Ford's experience, discuss the role of standards in EDI.
3 Find some other examples of early use of EDI.

number of companies in this category. It represents the variety of sectors involved in e-commerce and how a website can spring from very varied company backgrounds, but no significance is attached to how each site ranks in terms of success.

SOME E-COMMERCE COMPANIES

Amazon.com[5] (www.amazon.com or www.amazon.co.uk). Founded in 1995, this company was one of the pioneers of e-commerce and the first to sell books on-line. Jeff Bezos, the entrepreneur who started it, anticipated the attraction for the customer of searching for books to buy on their PC, reading comments, reviews and excerpts on-line, and selecting and buying without having to visit the store. The company also offers significant discounts in sale price made possible by the low overheads as a result of the savings they make by supplying books from a warehouse with no public bookstores to maintain. At present, Amazon have a significant share of all US book sales (De Kare-Silver, 1998) and a number of other booksellers are now following their footsteps. Amazon.com

Amazon.com is an example of the potential of e-commerce for entrepreneurs with the right vision. It shows how a small company can be a threat to the large and established ones with the help of e-commerce.

[5] Arguably, the example of Amazon is overused in the literature on e-commerce. However, it is often used in this book because it is expected that many students have an experience of buying from this company. It also provides an easy-to-understand context as it sells goods that students relate to easily.

is one of the many so-called dotcom companies arising out of the phenomenon of venture capitalism, under which a small team of people, or sometimes just one person, who saw the potential of an on-line business market and made a bid to investors for financing. Many companies have been set up this way in the last few years. Some of them have become very successful thus producing a new generation of mainly young (prospective) millionaires. However, there have been many, often high-profile, failures at the same time (e.g. Boo.com) which remind us of the importance of some of the questions raised previously in this chapter. We will attempt to deconstruct the risky environment of site development and launches later in the book.

Vauxhall (www.vauxhall.com): Although the automotive industry has been one of the first users of e-commerce, the business has really been limited between the company and its trading partners. However, this is changing. One example is Vauxhall which has set up a company website to provide direct car sales to customers. In the process they are attempting to establish a faithful customer base by providing 'on-going' information, services and support on-line, the same way they have always done via the physical outlet. This has enabled them to build a personal relationship with their customers and has increased the number of serious enquiries by about 40 per cent (Vernon, 2000).

Tesco (www.tescodirect.com). This well-known fast-moving consumer goods retailer started their on-line business site with Tesco Direct, the home shopping scheme. Customers use Tesco's website to see details of the products available and order goods which are then delivered to their door by the local store. Using email, Tesco informs customers of the latest launches, special deals and so on. Following a period of disappointing returns, the company has relaunched the site with plans to expand the system to link with suppliers for just-in-time delivery of products, competitive pricing strategies and other facilities.

Newham Online (www.newham.org.uk). Started in 1997 as a collaboration between Newham Community Education, Borough's Youth Service team and certain other agencies, this is an extranet created to integrate East London's local organisations and its people. The aim is to generate a cyber-environment with a view to creating an on-line community for users to access Newham related information, contribute to discussion groups and publications, attend courses, share resources, and take advantage of the link with local organisations such as Ford Motor Company and the University of East London. Thus this could be described as an on-line shopping mall which facilitates the exchange of goods, services, education and entertainment amongst other things.

Large companies such as Vauxhall and Tesco have gained a competitive advantage by using their websites to establish better customer relationships and faster movement of goods. At the other end of the scale are the Flying Noodle, an example of a small company competing on almost equal footing with the larger ones, and Priceline.com, a new service offering intermediation between a customer and the larger companies, made possible by the Internet.

Priceline.com. This is a unique and buyer-driven company that attempts to match a customer's request for a product and price to the goods. Users offer a price they are willing to pay for a product, for example a hotel room or a ticket for an airline flight, using the company's website, and the company searches for a seller willing to accept the price (Gupta, 2000). This is an example of how, on one hand the Internet has enabled companies to reduce the number of organisations they have to use (intermediaries) in order to get the product to the customer (e.g. dealers and distributors), on the other, new companies are being created to connect a buyer and a seller by providing an information-based intermediation.

The Flying Noodle (www.flyingnoodle.com). Reymond Lemire, a young American, set up a one-man company operating out of his bedroom in Duxbury, Massachusetts. He sells products required for cooking pasta and noodles by using a quirky and easy-to-use

hmv.com

HMV decided to launch an e-commerce site when they started getting about 500 emails a day from customers asking about buying over the Internet. It introduced a quick-fix solution in 1997 based on software from Microsoft to tide the company over for a year. They installed an IBM system later on which was more robust and scalable. The one-year pilot was very successful in that it enabled the company to realise that it needed to create a strong organisation-wide IT system to support the venture and offer a wide range of products. It also had to implement an email filtering software to deal with the large number of emails users were receiving. At the time, there were very few filtering products in the market, and the company had to opt for one of those. The business leaders realised very soon that the environment was very unpredictable and the rate of growth of e-commerce meant that projects tended to be under-resourced. Being the first or the best in the market was no guarantee for success; how much to spend and where to spend it was a crucial business lesson the company learnt from the experience. Some other lessons it learnt were: the importance of hiring people with a good sense of humour and tenacity, the importance of adequate investment, and the need for patience and flexibility. Stuart Row, the general manager of HMV e-commerce admitted that they knew there would be a lot of back-catalogue demand but didn't realise just how deep or specialist this would go. HMV's biggest store in Oxford Street had 140,000 products while its website had a quarter of a million.

(Adapted from Beckett, 2000, with permission from Reed Business Information Ltd.)

Questions

1 Discuss the added benefits of selling records on-line.
2 Why do you think the company decided to use an intermediate system for a year?
3 What benefits did it achieve from the temporary system?
4 Why do you think a company needs the things mentioned in the case study?
5 What lessons should we learn from this case study?

website that offers recipes, information on the ingredients amongst other things and also enables users to order on-line by guiding them through the variety of products available.

Working with a group of other students, design an e-commerce website for a fictitious company of your choice on paper.

The above are just some examples of companies using the Internet to do business. According to Forrester Research, a company engaged in surveying corporate performance, almost half of all business websites in the UK are attempting to engage in e-commerce (*e.business review*, June 2000). Another survey published by the same magazine in July 2000 announced that many companies (45 per cent of those with a website) are not yet generating any sales through their websites, although this is expected to change soon. They quoted from research by Internet market research company MMXI Europe that in the UK Egg.com, an on-line bank created in conjunction with the Prudential (a finance company), have the most successful e-commerce site in the financial market and Amazon.co.uk have the most successful retail site. The companies mentioned in this chapter are mostly successful e-commerce providers; there are others who are not so successful. We will discuss the criteria behind the success of e-commerce in later chapters.

Which products do you think are not suitable for on-line purchase? What are the problems associated with them?

Just the ticket for Nottinghamshire County Cricket Club

(www.trentbridge.co.uk)

With its main ground – Trent Bridge – a leading venue for international cricket, Nottinghamshire County Cricket Club was quick to recognise the potential of the Internet to communicate with supporters around the world. The message was driven home during the 1999 Cricket World Cup, when the club's website was bombarded with requests from supporters looking to purchase tickets on-line. Since the majority of the club's sales were already made by credit card, with a sizeable proportion made over the telephone, web-based sales seemed a natural progression.

The club therefore scrapped its first, information-only website, created around two years ago, and developed a new one providing on-line sales of tickets and merchandise, using BT's StoreCentre catalogue service. Lynn Steel, the club's membership secretary and ticket office manager, explains that StoreCentre was chosen because the club felt it would be simple to set up and easy to maintain, as well as cost-effective.

The revamped site was launched last November to coincide with the release of tickets for this year's international matches. Tickets for all international and domestic games, as well as coach travel and club memberships, are now available through the site. Web customers can also purchase club merchandise and around 250 items of cricket equipment, building on a limited mail-order service already being operated by the club shop.

Development of the site was handled entirely in-house by the shop and ticket management team, who have only limited technical expertise. According to Steel, they were amazed at how easy it was to set up StoreCentre. The major drawback, she explains, is that the visual appearance of the StoreCentre part of the system can't easily be customised to look like the rest of the Nottinghamshire County Cricket Club site. The club is now pressing BT to develop StoreCentre to make this possible.

In the site's first six months of operations, around £20,000 of business has been received, mostly for international tickets and club memberships. Steel is delighted that the website appears to have tapped into new markets, since a high proportion of people booking through the site have never previously visited Trent Bridge. Sales of cricket equipment are also starting to take off as the domestic season opens.

The club hasn't yet received any international orders from customers in the two countries whose test sides are touring England this year – the West Indies and Zimbabwe. However, Steel expects to see significant overseas traffic through the site next year, when Pakistan and Australia are playing, since the company normally receives a large number of telephone-based orders from Australian supporters.

(Adapted from Warren, 2000, with permission from Reed Business Information Ltd.)

Questions

1 Find some information on BT's StoreCentre: what it is, what facilities it offers, how it is run and managed, how a company can access it and so on.
2 What do you think are the pros and cons of using the services of another company this way?
3 Try to get into their site and critically evaluate it on the basis of its usability.
4 The cricket club is small compared to some other examples of companies trading electronically at present. What do you think are the benefits and drawbacks for small companies engaged in e-commerce?

SUMMARY

E-commerce has its roots in electronic data interchange (EDI), the process of transmitting data nationally and internationally using linked computers, performed by large companies from the mid-1970s. True e-commerce established itself as an important means of buying and selling products on-line and world-wide following the ascent of the Internet and the appearance of the World Wide Web. Companies in all spheres of the commercial world use their websites to advertise merchandise, display product details and offer methods for on-line payment. Buyers logged on to the Internet choose a suitable site, browse through details, select the products they want to buy, then order and pay electronically. Goods are delivered by physical or electronic means depending on their nature. The parties involved in this process could be two companies such as a car manufacturer and its spare parts suppliers, or a company and consumers, for example a supermarket and its home-shopping customers. The companies engaged in e-commerce could also be large multinationals or one-person firms. Starting with EDI used successfully in 1975 by SABRE, the airline reservation system, and in 1985 by FORDNET, a proprietary EDI network used by the Ford Motor Company, now e-commerce is used by a very large number of firms including Amazon and Tesco Direct. Some of them have managed to use it to gain a considerable competitive advantage in the market, while others have failed. The success of e-commerce depends on many factors which will be discussed in the rest of the book. In the next chapter we will go on to discussing the role of the Internet in the emergence of e-commerce.

Revision Questions

1 Describe the origin of e-commerce.
2 What is e-commerce and how does it differ from EDI and TDF?
3 What contribution did the Internet make to the proliferation of electronic communication?
4 Describe the steps involved in e-commerce clearly. How do the steps differ for different modes of e-commerce?
5 On the basis of your understanding so far, explain what you think are the contributing factors behind a company's success in e-commerce?
6 What questions do we need to answer to understand the nature and consequences of e-commerce?
7 Can you find the answers to these questions?
8 What observations could you make from the variety of examples of e-commerce companies used in this chapter? In answering this question, consider their size, type of business, the user base of the company etc.

Discussion Questions

1 Conduct a survey of people's perception of Internet-based buying and selling. What conclusion do you make from it?
2 E-commerce has been referred to as 'a phenomenon' here and by many other authors. Critically review the use of this description in the context of businesses and society.

Bibliography

Beckett, H., One year on . . . , *Computer Weekly, e.business review*, May, 2000, p. 21.

De Kare-Silver, M., *E-Shock: The Electronic Shopping Revolution: Strategies for Retailers and Manufacturers*, Macmillan, Basingstoke, 1998.

e.business review, Computer Weekly, June, 2000, p.12.

e.business review, Computer Weekly, July/August, 2000, p. 20.

Fellenstein, C. and Wood, R., *E-commerce, Global E-business and E-societies*, Prentice Hall, New Jersey, 2000.

Graham, I., Spinardi, G. and Williams, R., Diversity in the emergence of electronic commerce, *Journal of Information Technology*, 1996, pp. 161–172.

Gupta, U., *Information Systems: Success in the 21st Century*, Prentice Hall, New Jersey, 2000.

Hopper, M. D., Rattling SABRE – New ways to compete on information, *Harvard Business Review*, Reprint 90307, May–June, 1990, pp. 118–125.

Laudon, K. C. and Laudon, J. P., *Essentials of Management Information Systems: Transferring Business and Management*, Prentice Hall, New Jersey, 1999.

Lucas, A., What in the world is electronic commerce? *Sales and Marketing Management*, June, 1996 (http://proquest.umi.com).

Newham Online Report, 1999.

Vernon, *Computer Weekly, e-business review*, July/August, 2000, p. 20.

Ward, H., E-commerce tops IT agenda, *Computer Weekly*, 27 July, 2000, p. 14.

Warren, L., Size doesn't matter, *Computer Weekly*, 18 May, 2000, p. 54.

Webster, J., Networks of collaboration or conflict? Electronic data interchange and power in the supply chain, *Journal of Strategic Information Systems*, 4(1), 31–42.

The Internet and the World Wide Web for E-Commerce

Chapter Two

Objectives

By the end of this chapter you should have an understanding of:

- The history of the Internet.
- The role of an information infrastructure in electronic communication.
- The influence of the Internet on the commercial market.
- The concept of cyberspace.
- The Internet as a business environment.

INTRODUCTION

In chapter 1, we had a brief look at how the concept of electronic data transfer gave birth to the e-commerce phenomenon, and the extent of the use of e-commerce in the world today. But what made e-commerce, the way we know it today, possible?

In the late 1980s the arrival of the Internet in the commercial arena had a profound effect upon organisational environments. The possibility of making centrally held information available on computer screens caused a radical shift in the way businesses perceived the role of electronic communication in gaining a competitive advantage. This was enhanced by the development of the world wide web (WWW) in 1993 which provided a graphical user interface to the Internet and brought it to the mass market. This opened the doors to on-line business activities – a virtual marketplace (commonly known as cyberspace) – in which organisations could perform without the restrictions of time or space. This created many opportunities for businesses and consumers but raised many technical and organisational issues. In this chapter we will discuss the origins of the Internet and its nature today, the factors that helped to make the Internet a reality, the infrastructure required to underpin the concept of cyberspace, and the potential for the Internet as a business environment.

THE ORIGINS OF THE INTERNET

Increasingly worried by the activities of Soviet Russia in the area of space research and the launch of the first satellite in the late 1950s, President Eisenhower endeavoured to improve military intelligence in the USA. In consultation with the Secretary of Defense, he approached some key people from the country's mainly scientific community to develop a programme of research and development activities for the Department of Defense (DOD) to ensure that the country improved its technological capability in order to maintain security on the international frontier. Neil McElroy, the person the president put in charge of the initiative, set up the Advanced Research Project Agency (ARPA) in 1958 to co-ordinate the research programmes of different branches of the military. Following a period of uncertainty over the survival of ARPA due to controversies over who should be involved in space research – ARPA or the National Aeronautics and

Space Administration (NASA) – ARPA eventually beat NASA in the bid to become the organisation which pioneered political–academic research links.

This collaboration required a close link between the participating institutions so that they could share resources and results. This gave rise to the idea of connecting the universities and ARPA headquarters electronically. Following a considerable amount of negotiations between individuals, teams of researchers and networking companies, ARPANET was set up in the late 1960s to connect ARPA with the Stanford Research Institute and University College Los Angeles. Necessary protocols were established and the technique known as packet switching – suitable for the transmission of data over long distances – was developed. We will discuss networking technology in further detail later on in the book.[1]

ARPANET was the early version of the Internet. It was created in the 1960s in the USA by the collaboration of ARPA and some academic institutions involved in joint research on defence technologies via interconnected networks.

Soon other universities were connected to the network and satellite technology was applied to facilitate wireless communication. Many countries in Europe joined these research activities via satellite communication which led them to consider connecting the countries' networks together to form a network of networks. Technologies and protocols for transmission of data internationally were established. By 1975 the National Science Foundation (NSF) of the USA had taken an active role in expanding ARPANET into the academic community contracted to its services, and electronic mail systems were set up to improve communication between researchers.

In 1980, NSF supported a new initiative by a group of universities to create an academic network called CSNET. Although loosely connected to ARPANET, it was slower and cheaper. By 1986 the computer science departments of nearly all universities in the USA as well as some independent research laboratories were connected to CSNET. NSF supplied the backbone (supporting) network called NSFNET. Six supercomputer centres were scattered around the country, each supporting those institutions in its own area which were connected to CSNET. Nearly 2000 host computers holding large databases supplied the information circulating through the network. Since then the number of host computers doubled each year. Following the success of NSFNET, other co-operative networks were set up to serve different communities in the USA and many European countries. At the beginning they used NSFNET as the backbone to which they made connection by a local link. Soon this became unsatisfactory to both parties and the major networking companies set up their own nationwide links to carry the traffic independent of NSFNET. They all used the same protocol (TCP/IP) and could communicate with each other using the Unix open operating system, thus creating a network of networks: the Internet. By the early 1990s, access to the Internet was not just limited to government and government-sponsored organisations but also to the corporate world; by 1995 there were an estimated 4,852,000 host computers connected to the Internet (Gerace, 1995).

In 1980, NSF, the body which took an active role to support ARPANET, created an academic network called CSNET to connect the computer science departments of some universities. Initially CSNET used a backbone supported by NSF but in the early 1990s, it set up the Internet with TCP/IP with the support of the country's major networking companies.

Find out more about the history of the Internet, especially the role the American government played in this. Discuss the political issues surrounding the initiatives.

In addition to enabling users to retrieve information, the Internet also offered many other applications and services. *Usenet* is a service provided for groups of people, called newsgroups, who want to share information, comments etc. on specific topics. There are many computer systems world-wide which hold computer programs and other useful files in archives for public distribution through the Internet. A program called Archie, also available on the Internet, gives a list of all archives and their addresses. These files can be

[1] You can consult the glossary at the end of the book for a brief definition of some of the technical terms used here.

downloaded (retrieved) by using a service called file transfer available on the Internet. Using a protocol known as the *file transfer protocol* (FTP) it checks and transmits files of any format over the Internet. *Telnet* is a service which allows a user to login from a remote Internet Service Provider (ISP) and use it as his/her own. It works by transferring a user's files, using FTP, to the remote system. This is an easy way to access remote databases, libraries etc. Email has also been available on the Internet since the 1980s even though it was mainly text-based and therefore, less popular.

As we can see the Internet existed since the 1980s but its uses remained limited to the academic community until the early 1990s. The main reason behind this was the 'user-unfriendly' nature of the system and the lack of an infrastructure that would enable a user to connect to the network from anywhere in the world. Searching for information was difficult and required a high level of familiarity with the technology. Some services existed to facilitate searching: one example of this is Gopher, which is a multi-level index organised by the source of the information which enables a user to locate a document by searching through menus. This was very useful before the WWW and browsing programs such as Netscape were introduced because it was the only way to organise a search amongst the vast store of information available on the Internet. Wide area information server (WAIS) was a similar service offered by the Internet except that the index was organised by content rather than the source. However, if the concept of the Internet was to provide connectivity throughout the world, this would not work unless all networks could communicate with each other effectively, easily and inexpensively. This required an interface designed to make the Internet user-friendly – the world wide web, and an information infrastructure that facilitates true world-wide communication.

THE WORLD WIDE WEB

Until the WWW came onto the scene in 1993, the Internet was a territory for users with a specialised knowledge of technology. Commands were text-based and finding any information was difficult and time consuming. The Internet was linked to a large number of databases holding valuable academic and technical information but there was no easy way to search and therefore, narrow down the amount of information one had to plough through. Documents were not linked the way they are now and the only way to find information was to either browse through very long lists of titles or know the exact address.

Users recognised the potential of the Internet but grew increasingly frustrated by its limited usability. The situation was transformed in early 1993, after a researcher called Tim Berners-Lee working on Internet software protocols at the CERN atomic research centre in Switzerland, developed hypertext transport protocol (HTTP). Http enables a designer to use a programming language called hypertext markup language (HTML) to design a webpage with text, graphics, animation and many formatting techniques to create an interesting layout, as well as link a document electronically to other documents in the same way that files are linked in a relational database. Once connected this way, a link in one document can be used to access other linked documents anywhere in the world-wide network. Thus, this new technology created the possibility of virtually connecting all relevant information on a topic together; it created a world-wide web of information.

Introduced in 1993, the WWW improved the usability of the Internet by enabling designers to design and format a webpage. HTTP and HTML could be used to link documents electronically. This revolutionised the Internet by creating a web of information in which any document could be linked to any other.

However, the hyperlinks alone were not able to lift the Internet to the level of its popularity today because it ran on Unix and the interface was command-based and therefore still difficult to use. In the early 1990s, PC applications were in the process of adopting windows-based technology and using the same philosophy for the Internet was considered a natural progression. Work was going on to achieve this; the most successful of the initiatives taken was by a team led by Marc Anderson at the University of Illinois. In October 1993 they developed a browser, a windows-based graphical user interface for the Internet, called Mosaic. This was the first step towards freeing the Internet from the limited arena of the academic world and creating a true world wide web. The majority of the webservers which delivered the Internet service to consumers adopted the browser and by July 1996, 150,000 server computers were 'web-enabled' (Reid, 1997).

In October 1994, the same team developed Netscape, a web browser equipped with a 'search engine', a program that enables a user to perform a keyword search. They used an advanced version of HTTP to produce an attractive and intuitive graphical interface that used text, graphics, sound and animation to facilitate a search. They adopted pricing and marketing policies that gave Netscape a near monopoly amongst users in a very short period of time. A rapidly increasing number of commercial users saw the benefit of using the Internet and the WWW, not just for publishing marketing information but also for conducting on-line transactions. Other browsers were soon introduced to compete with Netscape, the most prominent of them is Internet Explorer by Microsoft. Although the latter gained a considerable proportion of the home PC market, Netscape has remained the favourite of the business world.

Real usability came soon after the introduction of the WWW by the development of Mosaic, a graphical user interface for the Internet to facilitate point and click navigation (browsing). In 1994, Netscape, the browser most commonly used today, was developed to enable users to perform keyword searches. This increased the popularity of the Internet enormously.

Find some information on the level and type of usage of the Internet at each stage of the above developments. What comments can you make about consumer preferences from your findings?

Following the integration of web browsers into the market, a number of websites dedicated to facilitating keyword searches from within a browser were developed; Yahoo!, AltaVista, Lycos and Excite are a few of the many such websites. However, a keyword search normally results in a long list of sites; finding a company this way is like walking through a very long high street shopping centre hoping there will be a branch of Marks & Spencer. A more effective way for organisations to attract visitors is to advertise on a portal – the first page presented to a user when he or she logs in, or advertise with a link on the homepage of a search engine, a tactic widely used by Amazon.com. Most companies have their own homepages now and in the majority of the cases the address is predictable; for example, the homepage of the weekly computer magazine *Computer Weekly* is 'www.computerweekly.com' (always following http://). This enables a customer to access a website directly without the need for a search.

The WWW also provided an increased level of data security by encrypting the messages moving between servers. Today, the security of data travelling on the Internet is a serious topic of debate, and there have been a number of reported cases of breach of security. However, the threat is no more acute than any other form of transaction. In reality, the security features used in the WWW and the measures taken to close any security holes found by dedicated hackers have been said to have made it one of the safest media of communication (Reid, 1997). We will discuss the finer points of Internet security later on in the book; at this point, we will move on to the most crucial aspect of successful communication of information – an infrastructure.

INFORMATION INFRASTRUCTURE

An infrastructure is a support system which enables a service or an enterprise to work. For example, the world-wide transport system which is expected to take people and goods from one location to any other in the world needs an infrastructure that does not only ensure that the vehicles exist but also that the facilities for transportation are set up.

Portals at Freeserve

Currently Freeserve is the UK's largest Internet service provider, with 35 per cent of the total ISP market and it needs to hold on to that very fickle customer base.

The problem is that the free Internet access model, which Freeserve launched and rode to dizzying heights of success in 1998 and 1999, is now a standard offering. The number of UK ISPs is growing exponentially, and call charges and subscription rates are no longer a viable revenue model. Freeserve's strategy over the past few months has been to move from being everyone's favourite ISP to becoming a valued source of information and services that its customers want to come back to again and again – in other words, a portal. Eventually it wants to run a whole series of portals – and to this end has recently launched two standalones – an auction site called FS Auctions and one aimed at women called iCircle.co.uk.

Any company can launch a website and call it a portal, but to make a successful one, Freeserve is going to try and squeeze every drop of business value out of its information.

Helen Litvak joined Freeserve in August 1999 as marketing data manager with seven years' experience of marketing databases. Litvak describes Freeserve's goal succinctly: 'We want to get to know our customers and in turn earn more revenue.'

Litvak's arrival at Freeserve saw the ISP launch an initiative to deploy new customer and site tracking software which will enable it to analyse users' interests and demographics to a level unmatched by its competitors: 'the aim of this initiative is to develop and organise content, enabling us to provide our customers with access to everything they need from the Web within one click on Freeserve.' Eventually Freeserve hopes to be able to gain an insight into the stickiness of its site, seasonal trends, on-line and off-line purchasing behaviour and customer acquisition and loyalty.

Once gathered, it will be able to use this information to maximise its advertising revenues by attracting the right visitors to particular parts of its site, thus being able to identify where adverts should be placed and what rates each area of the site should command. By understanding the intersets of its subscribers, Freeserve will also be more able to launch e-commerce services at them.

(Adapted from Paston, 2000, with permission from Reed Business Information Ltd.)

Questions

1 What advantages are Freeserve expected to gain from the above initiatives?
2 How do the customers gain from the new portal?
3 With reference to the comment 'Any company can launch a website and call it a portal', discuss how a portal should be different from a website.
4 What does the case study tell you about the qualities of a good website?
5 What does the case study tell you about how companies should act in the current climate of intense competition?

This includes direct links by road, air or water between places, necessary regulations and agreements between authorities in different places, facilities for the transfer of vehicles and drivers and so on. 'An infrastructure provides not only the physical links but also clearly stated rules and a carefully laid out structure which enable the system to function' (Bandyo-padhyay, 2000: 195). Without the infrastructure, the system falls down, and the Internet is no exception.

The Internet is often referred to as the information superhighway. This is not strictly true: whilst the Internet provides the scope for building an information superhighway, we are still far away from this for a number of reasons. First, we still need a computer to do this and the people who have access to a computer are still in a large minority; second, large parts of the world are not connected to the Internet; most importantly, the infrastructure is not fully developed yet. The world's developed countries have been attempting to build their own national information infrastructure (NII) to facilitate connectivity between all homes and offices within the country through initiatives backed by the government and some private companies. However, such initiatives have not proven to be adequate for the Internet for various reasons; amongst these are the inability of government-backed monopolies to meet the needs of the varied groups of customers effectively and doubts over whether or not private companies would consider all areas of the country equally suitable for investment. Whilst an NII works within the country, the Internet requires connectivity at a much wider scale.

A country's national information infrastructure (NII) should support connectivity between all offices and homes within the country. It must be prepared to cope with increasing numbers of users, and continue to provide reliable, fast and inexpensive communications.

Find some examples of the state of the infrastructure for electronic communication in some developed and developing countries in the last 20 years. Make comments on how the economic and political differences between countries affect the development of connectivity.

The Internet is different from all other networks we have used in the past in that no single person or organisation owns it; it is owned by almost everyone who uses it. A large company tapping into the country's telephone system to connect to the Internet has the same claim to the ownership of the network and the material passing through it as an individual who connects to the Internet via a modem. The 'backbone' of the Internet (see Fig. 2.1), that is, the physical electronic connections between large (super)computer centres all over the world, are normally built by governments (or their authorised bodies), telecommunication companies and private organisations, in order to carry the bulk of the data traffic. Smaller, regional networks (sometimes consisting of groups of even smaller networks) called service providers sell Internet access to users by connecting their computer systems to this backbone. There are other organisations which also use the backbone in order to support the system, for example, organisations which control the provision of addresses and domain names, the regulatory bodies which oversee standards, security and so on, and private and government-sponsored information centres which provide support and information (Gupta, 2000). Together, they provide the technical infrastructure.

However, an information infrastructure suitable for supporting a concept as big as the Internet requires much more than this. It has to be prepared to cope with phenomenal growth in the number of users, rapid increase in the power and variety of the Internet services, the demand for ease of use and speed, and the revolutionary innovations in information and communication technologies (ICT) which advance the parameters of the Internet continuously.

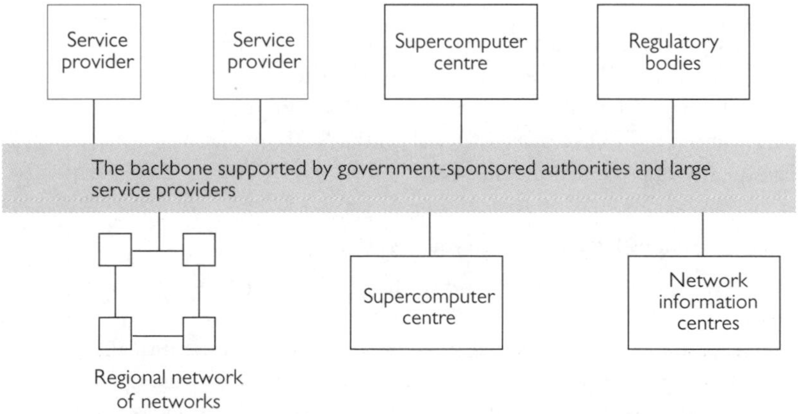

Fig. 2.1 The structure of the internet

The physical network supported by the bodies mentioned above can only be transformed into an information superhighway by a set of standards and policies agreed upon by the different communities involved in the process of communication. This has always been a major issue for the Internet but the proliferation of e-commerce has emphasised the importance of such an agreement. Amongst the decisions to be made are the following:

- How the system handles the rapid increase in the number of websites which necessitates the allocation of new addresses at an incredible rate.
- Who should be in charge of the expansion in hardware and software resources required by such a fast-growing system.
- A few years ago, only text and graphics were transmitted through the Internet. Now data is sent in various forms, for example, audio, video and animation. How do we ensure fast and reliable data transfer as an increasing number of businesses and consumers depend on the reliability of the network?
- Connectivity and operability between countries is the key to effective communication. A common standard is essential for this purpose. Effective e-commerce cannot be established unless trading partners in different countries use the same standard. So far, there has been friction between partners in global trading due to regional standard setting which did not serve the common purpose.
- Security is a major concern for Internet users. Threats do not only come from hackers who can bring even large and powerful service providers down by a simple email message (recently a hacker in the Philippines created mayhem by sending an email entitled 'I love you' to a number of major service providers), frauds in many forms have infiltrated the Internet, thus making security a major concern for e-commerce users. In addition to this, government authorities are increasingly concerned about the role of the Internet in international terrorism, criminal activities and unlawful transactions. The information infrastructure needs to establish measures to secure data against such threats in order to build customer trust in e-commerce. We will discuss security in more detail in a later chapter.
- Closely related to security is concern over the privacy of the users of e-commerce. Every time we buy something on the Internet, we must provide personal details such as a credit card number and home address that, if they fall into the wrong hands, can be used to our detriment. Policies and regulations designed to alleviate such risks are essential for the success of e-commerce.
- Effective Internet provision is still a problem for many users. Issues that an information infrastructure should address include access to the network, access to the full range of facilities, the problem of information overload (as there is a large amount of unnecessary material on the Net), quality of information, quality of presentation and so on.

What is currently wrong with the Internet in your view/experience?

The roots of the Internet are closely embedded in academia which has traditionally nurtured free speech and self-governance based on a consensus-building process open to continual innovations and growth. This is the strength behind the Internet – the imagination and enthusiasm of ordinary people who pioneered its many services.

However, this is also its weakness: the free spirit which created it is also responsible for a type of 'anarchy' which is behind many of the factors which weaken the suitability of the Internet as a business medium. Examples of the problems behind setting up an NII are the monopoly created by large telecommunications companies which resist openness and competition, and the absence of agreements between the government of a country and its citizens over the balance between accessibility and civil liberties. Heated debates are currently going on both in the USA and in the UK over respective governments' proposals to hold the keys equipped to decrypt the encrypted data transmitted via public networks. To create an effective information infrastructure we need to exploit the entrepreneurial energy that created the railroads in the nineteenth century while avoiding the concentration of power that can distort our society (Miller, 1996).

Many issues must be resolved before effective world-wide communication is possible. Amongst these are the problems of the growth in data traffic, management and control of the technology, security of data, privacy of users, and connectivity to all parts of the world. There is also a debate over whether or not there should be a control over the content of the WWW in order to avoid the transmission of 'improper' messages.

The purpose of a well thought-out information infrastructure is to address the above issues. In order to utilise the enormous power of the Internet in developing a healthy e-commerce environment a world-wide infrastructure must be created by co-operation of government authorities, business communities and consumers. There are already lively discussions on some of the issues while some others need a lot more awareness and attention. We will come back to the subject of the Internet technologies which support an information infrastructure as well as the criteria for successful implementation of e-commerce later on in the book. The following is a brief overview of the progress made so far in the creation of a global information infrastructure.

GLOBAL INFORMATION INFRASTRUCTURE – SOME EXAMPLES

Until the middle of the 1990s, the initiatives taken by countries to maintain an NII were concerned with, in most part, the country's telephone links which, in addition to maintaining a voice network, also provided the backbone for their national electronic connectivity. The NIIs worked collectively to a certain extent, especially for the Western world, to provide transborder data flow via the Internet. However, as the Internet became larger and countries new to the game started joining the phenomenon, governments faced a different challenge: how to achieve global communication. Somehow the NII had to be extended across national boundaries to form a global information infrastructure (GII).

Some governments resisted this in the name of maintaining national cultures and thus restricted the potential of the Internet in promoting global economy. '. . . governments faced friction between their NIIs and those of other nations, the economic uses of the network on the one hand and the political and social consequences on the other, and the thriving information world enabled by the NIIs and the physical world it threatened to leave behind' (Lodge and Reavis, 1999). Ideally, they needed to relate the NIIs to form a GII; according to some critics, this remained far from being a reality. However, attempts were being made by the authorities to address some of these issues; the following are a few examples.

GII is required to facilitate world-wide Internet connectivity. This can be achieved if efforts are made by each participating country to improve their NII in order to accommodate global communications. In the UK and the USA this was done by liberalisation of the communications policies which enabled the telecommunications companies to open their services up to a wider market and also encouraged them to provide cheaper and better services.

The realisation that the creation of a GII required financial investment which could only be provided by private companies made governments in technologically developed countries advocate a liberalisation of their telecommunications services. This led to a process of deregulation, driven mainly by consumer demands, in the mid-1980s; by the mid-1990s competition from private companies ended the long-established monopolies such as that of AT&T in the USA and BT in the UK. Governments concentrated on improving their NII in order to contribute to the GII. In the USA, the Clinton government created the National Information Infrastructure Advisory Council in 1994 with leaders from the government, education and the public services. They made consumer demand their main priority and advocated competition between telecommunications companies by liberalising regulations concerning telecommunications services and the international trading of electronic components. Consequently, many new companies entered the arena resulting in cheaper and easier Internet access; many small and medium sized companies benefited from world-wide connectivity, and there was an enormous increase in mass entertainment and information media – TV, films, publishers and so on who took advantage of better communications facilities. Critics argued that such a policy failed to acknowledge 'real' community needs such as narrowing the gap between the rich and poor, controlling the activities of neo-nazi affiliations, and ensuring privacy and security for the citizens of the world. However, the newly improved connectivity served to improve the potential of the Internet as a business medium.

Deregulation in the UK began in 1983 with the creation of a duopoly between British Telecom (BT) and Mercury operated by Cable & Wireless (C&W). BT was privatised in 1984 and Oftel, a government-sponsored regulatory agency, was created at the same time in order to monitor the activities of telecommunications companies. Later on, they allowed more companies to enter the competition and by 1997, there were 115 cable franchises, of which all but five also offered telephone services (Lodge and Reavis, 1999). This resulted in an improved communications infrastructure and, in some cases, by joint ventures between BT and cable companies. Although this restricted BT's market share in the UK, the newly liberalised infrastructure encouraged the company to enter the global arena and develop a strong presence on the international market. This in turn contributed to the GII which was crucial for the business world.

Competition was also encouraged by the European Union (EU) and by the 1998 many EU countries opened up their telecommunications markets. Like BT, many companies in the EU also expanded their services internationally, reaching a number of developing countries as well. However, the intended goal of a GII was not achieved fully as there were no adequate policy agreements appropriate for the interconnection of services between countries in relation to standards, licensing, compatibility of dialling codes, national regulations and so on.

Find some information on what initiatives have been taken in some other countries not mentioned above. How have they affected the countries' telecommunications infrastructure?

Some Asian countries such as Japan, Singapore and China reacted to the Internet phenomenon in unique ways. Japan achieved a high level of NII quite early but demonstrated a low demand for Internet access. The governments of Singapore and China, although technologically equipped to use the Internet, expressed caution over the issue of content for reasons of security and community values, and maintained some degree of control.

Japan experienced a different phenomenon. In spite of the fact that its information infrastructure aimed to achieve full cable network connection to all institutions and every home by 2005, and that it already had efficient communication services, demand for Internet connection remained low. A number of reasons have been given for this: the high cost of telecommunication, slow Internet development due to a certain over-regulation which restricted the allocation of domain names, alleged cultural attitudes, use of English as the main language for the WWW while computers in Japan have keyboards based on their own script and so on.

Singapore followed a unique route. It had a well-developed NII since the early 1990s with the visionary aim of creating an intelligent island capable of competing in the global business environment. It allowed a monopolistic telecommunications service operated by the country's privatised telecommunications company till the year 2000. In the meantime it established fibre-optic cable lines throughout the country to ensure nationwide connectivity for every citizen. However, the government controlled access to information for citizens because it believed that it had the responsibility to screen out what it thought was unsuitable for maintaining 'community values'. It restricted access to international broadcast by prohibiting home satellite dishes. At the same time, it encouraged 'home' media companies to broadcast in the whole Asian region. It facilitated Internet access in the early 1990s but did not allow widespread use until the mid-1990s, and even then a series of measures was taken to control the content before it reached consumers.

China exercised an even more cautious approach. In the mid/late 1990s, all Internet service providers were supervised by a government agency, all international connections had to use a channel designated by the Ministry of Post and Telecommunications, people with Internet access had to register with the police, and Internet content was checked for national security. In effect, they created a Chinese intranet. There was strict control over any foreign influence upon the IT equipment and services industry. However, nearer the end of the millennium, restrictions in this field – along with all aspects of the Chinese society – also began to be relinquished. Foreign investment in IT started to be encouraged, resulting in lower prices for phone lines and Internet access. However, control over content remained, for example, there was a drive to encourage the use of Chinese-language material on the Internet. Other factors that still limit the use of the Internet in China include the absence of credit cards and restrictions on delivery across cities.

Find examples of other countries which are exercising control over the Internet and in what ways. Discuss the pros and cons of such controls.

Developing countries remained largely neglected in the drive for Internet access. The lack of a private sector and foreign investment in some of these countries was the main reason. Even when attempts were made by the USA to improve the situation, they were often not trusted to be in the best interest of the receiving countries. Although countries such as India and Brazil have made phenomenal progress in their IT (mainly software) industries, their telecommunications infrastructure did not manage to make the Internet a viable business option as the majority of the people in the country did not have a telephone connection. However, there has been a growing level of recognition amongst the governments of the developing countries that a well-developed national information infrastructure has the potential to improve the way people work, learn and live. This has prompted many of them to introduce policies and plans to meet the challenges of the global information society. For example, the widespread realisation that information is the major precursor for alleviation of poverty in Africa has become the primary driving force for the formulation of national information and communication policies. As a result, the number of African countries with Internet access jumped from four in 1995 to 50 in 1999 (Adam, 2000). It has been suggested that digital technology and satellite communications have the potential to bring these countries up to date as they do not necessarily require point-to-point cable connection. '. . . in building their infrastructure LDCs [less developed countries] could "skip the 20th century" by installing the same technologies with which advanced countries were replacing copper wire' (Lodge and Reavis,[2] 1999: 21).

The different attitudes taken by different countries created some international friction in terms of competition, collaboration and community needs. For example, some of the policies restricted the free flow of information essential for global e-commerce, standards remained an issue in many parts of the world, poor technological infrastructures restricted communication, communities affected by job losses as a result of Internet-based commerce were neglected, and developing countries continued to be bypassed in the initiatives. A global debate on how to manage e-commerce started at this time because

[2] Much of the information in this section has been taken from: G. C. Lodge and C. Reavis, *Global Friction Among Information Infrastructure*, 9-799-152. Boston: Harvard Business School, 1999. Copyright © 1999 by the President and Fellows of Harvard College. Reprinted by permission.

the GII did not succeed in resolving the problems associated with e-commerce activities. In 1995, the Global Information Infrastructure Commission (GIIC) was set up in the USA. Made up of delegates from a wide range of technology companies, its mission was to provide leadership in the development of e-commerce with minimal government involvement. They worked closely with trade associations, intergovernmental organisations and public interest groups to achieve the following goals:

- To strengthen the role of the private sector in the development of an effective GII.
- To promote the involvement of the developing countries.
- To identify the necessary policy options and facilitate activities which would encourage widespread global telecommunications services.

Find out to what extent the above goals have been or are in the process of being met.

Due to the differences in the attitude of different countries and the lack of support for developing countries to build an effective infrastructure, the GII did not fully materialise. The GIIC was formed by some technology companies to improve the situation with minimal government involvement.

THE INTERNET REVOLUTION

The increased popularity of the Internet, prompted by improved cheapness and convenience, gave users access to almost unlimited amounts of information. This brought about a remarkable change in corporate and institutional culture throughout the technologically developed world. New technology has always been an enabler of change: the introduction of the steam engine transformed the nature of an organisation by expanding the 'reach' of businesses from local areas to the rest of the country, the use of automatic teller machines (ATM) changed the nature of banking for ever, and the introduction of the PC revolutionised the office. The Internet and the WWW started another revolution by stimulating profound changes in the business world. Reid (1997) expressed this as a phenomenon that is not concerned with doing things on the Internet, but rather about using the Internet to do things differently in the wider world. Universities can now teach a group of internationally situated students, teams of dispersed employees can work on a project using groupware running on the Internet, a multinational company can transfer its manufacturing base to countries with a cheaper labour cost and keep in constant touch with them, and ordinary people can communicate with friends and relatives world-wide without having to pay large telephone bills.

At the root of most of the changes in the business world is a drive towards consumer power; consumers rather than products are the focus of today's organisations. As new companies are entering the market and old companies are adopting Internet-based activities, it is becoming increasingly clear that the market for goods is now saturated and the winning strategy lies in a company's ability to attract customers. Customers are now in a position to demand better services and quick and easy access to information and goods. On the one hand the Internet has facilitated the delivery of such services; on the other, it has created an environment of instability in which a company incapable of meeting such demands is unable to compete. Thus, the Internet has not only revolutionised the way businesses are run, it has also revolutionised the concept of the relationship between businesses and their customers. We will come back to these concepts later on in the book.

The Internet revolutionised the way organisations run their business. In a highly competitive market, companies had to act to attract customers. This led to a situation in which customers were in a position to demand better services and quick and easy access to goods and information.

Pick an industry – pharmaceutical, retail, banking – and describe how the Internet could be said to have revolutionised it.

THE CONCEPT OF THE VIRTUAL ORGANISATION AND CYBERSPACE

The concept of the virtual organisation is not new. For nearly 15 years academics have exchanged emails between institutions in order to share information and knowledge; multinational corporations, especially banks, have used EDI to communicate with partners world-wide; and companies have outsourced specific functions of their business, thus extending the physical boundaries of the organisation and creating a virtual workforce. For example, Microsoft outsource the help-desk technical support for their employees to take advantage of external expertise (Gates, 1999). Bill Gates calls it the 'studio' model: the number of permanent members in the working team of a film company is very small; when a new project starts the core team employs technicians, actors and directors with the appropriate skills. The rise of the Internet has increased the scope of such models by linking companies electronically with their partners, buyers, suppliers and customers to create a market which is fluid in construction and unlimited in geographical extent. This global market is facilitated by technology and its main resource is information; it is often called a marketspace or the cyberspace to distinguish it from the physical world of 'bricks and mortar' that one can see and touch.

Until the mid-1970s, most large organisations followed a hierarchical model because it enabled them to standardise the mass production of goods and exercise strict managerial control over their activities. It also provided managers with clarity between different production processes. However, hierarchical organisations tended to be highly bureaucratic and inflexible with only top-down communication. They concentrated on mass-produced goods to cater for majority tastes. Such firms were in danger of excluding themselves from the emerging market of consumers who, enlightened by wider transborder communication facilities, wanted more specialised products. In the 1980s a dynamic network structure of organisation started to appear in which such hierarchies gave way to teams. In this model, each new project was allocated a team of people with the appropriate expertise, thus utilising the best and the most appropriate talents from a pool of managers and workers each time. Such organisations had a decentralised management structure and a flexible and informal division of labour. They used advanced technology and were capable of responding to market demands quickly. This dynamic network model was also more democratic than the hierarchical one, as employees had a better scope for expressing their views in small teams and improving their interpersonal and leadership skills.

With the help of further investigation, discuss the relative strengths and weaknesses of the hierarchical and dynamic network models, especially in the light of e-commerce.

The effectiveness of the dynamic network structure was enhanced by the emerging ICTs in the 1980–90s because it enabled teams to work over wide geographical locations. A virtual organisation is a progression of the same philosophy: teams in such an organisation can include people almost anywhere in the world, they can work together at any time of the day, and they can use technology to share files and documents in real time as if they were sitting round the same table. The office in this organisation exists in 'cyberspace' – a term '. . . . used to refer to the concept of global systems interconnection whereby every computer and telecommunications network . . . have access to the same "information space"' (Barnatt, 1996: 208). The primary resource of a virtual organisation is its communications link among collaborating workers. Nohria and Berkley (1994: 115) listed five characteristics of a virtual organisation: (1) electronic files replace material files; (2) electronic communication is used for primary activities and face-to-face communication is used mainly for maintaining organisational cohesion; (3) structure is defined by the organisation of technology and information rather than hierarchy; (4) external boundaries are ambiguous as a result of networking across firms; and (5) jobs are global and cross-functional 'such that individual members of the organisation may be considered holographically equivalent to the organisation as a whole'. An example of an organisation which demonstrates these characteristics is a virtual classroom in which teachers are connected electronically with students. Here, all participants share a common information resource stored on disk and communicated via a network, while face-to-face communication is used only occasionally. The architecture of the interconnecting network and the organisation of the information available to the participating members are based upon the needs of the classroom. While different courses comprise different (sometimes overlapping) groups of students and teachers, they can still be served by the same system, thus creating a boundless organisation in which each of the participating members represent the whole organisation.

Early forms of virtual organisations depended on the electronic mail system which came into the academic world in the mid-1980s and became a common phenomenon in commercial organisations in the early to middle 1990s. Now email is an essential software tool for employees in all types of organisation and for workers at all areas and levels. Together with the Internet, email is now the single most important contributor to the concept of cyberspace because it facilitates teamwork without the constraints of space and time. Other technologies that played an important part in this phenomenon are video-conferencing, which enables workers in separate locations to hold meetings by connecting via communications technologies incorporating a camera, and groupware – a suit of software developed in the mid-1990s to enable people to work interactively on the same electronic documents. Groupware was the result of an academic initiative of the late 1980s called computer supported co-operative work (CSCW) which addressed the issues arising from people working together in physically dispersed locations using technology. It considered how group dynamics, organisational behaviour and communications technologies relate to each other to provide a tool for effective teamwork in large organisations.

Organisational structures have been changing from a hierarchical to a distributed team-based model since the 1980s as a result of the improvements in ICTs leading to customer demands for better services. Equipped with the Internet, companies in the 1990s moved further in this direction by the creation of the cyberspace in which teams used technologies such as email and groupware to share a common information space from dispersed locations, thus creating a virtual organisation.

In the wake of the new millennium, mobile technology set a new agenda for e-commerce with third-generation WAP phones. Mobile communication was first introduced in the 1980s with voice-based (analogue) data transmitted via radio waves. Following this, the first-generation mobile network, came the second generation in the 1990s which made it possible to turn voice into digital data, thus improving the quality of transmission. This enabled mobile phone users to send short text messages to each other. It also saw the beginning of mobile e-commerce (other than what companies could do using laptops and notebooks) as some companies offered services such as stock quotes and horoscopes. But the service was limited by the length of the messages and slow speed. With the introduction of the third-generation mobile technology (referred to as 3G), consumers can now surf the Internet using wireless applications protocol (WAP), an international standard for transferring Internet content to mobile phones and palmtops. This development has an enormous potential especially in the business-to-consumer e-commerce market. We will come back to this subject in the later sections of the book.

In recent years, the concept of a virtual organisation has been taken much further by the upsurge of e-commerce companies, especially by the rise of the so-called dotcom firms because many of them have a very small physical existence: they are almost entirely 'virtual'. Most of them use the country's communications infrastructure to sell to individuals using PCs connected to a modem. Technologically, this is a relatively uncomplicated situation and the success of the companies depends on the strength of their vision and business resources. For larger organisations trying to establish a virtual relationship with their trading partners there are many other important issues: they must accommodate users whose IT sophistication may vary enormously; security must be maintained at every stage of communication; they must establish good working relationships with a constantly changing pool of customers and suppliers; and the technology must be capable of handling the flow of information speedily and reliably (Upton and McAfee, 1996). We will return to the subject of how to achieve success in e-commerce later on in the book. At this stage we are more interested in discussing the role of the Internet in providing an environment for virtual commerce.

In recent years, the introduction of mobile phones, WAP technology and the upsurge of dotcom companies have extended the concept of a virtual organisation by facilitating on-line business activities anywhere and by anyone. However, they have also presented companies with a lot of challenges.

Discuss the strengths and weaknesses of a virtual organisation for national and international business relationships.

THE INTERNET AS A BUSINESS ENVIRONMENT

Amongst the main advantages of the Internet in a business context are its ability to facilitate business activities without the restrictions of geography and time zones, and the ease of transaction in terms of speed and cost. The Internet started an era in business in which many new companies entered the market and ran their entire business on the Net, thus causing considerable consternation for some older, established companies. The challenge faced by traditional booksellers against competition from Amazon.com is a typical example. It is a well-publicised fact that many of the new Internet-based companies are yet to make a profit because their main emphasis is on growth and experimentation. However, the Internet offers them the scope to present themselves as a potential threat to the traditional business world which, in turn, is increasingly adopting the Internet business philosophy to maintain a competitive advantage.

Yet how is this done? Evans and Wurster (1999) use the concept of navigation as the tool that determines success in the battle for the largest market share. In a market crowded with competing products, customers must find a way to navigate using time-consuming and sometimes inconvenient methods. Traditionally, large companies used their economic strength to advertise their products and acquire knowledge of their customer base, in order to influence navigation in favour of their own brands. The automobile industry spends a large amount of money in advertising in an attempt to attract specific groups of customers to specific brands on the basis of the results of their extensive market research. The Internet facilitates the provision of cheap, easy and quick navigation facilities for customers without the companies having to spend much of their physical resources. This gives the new entrepreneurial companies an edge in the market.

Using navigational tools, companies can improve their business on three fronts: reach, richness and affiliation (Evans and Wurster, 1999). Using the Internet it is possible to reach and serve an unlimited number of customers regardless of geographical distance or the space required for the storage of the goods. While a traditional bookstore can perhaps hold a few hundred thousand books in stock and serve customers within a finite geographical area, Amazon.com offers 4.5 million books to customers almost anywhere in the world. This is possible because Amazon can store the books in a large warehouse without the overheads required by a traditional shop or even acquire them from the publishers as and when necessary. The navigation facilities of its website enable it to

First Direct

First Direct (FD) introduced the concept of a virtual organisation before the Internet became a practical viability. FD is a 24-hour telephone banking system introduced by the Midland Bank in the UK in 1989. This was the time when the customer opinion of branch services of all UK banks were low. Midland Bank was in further difficulty due to heavy losses in 1988; they had to find a way to improve the situation. Following extensive market research they decided that 24-hour person-to-person banking had the potential to woo customers back. However, in order to avoid the customer backlog resulting from a poor reputation, they started FD under a separate brand name. They went 'live' at one minute past midnight on Sunday, 1 October, 1989; by 1994 FD became profitable and by 1996 it became the largest 'virtual' bank in the world. The company depended on the 'personalisation' of services. They improved their human resources management, and established better communications technologies and customer information systems. Such changes enabled them to provide all types of banking service a lot more cheaply than their branch operations and they achieved a very high customer satisfaction level. Consumers could dial a freephone number or reply to a newspaper advertisement to open an account. FD used strict screening criteria to select customers with satisfactory credit records, but in return gave an excellent service which resulted in them retaining over 95 per cent of all customers registered since launch. They also used the customer data stored on their information system to build customer profiles which they could utilise in order to offer other relevant FD products to targeted customers.

(Source: Dickson, 1997. Copyright © 1998 by the President and Fellows of Harvard College. Harvard Business School Case 9-897-079.)

This case was prepared by Research Associate, Dickson L. Louise under the supervision of Professor Jeffrey F. Rayport as the basis of class discussion rather than to illustrate either effective or ineffective handling of an administrative situation. Reprinted by permission from Harvard Business School.

Questions

1. 'First Direct was one of the pioneers of the concept of cyberspace'. Discuss.
2. Why do you think FD enjoyed such high levels of customer satisfaction when most physical banks lost customer trust?
3. Compare the operations of FD with those of an Internet-based bank. In what ways are they similar/different?
4. How can FD's experience be translated into a cyberbank?

separate the function of searching for a product from its availability, thus increasing its reach enormously. 'Reach is the most visible difference between electronic and physical businesses, and it has been the primary competitive differentiation for businesses thus far' (Evans and Wurster, 1999: 87).

Find some other examples of companies taking advantage of the 'reach' made possible by the Internet.

While Internet-based companies have an advantage in reach, the story is slightly different on richness. Richness is the depth and detail of information a company holds on their customers as well as what it is able to give to its customers. Traditionally large companies have well-established procedures for collecting and storing customer data (data mining and warehousing respectively[3]), and their marketing machines are well

[3] We will cover these topics in chapter 6.

equipped to make product information available to the customers. For example a superstore can use data collected at the automated tills from customers' credit or store cards to build a database of customer habits and credibility. This can be used for distributing accurately targeted product information and for long-term planning based on projected trends. However, the Internet also has the potential to offer companies excellent facilities for advertising products and giving value-added information at a very low cost. For example, holiday companies can advertise their resorts with videos of accommodation, tourist attractions and so on (see case study on Hyatt Hotels, chapter 3); publishing companies can display reviews of the books on store, provide links to books on related subjects, and publish information on authors in order to impress customers; supermarkets can publish details of the ingredients in a product and their sources of supply or even recipes using products available in the store to add to their services. The greatest strength of the Internet is its ability to use information; Internet-based companies can exploit this to achieve richness. The Internet also offers the technical facilities required to collect customer information and use it for business purposes. For example, it is possible for a website to collect data on the types of product most frequently ordered by individual customers and email information on other similar products to them directly (see case study on 1-800-FLOWERS). Although, there are concerns over the legitimacy of such practices on grounds of privacy and security, the practice of collecting customer data by 'brick and mortar' companies is open to similar criticisms.

Affiliation is a new dimension brought on mainly by the power of a direct electronic link between a company and its customers. Traditionally, businesses operated within the sphere of their trading partners, and although customers had a role in it, their interests were not of high priority. As long as the product had a market and there were enough customers willing to pay the price set on it, businesses were not concerned about the opinion of the customers. This was mainly because customers did not have access to knowledge of the market and were not able to 'shop around' to a great extent. The Internet has changed all that; empowered by the wealth of information available on-line, consumers are now in a strong position to choose what they want, and disregard loyalty if necessary. Examining the potential of the Internet to streamline the financial services industry, John Riley (2000: 12) noted that, 'The Internet strikes at the heart of financial services by attacking its role as a middleman and empowering customers, who, far from being owned by their banks any longer, need merely to click to switch to a new account'. Such attitudes have forced businesses to shift their affiliation – the body whose interest they represent – from suppliers to customers. For example, a leading mobile phone retailer in the UK promised to give cash back on handsets if the price falls up to three months after purchase (Vernon, 2000). Such promises are the result of the change in the balance of power from company or product to the client. Another example of the utilisation of affiliation towards customers is the case of Microsoft's CarPoint program which provides car buyers with data and software to compare alternative models in the market for no cost. Microsoft use the power of technology to gather information on the automobile industry and exploit it to increase their own customer loyalty and, at the same time, to advertise MS products via the website. Whilst car dealers would not choose to publish information on competing models in their physical stores or the websites, they must accept the new trend and try harder to survive in the face of new consumer power.

In a market crowded with competing products, customers need to find a way to navigate. Reach: the number of customers a company can access; richness: the depth of information a company holds on customers and it can give to customers; and affiliation: the loyalty a company has towards its customers; are the three dimensions of navigation which can be used in businesses to gain advantage. The Internet enables a company to achieve all three.

With the help of further research, can you find examples of organisations which have been forced to alter their attitudes and practices as a result of the Internet revolution? Describe your findings.

1-800-FLOWERS
(www.1800flowers.com)

Run as a family business, 1-800-FLOWERS.com provides a broad range of gift products including flowers, gourmet foods, sweets, gift baskets and other items to customers around the world. The company built the business on the back of the powerful electronic marketing tool, the 1-800 free phone number, and became the world's largest florist with more than $300 million in sales and over 200 employees (De Kare-Silver, 1998). It was recently named the top gift site on the web by ClickGuide.com.

The company takes orders on-line from the customers and about 1600 partner florists worldwide, collectively known as BloomNet, supply the goods. Plow & Hearth, a subsidiary of 1-800-FLOWERS.com, is a mail order company located in Madison, Virginia which specialises in home and garden merchandise and publishes several seasonal catalogues throughout the year. 1-800-FLOWERS uses the Internet as its main communications channel with customers. From the orders submitted by customers, it collects and stores data on birthdays and invitations, as well as a record of gifts sent to specific recipients. It maintains a customer information file holding all such data which alerts them of the forthcoming events. At the appropriate times the company sends customised messages to the customers with suggestions for flowers and presents. Thus it uses the reach of its website to improve relationships with its customers and simultaneously promote its business by sending ideas before they have started thinking about a gift. Having started with the pioneering idea of making people comfortable with buying flowers over the phone, it went out of its way to build up consumer confidence by giving 100 per cent quality assurance guarantee and making follow-up phone calls to check on satisfaction. The company's infrastructure and know-how added to this philosophy of personalised service enabled it to build an interactive on-line business which won a reputation as 'the electronic flower seller'.

Questions

1 Explain how this case demonstrates the potential of the Internet in offering richness of information to promote businesses.
2 Find some other examples of companies using their website for offering customised services.
3 How does the company benefit from this in the long run?
4 Do the customers benefit? Discuss.
5 What are the political and ethical issues surrounding such practices?

Thus the Internet revolution has created a whole new arena in which companies can use navigation to gain a competitive advantage. They use it to improve reach and richness to attract new customers, and customers benefit due to the resulting shift in affiliation. A large number of new companies has been born as a result of the Internet's potential for navigation while search engines such as Yahoo! and AltaVista based their entire business on this concept.

BUSINESS PROCESSES IN THE ELECTRONIC AGE

A world-wide network has been considered a powerful medium for business communication for as long as it existed. The evolution of increasingly effective electronic distribution channels and payment mechanisms has enriched the quality of business transactions enormously in the last two decades. Especially in the Western world, the use of EDI by large multinational companies to re-engineer their businesses and improve supply-chain management processes (see below) demonstrates clearly the importance of electronic communication for trade. The Internet has championed the acceptance of the concept of electronic transactions by companies of all sizes all over the world by providing the necessary technical infrastructure (Bamford, 1997).

A businesses performs many activities from acquiring raw materials for products and services to serving the customer at the point of sale. The Internet has applications for these processes – to varying degrees – but before we discuss how or to what extent, we need to define the following terms which have particular significance to e-commerce and its relationship with technology.

Business process re-engineering (BPR)

This is the philosophy of '. . . tossing aside old systems and starting over. It involves going back to the beginning and inventing a better way to do work' (Chaston, 2001: 221). It entails a fundamental rethinking and redesign of business processes in order to achieve dramatic improvements in performance. 'The term BPR involves focusing upon the processes inherent in company operations – rather than the structures through which they are conducted – and rethinking them in the light of the industrial and technological revolutions of the late twentieth century' (Barnatt, 1996: 72). Different companies take different routes to re-engineer: some use it as an excuse to cut jobs in the guise of downsizing; others undertake a complete review of all operations and redesign activities wherever necessary in order to improve efficiency through a fresh look at business processes and their enabling technology. At the root of the initiatives taken by companies successfully engaged in re-engineering is the modern philosophy of consumer power – the increased demand made by customers who are now economically strong and technologically equipped enough to take their custom to the most efficient companies.

BPR is a concept geared towards reinventing business, and is not primarily a technological activity. However, IT plays a crucial role in BPR as an enabler of a re-engineering process. IT can be used to develop an infrastructure which would facilitate changes. One of the common outcomes of re-engineering in the current environment is a move away from a hierarchical management and technological structure to a 'dynamic network' which creates distributed, often virtual teams connected by telecommunications, thus giving rise to concepts such as telecommuting, hot-desking and hotelling. Another outcome is the development of a customer interface, for example a website, to create a convenient 'doorway' to the organisation for its customers. The Internet and its associated technologies have important roles to play in both activities.

Find examples of some companies not mentioned here which underwent a major re-engineering process. Describe what it did and what effects this had on the organisation.

Business process re-engineering (BPR), supply-chain management and procurement are some of the business processes which can be performed more effectively with the help of the Internet. BPR entails a fundamental rethinking and redesign of business processes, supply-chain management involves streamlining the involvement of the intermediaries, and procurement is the process of negotiating quality supply quickly and cost-effectively.

Supply chain

A product has to go through a number of stages between when its raw constituents are obtained and the final goods are delivered to the customer. A number of different agencies are involved in this cycle. For example, a tin of baked beans in our kitchen cupboard started its life in a farm as raw beans. The farmer probably sold the beans, amongst his other produce, to a wholesaler who sold them to the head office of a company such as Heinz, who cooked and packaged them. The tins were then sold to large distributors such as Sainsbury's who delivered them to their branches. There are other bodies involved in the process as well: the transport services which facilitated deliveries, the suppliers of the machinery required in the manufacture and packaging of the product, the companies involved in advertising and so on. Thus between the farmer and the customer there is a large number of *intermediaries* (mediating bodies) – and together they form a supply chain. Each stage of the process adds value to the product, thereby also creating a *value chain*; at each stage, the cost of the product rises because of the logistics involved in handling the goods and performing the necessary operations. The Internet enables companies to streamline the chain by 'skipping' some of these stages. This tactic is called supply-chain management, and should result in improved services and cheaper product development/procurement all of which benefit customers.

Procurement

In a business context, procurement is the process of negotiating quality supplies at an acceptable price and with reliable delivery. This is a manual, time-consuming and labour-intensive process involving requests for quotation, purchase order submissions, order approval and confirmation, shipping, invoicing and payment (Bamford, 1997). In the past these were performed via telephone or post; in recent years the use of technologies such as fax and EDI have contributed to a considerable improvement in the processes. The Internet has taken the situation further by offering the means to perform these functions electronically in a fraction of the time.

It goes without saying that there are many other processes involved in running a business. We have only described those which would help us to discuss the benefits of the Internet for businesses. We will come back to more details of these and a number of other business processes later on in the book (chapters 6 and 7).

THE BENEFITS OF INTERNET-BASED BUSINESS

According to a survey conducted by Forrester Research, almost half of all business websites in the UK are now attempting to engage in transactional e-commerce (e-business review, June 2000: 12). The survey also predicted that the value of transactions over on-line markets will rise from $54 billion in the year 2000 up to $1.4 trillion by 2004. A few years ago, most companies' websites were used for advertising – as an electronic brochure. This has now changed as organisations see the potential of the Internet as a medium for all forms of business activity.

The Internet offers a dynamic environment in which to interact with customers. This can be utilised in the marketing and promotion of products with the help of a website that takes advantage of the advanced software development tools available today. Extensive information about products on-line encourages customers to buy more readily than either printed catalogues or shop display could. Web catalogues can be updated immediately and cheaply and they can provide more information than printed brochures. The Internet has not only improved business opportunities this way, it has also increased the 'reach' of product information beyond all geographical and social boundaries. It is estimated that 1.18 million people in China have access to the Net and 80 per cent of them have purchased merchandise over it (Fellenstein and Wood, 2000). As well as the new, so-called dotcom companies who are taking advantage of it, traditional organisations are also increasingly utilising this phenomenon. Dell, a well-established computer manufacturer, has been one of the pioneers in web-based computer sales. They use their website to advertise and take orders from customers world-wide. They exercise a just-in-time approach by building the computers on receipt of orders, thus providing a tailored service as well as avoiding overstocking. Order entry and invoicing are performed on-line using Dell's innovative webpages; they even have 5000 especially designed Premier pages tailored to the needs of major customers (Gates, 1999). Dell used the Internet to re-engineer their business: they took a new approach to customer service and order processing, they used their hardware and software resources to create an improved IT infrastructure, and expanded their business to 36 countries and 18 languages, thus achieving extraordinary success.

Find an example of a company in an industry other than PCs and discuss how they can use the Internet to re-engineer their business.

The Internet facilitates transactions at a relatively low cost. For example, it costs banks more than 100 times more to provide face-to-face banking services as opposed to on-line transactions (Bamford, 1997). The Internet can cut procurement costs as it simplifies the process of finding the cheapest supplier, and even processing orders on-line is cheaper than the traditional methods. In recent years some retailers have joined forces to create global Internet exchanges that promise to link retailers with tens and thousands of suppliers world-wide. This should enable them to take part in global auctions for goods, thus driving down costs and pushing up profits while making the experience fun and unique. GlobalNetXChange (see case study at the end of the chapter) is such an exchange supported by French retailer Carrefour, J. Sainsbury and Sears. Fifty of the world's largest consumer products suppliers, including Coca-Cola and Kellogg, have joined forces to create Transora, an electronic exchange that dwarfs any other such developments Huber *et al.*, 2000). The Net also democratises the process of auctions themselves by taking it out of the 'closed' world open only to experts and making it widely accessible. The Internet facilitates cheaper supply-chain management as well, as companies can establish direct links with customers and thus bypass other parties involved in the process (intermediaries), a concept referred to as *disintermediation*. Research done by Cardiff Business School to examine the steps involved in delivering cola drinks to a supermarket chain found that the whole process took 319 days out of which only three hours were spent on activities that added value to the product (Chaston, 2001). Collaborative efforts such as the use of global exchanges for eliminating some of these steps demonstrates the use of the Internet to improve supply-chain management as well as reduce the time taken at each step, thus reducing the cost. In fact, some companies are taking advantage of the situation by eliminating previously valuable intermediaries. Ingram Micro is a distributor of PCs in the USA, they acquire computers from manufacturers such as Compaq and IBM to supply to high street retailers. They are now planning to sell on-line to consumers, thus bypassing the retailer completely, and are even in the position to build computers by buying the components directly from parts suppliers which would enable them to reduce the value chain to a minimum (Ghosh, 1998).

The Internet facilitates new modes of business activities such as the use of up-to-the-minute accurate electronic catalogues, tailoring of products according to customer needs, on-line banking, and on-line global auctions of any product.

Kraft Foods International is another company which used a trading exchange. Find out more about it and explain the benefits and drawbacks of the exchange system.

Although the Internet enables a company to automate many of its operations, it does not reduce the potential for better services. Many organisations use the opportunities provided by the Internet to add a value to their service which is not possible via a physical medium. For example, Marshall Industries, a distributor of electronic components in the USA, allows the search for a product by part number, by description, or by the manufacturer, and processes orders on-line; Staples, a supplier of office goods, have created customised supply catalogues that can run on customers' intranets (Ghosh, 1998). See case study below for further detail of the Staples system.

LIVERPOOL JOHN MOORES UNIVERSITY
LEARNING SERVICES

Staples

Staples, a supplier of office goods, have outlets to offices as well as to individual customers. They use personalisation to reduce the cost that large companies incur when ordering office supplies electronically. They do this by creating customised supply catalogues that can run on their customers' intranets. These catalogues contain only those items and prices negotiated in contracts with each company. The Staples system can maintain lists of previously ordered items, saving customers time when reordering. By searching and ordering electronically, Staples' customers can reduce their purchase order processing costs - which, through the traditional channels, can sometimes amount to more than the cost of the goods purchased. Over time, Staples could learn a great deal about its customers' preferences and use that information to offer other customised services that competitors, especially in the physical world, would find difficult to duplicate. For example, Staples could recommend new items to customers to complement what they have previously purchased or offer price discounts for items that customers have looked at in their on-line catalogues but have not yet bought.

(Reprinted by permission from *Harvard Business Review* from 'Making Business Sence of the Internet' by S. Ghosh, March–April 1998. Copyright © by Harvard Business School Publishing Corporation; all rights reserved.)

Questions

1 Discuss how Staples can gain a competitive advantage by providing services such as this.
2 How do customers benefit from the personalised services provided by Staples?
3 Ghosh lists four types of opportunities companies can obtain from the Internet: a direct link to customers, the ability to bypass others in the value-chain, a potential to deliver new products and services, and the possibility of becoming the dominant player in the electronic channel of a specific industry. Discuss to what extent the above case study demonstrate these points.

Companies can even create new services by including links to pages such as frequently asked questions (FAQ) to provide additional information on their products, profiles of other users of their products, customer comments and so on. For example, on-line booksellers (e.g. amazon.com, bol.com) provide an interesting array of additional information such as reviews, ranking in order of sales, and video interviews with authors.

The Internet provides the tools a company can use to achieve dramatic changes in business processes as a part of their re-engineering activities. It also facilitates better supply-chain management by enabling companies to do business directly with suppliers on-line. Companies can reach niche markets, provide unique services, and perform businesses at a global scale efficiently and cost-effectively.

The Internet also provides a convenient and inexpensive channel for the delivery of certain goods and services. Soft goods such as publications, software, audio and video material can be delivered over the Internet. There are also many websites which concentrate on information-based services. Internet service providers such as America On Line (AOL) exploit this philosophy to run a successful portal incorporating an information service, search tools, email and other on-line services. Some of these companies use advertising as a source of income to offer their customers a valuable and free service, while others operate on a commission basis. They utilise the reach the Internet has given them to profit from niche markets; they streamline the supply chain by acting as a one-stop company between the buyer and the goods, and they themselves become a new intermediary between the two ends, often referred to as *infomediaries* – the information brokers, thus allowing some new companies to enter the supply chain as *re-intermediators*. This is a growing market based on the new role of information in today's marketplace. For example, eBay.com, the on-line auction house, acts as an infomediary between sellers and bargain-hunters. Using information as a commodity, they enable the two parties to negotiate a price for the goods to be sold. According to a survey done in

Sainsbury's

Supermarket chain Sainsbury has been rethinking how it relates to its suppliers. As a result, it has developed Sainsbury's Information Direct, a portal site for 360 of its major suppliers, using technology including Lotus Notes email technology and collaboration software (groupware) from EQOS Systems.

EQOS Collaborator is a web-based planned and information-sharing toolkit that Sainsbury has used to build a collaborative planning system. One of the first applications is in measuring and evaluating product promotions.

Sainsbury's suppliers can go to the site and plan promotions in advance, or track how current promotions are doing in real time. Sales data is updated daily from the stores. This information also allows suppliers to deploy stock where needed, so promotions are fully exploited.

In addition to improving supply-chain management, the Internet is being used to provide new trading mechanisms which unite buyers and sellers within the retail industry - the so-called electronic marketplaces, trading hubs or business-to-business (B2B) exchanges.

For example, Sainsbury is hoping to purchase 75 per cent of its goods through GlobalNetXChange, a world-wide B2B exchange for retailers, within two years. Sainsbury has an equity stake in the holding company running GlobalNetXChange, along with US firm Sears Roebuck and French retailing giant Carrefour.

GlobalNetXChange allows members to buy, sell or auction goods and services over the Internet. 'The auctions in particular cut out the middlemen and focus suppliers on providing the right goods at the right quality and price,' says David Simister, supplier relations manager at Sainsbury. Having already seen savings through this process, the company intends to hold 100 auctions before next March.

(Source: Samuels and Phillips, 2000 with permission from Computing (www.vnunet.com).)

Questions

1 Does this case study demonstrate the management of any of the business processes described in this chapter? Explain your answer.
2 Find out how Sainsbury managed its product supplies before and discuss how the new system benefits the company.
3 Discuss how on-line auctions can contribute to better supply-chain management.

1999, eBay facilitates the sale of about 3 million products at any one time, and has a membership of about 7.7 million (Moon, 2000).

Many issues surround the efficiency of Internet-based services, at the root of which are the technical and organisational infrastructures available to the company. Problems in the areas of security, standards, the extent of Internet access available to consumers and bandwidth are some of the main obstacles to widespread acceptance of e-commerce on the Internet. In this chapter we discussed those characteristics of the Internet that make it a suitable vehicle for pursuing commercial activities. We will discuss what precise technology lies behind those characteristics, how they could be utilised and what needs to be done to make it a success later on in the book.

Often, a number of companies need to get involved in the supply chain of a product. These are the intermediaries. On one hand, the Internet has caused some disintermediation by enabling companies to streamline some of the above. On the other hand, some new, infomediaries have emerged which offer information-based services between two parties, thus creating re-intermediation.

SUMMARY

The Internet started its life in the early part of the 1980s (following more than a decade of developmental activities) as a network connecting the academic communities in the Western world and the research wing of the Department of Defense in the United States. By the early 1990s, the world wide web (WWW) was created in the form of a graphical user interface, and many services such as email, search engines and browsers were added to make the Internet a popular source of information. A global information infrastructure was set up to ensure that procedures and standards were in place to make this enormous network of networks perform effectively. Countries world-wide responded to the phenomenon in different ways: whilst some countries welcomed it and adjusted their telecommunications infrastructure to facilitate the use of the Internet, some other countries took a more cautious approach and allowed only partial use.

The potential for global on-line communication created revolutionary changes in the attitudes of both businesses and consumers. Many new web-based companies were started and traditional physical businesses began to use the power of the Internet to offer some of their services on-line. The world saw a new mode of business in 'cyberspace' where buyers and sellers far apart from each other took part in transactions using virtual organisations. The modes of operation within an organisation altered as well. Increasingly, organisations became flatter in structure where people worked in cross-functional teams, possibly in remote and dispersed locations (telecommuting) and using groupware for communication. The Internet enabled companies to increase the number of customers they could reach and the richness of services they could offer; it also shifted the balance of power from the supplier to the consumer as the latter could use the Internet to access information, which enabled them to choose the companies they wanted to do business with easily. Businesses also benefited as the Internet facilitated better supply-chain management and procurement facilities. Many companies utilised the benefits the Internet offered them to re-engineer the business in order to improve the cost-effectiveness of essential activities and provide better customer service. Often, a number of companies need to get involved in the supply chain of a product. These are the intermediaries. On one hand, the Internet has caused some disintermediation by enabling companies to streamline some of the above. On the other hand, some new, infomediaries have emerged which offer information-based services between two parties, thus creating re-intermediation.

On the one hand, the Internet was based on the ability of modern technology to transmit large amounts of information electronically regardless of the distance between the sender and the receiver; on the other, it utilised the power of information to create a new phenomenon in the business world. In the following chapter we will discuss the role of information in today's organisations and why businesses should treat information systems as a part of their strategic decision-making processes in order to benefit from the situation.

Revision Questions

1. Describe the history of the Internet before the 1980s.
2. Describe how the Internet proliferated in the academic community in the 1980s.
3. Describe the idea of the backbone of the Internet.
4. Explain the term 'information infrastructure'.
5. Why do we need an information infrastructure and which issues should such an infrastructure address?
6. Discuss the relationship between the Internet and the global information infrastructure (GII).
7. Discuss the current state of the GII by using examples from different countries.
8. Discuss the role of the WWW in the popularisation of the Internet.
9. Discuss how the Internet brought about changes in the attitudes of business and consumers.
10. Explain what we mean by cyberspace.
11. Discuss how the Internet contributed to the creation of virtual organisations and the difference this made to organisational culture.

12 What are the typical characteristics of a virtual organisation? Explain with examples.
13 Discuss the significance of cyberspace to the dotcom companies.
14 Using the concept of reach, richness and affiliation, explain how navigation can be utilised to conduct a business on-line.
15 Describe the terms supply chain, value chain, business process re-engineering and procurement in the context of a business.
16 Using suitable examples, describe and distinguish between the terms: intermediation, disintermediation, infomediation and re-intermediation.
17 Discuss with examples how companies benefit from use of the Internet. In doing this pay attention to a company's relationship with other organisations as well as with consumers.
18 Discuss with examples how consumers benefit from use of the Internet.

Discussion Questions

1 Discuss how the practice of controlling the content and/or the access to the Internet affects: (a) Society, (b) Businesses and (c) Consumers.
2 Discuss how SMEs are likely to be affected by e-commerce.

Bibliography

Adam, L., National information and communication infrastructure strategies in Africa, *Information Technology in Developing Countries, A Newsletter of IFIP Working Group 9.4 and Commonwealth Network for Information Technology*, 10(1), April, 2000, p. 2.

Bamford, R. S., *Internet-Based Electronic Commerce in 1997: A Primer*, Graduate School of Business; Stanford University, September, 1997.

Bandyo-padhyay, N., *Computing for Non-specialists*, Addison Wesley, London, 2000.

Barnatt, C., *Office Space, Cyberspace and Virtual Organisation; Management Strategy and Information Technology: Text and Readings*, International Thomson Business Press, London, 1996.

Bradbury, D., The generation game, *Computer Weekly, e.business review*, October, 2000, p. 54.

Chaston, I., *e-Marketing Strategy*, McGraw-Hill, London, 2001.

De Kare-Silver, M., *E-Shock: The Electronic Shopping Revolution: Strategies for Retailers and Manufacturers*, 2nd edition, Macmillan, Basingstoke, 1998.

Dickson L. L., *First Direct*, Harvard Business School, 9-897-079, 9 April, 1998.

Computer Weekly, e.business review, May 2000, p. 12.

Evans, P. and Wurster, T. S., Getting real about virtual commerce, *Harvard Business Review*, Product Number 4525, November–December, 1999.

Fellenstein, C. and Wood, R., *E-commerce, Global E-business and E-societies*, Prentice Hall, New Jersey, 2000.

Fulk, J. and DeSanctis, G., *Electronic Communication and Changing Organisational Forms*, Annenberg School of Communication, Organisations Science, 1995, Vol. 6, No. 4 (July–August), 337–349.

Gates, B., *Business @ the Speed of Thought: Succeeding in the Digital Economy*, Penguin Books, London, 1999.

Gerace, T. A., The Internet, 9-794-073, Business School, 19 June, 1995.

Ghosh, S., Making business sense of the Internet, *Business Review*, March–April 1998, 98205, pp. 125–135.

Gupta, U., *Information Systems: Success in the 21st Century*, Prentice Hall, New Jersey, 2000.

Hafner, K. and Lyon, M., *Where Wizards Stay Up Late: The Origins of the Internet*, Simon & Schuster, New York, 1996.

Huber, N., Ward, H., Goodwin, B. and Simons, M., The e-procurement dilemma, *Computer Weekly*, 20 July, 2000, p. 18.

Lodge, G. C. and Reavis, C., *Global Friction Among Information Infrastructure*, Harvard Business School, 9-799-152, 14 July, 1999.

Miller, S. E., *Civilizing Cyberspace: Policy, Power and the Information Superhighway*, ACM Press, New York, 1996.

Moon, Y., *Network Technology and the Role of Intermediaries*, Business School, 9-599-102, 19 January, 2000.

Nohria, N. and Berkley, J. D., The virtual organisation: bureaucracy, technology, and the implosion of control. In C. Heckscher and A. Donnelon (eds), *The Post-Electronic Organization: New Perspectives on Organizational Change*, Sage, Thousand Oaks, CA, pp. 108–128.

Paston, T., How Freeserve plans to create the Uberportal, *Computer Weekly, e-business Review*, June, 2000, p. 18.

Rayport J. F. and Svikola, J. J., Exploiting the virtual values chain; *Harvard Business Review*, Reprint 95610, November–December, 1995, pp. 75 85.

Reid, R. H., *Architects of the Web: 1000 Days that Built the Future of Business*, John Wiley, New York, 1997.

Riley, J., Finance industry slow on the e-commerce uptake, *Computer Weekly*, 19 October, 2000, p. 12.

Samuels, M. and Phillips, T., Retail goes e-tail – and more besides, *Computing*, 26 October, 2000, p. 37.

Upton, D. M. and McAfee, A., The virtual real factory, *Harvard Business Review*, Reprint 96410, July–August, 1996, pp. 119–134.

Vernon, M., Are they being served? *Computer Weekly, e.business review*, July/August, 2000, p. 16.

Whitely, D., *e-Commerce: Strategy, Technologies and Applications*, McGraw-Hill, London, 2000.

Information in Organisations

Chapter Three

Objectives

By the end of this chapter you should have an understanding of:

- The nature and purpose of an organisation.
- The concept of an information society.
- The role information plays in an organisation.
- The relationship between business strategies and information systems.

INTRODUCTION

In the previous chapter we discussed how the emergence of the Internet transformed the environment for businesses and how it created the concept of cyberspace. Due to the Internet, organisations today have access to an enormous amount of information. What does this mean for them and how can they utilise the information available for business advantage?

In the last four decades rapid development in information and communication technologies (ICT) has forced organisations to change the way they run their business. In the industrial age (the nineteenth to the mid-twentieth century), organisations relied on the use of machines and labour while productivity was measured in terms of the amount of goods manufactured. In the late 1950s, Daniel Bell, the eminent American sociologist, and other scholars of the time suggested that organisations were no longer dependent on the application of labour to produce goods, but relied instead on the utilisation of information and knowledge. They christened this development a feature of the post-industrial society, in which prosperity is directly related to the acquisition, storage and communication of information. The survival and growth of an organisation would therefore depend on its ability to use information intelligently and efficiently. Thus the 'information society' was born! To a large extent, the e-commerce revolution is a result of the initiatives taken by companies eager to succeed in the information age. Therefore an appreciation of the nature of e-commerce is dependent on an understanding of what we mean by the term 'information society', how an organisation can be situated in this society and how information can be utilised to meet strategic goals.

In this chapter we lay the foundation for a discussion of the importance of managing information and its relationship with management strategies. We will examine the basic principles of organisational theories, the nature of the information society, and the management issues in today's organisations. We will come back to the question of how these concepts may be applied to e-commerce implementation and development in the concepts section of the book.

UNDERSTANDING ORGANISATIONS

An organisation can be defined as a stable, formal and social structure that takes capital and labour as inputs and produces goods and services as output. According to this rather traditional school of thought, an organisation is stable because it is normally long-lasting and its functions are predictable; it has a formal structure with internal rules, procedures and regulations bound by national and international laws; and it is a social association because it is serviced by people from varied backgrounds. However, a more contemporary description of an organisation (called the behavioural description) takes the real-world view that like everything else, an organisation exists in an environment which comprises stakeholders (customers, suppliers, dealers etc.), innovation, culture and support as well as competition from other organisations. An organisation functions within the framework of various inter-relationships between a number of elements active within its environment. In order to understand the true nature of an organisation we need to have a clear understanding of what we mean by 'environment'.

The 'environment' of a modern organisation includes those entities which co-operate, compete with or challenge its market status, but also the bodies or individuals which supply raw materials, provide labour or contribute knowledge to the organisation's end product. It also includes other associates in the overall production process: customers, regulatory bodies and trading partners. Most of these entities are themselves organisations or are part of an organisation: raw material is supplied by an external company; employees may be a part of a trade union; customers may belong to an interest group such as the Consumer Association. Thus it could be said that the environment of an organisation comprises other organisations with which it interacts, and each organisation in this network has, as its environment, the network of all other organisations. In other words an organisation exists in the environment of an inter-organisational network (Fig. 3.1) in which the survival of each element of the network depends on the other elements.

The traditional definition of an organisation describes a stable, formal and social structure that utilises labour and capital to produce goods and services. The contemporary (behavioural) definition refers to an organisation as an entity existing in an environment comprising stakeholders, society, innovation, culture and support as well as competition from other organisations.

The environment of an organisation consists of entities such as labour, availability of raw material and other resources, knowledge, trading partners, customers, regulatory bodies and so on. Some of these entities are organisations themselves.

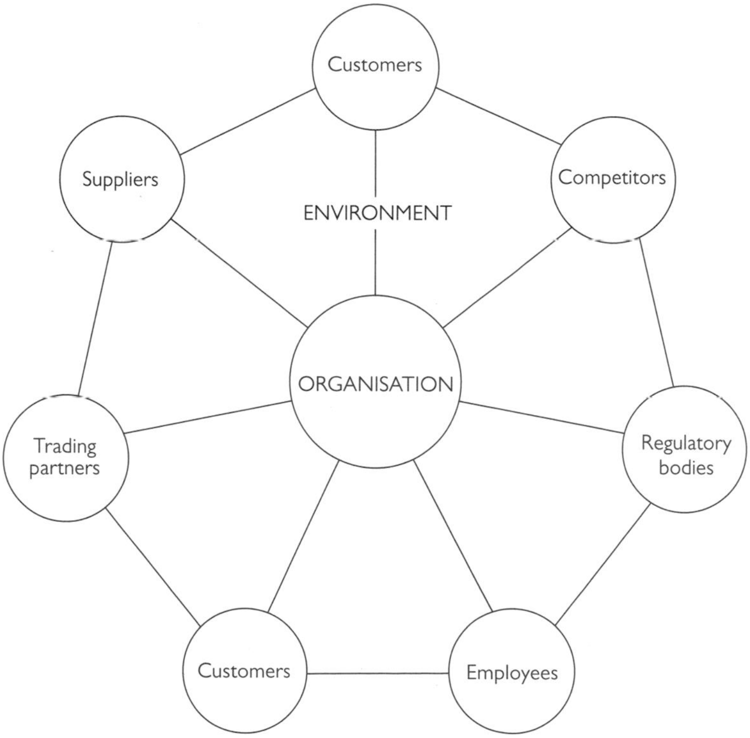

Fig. 3.1 The inter-organisational network

Pick an organisation and list the organisations which comprise its environmental network.

The environment of an inter-organisational network in the above model operates within the framework of a number of external forces that influence the way an organisation functions (Fig. 3.2). These forces are caused by formal and informal agencies which constitute the 'general' environment of the country within which the organisations have to conduct their business. This is determined by the social, political, legal, cultural, technological, economic and physical and natural resources within the boundaries of which an organisation has to conduct its business (Hatch, 1997).

Describe the general environment of your chosen organisation.

However, in the modern world, the environment of an organisation cannot remain limited to the boundaries of one country. With efficient transport links and an advanced telecommunications infrastructure organisations can operate on a global scale. They can buy material from a supplier in a foreign country, employ an organisation in a country where labour is cheap to manufacture their goods, and sell their products world-wide. Every organisation operating in the post-industrial world has a global dimension, either because it is operating with global trading partners or because the organisational network surrounding it is influenced by the global environment, or both.

The global dimension of an organisation's environment has been facilitated by certain advances in ICT which have revolutionised the way information is collected, stored, processed and transmitted. In this information age, the manufacturing industries have taken a back seat; a 'service sector' has risen in prominence in which technologists and knowledge workers are the most valued labour force. The potential of ICT for the service sector has given birth to numerous e-commerce businesses, some of which were mentioned in chapter 1. In the information society social and economic development depend on the utilisation of information, just as capital and labour did in the industrial age. E-commerce is founded on this philosophy and its success depends on the existence

An organisation has a network of other organisations in its environment. Each of the organisations in this inter-organisational network is in the environment of all other organisations. Additionally, all organisations in today's wired world, belong to a general environment of a global nature.

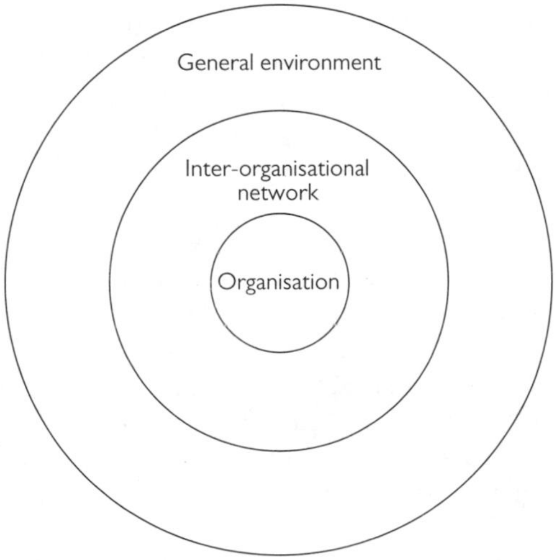

Fig. 3.2 The general environment

of the infrastructure which enables the sharing of knowledge. We will come back to this subject later on in the chapter; let us first take a brief look at the other ways in which an organisation has been conceptualised and how they relate to e-commerce.

DIFFERENT VIEWS OF AN ORGANISATION

Defining society in terms of industrialisation is based on one view of organisations. Another method would be to follow the theories presented by scholars at different periods of history. The first half of the twentieth century is seen as the classical period influenced by the philosophies presented by Adam Smith in 1776, Karl Marx in 1867, Fredrick Taylor in 1911, and Max Weber in 1924 amongst others who studied the influences of industrialisation on the nature of work and workers, and the management of organisations in the industrial age. The later part of the century is associated with the post-industrial age and the perspectives taken are known as modernist (1950s onwards), symbolic interpretive (1980s–) and post-modernist (1990s–). In the following discussion, we will concentrate on the post-industrial philosophies with the acceptance that e-commerce is a phenomenon of the post-industrial society; we will attempt to understand each philosophy and how it views the environment for an organisation.

The *modernist* perspective took the view that all natural and social phenomena belong to a set of nested systems, called the general system with each phenomenon forming a sub-system to the system above. In this scheme, organisations belong to the level of the so-called open (living) systems which survive and grow by taking input from their environment, processing it and producing output that goes back into the environment for other systems. Each such system has sub-systems, for example, an organisation has many departments and each department has many employees. In the modernist perspective, a system provides the environment for all sub-systems embedded within it. Thus each organisation belongs to an environment which consists of other organisations and their environments. This view fits very well with our previous discussion of an inter-organisational network as the environment for an organisation. Such an environment is vast and uncertain, and in order to survive, an organisation has to adapt constantly to external elements. The global dimension of today's organisations, especially those doing business electronically, are most acutely affected by such an environment and information is the most valuable commodity for them.

According to the modernist perspective, an organisation is a part of nested systems in which it takes input from its environment and produces output which is released back to the environment for its sub-systems. In this view, each organisation lives in the environment of all other organisations.

The *symbolic-interpretive* perspective is more abstract in that it views the environment as a socially constructed concept. Thus an organisation generates its own environment by the way information is collected and analysed, and the way it is used to make decisions. Actions taken on the basis of these decisions contribute to further constructions of the environment (Hatch, 1997). In this view, managers of an organisation seek information if they see it as important which, in turn, creates the thirst for more information. This process of continually acquiring information perpetually changes the nature and complexity of the environment. This perspective fits in well with the rate at which the Internet grew; firms saw it as a vital medium for distributing, acquiring and sharing information, which in turn increased the availability as well as the need for further information, eventually giving rise to the e-commerce phenomenon.

In the symbolic-interpretive perspective, an organisation creates its own environment by the way it collects, analyses and uses information to make decisions.

The *post-modernist* perspective argues against the concept of a unified truth and searches for one best way by confronting contradictions and ambiguity. It challenges the concept of certainty in anything and promotes the value of continual deconstruction of the established notion by the use of new information and analysis. It therefore refutes the concept of any fixed boundary between an organisation and its environment and introduces the concept of the network model in which an organisation is in intermittent partnership with other organisations in the face of rapid technological innovation.

This brings us very close to the situation of e-commerce sites which are required to adapt constantly to new customers, competitors, trading partners, cultures, values, regulations and so on. Their survival depends on the acquisition and sharing of information as well as the analysis and re-analysis of it.

The post-modernist perspective of an organisation argues against a boundary between itself and its environment. It views uncertainty as a challenge and a catalyst for flexibility and innovation.

All three perspectives described here are applicable to today's organisations. Whilst they might sometimes present conflicting views of an organisation and its environment, they can also expose different aspects of the same organisation. Thus, they enable us to understand an organisation from the poly-faceted perspective which is essential for today's global market. Of course there is a lot more to the theory of environments; we have presented some of the arguments relevant to organisations affected by e-commerce in order to establish the importance of environment which is continually transformed by technological innovation.

Analyse your chosen organisation in the light of the above discussion. Which perspective does it fit best?

THE INFORMATION SOCIETY

Both the modernist and the post-modernist viewpoints address the question of environmental uncertainty, albeit in different ways. In the modernist perspective, uncertainty prompts rapid change and causes an increase in the complexity of an environment, two characteristics which typify today's electronically driven organisations. Postmodernists recommend that nothing is taken for granted and that uncertainty poses a challenge. In either view, uncertainty is an active variable counteracted only by the acquisition of information. The global market which has been facilitated by the advances in communications technology, has increased the need for and the availability of information enormously. In the nineteenth century, when society developed from an agricultural into an industrial economy, there was an exodus of people from rural to urban areas, a shift from craft-based work to mass production, and replacement of small family firms by large companies. A similar upheaval has been caused by the change from an industrial to an information society. We are witnessing a revolution as the cumulative effect of radical changes in technological, social, organisational and economic environment is giving rise to new business models (Applegate and Gogan, 1996). In order to understand the role of an organisation in this environment, and hence the nature of e-commerce, we need to understand the concept of the information society.

So, what is an information society? It is a society in which economic development and therefore quality of life depend on the exploitation of information and advances in knowledge. In this society, information is a resource (just as capital and labour were in the industrial society) and its fast and reliable communication is essential for producing the goods and services required for progress.

An information society is a society in which economic development and therefore the quality of life depends on the exploitation of information and advances in knowledge.

Writing on information society, Webster (1995) presented five different definitions of an information society advocated by theorists who used different criteria for analysis. These can be classed as the technological, economic, occupational, spatial and cultural definitions, and they all contribute to the viewpoint that information is the most important resource for today's electronic market.

The *technological* definition is based on the view that we now live in a society where it is easy and economical to access, process, store and transmit information over a large distance quickly and reliably. Advances in ICT, and the consequent developments of the Internet and the WWW, have made it possible to link organisations and individuals world-wide. This has given rise to a so-called 'wired society' in which data and information[1] in any format (text, graphics, music etc.) can be passed on from one location to any other at any time of the day or night. This has revolutionised the definitions of work, business, daily life, leisure and so on. Now an individual or a company, a multinational or a one-person firm, can buy and sell products and services of all kinds without leaving their desk using e-commerce. Thus, although some authors have objected that in this view technology is seen as a privileged entity that shapes the world (technological determinism), the technological definition of information society elucidates the connection between information and e-commerce very well. For example, the Internet has forced organisations to improve their customer focus by providing customers with on-line information and services, making it easy for them to compare prices and services. At the same time, access to timely market information is essential for companies to attract and retain customers.

The technological definition of an information society advocates the view that the advances in ICT have created a society in which it is easy and economical to access, process, store and transmit information over any distance at any time.

The *economic* definition suggests that information has an economic value. According to scholars such as Fritz Machlup (1902–1983), the industries which create and communicate information and knowledge[2] – education, the media, computing and musical instruments, information services such as the law and medicine, other information activities such as research and development work – contributed to more than a quarter of the national income in the USA in 1958 (Webster, 1995). Companies which sell information-based products have been quick to cash in on the value of information by delivering their products over the Internet (Applegate and Gogan, 1996). For example, *San Jose Mercury News* (see case study), previously only a print-based news service, created a webpage with news stories and full-text searchable classified advertisements as early as the middle of 1995 to take advantage of the savings in cost of delivering a news service over the Internet. Information has become the foundation of the modern economy as a result of the advances in technology which, in turn, necessitate further knowledge production and communication. The information industry is supplying an economic service to the newly created e-commerce companies by making up-to-date information available on-line.

According to the economic definition, information has an economic value and companies which create and communicate information form the foundation of the modern economy.

The notion of the *occupational* definition of an information society arises from the fact that the information sector occupies a larger proportion of the workforce than any other. Thus, the people working in the knowledge sector outnumber those working in sectors involving physical skill, such as farmers, factory workers, coalminers and builders. Of course, workers in the latter category also process information and use knowledge; but they use practical rather than theoretical knowledge. It is also true that a large number of people in these sectors have lost employment as a result of the introduction of information technologies. In any case, information society has made a considerable difference to occupational patterns. E-commerce carries on the same trend as established companies employ more people to service their on-line activities and new companies emerge to provide goods and services electronically. The rapid growth of e-commerce companies has given rise to a new occupational sector called 'new media' which employs a large number of people to service the technical infrastructure as well as the content of the websites.

The occupational definition is based on the fact that the information sector occupies a larger chunk of the modern workforce.

The *spatial* definition of an information society considers the geographical aspect of the information networks which connect companies nationally and internationally, irrespective of time and space. This is also at the root of the e-commerce phenomenon.

The spatial definition of an information society acknowledges that organisations use information as a key resource to communicate in a market which spans nationally and internationally.

[1] The word data is used to mean raw facts which, when processed, becomes information. Thus, information is data with added relevance and purpose.

[2] Knowledge is the result of the understanding and internalising of information. For example, what you read in a textbook is information; when you understand the information and internalise it, it becomes knowledge.

The global market facilitated by ICT has forced many companies to use information as a key resource. Keeping up with information has become one of the most important issues for businesses because their survival in the competitive global market is dependent on the transmission and presentation of accurate and up-to-date information.

Finally, the *cultural* aspect of the information society concentrates on the extent to which individuals have been influenced culturally by the proliferation of information, again facilitated by ICT. Using the telephone, television, computers and the information superhighway, we can receive information we need without having to leave home. The films we see, the books we read, the food we eat and the music we listen to are influenced by what is happening elsewhere in the world because information from those places can be obtained easily. E-commerce takes advantage of the fact that information can be accessed from home, using a PC; we can be 'bought', 24 hours a day. The sale of goods and services is not restricted to companies, adults or professionals; e-commerce sites now target children and teenagers as well.

The cultural definition recognises that in today's wired society, everything we do is influenced by what is happening elsewhere in the world as information from anywhere can be obtained easily.

All these definitions are the result of innovations in technology and are therefore inter-related. Each of them take information to be a 'resource' capable of generating revenue by itself. This is one of a number of metaphors used to describe information in academic literature; the use of such metaphors[3] needs some explanation.

Produce an examination of your organisation, as analysed from each of the five viewpoints.

NEW PERSPECTIVES ON INFORMATION

In discussing the role of information in organisations, it has been described as a resource, a commodity, and an asset amongst other things. The use of these metaphors is useful for understanding the value of information in business and therefore in the economy.

Many organisations today are so-called information intensive. They do not just depend on easily accessible and accurate information, information has taken the place that resources such as money, labour, raw material have done traditionally. For some companies, information is the 'bread and butter' of the business, for example, a publisher, a credit card company or an on-line insurance service. This gives rise to the information as a resource metaphor because increasingly information is being used as the key to economic growth. If information is not available or is not of good quality, the company loses business and therefore money. This is inherently true for e-commerce companies as information is one of the main ingredients for their business. Some companies conduct a large part of their business by transmitting data and information electronically, for example, on-line banks; companies such as amazon.com rely heavily on information to sell books. For them, loss in quality or accessibility of information results in the loss of profit.

In the information society, information has taken the place in an organisation traditionally occupied by resources such as labour, capital and raw material. Information rich companies gain financially in today's market, thus giving weight to the asset metaphor of information. Information is also a commodity as it can be traded and can increase in value.

The economic aspect of information also contributes to the asset metaphor because a company in possession of valuable information gains financially in today's market. Some scholars have described information as a country's greatest source of wealth, its principal asset (Mosco and Wasko, 1988). Information has also been described as a commodity because it can be traded and can increase in value. Some e-commerce companies are based solely on this concept of information, for example, lastminute.com which sells

[3] A metaphor allows you to understand one kind of experience in terms of another by using a parallel between the two, for example, 'the evening of life' to describe the later part of one's life.

The Mercury News
(www.mercurycenter.com)

San Jose Mercury News repackaged its traditional newspaper in July 1995 to offer an entirely new product to a new market. This is The Mercury News, an on-line service, which publishes news, articles, columns and all other items normally seen in a newspaper. This is an innovative website with facilities for accessing archived articles, further details on chosen items, and sending responses to comments and questions amongst many other features. By combining the interactive, information-rich nature of the Internet with up-to-date news stories, full-text searchable classified ads, and even a colour comic section, this on-line publisher proved that it can attract both readers and advertisers. The cost of delivering the product over the Internet is significantly lower than delivering a physical newspaper to the front doors each morning.

In 1997, the company joined a national network called Real Cities.Com that provides the Internet infrastructure for a number of sites one of which is BayArea.com. This is the parent company that acts as the 'home' for a number of local on-line news services – The Mercury News is the one based in San Jose. The website also provides links to national and international news. Thus the company saved the cost of their service provision by joining a larger conglomerate which also helped them to reach a large consumer base.

Given the interactive nature of the Internet, it is easy for *San Jose Mercury News* to create an on-line customer survey that could be used to build a personal interest profile, which could then be used to create a customised newspaper delivered to customers' PCs every morning.

(Source: Applegate and Gogan, 1996. Copyright © 1995 by the President and Fellows of Harvard College.Harvard Business School Case 9-195-202. Rev. 22 July , 1996.)

This case was prepared by Lynda M. Applegate, Harvard Business School, and Janis Gogan, Bentley College as the basis for class discussion rather than to illustrate either effective or ineffective handling of an administrative situation. Reprinted by permission from Harvard Business School.

Questions

1 What are the benefits for *San Jose* of publishing their product on-line?
2 What are the benefits for the customers?
3 Can you see any disadvantages of reading a newspaper on-line?
4 Do you think on-line newspapers will ever replace printed papers delivered to your door each morning?
5 How does this case study demonstrate the existence of an information society and its different definitions?

theatre tickets and hotel bookings amongst other things on-line obtains information from vendors and sells directly to customers, thus using information as a commodity.

Find out how your organisation uses information. How does your finding compare with the comments made in the chapter about the resources and commodity metaphors of information?

Some information theorists would argue against the use of such metaphors and would hold in-depth debates over their validity. However, at a simple level they help us to understand the value of information as a key to economic development. E-commerce is made possible by the emergence of the information society and its survival depends on the use of information as a primary resource. Advances in communications technologies have made it increasingly easy to access, store and transmit information. Harnessing the power of digital information and transforming it into goods and services of economic value is at the root of the e-commerce industries. Organisations in all sectors are adopting this new economic paradigm as they come to realise that the commercial value of information has increased dramatically. Applegate and Gogan (1996) listed the following properties of digital information that contribute to its economic value:

- Information can be used to create new products and services or to add value to the existing ones. 'Byte size' pieces of data processed by a computer can be transformed into new information; products and services can be infused with added value by adding useful information; new products and services can be created by using information collected during the course of doing business. For example, Hyatt Hotel's (see case study) electronic brochure enables consumers to explore the facilities offered interactively thus offering far more value than a printed brochure could. It also enables the company to collect data on consumers surfing the website to improve their customer knowledge base.
- Information is reusable. It can be 'sold' without transferring ownership and 'used' without being consumed: it can be shared without the problems of ownership or obligation. Thus, unlimited number of consumers can visit Hyatt Hotels' website without having to progress to the booking stage.
- Information is highly customisable. The same information can be presented in different forms (text, graphics, video and audio) and can be combined with information from other sources. Information from various sources can be combined to create a new product. For example, an on-line publisher can supply a customer with material from different publications or selected parts of the same publication. The product can be delivered as printed text, as an electronic file, or perhaps in audio form.
- Information has an inherent 'time value'. The economic value of information is highly dependent on its timeliness. For example, the website of Heavenly Valley Ski Resort provides its customers with real-time weather forecasts and ski conditions by using multimedia technology and video-conferencing. They link their website with video cameras pointing to the slopes to provide up-to-date information.

Some properties of information, for example, that it can be processed to add value, that it is reusable, that it can be shared without loss of ownership, and that it has a time value, contribute to the economic importance of information.

Find out if your chosen company is using the above properties to gain advantage.

Advances in ICT have caused a fundamental shift in the economics of information. As people are increasingly more able to communicate electronically by using universal standards, managers are forced to adapt their operating procedures to new information technologies. For example, for many years *Encyclopaedia Britannica* (EB) have sold their set of printed volumes for £1,000 to £1,500. Many parents bought the full set as an important learning tool that they thought they 'ought' to buy for their children. Since Microsoft developed Encarta, an encyclopaedia on CD-ROM the content of which they licensed from Funk and Wagnall and added on-line illustrations to, the sale of EB has suffered severely. The CD-ROM costs very little to produce and is either supplied free with a PC or can be bought for about £30. The content of Encarta is not as full as that of EB. However, as Evans and Wurster explained in their article, parents now saw the computer as *the* important learning tool, the quality of the encyclopaedia was not of importance. This forced EB, who did not take Encarta seriously for a number of years, to change their strategies and rebuild their business around the Internet. 'It demonstrates how quickly and drastically the new economics of information can change the rules of competition,

Hyatt Hotels (www.hyatt.com)

Hyatt Hotels, a company providing hotel accommodation in holiday resorts, has established an electronic brochure packed with photos, video clips, and descriptions of its resort hotels. Instead of reading a static brochure, consumers interactively explore Hyatt's pages to find what they want – one person might want to know the exact facilities available in the different categories of rooms, someone else may be interested to see the layouts of adjacent golf courses, while another wants to know about beach conditions and off-shore snorkelling opportunities. The electronic brochure can be easily updated to reflect changing conditions or new promotions. If a resort in Hawaii is devastated by a hurricane, Hyatt can easily steer travellers to its other resorts, and keep them aware of the progress of the clean-up in Hawaii. As the potential customers browse, the system collects information such as which are the most frequently accessed features of the website or the most popular destinations in each season. The information is then fed to the market analysts who evaluate what information people look at and what patterns of viewing characterise those who make reservations. The results of the analysis can be used to improve the design of the website as well as the services offered by the company.

(Source: Applegate and Gogan, 1996.
Copyright © 1995 by the President and Fellows of Harvard College. Harvard Business School Case 9-195-202. Rev. 22 July, 1996.)

This case was prepared by Lynda M. Applegate, Harvard Business School, and Janis Gogan, Bentley College. This case was prepared by the authors as the basis for class discussion rather than to illustrate either effective or ineffective handling of an administrative situation. Reprinted by permission from Harvard Business School.

Questions

1 Assume you are planning a holiday. What features would you like to see in a website such as Hyatt's?
2 What do you think could be the problems associated with on-line booking of a hotel room?
3 Can you think of anything else Hyatt Hotels could add to their website to give its customers further benefits?

allowing new players and substitute products to render obsolete such traditional sources of competitive advantage as a sales force, a supreme brand, and even the world's best content' (Evans and Wurster, 1997: 72).

This is not true only because EB is in the business of selling information; only a very small fraction of EB's cost structure came from its content. Evans assigns the vulnerability of EB to their dependence on another kind of information economics – that of personal selling – which was made redundant by technological innovation. At this age of advanced ICT, every business is an information business because a large proportion of an organisation's cost comes from capturing, processing and storing information: '. . . information is the glue that holds together the structure of all businesses (Evans and Wurster, 1997: 72). The ability of electronic communications technologies to carry information from one place to another adds a dimension to a product's value that physical transaction does not offer. The image of a product is based on information that customers have of that product. When information is carried by a salesperson or by mail, it cannot go any further than the carrier. But, electronic communication of information on a product is not constrained by the extent of the physical movement of the product itself. This allows the economic value of information to be freed from physical barrier; widespread connectivity has the ability to unbundle information from its carrier, thus offering competitive advantage to its owners. E-commerce takes advantage of this phenomenon by claiming 'retail space' on the Internet in order either to extend their business opportunities or to create new e-business. Companies are presented with a challenge

The ability of a network to carry information from one place to another adds a new dimension to a product's value. Information on a product is not constrained by the extent of the physical movement of the product itself thus allowing the economic value of information to be freed from physical barrier.

for a new business model in which information is seen as the most important commodity and the management of information is one of the most important business functions.

Michael Dell, the chairman of the PC manufacturer Dell Computers, utilised his experience of direct selling to create successful on-line strategies. Find out more about it and comment on the relevance of his strategies for companies such as Encyclopaedia Britannica.

INFORMATION MANAGEMENT AND THE MODERN ORGANISATION

Information has played a major part in organisations for a long time. The beginning of the information society merely emphasised the relative importance of information over other resources. Until the mid-nineteenth century, most firms were owned by individuals who managed the business. These were small companies and oral communication was adequate for internal operations. A small amount of written documentation was required for communication with suppliers, customers and so on. However, some textile manufacturers had larger businesses and were managed by paid employees. Management of business information was seen as necessary by these companies.

By the middle of the nineteenth century, innovations in communications technologies, especially, the introduction of telegraphy and the development of the railroads encouraged businesses to expand. This resulted in the need for improved communication between trading partners. As the companies grew in size, written instructions and documentation were also passed between employees vertically at different levels of the hierarchy, as well as, horizontally between departments and managers. Companies started to generate large amounts of information which needed to be managed. One example of such a company was the British railway system. During the 1830s, lines between parts of the country were owned by different companies. So, a person wanting to travel a long distance had to buy a separate ticket for each part connecting the two ends of his/her journey and sometimes had to break their journey to buy a ticket for the next section of the route. This resulted in an enormous amount of confusion and inconvenience for both the passengers and the companies involved. High-ranking executives in the railway and other business sectors saw the need to establish an information management system which would take care of the communication between companies. This led to the introduction of the railway clearing house in the middle of the 1800s. Other sectors such as the banking and coach companies also had their own clearing houses (Campbell-Kelly in Bud-Frierman, 1994). By 1920 the management of information, that is, the collection, storage, processing, analysis, presentation and communication of information became one of the most important functions of organisational management.

Traditionally, businesses depended on oral communication. By the middle of the nineteenth century, when widespread railroads were set up, the need for formal communication and management of information grew. Aided by the advances in ICTs, the trend continued in the twentieth century.

Today, organisations are much larger and information management in these organisations involves the management of global data flows electronically or otherwise, or of communications internally as well as with outsiders, or of information services such as marketing and publicity. Some have suggested that the so-called information technology revolution in recent years has been driven by an information revolution that has taken place as a result of the increased need of communication between a business and its trading partners. This, in turn, has changed many of the work processes and the speed at which they have to be performed. Managing information is one of the major business functions involving people at all levels of a company. It is as important as the management of other corporate resources and requires carefully thought out strategies. Although information technology plays a large part in facilitating this, managing information is a key corporate activity fundamental to the health and survival of organisations (Martin, 1997) and therefore has to be seen as major part of strategic business management and not as IT management.

One of the effects of the proliferation of electronic communication has been a gradual flattening of the hierarchy in organisations. Responsibilities are often decentralised and middle and junior level managers have increased autonomy. In some cases, old departmental structure has given way to small teams with the responsibility to see a job from the beginning to the end. Thus companies have adopted a pattern of distributed processing of jobs with cross-functional links between teams. Individuals in an organisation, equipped with desktop computers connected to a wide area network, are also empowered with easily available information. New organisations are being born every day and the relationship between buyers and sellers is changing. Information is now shared between an organisation and its users, customers, suppliers and other trading partners. Some have called it the 'information democracy': boundaries that used to delineate corporate authority are becoming increasingly permeable (Hamel, 2000). Intelligent use of information is of vital importance for the growth of such companies as they make a transition from old ways of running a business to becoming e-commerce companies. At the forefront of their business is a website because this is the point of entry for its customers and suppliers, the vehicle through which the company presents business information to its stakeholders. Users of the website evaluate the products or services sold by the company on the basis of the information presented on-line. The management and presentation of the information are at the basis of the success of the company. The situation is made more complicated by the global market in which such companies have to operate. 'The global organisation seeks to manage the interdependencies among geographically dispersed multi-site operating units, for example between manufacturing facilities, distribution centres and sales offices all at different locations. Information is the mechanism through which this integration is achieved and IT is increasingly being used to integrate and manage geographically dispersed operations' (Pepperd, 1999).

The information revolution that has taken place in recent years has changed the structure of many organisations and their work processes. Managing information has become a key corporate activity. Therefore IT management must be seen as a major part of a company's strategic functions.

Processes that took months or weeks before are now taking a few seconds, thus creating a short circuit between companies (Information Society, 2000). This has resulted in an explosion of an almost unlimited amount of information available to companies and created an enormous scope for information interchange via the Internet. This has enabled a growing number of companies to move towards a paperless environment. E-commerce is a unique example of this phenomenon. It is predicted that about 75 per cent of all document-based information is now stored electronically (Fellenstein and Wood, 2000). This has led to the following consequences:

- The availability of free and uncontrolled access to information. This has encouraged, on one hand, freedom of expression by individuals and groups giving rise to a rich medium for debates and communication, and on the other, anarchy exercised by some people willing to take advantage of technology to express personal views not acceptable to many others.
- An opportunity for poorer countries to use the Internet to take part in the global market. However, this has also created further divide between the rich and the poor in those countries and widened the gap between them and countries who do not have the technology to join in.
- The creation of multinational companies which take advantage of low labour cost of poor countries for manufacturing their goods but keep the processes of knowledge-intensive development and management in the head office.

Whilst this has given poorer countries some economic advantage, it has also led to exploitation in many cases.

- Some openness in businesses between management and the other employees as well as between an organisation and its customers.
- The ability for people to become mobile employees as they can use technology to work from anywhere by remote contact. This also has its advantages and disadvantages.

We will discuss all these issues in more detail in the consequences section of the book.

The wired world and the availability of free and uncontrolled information over the Internet have, on one hand, divided communities and countries, opened doors to exploitation and rivalry, and on the other, increased the scope for economic advantage and corporate democracy.

What are your personal views on the above matters?

Whilst information is an asset companies can use to create new market for themselves, they also live in the threat of other, often new companies, entering the market. As ICT offers an easy route to unlimited amount of information, it is relatively easy for even small organisations to enter into competition with large and established companies. Amazon is an example of such threat to other booksellers. According to Smithson (1994), the position of ICT in the global organisation is twofold. On one hand ICT are at the foundation of the new organisation. They are driving the globalisation process with the Internet and the WWW allowing even the smallest company to operate globally. On the other hand, the pace of technological change and the growing dependence of organisations on a technology that has so far remained alien to most of its users has meant that IT is viewed as a contributor to the uncertainty of the environment that we discussed before. The successful management of an organisation today entails the strategic management of its information as well as its ICT infrastructure.

An e-commerce site in an organisation is a computer system geared towards doing business with other organisations using information. Thus, it is an information system – a computer application based on database technology which processes business data to provide information to users in a presentable format. An information system uses and integrates technologies to meet the information needs of a company (Gupta, 2000). Technology as such does not have the power to serve users, the way it is used to build and maintain an information system makes their existence meaningful. In the past an information system was seen as a support service and not as a part of the mainstream operations of an organisation. This needs to change as information is now the most important commodity and the main tool for the survival of a business.

The contemporary approach to the design and development of information systems stems from an overall strategy that is specifically designed to look at the corporate information needs. It argues against treating systems design as a part of IT management, rather an essential element of overall business management.

The contemporary approach to the design and development of information systems stems from an overall strategy that is specifically designed to look at the corporate information needs. As a corporate resource, information costs money; collecting raw data and processing it are expensive operations as setting the system up and running it involve complicated processes. It should not be a resource that is managed in isolation but, like all other resources in the organisation, it should be included into the overall strategic planning and management process. Bill Gates included the following in his list of business lessons from the chapter on 'IT as a strategic resource' in his book on how to succeed in the digital economy: 'The CEO must regard information technology as a strategic resource to help the company generate revenue' (Gates, 1999: 367).

IT STRATEGIES IN THE INFORMATION AGE

Adopting and implementing ICT can lead to widespread organisational change. Whilst e-commerce simply means buying and selling products electronically using ICT, this

e-business for Unilever

In June 2000, Anglo-Dutch food giant Unilever, the company with an IT budget of £600m, sketched out a future for IT in supporting e-business that will bring home to many how the business world has changed. For many organisations, e-business has so far only been about setting up a website and preparing to engage in some form of electronic commerce. But for Unilever, e-business is just 'business'; it pervades the whole of the organisation; it is paramount and pervasive. According to Unilever's director of electronic commerce, Martin Armitage, e-business now impacts internal processes, partners, customers, and suppliers. 'It is just too important to be a special project'. Imagine, Armitage suggested, an IT world where 50 per cent of applications are outside the firewall, and where there is no differentiation between internal users, customers, suppliers and consumers, and where your service desk answers queries from all of them. Meanwhile you are managing over 200 firewalls, and your network is simply 'the Internet'. This is the world of e-business that IT has to manage.

Today IT customers are internal, in a standard, controlled environment, where volumes are predictable. In the future, the customers will be internal and external – customers, partners and suppliers. Volumes will be unpredictable, and the only common element is likely to be the web browser. There will be e-exchanges – and they will be mature and transaction loads will escalate beyond any plan. Suppliers and partners will be different too. Instead of traditional hardware and software suppliers such as IBM and Compaq, companies will be using applications service providers (ASPs). In place of global telecommunications suppliers, there will be e-business service companies who provide the content of the website with a focus on customer service. That will mean a massive impact on the infrastructure.

(Source: Bicknell, 2000, with permission from Reed Business Information Ltd.)

Questions

1. Discuss how the attitude of Unilever demonstrates why today's organisations need to take a strategic view of IT.
2. Discuss the role that the proliferation of information plays in the changing world of IT provision in the corporate world.
3. Explain the meaning of the statement 'e-business is just business'.
4. General Electric also announced its e-business strategies at the same time as Unilever. Try to find some information on this and compare the two sets of strategies.

cannot be done in isolation from the rest of the business. The emphasis needs to be on becoming an e-business, that is, adopting business strategies focused on meeting the overall business objectives by using the e-commerce philosophy. This fits in comfortably with the increasing awareness among senior business managers from the late 1980s that IT (and ICT) should be a key ingredient in strategic business decisions (Combs and Hull in Dutton, 1996).

Contemporary views on the introduction of ICT in a business advocates that it is treated as a part of a broader exercise of rethinking the organisation's overall goals. Thus IT needs to be a part of a company's overall communications infrastructure, that is, the foundation for its technical facilities and institutional arrangements that supports communication using electronic means. Thus, ICT must be included into the core strategic organisational agenda. As computers became increasingly common, a number of approaches have been used by scholars working on the role of IT[4] in organisations. The approach taken in the early 1980s which coincided with the emergence of the

[4] The term IT is used rather than ICT in some places in the text here because either, the discussion relates to the time when IT was more an issue than ICT or, it relates to a statement made by an author who referred to it as IT.

information society focused on the role of IT in improving communication in an organisation. This approach is concerned with the social as well as the technical aspects of communication with the belief that computer networks radically alter the way people work together. A number of initiatives resulted from this approach: amongst these are computer supported co-operative work (CSCW) which promotes the use of 'groupware' – software designed to enable a group of users to work simultaneously on the same documents; business process re-engineering (BPR) which focuses on the 'processes' involved in company operations and re-thinking (and re-designing, if necessary) the processes in the light of new innovations, in order to achieve dramatic improvements; and business concept innovation – the introduction of a dramatically different business concept to gain advantage in the market (Hamel, 2000). We will discuss these as well as some other business concepts later on in the book.

Research conducted by scholars working on the subject of strategic thinking at the age of electronic communications have used a number of frameworks at the root of which is the need to bring IT and business closer. Managers need clear business strategies where the use of information and knowledge are included as central elements. The focus should be on the integration of all information assets of an organisation – strategy, people, systems, operations and technology (Martin, 1997). Businesses need to address their strategic and operational goals and consider how they can use their information resources to achieve them. Information management should form the basis of an information system, that is, technology should be seen only as the facilitator of strategic decisions rather than making business decisions based on available technology.

Managers need clear business strategies where the use of information and knowledge are included as central resources. Information management should form the basis of an information system, that is, technology should be seen only as the facilitator of strategic decisions rather than making business decisions based on available technology.

The increasingly competitive global environment creates uncertainty for a company, but at the same time, presents it with exciting challenges by providing new opportunities. In this environment businesses must develop core competencies which meet the needs of their growing customer base. At the heart of such competencies is the organisation's ability to use information effectively and improve knowledge. Acquiring and sharing knowledge are important for all companies but they are crucial for the survival of e-commerce firms. We will come back to the topic of knowledge and its relevance to organisations in the following chapter.

How does your organisation deal with the management of information and information systems? Do they believe in the philosophy described above?

SUMMARY

The contemporary theories of organisation takes the real-world view that it operates within an environment of a number of entities such as culture, society, procedures, competition as well as support from other organisations, and so on. The environment includes other organisations and exist in the form of an inter-organisational network. Advances in ICT have made it possible for an organisation to operate at a global scale thus creating a general environment for the inter-organisational network. Such an environment presents an e-commerce company with a lot of opportunities for expansion and co-operation as well as threats of competition from existing and potential rivals.

Scholars have identified the second half of the twentieth century as post-industrial. This is characterised by a shift from an emphasis on capital and labour as the main resources to information for economic success. Thus, the post-industrial society is also an information society. Theorists using different perspectives (such as modernist, symbolic-interpretive and post-modernists) have also acknowledged that today's environment creates much uncertainty for organisations and survival is dependent on the amount

Kao Corporation: A Learning Organisation (www.kao.co.jp)

Kao was founded in 1890 as a soap company. In the 1940s, Kao had launched the first Japanese laundry detergent, followed in the 1950s by the launch of dishwashing and household detergents. The 1960s saw the expansion into industrial products to which Kao could apply its technologies in fat and oil science, surface and polymer science. The 1970s and 1980s, coinciding with the presidency of Dr Maruta, saw the company grow more rapidly than ever in terms of size, sales and profit, with the launching of innovative products and the start of new businesses. Between 1982 and 1985 it had successfully diversified into cosmetics, hygiene and floppy disks.

Dr Yoshio Maruta introduces himself as a Buddhist scholar first, and as President of the Kao Corporation second which reveals the philosophy behind Kao and its success in Japan. He sees Kao as a learning organisation: an educational institution in which everyone is a potential teacher.

Managing information in Kao

In Kao, information is regarded not as something lifeless to be stored but as knowledge to be shared and exploited to the utmost. Every manager repeated Dr Maruta's fundamental assumption: 'In today's business world, information is the only source of competitive advantage. The company that develops a monopoly on information, and has the ability to learn from it continuously, is the company that will win, irrespective of its business'.

Through the development of computer communication technologies, the same level of information is available to all. Terminals installed throughout the company ensures that any employee could, if they wished, retrieve data on sales, research and product development records on any of Kao's products. Employees can even check on the president's expense account. The task of Kao managers is to take information directly from the competitive environment, process it, and by adding value, transform it into knowledge. 'Learning through co-operation' is the slogan; the emphasis is on information exchange.

Information technology in Kao

Kao has maintained a close link with its retail stores via leased lines since 1982 and built its own VAN[5] in 1986 to keep a close link with its trading partners. Fully integrated information systems controlled the flow of materials and products; from the production planning of raw materials to the distribution of the final products to local stores. Kao's electronic links enable them to maintain a symbiotic relationship with its distributors. Its Logistics Information System (LIS) consisted of a sales planning system, an inventory control system and an on-line supply system. It linked Kao headquarters, the distributors, and Logistic centres, and dealt with ordering, inventory, production and sales data. Other supporting information systems helped the wholesale houses in ordering, stocking and accounting and worked with Kao's nine distribution information service companies (ISC). These ISCs had about 500 customers, mainly small and medium sized supermarkets who were too small to access real-time information by themselves. Thus the ISCs served to bring the benefits of information available in Kao to those stores. The ISCs also offered the stores the analyses of customer buying trends, shelf space planning and ways of improving sales among other benefits.

It created a number of other information systems and on-line services that enabled it to expand in other areas of business. It presented a serious challenge to its traditional competitors such as Proctor & Gamble, Unilever and L'Oreal, as well as to new markets such as software development. Kao started as a small company and by 1990 they had a global market spreading over 50 countries. At the root of their success was their ability to manage the flow of information. They used communications technologies to form a chain with their trading partners to exchange information. The knowledge they gathered was exploited for the development of new products. Thus, they were one of the forerunners in EDI. They used technology and a philosophy of sharing information and continuous learning to become a confident challenger of big

[5] Value Added Network – see glossary for an explanation.

businesses. One IBM sales engineer forecast in 1992, 'by 2000, Kao will have become one of our major competitors, because they know how to develop information technology, and how to combine it with real organisational systems'. Kao is on its way to fulfilling this promise.

(Source: Butler, C. and Ghoshal, S., *Kao Corporation*, INSEAD Euro-Asia Centre, 03/92-213, 1992. Printed with permission from S. Ghoshal.)

Questions

1 Discuss how Dr Maruta's concept of a learning organisation can relate to organisations of different sizes.
2 Discuss how the technology route taken by Kao helped to give them an advantage over their competitors.
3 How does Kao's experience in information systems and EDI give them a headstart in e-commerce?
4 This case study was done in 1992. Check their website and try to find more information on the company. On the basis of your findings, discuss if the forecast made by the IBM sales engineer came true.

of information they can access, use and transmit. Information must be seen as the raw material and the main asset for a company. This is particularly relevant to the global environment most e-commerce companies operate in and management of information is one of their most important business functions. The success of e-commerce is dependent on effective policies for handling the information asset of a company.

An information system (IS) is one way of managing information. In the past they were seen as an IT system dealt with by the IT department. Now, it needs to be recognised that an IS is the vehicle for the organisation and management of the most important resource of a company; therefore management of an IS must be seen within the framework of the main business functions of a company. Managers of e-commerce companies must move away from the concept of just buying and selling over the Internet to turning their business in to an e-business. This requires them to include IS management as a part of their overall business strategies rather than as the management of technology. Introduction of ICT into the business is at the core of the activities of an e-commerce company and needs to be seen as a part of a broader exercise of rethinking the organisation's overall goals.

In this chapter we discussed the importance of information in today's organisations. However, the information acquired can soon become useless unless organisations learn to use it to gain knowledge and make an effort to utilise, update and communicate this knowledge. This gives rise to the concept of an intelligent organisation. In the next chapter we will discuss this concept and the role of knowledge management in businesses in the world of e-commerce.

Revision Questions

1 What are the traditional and the behavioural descriptions of an organisation? What is the significance of two definitions?
2 What do we mean by the environment of an organisation?
3 Explain the nature of the environment in today's organisations.
4 Distinguish between the industrial society and the post-industrial society.
5 What are the modernist, symbolic-interpretive and post-modernist views of environment?
6 Explain what we mean by the term information society.
7 Explain the meaning of the five different definitions of information society.

8 Explain the significance of the different metaphors used for information.
9 Explain why information and information systems management should be considered as one of the central functions of running a business.
10 'The successful management of an organisation today entails the strategic management of its information as well as its ICT infrastructure'. Discuss.

Discussion Questions

1 How have the different perspectives of an organisation discussed in this chapter influenced the philosophy of information management in the twentieth century?
2 To what extent have the perceived changes affected the management style in (a) large companies and (b) SMEs?

Bibliography

Applegate, M. and Gogan, J., *Paving the Information Superhighway*, Harvard Business School, 9-195-202, 22 July, 1996.

Barnatt, C., *Management Strategy and Information Technology: Text and Readings*, International Thomson Business Press, Oxford, UK, 1996.

Bicknell, D., The IT department of tomorrow, *Computer Weekly, e.business review*, July/August, 2000, p. 13.

Bud-Frierman, L. (ed.), *Information Acumen: The Understanding and Use of Knowledge in Modern Business*, Routledge, London, 1994.

Butler, C. and Ghoshal, S., *Kao Corporation*, INSEAD EURO-ASIA CENTRE, 03/92-213, 1992.

Dawson, S., *Analysing Organisations*, Macmillan, London, 1992.

Dutton, W. H. (ed.), *Information and Communication Technologies: Visions and Realities*, Oxford University Press, Oxford, 1996.

Evans, P. B. and Wurster, T. S., Strategy and the new economics of information, *Business Review*, Product Number 4517, September–October, 1997, pp. 71–82.

Fellenstein, C. and Wood R., *E-commerce, Global E-business and E-societies*, Prentice Hall, New Jersey, 2000.

Gates, B., *Business @ the Speed of Thought: Succeeding in the Digital Economy*, Penguin Books, London, 1999.

Gupta, U., *Information Systems: Success in the 21st Century*, Prentice Hall, New Jersey, 2000.

Hamel, G., *Leading the Revolution*, Harvard Business School Press, 2000.

Hatch, M. J., *Organisation Theory: Modern, Symbolic, and Postmodern Perspectives*, Oxford University Press, Oxford, 1997.

Information Society 2000, *The Global Short Circuit and the Explosion of Information*, http://www.fsk.dk/fsk/publ/info2000-uk.

Martin, W .J., *The Global Information Society*, Aslib Gower, Hampshire, England, 1997.

Mosco, V. and Wasko, J. (ed.), *Political Economy of Information*, The University of Wisconsin Press, 1988.

Pepperd, J., *Information Management in the Global Enterprise: An Organising Framework*, Information Systems Research Centre, Cranfield School of Management, Bedford, UK, 1999.

Reponen, T., The role of learning in information systems planning and implementation. In R. D. Galliers and W. R. J. Baets (eds), *Information Technology and Organisational Transformation: Innovations for the 21st Century Organisations*, John Wiley, Chichester, England, 1998.

Smithson, S., New organisational forms for an information rich society, International Conference on Information Technology (ICIT94), Kuala Lumpur, Malaysia, August, 1994.

Webster, F., *Theories of the Information Society*, Routledge, London, 1995.

The Intelligent Organisation

Chapter Four

Objectives

By the end of this chapter you should have an understanding of:

- The need for communication in an organisation.
- The concept of the knowledge economy.
- The importance of managing knowledge in the global market.
- Knowledge management strategies and methods in today's organisations.
- The role of communication for business-to-business and business-to-consumer e-commerce.
- The relationship between communication and competitive advantage.

INTRODUCTION

In the last chapter we discussed the concept of an information society and how organisations must utilise their information resources to meet strategic needs. We discussed the importance of managing information and how an information system contributes to the management of the overall business goals. But how does an organisation ensure that the information acquired continues to be useful and to contribute to the company's overall performance in today's global business environment?

We argued in the previous chapter that the survival of an organisation in the information society depends on its ability to share information and utilise it in the provision of customer services. As the most important asset to a company, information must be used to create knowledge and improve the 'intelligence' of the organisation, applying it to meet the challenges of a global market. In this chapter we will discuss what is meant by an intelligent organisation and a knowledge economy, and how the management of knowledge enhances business performance. We will then take a closer look at the relevance of knowledge management for e-commerce and discuss how technology provides the infrastructure required for the management and communication of knowledge within and across businesses. In an attempt to explain the importance of knowledge management for e-commerce companies, we will need to introduce a number of technical concepts at this stage. However, we will not discuss them at any depth but will come back to them in the concepts section.

ORGANISATIONAL BEHAVIOUR IN CYBERSPACE

In defining the new methods followed by the Japanese companies which attempted globalisation following the Second World War, Nonaka (1990) used the concept of 'self-renewal' (Fig. 4.1) in order to explain the radical thinking required when reinventing a company. Companies at that time had to expand their product market from the domestic to the international arena; these challenges were similar to those faced by today's organisations who are required to cope with a market in which the notion of a boundary between a company and the rest of the world has almost vanished. We will use this model to discuss the phases e-commerce companies are required to go through in order to establish a presence in cyberspace. It is not suggested that all companies are following this path or that those not following it are unlikely to make a profit. The model demonstrates the importance of a vision that creates an environment of knowledge creation and management in the enterprise in order to make the most of the opportunities presented in cyberspace.

Phase 1: An organisation facing change, especially on the scale faced by those in cyberspace, often adopts a new strategic vision. The uncertain environment generates the challenge to create a new direction for the company. In 1954, the new president of Honda Motors, a company with only about 50 employees, decided to enter the international motorcycle races as a means of winning global recognition. This was considered to be extraordinarily over-ambitious by the outgoing management of the company, and yet it worked. Such a vision kick-starts a revolutionary change in organisational behaviour, and often creates some chaos. Companies entering the e-commerce world, especially the small and medium size enterprises (SMEs) starting in e-business, face the same phenomenon. For example, Fabulous Bakin' Boys, a muffin manufacturer in the UK with a traditional dusty baker's image, took the unusual step of going on-line to attract young customers. Following a period of instability with a dull website which failed to attract customers, they redesigned the website with a database comprising 1000 jokes and downloadable games. This resulted in a tremendous upsurge in the web traffic and publicity, and led to a significant expansion of the business (Vernon, 2000).

Phase 2: This phase in the self-renewal process amplifies chaos in order to find the contradictions between traditional ways and the new vision. The organisation then focuses on the contradictions and begins to seek a solution. This is effected by the generation of information on new products, markets, technologies and so on, and by organisational learning. Organisations planning activities such as the development of new designs, or the use of new technologies, capitalise on their existing information resources and continue to search for new information. This is true for bricks and mortar organisations trying to establish a presence in cyberworld such as the muffin manufacturer described above, as well as for new 'dotcom' companies trying to enter a niche market. For example, within two years since its launch, Priceline.com (see chapter 1) has changed the way many people shop for airline tickets, hotels, mortgages, and even cars. Until then there was a firm belief that brand loyalty would prevent an organisation from convincing customers to accept a product unknown to them even if the price is lower. Priceline.com challenged this notion and created a new direction in the buying habits of consumers. Its success was based on its ability to tap into all sources of information in the environment in order to find their customers the cheapest product. KPMG, an accounting firm based in the USA, created an information network that would link all KPMG professionals to each other and to the enterprise-wide databases and information

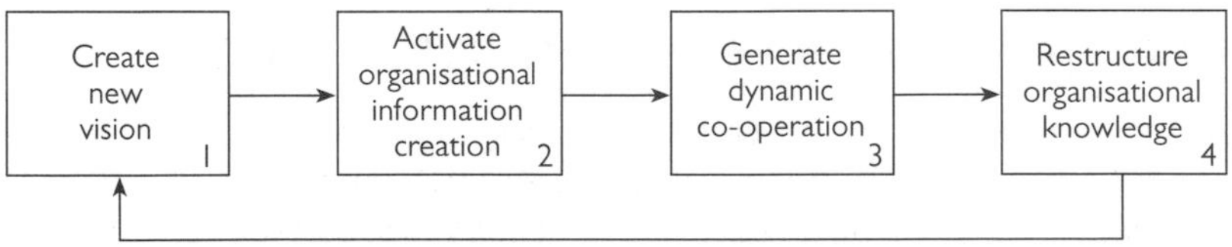

Fig. 4.1 The phases of self-renewal (Source: Nonaka, I., Managing globalization as a self-renewing process: experiences of Japanese MNCs. In C.A. Bartlett, Y. Doz and G. Hedlund (eds), *Managing the Global Firm*, Routledge, London, 1990. Reprinted with permission)

services. They called it the 'shadow partner' as, like a partner, it would keep them informed of all developments, only electronically (see case study later on).

Phase 3: In the dynamic co-operation phase, the members of an organisation use the information gathered in order to communicate with cross-functional teams. At this stage the company must discard old hierarchical or localised patterns of communication and adopt the dynamic network structure discussed in chapter 2. KPMG's shadow partner is an example of such dynamic networking. Another way of doing this is to follow the model of a spider's web, a new network of professional intellect created each time the company faces a new challenge, as done by Merrill Lynch (see case study later on).

Phase 4: This is the process of transforming the collective information into organisational knowledge. An organisation engaged in implementing a new vision uses the opportunity to acquire information and internalise it in order to turn it into knowledge, thus becoming a 'learning organisation'. 'A learning organization transforms the flow of information into a stock of knowledge, and at the same time, spreads it to other departments and stimulates the systematic transfer of information which has been generated and stored. The information generated is shared by all members of the organization and becomes knowledge at the organizational level' (Nonaka, 1990: 71). McKinsey & Company, founded in 1926 as the firm of 'accounting and engineering advisors', transformed itself into a highly successful consulting firm by the early 1990s on the basis of the belief that knowledge development must be a central, not a peripheral firm activity (Bartlett, 1998).

The phases of self-renewal represent the four stages an organisation facing a major change goes through. At the beginning there is a new vision, next it engages in acquiring information in order to face the resulting uncertainty, it then uses the information to communicate with dynamic cross-functional teams, and finally it uses the collective information to create corporate knowledge.

However, the knowledge stored this way loses its value as the environment changes. This is particularly true in cyberspace because the information generated anywhere in the world affects all organisations. The process of self-renewal must therefore carry on as a company strives to gain a competitive advantage in this environment by continually re-examining its mission and using information to increase knowledge which it feeds into the business processes; this leads us to the concept of the knowledge economy.

Using a suitable company as an example (such as Dell), find out if it faced the same phases and if so, how it coped with the chaos.

THE KNOWLEDGE ECONOMY AND THE INTELLIGENT ORGANISATION

In spite of the emergence of the information society in the middle of the twentieth century, computers continued to be seen as simply data-processing machines until the late 1970s. Strategic decisions made in the boardroom had no relationship with the IT department, whose only job was to support the record-keeping functions of the company. Managers and operators in charge of computer departments ran large centralised systems and made technical decisions on the basis of the organisation's data needs.

This changed in the 1980s and 1990s as, with the introduction of PCs on desktops, organisations began to note the importance of computers in the management of information for all areas of the business. Centralised data-processing units gave way to distributed systems throughout organisations. Instead of using computers to run large 'batch' jobs such as the company payroll or accounts, the newly created distributed architecture enabled companies to focus on the information needs at all levels of the business. This led to a drive towards the provision of an infrastructure equipped to support information systems customised for each aspect of an organisation's activities and integrate them through a central link in order to extract overall business information crucial for strategic decision making. Businesses therefore progressed from the computer era to the information era. Information rather than data processing became the basis of technology management. The chief information officer (CIO) replaced the data processing manager as the person in charge of the technology provision in an organisation. This CIO, who was expected to have a grasp of both business and technology, became an essential part of the executive decision-making team, and led the company's strategies for the use of information as a valuable resource.

Aided by the improved national and transborder telecommunications links, organisations began to realise the value of sharing information internally as well as with partners world-wide. Consequently, organisations became both more complex in nature and global in extent. Today, they exist in a dynamic environment and are forced to interact with customers, suppliers, consumers, competitors, law enforcing agencies, and various support services (such as transport, telecommunications providers etc.) in a diverse market. Their survival and growth are dependent on their ability to process information and to turn it into knowledge that enables them to adapt effectively to external change (Choo, 1998). Currently, the value of a company's intellectual capital is considered to be much higher than its material assets because knowledge-intensive industries are responsible for a steadily increasing proportion of the national income of the developed nations. For example, Netscape, the company which started life as an Internet browser and then progressed to a successful portal for the WWW, has achieved a higher stockmarket position than Apple and Microsoft (Probst *et al.*, 2000). Thus, we have a global commercial environment in which companies that recognise the importance of knowledge as a business resource have a competitive advantage: we have a knowledge economy.

In a knowledge economy the value of a company's intellectual capital is considered to be higher than its material assets. Companies which recognise that their survival and growth are dependent on their ability to process information and to turn it into knowledge have a competitive advantage.

The value of old information diminishes fast, reducing a company's knowledge reserve. An organisation which strives to succeed in the knowledge economy must therefore become an intelligent organisation – one that is capable of constantly updating its information and knowledge – in order to deal with the changeable environment. This prepares them to meet the growing expectations of customers, trading partners and workers. The intellectual network at Merrill Lynch was established on the basis of this philosophy. On the one hand information and communications technologies (ICTs) are the reason behind the phenomenal rate of change, and on the other, they play a vital role in enabling the organisations to introduce a mechanism for an intellectual network: e-commerce reflects both these aspects.

It is important to note that the term learning organisation has been used in the published literature both in terms of the skills development of the employees, as well as the improvement of the knowledge reserve of an organisation. Both definitions are important for e-commerce. As companies embrace the e-commerce philosophy and use technology to facilitate an increasing degree of on-line activities, employees need to update their skills accordingly so as to be able to cope with the situation. At the same time, in order to survive in the information-intensive environment of e-commerce, companies must constantly update their information/knowledge base by maintaining an information infrastructure strategically, innovatively and efficiently. In this chapter we are going to concentrate mainly on organisational knowledge, and will come back to the subject of employee skills in the consequences section of the book.

A learning organisation is capable of constantly updating its information and knowledge in order to deal with the changeable environment. This helps it to become an intelligent organisation and prepares it to meet the growing expectations of customers, trading partners and workers.

Communication is an important aspect of business activity in the knowledge economy. Possessing a large and reliable knowledge base is beneficial only when a company has effective strategies for the communication of information both internally and across its external environment. This is especially relevant for e-commerce businesses as their success depends on their ability to provide information of both depth and volume

The intellectual network at Merrill Lynch

In order to overcome complex problems which no one person in the organisation could fully understand or solve, Merrill Lynch (ML) created a so-called spider's web. A spider's web is a form of self-organising network designed to leverage the intellectual assets of the company to the maximum. Typically, a spider's web brings people together quickly to solve a particular problem and then disbands just as quickly once the job is done. In ML's mergers and acquisitions group, specialists work primarily with others in their own disciplines, for example, acquisitions, high-yield financing, or equity markets. But when large financing opportunity emerges, the product becomes an intellectual focal point and a team of specialists from different locations forms to pursue each individual deal. Such projects are so complex that, as one executive says, 'No one can be a know-everything banker. You can't have only specialists doing their own thing, and the client is not interested in dealing with multiple specialists'. The key problem is focusing ML's rich but dispersed talents on a single customer's problem. Client-relationship managers, who best understand the customer's integrated needs, usually co-ordinate these teams, but they do not have direct control over team members.

Despite the current popularity of virtual organisations and networks, few companies understand when and how to use networked forms to leverage professional intellect. As ML's experience shows, networks can flexibly combine high specialisation in many different disciplines with multiple geographical contact points and a sharp focus on a single problem or customer set. At ML, individuals work with many different colleagues on a variety of projects. People are willing to share knowledge and co-operate because their compensation is attached to this mosaic of peer relationships. According to one vice president of the mergers and acquisitions group, 'In addition to profits generated, people are evaluated on how well they throw themselves into various projects, work with different groups to meet priorities, and meet clients' needs. The culture penalizes those who fail to be team players or to meet clients' needs'.

(Reprinted by permission of *Harvard Business Review*. From article 'Managing Professional Intellect: Making the Most of the Best' by Quinn, J. B., Anderson, P., and Finkelstein, S., March–April 1996, Copyright © 1996 by The Harvard Business School Publishing Corporation; all rights reserved.)

Questions

1 Using examples from other published case studies, explain the concept of a spider's web.
2 What are the benefits of sharing knowledge in this way for the organisation?
3 What are the benefits of sharing knowledge in this way for the customers?
4 In what way can Internet technologies contribute to the above concept?
5 Are there any disadvantages of this model of knowledge sharing? Explain.
6 Find examples of other models of communication used by organisations.

cost-effectively to all the relevant parties. Traditionally, the communication of information used to be restricted within a company as 'proprietary knowledge'; the potential of the WWW to enable firms to acquire and disseminate information has redefined the dynamics of information distribution (Papows, 1999). An intelligent organisation utilises modern technological concepts designed to capture and manage information, acquire knowledge by absorbing it, and communicate it to customers, suppliers, and other stakeholders in a way that gives them an advantage in the global market.

Find out how a company which uses information as a commodity, as well as its main asset (such as Priceline.com), uses it to improve its knowledge base.

TECHNICAL AND BUSINESS CONCEPTS UNDERPINNING THE KNOWLEDGE ECONOMY

Choo (1998) has described an organisation as an open system which takes information, material and energy from the environment, and converts them into knowledge, processes, and infrastructures. Those are then used to produce goods and services which are in turn consumed by the environment. Organisations must understand today's complex and volatile environment well enough to be able to use their knowledge in order to formulate the steps necessary to make progress. Companies capable of doing this are intelligent organisations; they can acquire, screen, store, process and communicate information for decision-making purposes. Choo uses the analysis of Haeckel and Nolan (1993) to describe an organisation's 'intelligence quotient' as its ability to: *connect* (link) the sources of information in such a way that accurate information can be captured and made available to the right users at the right time and place, *share* data and information, and *structure* it by organising and inter-relating these resources. These form the core activities associated with the management of technology in e-commerce firms: a network infrastructure provides the *connection*, the interface and the content of a company's website provides the means of *sharing*, and *structuring* is achieved by organisational information systems. Thus an intelligent organisation possesses the ability to utilise the available technologies in order to establish the mechanisms for managing information and knowledge.

The intelligence quotient of an organisation is its ability to connect the sources of information, share it, and give it a structure suitable for the use of the organisation as a whole.

Organisations learn from past experience as well as by vindicating their vision for the future. E-commerce exists in an unstable environment and therefore is heavily dependent on an organisation's ability to learn and act quickly. An intelligent organisation does not only use information to acquire knowledge, it can also modify its behaviour as it gains new knowledge. Additionally, it is capable of developing foresight by understanding and interpreting the trends in technology, customer demands, economic growth and so on. Today's customers exhibit a complex pattern of behaviour; the Internet enables them to access market information easily and thus become knowledgeable. They are in a position to demand good service, and, if not satisfied, to shift loyalty. In this environment, businesses need to conduct market research to glean information on customer expectations in terms of goods and services. Data warehousing (archiving a large amount of inter-related data) and data mining (the automated analysis of stored data) are techniques used by companies to gather, analyse and store information on customers. They require technology to tap into large databases to find information on customer habits and trends. For example, a website can keep a log of all customers who place an order on-line. From this, a company can interpret customer profiles such as the most frequently ordered goods, the specific taste of frequent buyers etc. which they can use for targeted marketing. A relatively new concept in the corporate world, supported by the practice of data mining, is customer relationship management (CRM) which involves the use of business intelligence and computer technology to interrogate the vast amount of customer information coming in through every channel of a company's computerised systems, analyse it, and feed it into the decision-making process in order to improve customer services.[1]

Data warehousing is the technique of storing large amount of inter-related data electronically; data mining is the analysis of the stored data; and CRM is the use of the above to create information on customers and feed it into the decision-making process in order to improve customer services.

A major consequence of the availability of the vast amount of information over the Internet is the problem of information overload. Anyone can place information on the web thus leading to a situation in which information may be repetitive, incorrect, irrelevant or overwhelming. A company's strategies for managing its information

[1] We will discuss data warehousing, data mining, CRM etc. in more detail in the concepts section of the book.

resources, learning processes and knowledge distribution determine the extent to which its intelligence is likely to benefit itself and its customers. Content management is an important aspect of a company's responsibilities for the maintenance of an on-line business profile which ensures that end-users are not confused or overwhelmed by the amount of information presented to them.

The job of becoming an intelligent organisation is made more challenging by the enormity of the e-commerce arena. Dealing with the varied legislative structures in countries world-wide, cultural differences and political and economic situations, for example, requires that companies acquire enough knowledge and manage their transition into the global market. The management of change is a business process forced upon most companies in the e-commerce era. In the past, an organisation had to go through a process of change only when they made a decision to venture into new territories. This could be to expand their business provision to a new arena, introduce major new technologies or systems, engage in widespread business process re-engineering, and so on. Now a permanent state of environmental uncertainty means that those companies which are capable of acting positively in order to manage continual change will be the winners in the information age. An information system designed to support e-commerce is inter-organisational by nature; any change in the environment affects a long chain of value-adding activities. In these circumstances, an intelligent organisation uses its knowledge and strategies of leadership to manage change.

An intelligent organisation establishes a link with its partners, shares data and information, and gives it a structure suitable for organisation-wide use. It also maintains an archive of data, which it analyses and uses to improve customer services. It manages the information to make it useable and useful, and, using it, learns to provide leadership at the time of change.

Thus, an intelligent organisation survives in the knowledge economy by an on-going process of acquiring information, turning it into employee skill and organisational knowledge, and sharing it with its customers and business partners. In order to do this an organisation must establish an infrastructure that enables it to link effectively with its trading partners, maintain a well-equipped corporate information system to support the company's information needs, provide the facilities for the maintenance of an efficient on-line interface, introduce data management strategies capable of facilitating appropriate CRM systems, incorporate marketing strategies to take advantage of the vast amount of information available, and ensure strong leadership for managing change in the environment of instability. We will discuss the techniques behind these processes in the concepts sections of the book. At this stage we need to understand how the Internet facilitates the sharing of knowledge for an e-commerce organisation.

Companies House, the organisation that deals with legal information on companies, recently introduced Internet access to its resources to the customers. Find out what strategies it used to move an almost secret organisation to this stage.

SHARING KNOWLEDGE IN THE INTERNET AGE

Commenting on the effect of technical innovation on economic growth and fluctuation, neo-classical theorists (those working since the end of the Second World War) such as Joseph Schumpeter (1883–1950) argued that innovation places companies in a state of dynamic disequilibrium. In this state, companies continually dismantle the old order of economic activity (technological, organisational and managerial) and simultaneously invent and build a new one (Nolan, 1996). Thus organisational behaviour in this climate is determined by an attempt to create new equilibrium by destroying the traditional hierarchical communication infrastructure and constructing an IT-enabled dynamic network of shared intellectual resources. Internet technologies have provided modern organisations with the facilities required to generate new ideas and learn continually

In the state of dynamic disequilibrium, companies continually dismantle the old order of economic activity (technological, organisational and managerial) and simultaneously invent and build a new one.

from their own experience and that of others. In the information society, perceptions of a universal truth and static knowledge are discarded. Bill Gates uses the term 'corporate IQ' to indicate how easily a company shares information broadly and how well people within an organisation can build on each other's ideas, (Gates, 1999: 266). In the dynamic environment of e-commerce, an intelligent organisation makes progress by sharing its knowledge within the company and across environmental boundaries. It can utilise the knowledge to improve every aspect of the business: this could be to improve product quality, tighten relationships with trading partners, or gain important knowledge of rival products.

Networks enable firms to share vision, expertise, tasks and responsibilities, and participate equally in the decision-making processes. The quality of decisions depends on the reliability of the information transmitting through the network. Malone refers to the companies in cyberspace as the 'connected decentralised' because although decentralised in their organisational structure, they are connected by the network. 'Sharing information with each other, these decentralised decision makers can combine the best information available anywhere in the world with their own knowledge, energy, and creativity' (Malone, 1998: 262). The Internet is in a unique position as the enabler of such decentralisation, as well as being a completely decentralised organisation itself. Decision making is facilitated by a team of employees working together from different parts of the world and the communication between a network of buyers and sellers in the cybermarket. In the world of e-commerce buyers can influence, and thus take part in, the decision-making process by specifying their requirements or by using their knowledge-able status to exert pressure on the seller for changes. In such a world, information is easier to communicate when it is quantifiable, for example, share prices or account balance. It is harder when it is based on implicit knowledge, for example, individuals' experience and judgement. The challenge for the organisations in cyberspace is how to utilise such knowledge.

At the root of an organisation's success in the twenty-first century lie the technologies that provide the means for the sharing of intellectual capital. This occurs in two ways: internally, with co-workers via organisational information systems, intranets, and groupware; and externally, with customers, suppliers and other trading partners via the WWW, and extranets. By providing the platform for sharing each other's knowledge base, such technologies enable companies to collaborate widely with other organisations, sharing core capabilities and thus creating a state of industrial convergence. At the same time, this co-dependence is based on an information infrastructure (see chapter 2) that supports a company and its competitors equally, thus making its on-line capability as good as that of its competitors (Papows, 1999). The companies that survive in this environment of public infrastructure are those who are not only capable of using technology to create, utilise and communicate knowledge throughout the organisation but also exercising competitive collaboration by sharing some of their knowledge with rivals. This can be achieved by environmental scanning – a term used by researchers (for example Choo, 1998) to mean the acquisition of information about an organisation's external environment, and using the knowledge gleaned for strategic decision making. At a time of information overload, an organisation must use technology to scan the environment and process all useful information obtained to gain knowledge. Such scanning might result in sensing scanners from other organisations; a competent organisation collaborates with them rather than regarding them as a threat in order to gain a competitive advantage. The search facility provided by the Internet is an excellent platform which companies can use in order to undertake these activities.

Such collaboration has resulted in a market where there is very little distinction between the quality of the goods produced. Under these circumstances, the profit-making capability of a company depends largely on its ability to provide customer service. One of the ways to do it is to make reliable information available on-line because 'customers place an extremely high value on their ability to access supplier knowledge platforms when confronted with the need to resolve complex operating problems' (Chaston, 2001). The use of intranets and extranets to accommodate partners in business-to-business communication has been adopted by many companies to great advantage. The creation of business exchanges (also known as marketplaces) such as the GlobalNetXChange (see chapter 2) is a reflection of this philosophy. Business-to-consumer use of these technologies raises questions regarding the security of data. FedEx, the international goods delivery company, allows customers to access their intranet to track the position of a package. Firewalls enable companies to separate important corporate data from the rest of the system, thus making consumer access to company information a viable option.

Organisations attempting to share knowledge with business partners world-wide face the challenge of managing their knowledge resources. This necessitates an understanding of the building blocks of knowledge management – the processes involved in the acquisition, communication and distribution of knowledge at all levels of the business activities.

In the Internet age, companies cope with disequilibrium by sharing information via dynamically created teams. They use their resources of information, knowledge and experience, and utilise Internet technologies such as intranets, extranets, WWW and groupware to communicate them. At a time when all organisations have equal access to information, they use scanning techniques to acquire information on competitors, as well as to share it with them.

Covisint is an exchange for some automobile manufacturers (see later). Find out what techniques it uses for the collaboration between the companies it represents. How does this approach compare with the way business is conducted in the bricks and mortar world of the automobile industry?

THE CONCEPT OF KNOWLEDGE MANAGEMENT

For a virtual organisation, sharing knowledge with trading partners to include not only people all over the world but also those with varied relationships with the company requires an efficient knowledge management infrastructure. Bill Gates (1999) describes knowledge management as those objectives and processes introduced in a company which recognises the need to share information. It concerns managing information flow: getting the right information to the people who need it so they can act quickly.

Knowledge in an organisation can be of three different types. *Tacit* knowledge, the knowledge and expertise held by individuals, is often informal in nature and undocumented in format. Thus, familiarity with customers and acquaintance with their personal preferences acquired by a person serving at the counter of a bank is a form of tacit knowledge which enables him or her to provide a satisfactory service. Such knowledge is crucial for business performance and is difficult to transfer to an on-line format. *Rule-based* knowledge on the other hand is organisational and formal in nature; it is documented in the form of operating procedures and stored in the form of databases. It promotes control over organisational information and improves the quality of performance of the company. The third type is the *background* knowledge belonging to the organisation at a higher level: it is contextual in nature and exists in the form of the experience, vision and mindset of usually senior managers. Dell's success on-line is the result of the knowledge and vision of Michael Dell, its founder; by sharing this knowledge with his workforce he obtained their commitment and achieved a common value. An intelligent organisation is skilled at continuously expanding, reviewing, renewing, and refreshing its knowledge in all three categories (Choo, 1998). This entails the integration of organisation-wide knowledge, moving away from the concept of specialised web pages for specific groups and toward web content generated

Tacit knowledge is held by individuals in the form of expertise and experience; rule-based knowledge is formal and documented as procedures; background knowledge exists in the vision and mindset of the decision makers.

automatically from all business activities. By doing so, an organisation moves on from a traditional business with a website to becoming an e-business.

The table in Fig. 4.2 represents an adaptation of Papows' (1999) 'enterprise framework' model and shows the levels in an organisation and the activities related to the acquisition of data, information and knowledge at each level. The last column represents the actions an organisation should finally take when in possession of knowledge. In most organisations data is given a structure before it is used or added to a database. The information the organisation extracts from the database, for example, the management reports or the documentation passed round for cross-functional communications, is unstructured. The knowledge acquired from these reports is also unstructured in nature while the work done on the basis of the knowledge is structured. An example would make these classifications clearer. An insurance salesperson visiting a customer at home can access structured data from the products file of a database; having discussed the products with the customer s/he compiles a list of suitable policy options (unstructured information); this is used to make a judgement for an appropriate policy (unstructured knowledge); and finally an insurance quotation is produced for the customer (structured [or mostly structured] action/work). The tasks involved in relation to these four activities (data-to-work) vary according to their roles in the organisation. Figure 4.2 identifies them separately but the following discussion will address them as a continuum of distinct processes.

Structured data is processed to turn it into information which is unstructured. This is translated into unstructured knowledge which is used to take structured action.

Level 1 in the enterprise framework stands for the empowerment of individual employees in the organisation. They use software such as a database, email or the Internet to access data, create and distribute information, use the information to acquire knowledge and expertise, and use all these resources in order to improve the nature of the work. The company can use the environment provided by the WWW to create an intranet or an extranet in order to facilitate all of these activities. These are particularly useful for the on-line education and support essential for the improvement of individual expertise; they are also invaluable to the creation of an integrated organisation in which users can collaborate with each other and share knowledge.

Level 1 of the enterprise framework represents the role of the individuals in creating and disseminating knowledge and using it for work.

Level 2 is concerned with the same processes performed by workgroups supported by groupware. Technology is used at both levels but for different purposes.

Level 2 is concerned with workgroups – teams working on projects using centrally stored information. In the Internet age, a workgroup often involves people in dispersed

4. The virtual organisation	On-line transactions	Communication with stakeholders	Ecosystem development	Cybermarket development
3. The intelligent organisation	Organisational data systems and applications	Organisation-wide communication	Enterprise-wide knowledge management	Improved business process
2. The organisation with empowered teams	Workgroup data systems and applications	Workshop communication	Workgroup collaboration	Improved conduct and control of workflow
1. The organisation with empowered individuals	Data creation, access and usage	Information access	Training, education and expertise	Integration of knowledge into work processes
	Data (Structured)	**Information** (Unstructured)	**Knowledge** (Unstructured)	**Work** (Structured)

Fig. 4.2 The enterprise solutions framework (Source: Papows, J., *Enterprise.com: Market Leadership in the Information Age*, Nicholas Brealey, London, 1999. Adapted with permission)

locations communicating via groupware. Lotus Notes was the first commercially successful groupware product – software that used relational database technology to store linked documents to be shared by people working together using a network. It incorporates email, electronic calendars, and a repository of corporate data in both text and graphical formats. Using groupware participants can access departmental databases and applications to find data, hold virtual meetings, share ideas, create and update documents together, work on a project, and discuss a problem. Thus it facilitates the processes involved in generating information and knowledge via communication and collaboration, and deciding on a course of action. Groupware enables people to work in groups in a relaxed environment and express opinions without intimidation. This was an important vehicle for organisations which moved from the old hierarchical to the dynamic network architecture of the information age. Workgroups formed with people from different departments enable companies to create integrated work processes that cut across specialist areas in order to establish improved workflow. For example, a team designing a new product can incorporate product information from the manufacturing department and customer information from the sales department in order to assess the market trend.

Level 3 of the enterprise framework involves enterprise-wide communication between teams and locations. It entails the building of communities which share knowledge and ideas by using technology.

At level 3, the organisation attempts to become an intelligent one by integrating data, information and knowledge across teams, departments and locations. Enterprise-wide databases and applications are used via client-server technology, and teams increasingly work together across geographical and national boundaries via email, video-conferencing, and groupware. This is the stage at which organisations begin to take positive steps towards knowledge management: they create on-line communities and use them to increase organisational knowledge, make decisions based on enterprise-wide knowledge, establish procedures for data mining and customer relationship management (CRM), and build an infrastructure for effective knowledge sharing.

Communities are created to facilitate internal company communication and knowledge management, and for meeting external business partners and information providers. 'Virtual communities are places where people come together online. They are brought together by a variety of organisations to fulfil any function' (Guthrie, 2000: 66). Academics have been sharing ideas via emails, and users of all categories have participated in on-line discussions via chat lines and bulletin boards for quite some time. With the help of Internet technologies, this has been extended to the world of business, where workers involved in similar projects share expertise and ideas. ICT enable companies to automate such activities with applications such as intranets, groupware, and enterprise resource planning (ERP) – software that links databases on different elements of an organisation, for example, marketing, manufacture, finance, procurement, and so on. Software developers such as Oracle and SAP supply generic ERP systems to facilitate access to information by all users on any aspect of a product's life cycle. They form the basis of the infrastructure for an organisation to share ideas, information and knowledge in order to make decisions. They also provide facilities for CRM by enabling a company to add the customer database to their ERP system, thus facilitating data mining. Also available are independent CRM products which enable a company to collect, share and analyse customer data in order to gain a deeper understanding of customer habits and demands, and utilise such knowledge in planning customer services. Companies in possession of an effective knowledge infrastructure can also improve their business processes by re-engineering some aspects of their activities. For example, they can introduce a new product information service for customers by integrating information on order processing, manufacturing schedule, and delivery arrangements. Such community-building organisations can also provide customers with the facility to communicate with each other via the company websites thus enabling them to form electronic consumer communities. On-line communities based on common interests, needs, fantasies, and life experiences create company loyalties and linkages which organisations can utilise; they also enable businesses to gather information on customers in order to improve their services.

Level 4 of the framework looks toward an extended organisation; it incorporates the idea of using Internet technologies to share knowledge in cyberspace. At this level, it uses corporate information systems to provide on-line services to customers and suppliers. This could be to facilitate home-shopping for individuals, remote order processing for suppliers, or participating in on-line auctions themselves for the best prices of raw materials. Using an extranet and the Internet, a company shares information and knowledge with stakeholders world-wide. This could be in the form of group emails, hyper-linked documents with information on new company policies, or on-line invitation to tender for prospective suppliers. Through this process, an organisation creates an ecosystem, a web of partners, suppliers, and customers whose success is important for itself (Papows, 1999). This enables virtual communities to liaise with their stakeholders, for example, supermarkets can use an Internet exchange to join in a global auction for suppliers, or a global academic community can perform collaborative research. In these examples all members of a community belong to one ecosystem; they share knowledge for mutual benefit. The result of such communication for an organisation is the establishment of a virtual organisation. Papows calls it the market-facing enterprise (MFE), a company that integrates various services with the help of technology in order to conduct business electronically; it enables a customer's market experience to be defined entirely on-line. This is when a business becomes an e-business in which electronic technology both defines and manages the business: amazon.com is a typical example. Physical organisations can also become MFEs by providing complete e-business solutions to on-line customers; this does not exclude the maintenance of their bricks and mortar existence in parallel.

Level 4 of the enterprise framework looks towards an extended organisation in cyberspace. At this stage the company becomes a market-facing enterprise (MFE) and shares its knowledge with customers and trading partners using technology.

An MFE faces a number of challenges due to the changes in the nature of knowledge development. All three types of knowledge (tacit, rule-based and background) in an organisation originate from individuals to a large extent which complicates the process of sharing knowledge. On the one hand, technology has improved the scope for intelligent organisations to share knowledge on a global scale, on the other, it has also complicated the process. Communication in the global market entails the sharing of vast amounts of information, at a high speed, with people and systems at dispersed locations, and in an environment in which customer demands are the foundation of a company's success. Modern technologies do facilitate these activities, but the fast pace of innovation and the resulting competition from companies of all sizes puts all organisations under increasing pressure to update their capabilities and improve their knowledge base continuously.

Commenting on the strategies for knowledge management, Davenport (1996) talks about the inter-relationship between four aspects of information all of which have an important role to play in a company's success in the utilisation of knowledge: politics, culture and behaviour, support structure, and technology – the so-called information ecology. Information *politics* advocates that the company managers discuss and agree on the types of information to share. The subsequent decision ensures that information is no longer the capital of the computer department, but the source of knowledge for the whole organisation. Thus, the political model treats information as a strategic resource, and encourages an ongoing debate in which items of information cease to remain local and contribute to the global knowledge base. The *cultural and behavioural* aspect puts the emphasis on learning and on leveraging knowledge. This can be achieved by widespread communication in order to enable employees to perform on the basis of knowledge rather than on intuition, and the establishment of a culture in which communicators are rewarded and information hoarders are reprimanded (as demonstrated by the case study on Merrill Lynch). The above strategies must be encompassed within an infrastructure that provides the intellectual support *structure* and technological backbone for the management of knowledge. *Intellectual support* could be provided by the appointment of information co-ordinators who have the responsibility for gathering information from internal and external sources, putting them in structured, usable formats, and bringing them to the attention of those who need them. Thus, these people should be in charge of using data and information from the organisation's information systems, and making them available to the others as a source of knowledge. The *technology* dimension comes in the form of a system which integrates the knowledge base of the organisation and uses technology to make it accessible to the whole organisation. The system must be easy to use, continually updated with new documents added as soon as new information is generated so that all aspects of company information can be obtained via the same system, and ensure that information provided on-line is structured in such a way that it is easy to find. The WWW provides an efficient platform for such an integrated approach.

Effective knowledge management pays attention to the information ecology: the politics, culture and behaviour, support structure, and technology of the communication of information. It makes sure managers agree on the strategies for information sharing; it establishes a culture of learning; and it gives technical and organisational support to facilitate learning.

Various writers (for example, Cerny, 1996) contributing to the debate of communication in organisations advocate the following methods for knowledge management: keeping an up-to-date database of case histories, appointing a consultant with expertise in the field of corporate culture, and adopting a global life form. A global life form enables a company to become globally efficient and locally sensitive: 'This is the so called transnational model, which combines global efficiencies with local sensitivity by creating an interdependent, highly collaborative, and responsive network of global teams' (O'Dea, 1996: 14). A transnational company is different from a multinational (MNC) in the sense that the latter sees the head office as the parent of its partners world-wide. Thus, there tends to exist a uniformity in the treatment of the subsidiaries with little regard to the local variations. Thus these companies have two distinct roles: a global role for the headquarters and a local role for the subsidiaries. This model restricts an organisation's capacity to facilitate all the different local, central and global innovation processes simultaneously, and goes against the philosophy of interdependence through the communication of knowledge and expertise. The transnational model (Bartlett and Ghoshal, 1990) supports the dynamic network structure of an organisation; it recognises the importance of multinational teams working in collaboration with local market partners. These are today's virtual organisations; they use technology to work in teams across national borders and incorporate local knowledge and expertise into the knowledge base of the entire company.

A transnational organisation recognises the importance of multinational teams working in collaboration with local market partners.

In summary, a learning organisation in the virtual business world aims to transform itself into a 'knowledge-based' organisation by creating, acquiring, and transferring knowledge continually. It adopts a market-facing approach in order to ensure that knowledge is communicated as required and it attempts to establish an understanding of the political, cultural and behavioural patterns of communication of its trading partners world-wide. Organisations of all sizes in the cyberworld have the potential to trade internationally; this is the transnational rather than multinational business model in which firms must develop an infrastructure that enables them to share human and technical intelligence to maintain their knowledge base. This requires effective strategies for knowledge management.

Using the example of an organisation of your choice, explain how the concept of knowledge management could be applied to each level and for each activity within a level.

The World Bank (WB)

After more than half a century of providing lending and advisory services in every region of the world, the World Bank Group had become an unmatched source of development experience. A key component of WB president James Wolfensohn's agenda was to create a knowledge bank – a world-class repository of development experience and knowledge that would benefit all entities that did business with the bank.

To address this challenge, they wanted to build a world-class knowledge management system throughout the bank, to capture and organise their knowledge, make it more accessible to staff, clients, and partners, and strengthen their knowledge dissemination and capacity building efforts. It would interconnect with universities, foundations and other world-class sources of knowledge so that the bank became a clearinghouse in knowledge about development. The preliminary focus of the system would be on improving the effectiveness of WB staff through providing just-in-time, just-enough knowledge to meet demands of both internal and external users.

In late 1996 it was clear that the bank's IT infrastructure would not support the type of knowledge management required to implement their vision. Among other problems, the duplication and fragmentation of data created serious business problems. Many of the weaknesses of the bank's IT system had been well known for years but had been masked by the creation of a series of compensatory administrative procedures. Consulting reports also confirmed that there was little business sponsorship of important IT initiatives, that IT costs were high, and that the bank suffered from a lack of IT governance.

Following a discussion in July 1994 at the executive level, WB decided to go ahead with an enterprise network (EN). The EN provided an infrastructure for an organisation-wide IT solution integrating all systems of the bank. It contained a suit of software that could be expanded to incorporate the tools that people would need to work together. Until then, little co-ordination of technology initiatives had occurred across organisational lines. The EN facilitated co-operation among parts of the information systems community at the bank.

It was the bank's mission to be more than a corporate network; it should also be a global network, thus making bank work location independent. Its leaders believed that the bank's business environment demanded an increased capacity for quick response to changing external events, more diversity in product lines, greater use of information to leverage lending with learning, improved partnering and knowledge sharing with clients and shareholders, move more work into the field and improve the efficiency and effectiveness of internal operations. The system enabled the bank to share information, perform more collaborative work, and harness the power of 50 years of development experience and knowledge.

(Source: Knoop *et al.*, 1997.
Copyright © 1997 by the President and
Fellows of Harvard College.
Harvard Business School Case 9-897-053.)

This case was prepared by Research Associate Carin-Isabel Knoop, Professor Joseph Valor, IESE Barcelona, Spain, and Professor W. Earl Sasser as the basis of class discussion rather than to illustrate either effective or ineffective handling of an administrative situation. Reprinted by permission from Harvard Business School.

Questions

1 Discuss how the WB's knowledge management benefits (a) the bank and (b) its customers.
2 How could Internet technologies aid the creation of an EN in terms of (a) researching what the EN needs to include; (b) people interacting with the completed EN?
3 Explain how the WB's enterprise network fits in with the concept of an MFE.
4 How does the concept of a transnational organisation apply to the WB?

A FRAMEWORK FOR KNOWLEDGE MANAGEMENT

Probst *et al.* (2000) described knowledge management as a set of inter-linked activities as described in Fig. 4.3. Although a number of these activities have been mentioned before, it helps to organise them within the structure of a framework in order to describe the steps involved in the management of knowledge. An organisation must have clearly stated strategic goals for the management of each of the activities, as well as a strategy for the assessment of its success in these processes. The following is a brief description of the activities involved in each of the processes identified by Fig. 4.3.

Knowledge identification. This process represents a company's efforts to locate the data, skill and knowledge residing in its internal and external environment. This is a difficult task as the above resources are often not easily visible. Due to globalisation, remote teleworking and increasing staff mobility, organisations often lose sight of knowledge sources. On the one hand, the Internet has created a world of information overload; on the other, specific information is often difficult to find. An organisation must utilise its internal human and technological networks to locate corporate knowledge and take advantage of the searching facilities offered by the Internet to find information from its external environment.

Knowledge acquisition. This involves acquiring knowledge either from a company's experience of working with its customers, suppliers and other trading partners, or by buying knowledge and expertise from external sources. Active research programs designed to find knowledge from the environment can be an effective way to do this. The WWW is a rich source of information for such research.

Knowledge development. This process concentrates on the development of new capabilities. This could be done by a market survey, by using the company's department of research and development, or by capturing new trends emerging in the environment. It also involves the nurturing of individual skills, finding the means to utilise tacit knowledge to create new corporate knowledge, and building a communication infrastructure that encourages interaction between individuals, teams and business partners.

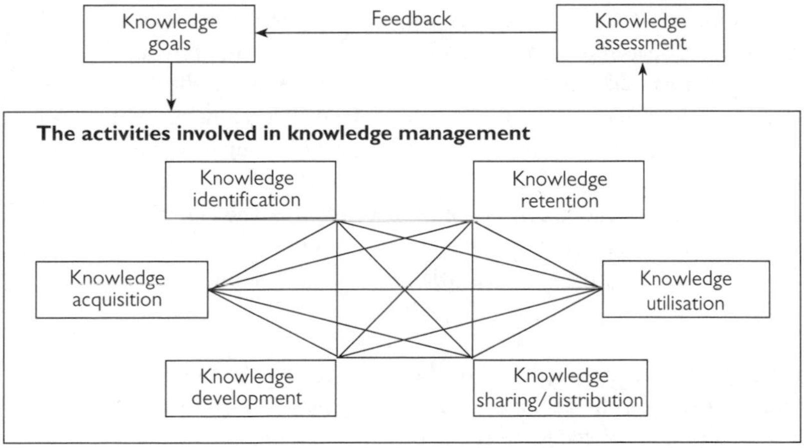

Fig. 4.3 The knowledge management framework (Source: Probst, G., Raub, S. and Romhardt, K., *Managing Knowledge: Building Blocks for Success*, John Wiley & Sons Ltd., 2000. Reprinted with permission from John Wiley & Sons Ltd.)

Knowledge sharing and distribution. The main purpose of acquiring knowledge for an organisation is to share it with those who need it. This could be to make decisions on business processes, to provide trading partners with information they require in order to do business, or to improve the on-line customer service provisions. Knowledge management strategies must establish policies on how knowledge acquired by the company should be communicated to the others, how it should be distributed, who should have access to which part of knowledge, and so on.

Knowledge distribution is of utmost importance for e-commerce. Technologies and procedures must be made available for those employees to share knowledge effectively, securely and speedily. On the one hand the developments in ICT provide an efficient platform for these tasks, on the other, they have also presented managers with many complications. Amongst these are: the overwhelming choice of technologies a company could adopt, how selective information can be distributed easily to selective groups, which groupware is best for virtual teams, whether or not there should be an enterprise-wide solution for knowledge distribution, how to ensure that those sharing knowledge have the technical skill required, and so on. The Internet provides an environment for effective solutions to most of these problems.

Knowledge utilisation. Knowledge is of no value unless there are clear strategies for how it is to be used. This part of knowledge management determines the steps necessary to ensure that the knowledge base of the company is usable and fully utilised. The design of the computer interfaces used for knowledge distribution is an important aspect of this activity. For example, pages of the intranet or the extranet used internationally must take into consideration different cultural and behavioural patters of the users, ease of use of the features available, the language used, the speed of access, technical infrastructure available locally to the users, and so on.

Knowledge retention. This is the combined process of selecting, structuring, storing and updating knowledge. It dictates the methods a company must use to collect and store useful knowledge, and continually update it in order to improve corporate memory. Organisational knowledge has a strong relationship with individuals. In spite of the use of technologies to store knowledge in the form of documents and expert systems, individuals often hold the keys to important knowledge in the form of experience and know-how. In the cyberworld of e-commerce, there is a tendency for people to move to different countries or companies. Retaining the knowledge of those individuals is an important part of knowledge management. This could be done by the establishment of procedures designed to document all types of knowledge, for example, in the form of minutes of meetings, case histories etc., by maintaining a formal relationship with people who have left the company, for example, as consultants, and by using techniques to store such knowledge, for example, in the form of databases. Additionally, in the global environment of e-commerce, knowledge becomes out of date very fast. The knowledge reserve of the company must be refilled continually by procedures that encourage new learning, acknowledge new ideas, document new knowledge, and add it to the corporate memory.

Knowledge management comprises a set of core processes consisting of the identification, acquisition, development, sharing and distribution, utilisation and retention of knowledge. These processes are all interlinked, and are placed within the context of the goals for knowledge management and the continual assessment of it.

As is obvious from the above descriptions, none of the processes can be performed effectively in isolation. For example, the acquisition of knowledge is fruitless without established procedures for storing knowledge; stored knowledge has no purpose unless the company has policies on how and on what basis people should have access to it; in the fast-changing global market, old knowledge must be refreshed continuously with new learning in order to be valuable. Thus, each process must be performed within the

Shadow partner in KPMG Peat Marwick

KPMG, an accounting firm based in the USA, created a 'shadow partner' – an information network that would link all KPMG professionals (partners) to each other and to enterprise-wide databases and information services. The databases on the network included information, updated daily, about the experiences and contacts of the partners in KPMG, public information such as directories, on-line news services, and Dow Jones report, and training courses on business topics. It also included standard functions such as word-processing, voice mail and resource scheduling functions. Partners, by sharing and gathering information through the shadow partner, would be able to use the entire company's knowledge and experience to serve clients. The results of a survey done in 1989 indicated that 80 per cent of the clients of KPMG wanted the firm to bring the full range of the firm's experience and knowledge to individual client needs. Firms also needed to respond to the expanded needs of clients who demanded solutions, not simply products. Solutions needed to be integrative, combining the knowledge of all the functional areas: tax, auditing and consulting. To provide integrated solutions, each partner needed to access knowledge of all the functions. Thus, they required cross-functionality, which needed a shift to an integrated information orientation, not a product and functional orientation.

Overall the shadow partner would allow partners to access the full range of knowledge in the firm, to grow professionally through learning about a wider range of partners' experiences, and to offer a superior service to meet clients' expanded needs. Bob Elliot, strategic planner, recognised within the firm as a visionary, saw this as 'a complete, concise, quality-controlled representation of the company's expertise'. Another executive described it as a 'reservoir of practice and knowledge'. Elliot believed that the information in the databases should be 'unstructured' because an unstructured database connected creative responsiveness to novel client issues. The data would come from public information sources, published company reports, and partners' reports, proposals, letters and other business-related material. Any structure imposed on the information would be based on past experience. Information in the database could be retrieved, looked at, and presented in whatever way imagined.

(Source: Gladstone, 1995.
Copyright © 1991 by the President
and Fellows of Harvard College.
Harvard Business School Case 9-492-002
Rev. 5 October, 1995.)

This case was prepared by Research Associate Julie A. Gladstone under the supervision of Professor Robert G. Eccles as the basis of class discussion rather than to illustrate either effective or ineffective handling of an administrative situation. Reprinted by permission from Harvard Business School.

Questions

1 Explain the role of a shadow partner.
2 Discuss the benefits of a shadow partner for KPMG.
3 Explain Elliot's comments about unstructured information.
4 What technological infrastructure does KPMG need in order to implement the shadow partner?
5 How can the concept of a shadow partner be extended to business-to-business e-commerce?

context of the others; and the methods used for each must be updated in the light of any changes in the rest of the framework. This necessitates that knowledge management is an essential part of the organisation's strategic planning process and is supported by a technological infrastructure capable of meeting the company's strategic goals.

In what way are the above steps relevant to the World Bank?

THE TECHNOLOGICAL INFRASTRUCTURE OF KNOWLEDGE MANAGEMENT

There are many tools available to organisations to facilitate knowledge management. Often referred to as intelligent tools, knowledge-based systems such as expert systems, artificial neural networks and case-based reasoning systems are designed to support organisational learning; information systems such as decision support systems (DSS) and management information systems (MIS) facilitate the communication of centralised information and knowledge between departments; and concepts such as data mining and warehousing facilitated by business intelligence software[2] enable companies to utilise customer information for enterprise-wide usage.

In the global environment of e-commerce, the role of technology is to provide the platform for the communication of information without regard to the physical location of the sender and the receiver. This requires widespread electronic communication at both local and global levels. In the past, companies had to rely on their local area networks (LAN) to connect via a modem to the country's telephone network, thus forming the international wide area network (WAN) for data transmission. Some multinationals maintained private data networks (PDN) at a high cost. Communication was slow and using the system was cumbersome. The introduction of the Internet and the associated development in technological standards changed all that by facilitating easy access to information world-wide. A number of new concepts followed to take advantage of the improved facility for sharing information; intranet, extranet and groupware are examples of such developments.

Corporate tools such as expert systems, DSS and MIS facilitate the sharing of knowledge in organisations. Networking technologies such as LAN, WAN, PDN enable electronic data communication. Programming languages and concepts such as OOP, HTML, XML, and Java, together with Internet protocols, enable communication via the Internet.

Accompanying innovations in software technologies supported the development of the content to be transmitted over the Internet: object oriented programming (OOP) methods were introduced in order to facilitate fast and efficient program development; new programming standards and languages such as Hypertext Mark-up Language (HTML), eXtensible Markup Language (XML) and Java were used to support web page creation and maintenance; and suitable protocols were established to ensure that the Internet is accessible easily via landlines as well as via the satellite network and mobile phones. We have already introduced some of these concepts in previous chapters; we will discuss their technical characteristics in the concept section of the book.

The main purpose behind the management of knowledge is to improve communication. E-commerce is founded on the communication of information; an intelligent organisation acquires knowledge in order to perform this function. Such communication has two major dimensions: access to information for customers communicating on-line (B2C communication); and the availability of enterprise-wide information for the consumption of an organisation and its business partners (B2B communication). Companies involved in e-commerce must take advantage of both in order to utilise the power of the Internet for business purposes.

Business-to-consumer (B2C) communication

Businesses have been communicating with consumers electronically since the late 1970s over the videotext system such as Prestel in the UK (1978) and Antiope in France (1981). Companies participating in these services made product information held in databases in text and graphics forms available on TV screens via telephone lines. Subscribing

[2] Programs designed to collect data from the company's order processing and other customer-based transaction systems, and analyse it to gather information on customers that can be used for targeted marketing.

customers needed a keyboard, a modem, an auto-dialler which would enable them to connect to the database as legitimate users, and the necessary electronics capable of formatting the data for display. Output devices such as a printer or a tape could be used for storing information permanently. This was an interactive system which enabled customers to place orders for goods and services on-line. Antiope, developed in the early 1980s and supported by participating retailers, used the same concept to enable customers to purchase services such as access to the national telephone directory, travel information and reservation, retailing and banking. Teletext, started in the 1970s and still used widely (for example, Ceefax), is a text-based, non-interactive service that provides information from corporate information systems to customers over national TV channels.

TV shopping via videotext and channels such as QVC and TV Travel Shop paved the way to electronic business transactions for consumers unwilling or unable to visit the shop. The Internet made use of this trend but with a greater scope and challenge for organisations to make use of this medium for a competitive advantage. Using a browser such as Netscape, a user connects to the company website either by entering the web address directly or by using a search engine to find suitable sites for the goods s/he is looking for. Thus the company is in competition with other firms at two levels: the availability of its website – unless it is easy to find, customers will go somewhere else; and the availability of information – if information is difficult to obtain or it is of poor quality, customers will lose interest.

The following factors influence how quickly customers can find what they are looking for.

The quality of the information systems – Companies using Internet technologies for business transactions make relevant data held in their information systems available to their websites. These systems must therefore be 'Internet-aware', that is, the database management system supporting these information systems must be compatible with the Internet. This is achieved by using object oriented programming languages and a filing system that supports a search through unstructured data such as web documents. XML has played a big part in enabling web interaction because it facilitates communication between incompatible systems. Software vendors such as Microsoft (for its SQL Server 2000) and IBM (for its DB2 7.1) are now using XML to web-enable their database servers. Databases created under this environment also follow web protocols such as HTTP and encryption techniques so that webpage developers can interact with databases easily and securely. Using a client-server model,[3] these databases are placed on a server with users at the client end accessing data via a webpage. A customer searching through a company's website expects to gain access to information quickly and reliably; web-enabled and well-integrated information systems form the foundation of such accessibility.

The availability of the webpages – Companies create webpages with links to information on their products for customers to access. An intuitive address makes it easy for customers to guess it. Users looking for the website of well-known companies will often try the format 'www.companyname.com'. Thus, hmv.com is a predictable name likely to attract customers familiar with the record shop to try the website. Inappropriate addresses which are completely different from a company's name in the physical world requires customers to either know the address via correspondence or find it by using a search engine. However, there are criteria for choosing a webname and smaller companies may not be in a position to use the name they want.

The other method used to find a website is to perform a keyword search via a search engine such as AltaVista and Yahoo!. Finding a website out of an incredibly large number

[3] Explained later. Also see Glossary.

Knowledge management in BG (formerly British Gas)

BG has given knowledge management a high priority and views the enterprise portal as an increasingly important part of an overall solution they created called Kite (Knowledge and Information To Everyone), particularly for organising information around project teams. 'If you have an enterprise portal for a function, it should be their (the teams') one-stop shop to go for everything they need to know to do their job,' says Tom O'Connor, BG's head of knowledge management.

BG's workgroup-centric approach to enterprise portals can be contrasted with an even more granular system where each user has a personal portal, providing links to all the virtual teams they belong to. O'Connor sees the two approaches as complementary, however, with the workgroup approach being a step towards the ultimate goal of individual portals which, in effect, are just windows on to other portals that may relate to specific projects or skills.

Although portals may be the centre of the knowledge universe, they are not the substance of it, and O'Connor emphasises the importance of training and incentives in getting users involved both with maintenance and exploitation of the system. Such incentives are not necessarily financial, and include a mixture of old-fashioned courtesy and efforts to deliver the information that users really want.

On this front BG is extending Kite to Palmtop computers and other mobile devices, so that travelling staff can be alerted to important new information identified as relevant to their function. This can be either internally or externally sourced information.

To begin with, the mobile service was restricted to about 200 senior managers, and requires synchronisation of Palms with desktop machines within a BG office to obtain updates. But the system is being extended to more junior staff, and to incorporate wireless access for delivery of updates. The key point, especially when delivering to Palm devices with limited display and memory, is to allow users to define what information they want so that they can hone it down to their needs.

(Source: Hunter, 2000. Copyright obtained from Reed Business Information Ltd.)

Questions

1 Discuss how BG's use of a portal helps knowledge management.
2 Find out more about personal portals and explain how they link to an enterprise portal.
3 Comment on BG's technical and organisational infrastructures. In what way do they support the users of the system?
4 What else could BG do in order to benefit from their knowledge management strategies?

of webpages on the Internet is a complicated process for search engines. They use a suit of software known as 'intelligent agents' which continuously scan the Internet and build databases of available information. When a user enters a keyword, the search engine looks through these databases, attempts to find a match, and presents the user with a list of links to the websites it found. Web-enabling a site is obviously essential for this purpose, but availability can be improved by other means such as a button on a portal, advertisement in prominent websites, and so on.

The success of B2C communication is determined by the quality of the information systems in the organisation and the quality of the website. An enterprise portal can enhance internal as well as external communication.

The communication of information between a company and its consumers can be enhanced by the provision of an enterprise portal which integrates internal and external sources of information within the framework of a website. A portal is the first page that a user is presented with when s/he logs on to the Internet and invokes a browser. Thus, this is the point of entry for the consumer to the Internet; from here users can use the portal's search facilities to find the information they are looking for. In fact AltaVista and Yahoo!, commonly referred to as search engines, are the pioneers in the portal business. An enterprise portal is such an interface owned by an e-commerce company which enables it to function as a single, unifying focal point for accessing and managing all sources of information and knowledge residing at different physical locations and formats within the organisation (Hunter, 2000). It gives users access to the WWW via the company's website and gives the company an environment in which to organise its knowledge management activities such as sharing files and information by workgroups, and monitoring customer interaction for warehousing.

Business-to-business (B2B) communication

Broadly speaking, B2B e-commerce involves a market in which companies communicate on-line with each other rather than with individual consumers. Dealing with each other directly in this way does not only enable businesses to streamline their value chain, it also forces them to establish a certain standardisation of procedures in order to operate electronically without complications. It transforms physical inter-business operations into a network of information-based activities, thus improving the transparency of business functions and therefore the efficiency of transactions and communication.

B2B is more than just company-to-company business on-line; it is a philosophy that creates the infrastructure for an electronic market equipped to handle a wide range of communications services over a supply chain. Large companies in a wide variety of sectors such as the automobile industry, finance and retailing have taken the initiatives to build B2B communities by participating with technology companies and service providers. This has resulted in B2B consortia: companies which act as an exchange for a specific sector. GlobalNetXChange, described in chapter 2, is a model for a consortium for the retailers; in February 2000 General Motors, Ford and DaimlerChrysler formed a consortium called Covisint for the automobile sector (Burgstaller, 2000). Burgstaller calls B2B an operating system designed to facilitate the communication between businesses engaged in the transfer of products and services in the same way a computer operating system co-ordinates the interaction of the CPU, the applications programs, and the peripherals in order to process data. In addition to the provision of a technological and procedural infrastructure for communication within a country, this also involves agreements on international logistics – the regulations involving customs, distribution, financing, transport and so on.

B2B communication involves the collaboration, aggregation, knowledge exchange and information-transformation between companies, thereby building communities of business partners. Sector-based exchanges or electronic marketplaces improve communication and help companies to maintain the quality of their goods and services.

The overriding goal of B2B is to facilitate automatic communication between all participating systems, in real time. Any event influencing the status of the provision of services must be communicated immediately to all affected systems. For example, if the shortage of raw materials is likely to affect production and therefore the supply of orders to companies, then the sales department must have that information immediately in order to plan the necessary action. B2B not only involves the transfer of information, it also necessitates the communication of business intelligence in order to maintain the quality of goods and services produced as a result. This requires widespread application integration: the leveraging of all existing systems and databases belonging to all the trading partners by letting them communicate seamlessly in support of a business purpose (Linthicum, 2000). This is enterprise resources planning (ERP) played out over the whole supply chain and is designed to integrate all systems of all the businesses taking part in communication.

Find out more about GlobalNetXChange: which companies use it, how it works, who runs it, and so on. Then comment on if and how it improves the quality of the businesses it supports.

INTRA-ORGANISATIONAL COMMUNICATION

The technical foundation of knowledge management is an efficient database management system and a network infrastructure that facilitates on-line communication over the Internet and is capable of serving business communities on a real-time basis. This necessitates the implementation of the technologies and procedures that enable not only business-to-consumer and business-to-business communication world-wide, but also strengthens the communication of information within an organisation. In the Internet-enabled world of e-commerce all companies today are global in nature, and all systems are potentially inter-organisational. Therefore, the characteristics of the communications systems for the transmission of information within businesses and between a business and its consumers must be seen as an extension of a company's intra-organisational communications infrastructure. An organisation must be viewed with all systems integrated with each other as one entity without functional or departmental divisions. This facilitates the sharing of knowledge within the organisation and also enables managers to communicate effectively with consumers and business partners outside. Thus, the philosophy behind intra- and inter-organisational communication is the same: how to access, digest and disseminate large volumes of information quickly across national and international boundaries (Gupta, 2000). The use of an intranet integrated with enterprise-wide systems as described in the MFE framework supports this ethos.

The philosophy behind intra- and inter-organisational (B2C and B2B) communication is the same: how to quickly access, digest and disseminate large volumes of information across national and international boundaries. Therefore, the support structure required is also the same.

E-commerce exists in an environment in which Internet technologies facilitate communication for all types of organisation. In an environment in which widespread collaboration between organisations has given companies equal access to the knowledge required to produce goods of high quality, using communications infrastructure to enhance customer services is the key for organisations to gain a sustainable competitive advantage.

Find out how a company which performs both B2C and B2B communication, for example the supermarket chain Tesco, manages its communications infrastructure.

COMMUNICATION FOR COMPETITIVE ADVANTAGE

In his book on the subject of competitive advantage, Michael Porter (1980) presented his five-forces model (Fig. 4.4) to describe the internal and external influences that define a company's position in the market.

Porter identified a number of external threats and opportunities faced by a firm: the threat of new entrants into its market, the pressure from substitute products or services,

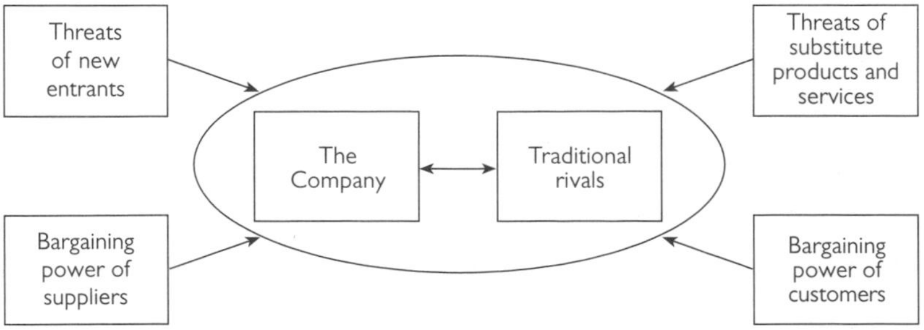

Fig. 4.4 Porter's five forces model

the bargaining power of buyers, and the bargaining power of suppliers. The firm exists within the environment of these forces plus the rivalry from its traditional competitors. Let us take a brief look at each of these forces in the context of Internet-based businesses.

New entrants. In the traditional world of business, this was a real threat only for small businesses. The Internet has changed that; any company is now in a position to compete with multinationals. Amazon.com and banking operations of a supermarket are prime examples of the threat presented by new entries into the business arena. While they pose a threat to established companies, they can also see these as a challenge and the motivation for innovation. Since the scope for improvement in the quality of a product is finite, the strategy for a competitive advantage must be based around the communication of information. Increased knowledge of the business philosophies of the new entrants and the market trend for new customer demands can be incorporated into the ethos of the larger companies. The other side of the argument is the opportunity this situation presents to the new and smaller entrants to the market. They must utilise the power of communications technologies and establish strategies to take advantage of such opportunities.

Substitute products and services. The Internet enables a company with a substitute product to compete with an established market. For example, the availability of downloadable music on the Internet has created a real threat to the physical CD market and has raised some legal issues. However, communication enhances the ability of existing players to deal with this situation. For example, record companies could acquire information on how to change the format of a CD which prevents easy duplication, and make deals with artists in order to enable them to supply music on-line legally themselves.

The bargaining power of customers. As discussed already, the Internet provides the means for its users to compare prices and conditions of service, thus enabling the buyers of products and services to bargain for the best deal. For example, banks are now in acute competition with each other to provide on-line services. It is now generally acknowledged that the cheapest deals in savings accounts these days are in Internet banking.[4] This encourages customers to shift their loyalty and go for the cheapest and most convenient provider of the service. Under these circumstances companies are obliged to utilise their business intelligence mechanisms to understand consumer demand in order to survive in the competition. According to a survey done by Delloitte & Touche (Whittle, 2000) even with the enormous advantages in cost savings for banks, only 22 per cent of the customers of those traditional banks who offer e-banking use the facility. On the other hand the on-line customers of First Direct are extremely happy with their services and 80 per cent would recommend them to a friend. This is achieved by the provision of customer services; for example, all systems in First Direct are integrated which enables a customer to make a transaction using a computer or a WAP phone, modify it on-line and check its progress on-line or at a branch.

Porter identified a number of external threats and opportunities faced by a firm: the threat of new entrants into its market, the pressure from substitute products or services, the bargaining power of buyers, and the bargaining power of suppliers. The firm exists within the environment of these forces plus the rivalry from its traditional competitors.

The bargaining power of suppliers. Suppliers in electronic transactions can aim for the best deal from the supply chain. They are also in a position to sell directly to consumers, thus dropping out of the supply chain entirely; the example of Ingram Micro used in chapter 2 demonstrates this point. This gives suppliers bargaining power against traditional retailers and encourages them to enter the market as retailers themselves. The use of

[4] This has been made possible by the enormous amount of the savings that banks can make in providing services on-line; transactions that cost 69p off-line cost only 2p on-line (Whittle, 2000).

consortia is one way to form a closer link with buyers and suppliers thus overcoming the threat.

A company exists within these threats and opportunities in addition to the environment of its traditional competitors. It can use a number of strategies to gain a competitive advantage under these circumstances. These are:

- Focusing on the aspect of the market that it has special strength in. For example, Microsoft used its reputation as a software developer for the PC industry to market its Internet browser program Internet Explorer bundled with its Windows operating systems in order to gain an advantage. The on-line customised sale of desktop computers by Dell (as discussed in chapter 2) is another example.
- Product differentiation, that is, concentrating on a specific aspect of a product quality that its rivals cannot match. The use of the automatic teller machines by Citibank in the 1970s gave the bank a considerable competitive advantage that its competitors took some time to catch up with.
- Creating tight linkage with customers and trading partners. This is the basis of all other activities since a close communications link enables a company to implement the strategies mentioned above. Communication is the foundation for gathering information on customers, competitors and the market; e-commerce presents organisations with the ideal opportunity to do so.

A company within an environment of threats and opportunities can use focus, differentiation and tight linkages in order to gain a competitive advantage. Internet technologies provide the means for doing so.

The development of an infrastructure capable of facilitating communication requires an understanding of the issues surrounding the design and implementation of information systems, as well as of the technologies of electronic communication. Managers must understand the importance of corporate knowledge and the role that the communication of information plays in knowledge management. In this chapter we discussed the concepts that underpin these concepts; we will discuss the technologies that facilitate communication and the methods an organisation should use to implement knowledge management systems in later sections of the book.

Amazon.com was a new entrant into the book-selling business when it started. Find out what threats and opportunities this created for the traditional book trade and how their business environment changed because of this.

SUMMARY

The survival and growth of an organisation in the Internet age depends on its ability to acquire, store and process information and turn it into knowledge. We now live in a knowledge economy; companies which recognise this strive to gather and communicate knowledge continually thus becoming the intelligent organisations. Using technical concepts such as data mining, ERP, CRM etc., organisations can gather knowledge and use it for inter- and intra-organisational communication. They must also survive in the unstable environment of cyberspace by learning to manage change. The key to such survival is in the sharing of corporate knowledge; Internet-based technologies such as intranets, extranets and groupware facilitate such sharing. Knowledge management in the e-commerce world can be seen within an enterprise-wide framework in which all organisations are market-facing, and knowledge is shared and utilised at all levels – between individuals and across organisational and geographical boundaries. Sharing knowledge must also be based on an understanding of the politics, culture and behaviour, technology, and a support structure – the so called information ecology. The process of knowledge management can be formalised as a number of inter-related stages: the identification, acquisition, development, sharing and distribution, utilisation, and retention of information. Intelligent organisations perform these processes within the framework of a set of strategic goals, and assess the results on a regular basis in order to gain a competitive advantage. Information systems such as expert systems, decision support systems and management information systems, together with Internet technologies and protocols such HTTP and XML support the infrastructure required for the acquisition and communication of knowledge. Using these technologies companies can communicate within organisational boundaries as well as for business-to-business and business-to-consumer transactions, locally and globally. In an environment in which the availability of information has empowered all types of organisation and presented them with a variety of threats as well as opportunities, the key to competitive advantage is communication. Companies must use the power of Internet technologies and appropriate strategies such as focus, differentiation and linkages as suggested by Michael Porter in his five-forces model in order to do this.

This chapter ends the context section in which we addressed the theoretical issues and the models that underpin the existence of e-commerce companies. We discussed the origin of e-commerce, the contribution of Internet technologies and the associated information infrastructure in facilitating e-commerce, the concept of the information society and its relevance to cyberspace, and the importance for organisations in cyberspace to improve their intelligence by the acquisition and effective management of knowledge. We established that organisations need to use information as the most important resource, and that information and knowledge management must be at the core of a company's strategic decision-making processes. In the next section we will discuss the concepts and technologies that facilitate the achievement of these goals.

Revision Questions

1. Describe the four phases of self-renewal for an organisation and explain how they apply to an e-commerce company.
2. Explain why we are said to be in a knowledge economy at present.
3. Explain the concept of an intelligent organisation and its relationship with e-commerce.
4. Describe the concept of the intelligence quotient for an organisation.
5. What does an organisation need to pay attention to in order to become intelligent?
6. Explain how the concept of dynamic equilibrium applies to the Internet age.
7. Why do organisations in the Internet age need to share knowledge?
8. In what ways do the Internet-based technologies help the collaboration between organisations?
9. Describe the concept of a market-facing enterprise.
10. What are the three types of knowledge and how can an organisation incorporate them into their knowledge base?
11. Describe the functions of four levels of the enterprise solutions framework.
12. Explain the activities in each level of the enterprise solutions framework.
13. In what way does the above framework explain knowledge management in the e-commerce era?
14. Explain the concept of virtual communities with examples.
15. Discuss the concept of information ecology and how it relates to knowledge management.

16 Explain the concept of a global life form for an organisation.
17 Describe the knowledge management framework and its constituent processes.
18 What are the characteristics of B2C communication for on-line businesses? How can such communication be improved?
19 What are the characteristics of B2B communication for on-line businesses? How can such communication be improved?
20 Describe Porter's model for competitive advantage. Use examples to demonstrate your points.
21 How does Porter's model help to explain competitive advantage for e-commerce companies?

Discussion Questions

1 It is well known that a large number of companies have entered cyberspace and many of them have managed to survive without paying any attention to the concept of knowledge management. Do a critical analysis of what this means in the light of what we discussed in this chapter.
2 With the help of further reading discuss the relationship between knowledge management and e-commerce.

Bibliography

Armstrong, A. and Hagel III, J., The real value of on-line communities, *Harvard Business Review*, Product Number 96301, May–June, 1996, pp. 134–141.

Bartlett, C. A., *McKinsey & Company: Managing Knowledge and Learning*, Harvard Business School, 9-396-377, 20 April, 1998.

Bartlett, C. A. and Ghoshal, S. In C. A. Bartlett, Y. Doz and G. Hedlund (eds), *Managing the Global Firm*, Routledge, London, 1990.

Burgstaller, S., B2B in 10 minutes, *Computer Weekly*, 9 November, 2000, p. 68.

Cerny, K., Making local knowledge global, *Harvard Business Review*, Reprint 96302, May–June, 1996, pp. 1–15.

Chaston, I., *e-Marketing Strategies*, McGraw-Hill, Maidenhead, 2001.

Choo, C. W., *Information Management for the Intelligent Organization: The Art of Environmental Scanning*, Information Today/Learned Information, New Jersey, for ASIS, 1998.

Davenport, T. In K. Cerny, Making local knowledge global, *Harvard Business Review*, May–June, 1996, p. 10.

Ferrill, P., Databases that focus on the Net, *Information Week*, 9 October, 2000, p. 151.

Galliers, R. D. and Baets, W. R., *Information Technology and Organisational Transformation: Innovation for the 21st Century Organisation*, Wiley, Chichester, 1998.

Gates, B., *Business @ the Speed of Thought: Succeeding in the Digital Economy*, Penguin Books, London, 1999.

Gladstone, J. A., *KPMG Peat Marwick: The Shadow Partner*, Harvard Business School, 4-492-002, 5 October, 1995.

Gupta, U., *Information Systems: Success in the 21st Century*, Prentice Hall, New Jersey, 2000.

Guthrie, P., Creating online communities, *Computer Weekly*, 23 November, 2000, p. 66.

Hale, R. and Whitlan, P., *Towards the Virtual Organisation*, McGraw-Hill, Maidenhead, 1997.

Hunter, P., Doing the knowledge, *Computer Weekly*, 26 October, 2000, p. 58.

Knoop, C., Valor, J. and Sasser, W. E., *Information at the World Bank: In Search of a Technology Solution*, Harvard Business School, 9-898-053, 17 September, 1997.

Linthicum, D. S., Application integration for real-time B2B, *e-Business Advisor*, September, 2000, p. 20.

Malone, T. W., Inventing the organisations of the twenty-first-century: Control, empowerment, and information technology. In S. P. Bradley and R. L. Nolan R. L. (eds), *Sense and Response: Capturing Value in the Networked Era*, Harvard Business School Press, 1998.

Nolan, R. L., *The Process of Creative Destruction: Business Transformation*, Harvard Business School, 9-196-018, 9 December, 1996.

Nonaka, I., Managing globalization as a self-renewing process: experiences of Japanese MNCs. In C. A. Bartlett, Y. Doz and G. Hedlund (eds), *Managing the Global Firm*, Routledge, London, 1990.

O'Dea, G. K. In K. Cerny, Making local knowledge global, *Harvard Business Review*, May–June, 1996, p. 14.

Papows, J., *Enterprise.com: Market Leadership in the Information Age*, Nicholas Brealey, London, 1999.

Porter, M., *Competitive Strategy*, Free Press, New York, 1980.

Probst, G., Raub, S. and Romhardt, K., *Managing Knowledge: Building Blocks for Success*, John Wiley & Sons Ltd, Chichester, 2000.

Quinn, J. B., Anderson, P. and Finkelstein, S., Managing professional intellect: Making the most of the best, *Harvard Business Review*, Reprint 96209, March–April, 1996, pp. 71–80.

Vernon, M., First steps, *Computer Weekly, e.business review*, April, 2000.

Whittle, S., On-line banking hangs on the balance, *Computing*, 7 December, 2000, p. 70.

Concepts

Part Two

Communications Infrastructure for Commerce

Chapter Five

Objectives

By the end of this chapter you should have an understanding of:

- Computer technologies in relation to business and communication.
- The significance of an infrastructure for e-commerce.
- The technologies of Internet-based communication.
- The important issues surrounding reliable communication.

INTRODUCTION

We explored the technologies, models and debates that underpin the e-commerce phenomenon in the context section of the book. We addressed the issues that influenced and contributed to the emergence of e-commerce, and discussed some of the frameworks introduced by those working in the areas of organisational behaviour, processes and strategies. So far, we have restricted ourselves to the technological and business models that make up the foundation of e-commerce, now we will discuss the technological and business concepts themselves at some depth.

E-commerce is founded on two things: a network of computer systems, and business strategies that use this network for a competitive advantage. This section deals with the former: it is about how things work, and what infrastructure is required to underpin the technology, management and operation of e-commerce systems.

In order to understand how e-commerce works, we must have a clear understanding of the role technology plays in the processing and communication of data. This chapter covers the technical issues behind Internet-based communication. Following a discussion of the importance of a technical infrastructure to support e-commerce, we will explore the advanced technologies that facilitate electronic communication and provide the basis for such an infrastructure. In this chapter we will concentrate on the technologies required for effective communication of data. The information systems that provide the foundation for the software support necessary for the infrastructure will be discussed in the next chapter.

It is expected that the readers of this book have a basic understanding of how computers work, what constitutes a network of computers and what role a network plays in the communication of data. However, in order to reacquaint ourselves with the important technical concepts relevant to e-commerce, here follows a brief account of the concepts of a computer system, and a brief description of the devices, trends, policies and techniques that provide the foundation for computer-to-computer communication.[1]

[1] Readers who are proficient in this area may like to skip to the section entitled 'IT strategies for e-commerce systems'. However, the links made here between the basic technical concepts and the introduction of e-commerce should provide a useful overview of the foundation.

THE CONCEPT OF A COMPUTER SYSTEM

A computer is a machine that accepts data, processes it, and produces information. It can also store data and information temporarily during processing. It enables us to store processed data (information) permanently for further use, and it also facilitates the printing of the information in human-readable form. Thus, a computer is an *input/process/output* device: it accepts data such as amounts of money deposited to a bank account as input, processes it, that is, uses programs to perform various calculations relevant to the data in order to produce information such as a statement in the form of output. Data can be entered into the system using a keyboard attached to the input end or via a disk containing files of data. The computer holds the programs and files in memory during processing, and can produce printed statements using a printer attached to the output end. Information produced can be stored permanently on a disk using a disk drive, the device for backing storage. These devices are connected to each other by channels (circuits) which facilitate the transmission of data and information.

The 'computer' in this system is the processing unit connected to input and output devices externally; it comes with some internal storage, referred to as memory, for holding data and programs during processing. The external storage, usually provided by disks, is normally incorporated into the computer system in the form of removable (known as floppy in the PC world) and fixed (known as hard) disk drives used for storing small and large amount of information, respectively.

A computer is an input/process/output device. It also provides facilities for storing data internally, during processing, and externally, for permanent storage.

As is evident from the above description, a computer works with two elements: the physical devices such as the processor and the keyboard, which are referred to as hardware; and the non-physical (or soft) elements – the programs and data – known as software. Without software, a computer is only a metal object incapable of doing anything. On the other hand, although software instructs a computer exactly how to process data, it has no function or ability without hardware. A carefully constructed combination of these two elements enables a computer to perform the tasks allocated to it. Additionally, in today's businesses, a computer system is of little use unless it can communicate with other systems in order to share resources and enable users to access the system locally, nationally and internationally. Thus, we need to understand the basic concepts behind three elements of a computer system: hardware, software and inter-computer communications.

Hardware

As shown in Fig. 5.1, a computer consists of a central processing unit (CPU) and memory with data travelling between the units within them via channels, each known as a bus. The CPU is the nerve centre of a computer, rather like the human brain: it co-ordinates the operations of the computer. The memory of a computer holds data and programs to be used by the CPU. It has two parts: the read only memory (ROM) to store the programs essential for preparing the computer to recognise the units of the computer system and to begin the initial operations; and the random access memory (RAM), the space reserved to hold the programs, data and processed information at runtime. The programs in ROM are permanent; users can use the programs but are unable to change them in any way. On the other hand, RAM is volatile, that is, its content is wiped out every time a computer is switched off or the programs and files held in it are closed. Thus, when a new task is started, users are presented with an empty RAM ready to accept the programs and data associated with the task.

The other hardware items associated with a computer system are the peripheral devices: input, output and storage. An input device is used to enter data into the computer. Following a long period (till the late 1970s) of data entry by bulky devices such as a punch card reader, the most common forms nowadays are the keyboard used for entering textual data and the mouse used for selecting options available on the screen by a method of point and click. Printers and monitors (also called visual display units) are the most common output devices. In the last 30 years, a rapid evolution in technologies transported computers from isolated computer centres in large companies to the stage where business of all sizes are able to benefit from their use for global business activities.

The processing unit of a computer mainly contains a processor, read only memory (ROM) for programs required to initiate processing, and random access memory (RAM) for holding programs and data during processing.

A computer works under the instruction of programs written by humans. Programs control the sequence of operations and feed data that the computer processes. All instructions and data inside the computer are interpreted as a series of 0s and 1s, referred to as binary digits; a 0 represents an electronic switch being off, and 1 means the switch is on. The electronic device that provides the switching is called a transistor, a large number of which are connected to the circuit board. In the early days of computers transistors were quite big in size and prone to overheating and malfunctions. Consequently computers were large and expensive – the mainframes and minicomputers of the 1960s and 1970s. They were powerful machines (for that time) and enabled large corporations to process their central legacy systems such as payroll and accounts. They were too expensive and specialised to enter small and medium size enterprises (SMEs), or make any impact on ordinary consumers. Transistors soon became much smaller and more robust due to the use of silicon – a crystal of a chemical element with special electronic properties. A small piece of silicon (a chip) could hold a large amount of circuitry comprising many such transistors etched onto it. Known as integrated circuits, they made it possible to produce a complete CPU on one silicon chip, called a microprocessor.

In the meantime, programming languages moved on from machine code (strings of 0s and 1s), to mnemonic code (abbreviations resembling instructions), to high level (using English words), called the third-generation language, to eventually, a fourth generation of language which provides a programming tool for non-specialist programmers. This contributed to the ease and efficiency with which programs could be written. Consequently, computers became much smaller, cheaper, and easier to use. This

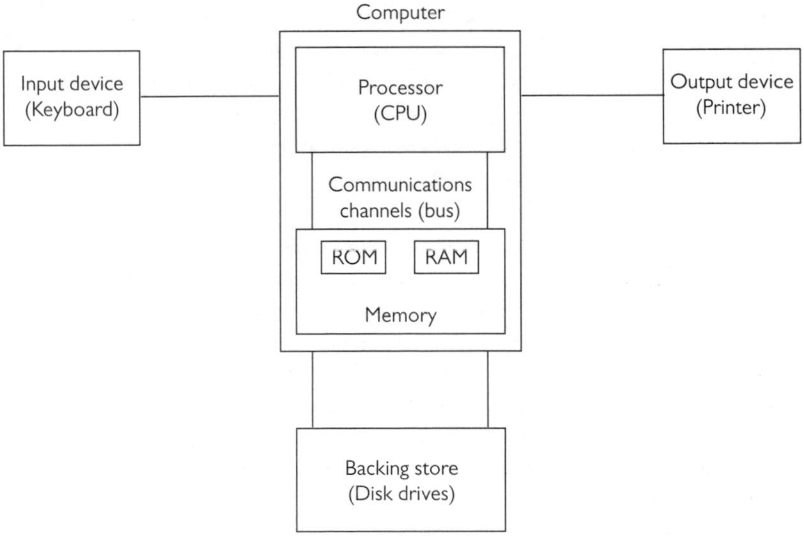

Fig. 5.1 The components of a computer system

paved the way for the birth of personal computers (PCs) in the early 1980s. Initially PCs had a small amount of memory, no hard disk, and limited processing power. However, thanks to the involvement of large companies such as IBM, Intel and Microsoft, as well as the pioneering spirit of some new young entrepreneurs who started Apple computers, PCs made fast progress. Rapid improvements were made in the specification in all areas: processors, memory, storage, input and output technologies, and the quality of software. This started the so called IT revolution, and by the early 1990s computers entered all spheres of society: large companies, SMEs, homes, schools and so on. PCs became powerful machines capable of running advanced programs designed for all types of business applications, as well as supporting a small network of computers. This enabled companies to use PCs to run distributed systems with mainframes and minis used mainly for the purpose of linking such distributed operations and supporting the company's larger IT infrastructure. This increased the flexibility of computer systems; smaller organisations could utilise the power of modern PCs to run e-commerce applications while larger companies used a combination of different sizes to support their front-end (distributed applications) and back-end (legacy) systems.

Incidentally, another class of computers called supercomputers appeared in the market at the same time. These are large computers containing rows of many small processors. Each instruction to be executed by a supercomputer is divided into a number of small ones all processed together in parallel with each other by the processors. This enables each computer to work very fast and process complicated instructions. These are powerful and expensive machines used mainly for computer systems for space research, geological surveys and so on. Although they may be used for global systems, their use in e-commerce is limited.

The trend in the size of computers is downwards. The introduction of laptops, notebooks, hand-held PCs (HPC), personal digital assistants (PDA) etc. represent a spectrum of personal computers with gradually decreasing size, processing power, memory, storage and so on. By taking advantage of innovations in networking technologies in parallel, these devices facilitate mobile computing by enabling users to communicate with the company's information systems from remote locations, and to conduct business activities regardless of their physical location. This has made a major contribution in the global environment of e-commerce.

Rapid innovations in technology resulted in the miniaturisation of hardware and advances in programming methods. This, in turn, led the way to smaller, easier-to-use computers. PCs are the consequence of this trend.

As computers became increasingly ubiquitous, hardware manufacturers came up with a number of innovations in input and output devices. Special-purpose keyboards tailored to a company's products such as the ones used in supermarkets for use by staff, or the hand-held devices for use by customers to log their own purchase, are becoming more common; a number of new mouse designs are also being introduced to take advantage of the advanced graphical interfaces used with e-commerce applications, for example a small rolling button fixed to the keyboard of a laptop, mouse pens which work in a very small area and also by directly pointing on the screen, and a mouse with extra buttons for specific functions assigned by the user. There are a number of other special purpose input devices such as light pens, touch screens, barcode readers, scanners for optical and magnetic character recognition as used by banks to read cheques and credit card slips, voice and handwriting input, a camera for entering photographic images, and smart cards holding personal data on the owner of the card. A number of these devices are used in businesses for quick and secure data entry, and therefore have an important role to play in e-commerce. Increasingly PCs are being made with multimedia capability incorporating input and output devices for handling data in various formats such as audio, video, graphics and animation. As the use of e-commerce grows, these facilities will become common features in all computers due to increasing demand for fast and convenient communication.

There have also been many innovations in output technologies. On the one hand, the use of printed output has become less important in business transactions as the popularity of on-line communication has increased. On the other, the quality of the monitor has become very important for e-commerce because of its contribution to the ease of use and versatility of webpages. Monitors with high resolution and colour range are now essential for organisations attempting to take advantage of the advanced techniques of web design available today. The quality of printers also improved; as organisations empowered by new technologies entered the global market, they needed to produce better quality documentation for the physical parts of their operation. Additionally, documents are often sent electronically by organisations using e-commerce, expecting the receiver to print them before use. Thus the printing process has been passed on from the producer to the receiver who, because of the elaborate use of colour and formatting, needs good quality printers. Thus, improvement in technology inspired e-commerce; however, e-commerce drove the initiatives for further improvement in technology.

As with the need for better quality input and output devices, the demand for high capacity storage devices has also been increasing. As the quality of software improved, the size of the programs increased as well, resulting in the subsequent increase in the hard disk space required to hold them. Storage in mainframes and minis come in the form of Winchester disks comprising a number of disks in a pack. Together they provide the space required by companies storing data and programs for large systems. They also use removable disks for back up. The storage available in PCs has been increasing steadily since their birth; now they provide more hard disk space than the minis of the 1980s. Currently PCs come with hard disks of sizes in excess of 40 GB (1 Gigabyte = about 1 billion characters), together with floppy disks (1.4 MB (Megabyte)), zip disks for compressed data (100 MB), and CD-ROMs and DVDs (Digital Video Disks/Display) for storing large multimedia applications.

As programs running on a computer have to be held in memory, the size of memory also had to increase with increasing sophistication of software. E-commerce applications with high quality graphics, animation etc. are extremely demanding in terms of memory, speed and processing power. Things are changing very fast and it is difficult to quote any specific figures. Nonetheless, typical memory in a modern PC is 128 or 256 Mb and the processor speeds are in the region of 800 MHz to more than 1 GHz.[2] Intel, the well-known chip manufacturer, in collaboration with Microsoft (for software) and IBM (for hardware), produced the PC in the early 1980s. This became the industry standard for microcomputers to the extent that the term PC became synonymous with machines compatible with the Intel/MS/IBM architecture. Intel enjoyed a monopoly in the CPU market for about 20 years. Its latest processor, the Pentium 4, has a speed of 1.5 GHz. In the meantime some other manufacturers, especially Apple, have maintained their own brand of hardware and software in the microcomputers market. They specialised in easy-to-use software with a graphical user interface and managed to enjoy the loyalty of a relatively small but dedicated group of users. However, now there are a number of competitors in the chip industry, such as AMD and Cyrix, who are also producing processors of high quality. As stated before, e-commerce is both the effect and cause of such growth.

Together with the processor technologies, there were improvements in memory and external storage capacity as well. On the one hand, such progress gradually led to the introduction of e-commerce, on the other, e-commerce encouraged further growth in technology.

We have quoted typical specifications mainly for PCs which are so powerful these days that they are extensively used in large as well as in small organisations. Top-range PCs can

[2] A processor speed represents how many times the crystal (signal generator) in the processor oscillates in one second. Thus 800 Mhz means the crystal oscillates 800 million times per second, which coincides roughly with the number of instructions it can execute in a second.

now be used for distributed processing as network servers, a computer that supports a network of smaller client PCs. However, large organisations need to use mainframes and mini (also referred to as midrange) computers for their backend systems; advances in hardware technologies have been equally significant in this market as well. They come with very fast processors and proportionately large memory and disk storage. These systems can use techniques such as multi-processing – using more than one processor to share the workload; multi-programming – running a number of programs at the same time by scheduling different parts of each job separately on priority basis; virtual memory – using the hard disk as an extension of memory; and various disk management procedures to optimise the disk space. As a result they can utilise hardware resources to an almost unlimited extent, thus achieving great operational flexibility.

Using examples from recent technological innovations, discuss the comment that e-commerce is both the effect and the cause of the growth in technology.

Software

Software[3] can be put into two main categories: systems and applications. Systems programs run the computer system; they co-ordinate the sequence of operations – from starting the computer, to running programs, the input and output of data, the interconnection between different parts of the computer system, and so on. A typical example of systems software is an operating system such as Microsoft Windows 2000 for PCs, and Unix, Linux and AIX RS/6000 – an IBM version of Unix – for the midrange. Applications programs perform specific tasks such as wordprocessing, creating websites and running games. It is anticipated that most of the readers of this book have some knowledge of these two types of software; in the following discussion we will give a brief description of the trends and concepts specifically relevant to e-commerce.

E-commerce has benefited enormously from the evolution in software. In the 1960s and 1970s, software had a problematic user interface. Operators with special training had to perform a number of manual operations in order to install software into the memory and enter text-based commands to run the computer. As computers came more into common use, the interfaces became progressively user friendly: from text-based, to menu-based, to graphical user interfaces (GUI). GUI is the use of graphical images that represent real-life operations. WIMP (Windows, Icons, Mouse, and Pull-down menus/ Pointers) is a term used to reflect this concept: software came with windows such as in the Microsoft operating system, icons such as the image of a folder to represent files, a mouse to point at the relevant part of the screen, and menus and buttons to point to. Initiated by the PC industry, mainly by software developers working for GEM (a company which supplied software used by Amstrad – a cheap and cheerful microcomputer platform introduced by Alan Sugar in the UK in the 1980s) and Apple microcomputers, and later on followed by Microsoft, it revolutionised the use of computers. Along with the growth of the PC hardware industry, such development in software brought computers to the common people which, in turn, paved the way to the widespread use of computers in business. Initially, the trend was restricted to the PC industry but gradually operating systems and applications software for larger computers also adopted the philosophy of usability. Unix and Linux, two popular operating systems for larger computers now come with GUI, and most applications programs for this sector also have a user-friendly interface.

[3] We are using the term to mean only programs and not data.

Another trend that made an impact, especially in the systems software market, is the movement towards open source. Initially, software used to be written for specific hardware; thus the operating system for an IBM machine would not work on any other. It was the owners of Unix who aspired to change that by making source code (program instructions) available to the buyers. It was sold very cheaply to encourage market penetration. This enabled users to change the program to suit their own system, thus eliminating the problem of incompatibility between systems. This was the beginning of the open source movement: Unix became the 'open' operating system, compatible with (almost) all machines. The trend was followed by Linus Torvalds when he and his team introduced Linux, free of charge and packaged it with the code, in the mid-1990s. Linux became very popular very fast and a lot of companies which were using other operating systems such as Unix shifted to Linux. The open source movement encouraged other companies to follow suit; examples of other open source operating systems are Perl, Python, Apache, and Samba (Langley, 2001). The interoperability achieved by open source initiatives increased the freedom of organisations to choose hardware and applications for their business systems, thus improving their opportunities in e-commerce.

Hand in hand with systems software, applications programs made an important contribution to e-commerce. They provided the platform for: the databases for the company's backend information systems; applications such as emails, intranets and groupware; on-line interfaces; and the usual business processes such as wordprocessing for documentation and spreadsheets for the presentation of financial data. Following the trend in user-friendly interfaces, application programs became increasingly easier to use enabling workers in all areas of an organisation to use a computer. This section of the computer industry has grown so fast, and there has been so much competition amongst software manufacturers to gain customer loyalty, that there is a continuous race to release new updates in rapid succession. This has improved the quality of software enormously; however, it has created some instability caused by the pressure felt by organisations to opt for new technologies with inadequate regard as to how it affects the company's overall goals. Employees are now expected to adapt to changing software environments with little training or support. We will come back to this topic in the next section of the book.

The trends contributing to the e-commerce phenomenon are:

- GUI-based software.
- The proliferation of applications programs.
- The open source movement in operating systems.

Despite certain issues such as training, innovations in software development have been invaluable for e-commerce because of its dependence on Internet-based applications such as browsers, search engines, websites, and so on. These are built by using hypertext handlers such as HTML and its updates, programming languages such as Java, and data in various formats such as graphics, music and video. The other major software essential for the support of e-commerce are databases which are required to support the backend information systems for organisations, and provide the backbone of the information retrieval process by the search engines (see chapter 2). We will give an overview of the technologies behind webpage design and search as well as database concepts in the next chapter.

Another type of software that has cropped up as a result of e-commerce is middleware – programs that integrate frontend e-commerce applications such as on-line catalogues and business transaction interfaces with backend activities such as existing databases and enterprise resource planning (ERP) systems. They are designed to hide the complications of the processes involved in interconnecting a company's complex e-commerce activities. In order to provide proper customer service, a company needs to web-enable its whole IT infrastructure to achieve full communication between all the systems.

E-commerce depends on some relatively new concepts in software:

- Web-development tools such as HTML.
- Middleware for front and backend integration.

All types of e-commerce system are now available from software vendors. This means that companies have the option of building systems themselves, buying solutions from a vendor or outsourcing the whole operation to another company. We will discuss these options and their implications in a later part of the book.

Look at the interfaces of some on-line companies and write a critical review of their level of usability.

Inter-computer communications

E-commerce cannot work unless computers can communicate with each other over wide geographical areas. This necessitates a network of computer systems sending messages to each other and sharing resources via communications channels. This could be only a few computers connected to each other within a small area – a local area network (LAN); computers communicating with each other over a large distance via interconnected LANs – a wide area network (WAN); or even global communication by connecting large networks together – the Internet. The communication involves the transfer of electromagnetic waves: pulses of electricity or light by physical (wireline) connection between computers or the wireless transmission of radio signals.

Communication channels

In order to understand inter-computer communication, we need to have some understanding of the nature of electromagnetic waves. For our purpose we can think of them as signals generating waves (Fig. 5.2) the same way a pebble moving up and down in water generates ripples. The intensity (strength) of the signal is represented by the amplitude (the maximum height) of the wave, and the time it takes it to complete one cycle (to move from A to B) is the time period. The signal is carried through air by a continuous repetition of this pattern; frequency is the rate at which the signal repeats the pattern, and is measured in hertz. A frequency of 1 MHz means the signal repeats 1 million times per second. The wave moves as a result of the repetition of the signals, hence the higher the frequency the faster the transmission of data.

Frequencies in the range of 30 MHz to 40 GHz are used for wireless transmission. The lower range of this spectrum (up to 1 GHz) is omnidirectional, that is, the signals go in all directions. Transmission and reception of signals are done via antennae: a transmitting one that radiates electromagnetic signals and a receiving one that picks them up. Omnidirectional signals can be 'caught' by an antenna easily and do not need a dish, thus making them suitable for broadcast radio. At the higher range, signals (known as microwaves) are highly directional, and therefore suitable for point-to-point

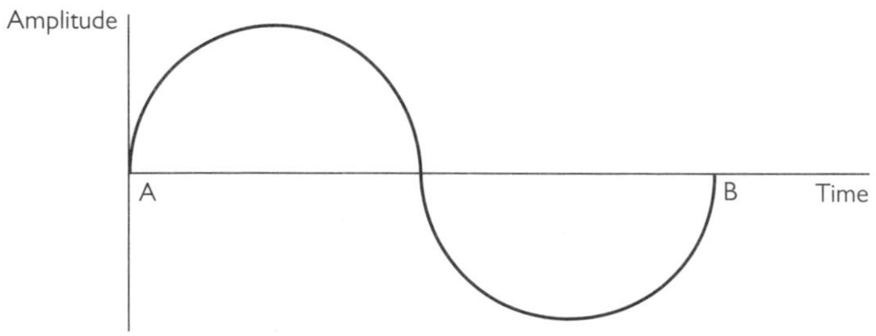

Fig. 5.2 An electromagnetic waveform

transmission. They require transmitting and receiving antennae to be carefully aligned. Normally, a large parabolic dish is used at a substantial height to transmit the signals to be received by antennas at the users' end. Sometimes it is necessary to boost the strength of the signal by using a number of microwave towers as relay points. Satellites are commonly used these days as microwave relay stations. We will come back to this topic later on in the chapter.

One term often used in a confusing manner in connection with data communication is bandwidth. For an analogue service this refers to the difference between the highest and the lowest frequency within which a transmission medium carries traffic, and is measured in Hz. Thus a channel carrying data at frequencies between 150 MHz and 250 MHz has a bandwidth of 100 MHz. For digital data, bandwidth refers to the rate at which bits are transmitted and is measured in bits/sec. Thus, frequency can be thought of as the capacity rating of a transmission medium. Some channels are said to be narrowband – providing lower speed than 1.544 Mb/s; wideband – supporting data rate of 1.544 to 45 Mb/s; and broadband offers speed in excess of 45 Mb/s. The article by Green (2000) gives further details on these.

Frequency represents the capacity rating of a transmission medium, and is measured in hertz (Hz). For analogue transmission, bandwidth refers to the range of frequencies of data traffic a medium can support; for digital transmission, it is the rate at which bits are transmitted.

Wired connection, also referred to as guided communication, sends signals through cables. In this mode, the transmission capacity depends on the distance to be covered, the quality of cabling, the number of simultaneous receivers, and so on. The cables can be of different types:

- Twisted wires – strands of copper wires twisted in pairs, as in telephone lines. This is easy to use and inexpensive as it enables electronic companies to utilise a country's telephone network to transmit data. However, it can only carry analogue (continuous, voice type) data, and the transmission quality is affected by interference in the lines.
- Co-axial cables – an insulated copper cable as used in television aerials. These are more expensive than twisted pair but can be laid under the ocean floor to connect systems internationally.
- Optical fibres – strands of transparent fibres bound together into cables. These can carry pulses generated by laser sources. Although this is an expensive medium, it is capable of carrying both analogue and digital data, and provides faster data transmission.

In addition to the channels, communication also requires a number of devices to facilitate the transfer of data. They vary widely in terms of format, speed, and medium.

Network devices

The signals produced by voice (as in a telephone line) or video (as for TV) are 'analogue' in form. They produce continuous electromagnetic waves as shown in Fig. 5.2. Computer-generated signals are a series of voltages (5 volts to indicate 1, and 0 volts to indicate 0); thus they are discrete bits, a stream of 0s and 1s. When data from a computer has to be transmitted via a telephone line, it needs to be converted into analogue form. A modem (modulator/demodulator) connected at the sender end of the telephone line converts the bits into an equivalent waveform and transmits it via the telephone line; another modem connected at the end of the line converts it back to a bit pattern before passing it on to the receiver.

Some other devices are used with networks in order to improve transmission in various ways.

- Often it is more efficient to send signals from a number of sources via one channel. This is achieved by a *multiplexer* – a device that interleaves the signals and sends them via one channel. At the receiving end, another multiplexer separates the signals and transmits them by individual channels to their destinations.

- Sometimes a signal loses its strength during transmission; a device called a *repeater* is often used in a channel in order to boost the signal.
- *Bridges* and *gateways* are used to interconnect two LANs: the former for LANs of the same type, and the latter for those of different types.
- While the above are designed to simply pass messages on from one channel to another, a *router* is a device which determines the best route between the sender and the receiver before a message is passed on.

A combination of all these devices is normally necessary in order to obtain widespread interconnectivity within a LAN, between LANs, and eventually to WANs. It is also possible to join a bridge and a router (referred to as a brouter) which tries to find the best route for a message; if it fails, it just passes it on to the next stage as a bridge. Together, all these devices ensure that messages are sent to the right place, along the best possible route, without delay, and with as little distortion as possible. In addition to the hardware devices, this requires protocols.

A number of hardware devices are used to enhance the movement of data in a LAN. They are: modems, multiplexers, repeaters, routers, bridges and gateways.

Why are LANs important for e-commerce?

Protocols

Avoiding errors in communication is of vital importance and further steps need to be taken to maintain the quality of transmission. Quality can be affected in two ways: inadequate facilities (which also affect the speed of transmission), and incompatibility between systems resulting in the message from one system being unacceptable to another. In today's world of global communication, reliability is crucial; there must be rules and procedures – protocols – to ensure smooth transfer of data.

Protocols in data transmission are established to check the passage of data at a number of fixed stages. It is similar to the way a letter sent by a postal system goes through stages beginning with the sender writing the address and posting it in a designated place through to the post office collecting it, sorting it, and delivering it to the addressee. There are rules to be followed at each of these stages, for example, writing the address using the correct format, putting the right stamp on, sorting the letter in address order correctly and so on. These rules are checked at each stage, and if any errors are found the letter is sent back to the previous stage or returned to the sender (speaking ideally). Thus the rules are divided into layers, each layer checking that the work done in the previous layer is correct before passing it on to the next one. Protocols for electronic messages are similarly divided into layers with the task of checking divided into sub-tasks, each to be performed by one layer.

The layers can be classified in three basic categories (Fig. 5.3): the network layer that looks after the exchange of data between a computer and the network to which it is attached; the transport layer concerned with the reliable transfer of the message, in the correct order during its passage through the communication system; and the application layer which ensures that the delivered message can be passed on to the intended application (email, file transfer etc.) at the receiving end. Protocols perform two tasks: at each layer of the network, it checks that the message sent follows the rules of the protocol before passing it on to the next layer and, it attaches extra (control) information

Protocols establish rules of communication to enable the data transmission to occur securely and speedily. The rules are divided into layers, each serving a stage of communication.

to the message to be read by the same layer of the receiver system in order for it to understand it. The control information related to a layer is removed from the message by its pair at the other end. Thus, according to Fig. 5.3, a message from system A is checked by the protocol of the application layer, control information is attached to it for the application layer of system B, and then passed on to the physical layer of A. This process goes on until the message reaches the communication network and travels to system B. The process is now reversed – from the network layer to the application layer of B – and the control information gets taken out in stages by the appropriate layer.

Protocols can be proprietary, that is, rules established by and followed within an organisation. This is of little use in the e-commerce world which requires protocols to be agreed by all organisations involved in data communication, that is, they require standards.

Figure 5.3 represents a model; a standard setting body adds details to it by subdividing the layers further for clarity, and by attaching specific rules with each layer. The International Organisation for Standardisation (ISO), the body involved in the open systems movement dedicated to finding a common standard for all aspects of computer systems, suggested the protocol known as the open systems interconnection (OSI) model. ISO expected this model to be accepted for all networked communications. Although they managed to discourage the culture of proprietary standards used by big companies such as IBM and Ford and advanced the move towards an international standard, they failed to persuade the Internet users to adopt OSI. Instead TCP/IP, Transmission Control Protocol/ Internet Protocol, the protocol established by the ARPANET project dominated the Internet. Although this is not an official model like OSI, it is generally used as the standard for the Internet. Figure 5.4 shows the two models with the positioning of the layers in the two representing the correspondence between their functions. We are not going into any more detail on this; recommended books on data communication (especially Stallings, 2000) can be used for further information.

OSI is the data communications standard introduced by the open sources movement; TCP/IP is a set of protocols (not officially a standard) for Internet-based communication.

The issue of standards affects all aspects of e-commerce. Interoperability between trading partners is essential for a company attempting to use the Internet to run its business processes. This requires agreed standards, not only for hardware platforms and operating systems, but also for communication between different systems, nationally and internationally. Predicting the future of communication in the next 5 to 10 years Whyte writes:

> Efforts in standardisation will mean that within the decade mobile and fixed-line telephony will be extensively integrated, sharing services and handsets (although the differing standards in Europe, the USA and the Far East may hold this back somewhat). It is perhaps doubtful that the distinction between connectionless and connection-oriented will have disappeared completely, as they have different virtues, but there will have emerged a common set of

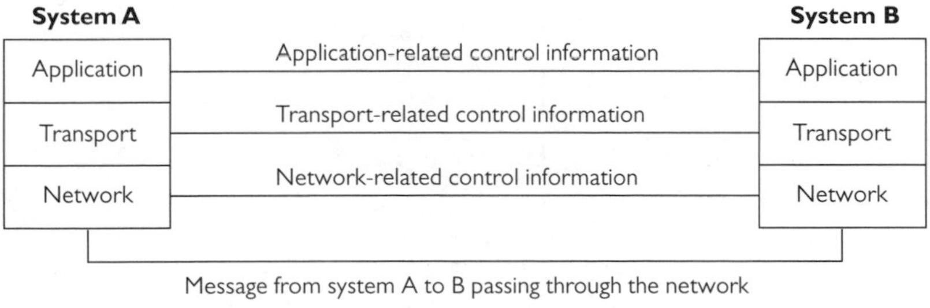

Fig. 5.3 The concept of layered architecture of protocols

> standards for control of 'computing' and 'telecommunications' networks and the latter distinction will have been lost.
>
> (1999: 356)

The issue of standards arises in most of the debates associated with Internet-based communication; we will address them at the appropriate points.

There are some other concepts that need to be understood in order to engage in the discussion of e-commerce related communication: in particular, the way data is sent through a physical medium, and the way computers in a network relate to each other. We will discuss the techniques used in data transmission later on in the chapter; the following is a brief description of the inter-relationships of computers.

Are there any problems associated with the use of a standard? Discuss in relation to Internet-based data transfer.

The relationship between computers in a network

Network terminals (computers and other devices connected to the endpoints of a network) can be connected to each other in three basic forms: star, ring or bus (Fig. 5.5). Referred to as the topology (architecture) of network, it determines how the computers

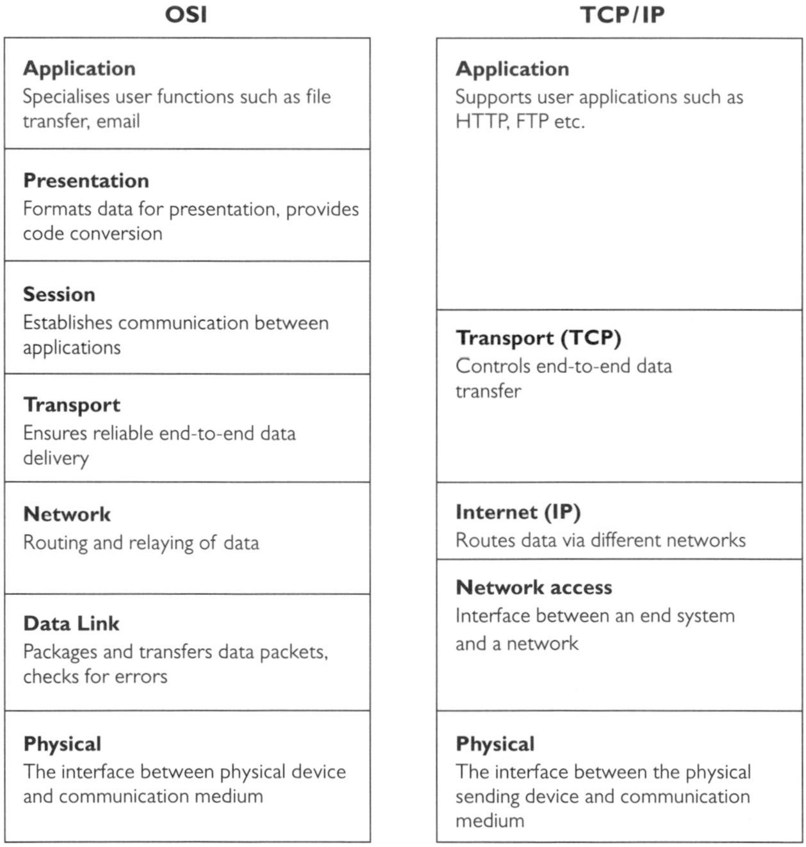
OSI
Application
Specialises user functions such as file transfer, email
Presentation
Formats data for presentation, provides code conversion
Session
Establishes communication between applications
Transport
Ensures reliable end-to-end data delivery
Network
Routing and relaying of data
Data Link
Packages and transfers data packets, checks for errors
Physical
The interface between physical device and communication medium
TCP/IP
Application
Supports user applications such as HTTP, FTP etc.
Transport (TCP)
Controls end-to-end data transfer
Internet (IP)
Routes data via different networks
Network access
Interface between an end system and a network
Physical
The interface between the physical sending device and communication medium

Fig. 5.4 OSI and TCP/IP models

relate to each other. *Star* follows the centralised model – a computer in the centre is the processor, with terminals (computers with low or no processing power, as well as other devices such as printers) at the end of the spikes. The terminals only act as the senders and receivers of information. The transmission of data is controlled by the centre, 'polling' the terminals as necessary. In the *ring* topology, all the terminals are connected in a ring shape with no hierarchy in the architecture. When a terminal wants to send a message it grabs a token – a standard bit pattern recognisable by all the terminals as a message carrier. A message with the address of the destination terminal is added to the token and passed through the ring in one direction via each terminal (which also acts as the repeater) until the addressee detects it. This mode of data transmission is known as *token ring*. A *bus* reflects the backbone model, the cable running at the background (as the route of a bus) with computers connected to it with short cables. Known as the *ethernet* model, a message passes through the backbone; each computer checks the message and accepts it if it is meant for itself. Networks can also be built by combining two or more topologies together. For example, a bus network can serve as the backbone for small star or ring networks attached to it. The Internet follows this pattern and even though ethernet was initially used in large LANs, with the invention of high speed ethernet (explained later), this technology is likely to become important for e-commerce.

Network terminals can be connected to each other in a number of ways:

- in a ring, all with equal status
- in star shape, with power lying at the centre
- in a bus with data travelling in the backbone and terminals 'hanging' from it.

In the days of mainframes, networks used to be centralised – a large and powerful computer (a main or a mini) holding all applications and files, and doing all the processing – connected to simple computers (terminals) with no or little processing power, used for accessing information from the centre. As PCs became increasingly powerful, the situation changed gradually; computers took on a dual role as network terminals as well as desktop computers running applications such as a wordprocessor. As computers became more integrated into the office environment and the management of information became a vital part of an organisation's activities, distributed processing gave way to centralisation. This was in keeping with the shift of organisational structure from a hierarchical to a distributed network architecture. In this mode, computing tasks are distributed amongst a number of smaller, often department-based, systems. For example, each section or department of an organisation has its own computer system for managing the information they require. The local systems, often supported by powerful PCs, are connected to each other, and often to a central system, for connectivity between different sections. Such architecture is normally run by a client-server networking model in which the central system acts as the server and the departmental systems are the clients. The server holds all the programs and data centrally. When a client requests an application, either a copy of the program and the necessary files are downloaded to the client for it to do its own processing or the processing is done by the server, the local PC only acting as a terminal. The exact division of tasks is determined by the organisers of the IT systems in the company.

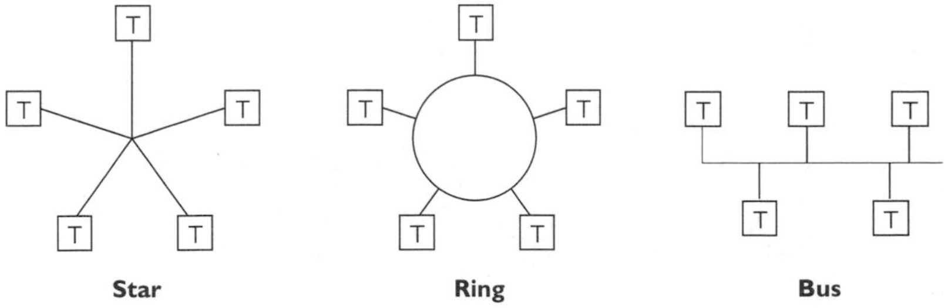

Fig. 5.5 The three basic architectures for a LAN (T = terminals)

The concept of a server is similarly appropriate for Internet-based communication as well. An Internet server holds the software resources which enable the computers in a company to communicate with the Internet. Additionally, one large computer system can have a number of servers for different purposes. For example, an organisation's central system may have an email server, a web server, a file server and so on (Fig. 5.6). Thus, when a user in the company wants to connect to an external website, it goes via the web server; if s/he wants to send/receive an email, it is handled by the email server. Thus an Internet server is a powerful processor that connects organisational computer resources and users with the Internet. IBM and Sun Microsystems are two well-known server manufacturers. Linux has become very popular as the operating system for a server, and Microsoft (MS Internet Information Server), Apache (Apache Server) and Netscape (Enterprise Server) are front-line web servers.

Before PCs became powerful, networks used to be centralised with all processing done by the central hub. Now, client/server networks are predominant; the server holds the programs and the processing is distributed to the clients as appropriate.

A server is also used as a storage device. Internet-based communication requires the system to store large programs and data; usually a server is used for this purpose. However, a storage area network (SAN), a separate network designed to handle storage needs, is sometimes used by large systems to create a shared storage facility across a high-speed network. It can include hard disks, magnetic tapes and CD-ROMs, and communication takes place via fibre optic channels. Another concept, known as network attached storage (NAS), initially used by small networks to store files required by communicating systems, is now being used more widely. NAS provides improved file sharing between users, economics of scale, compatibility with existing technology and so on. The two systems (SAN and NAS) are complementary to each other and are often used together in a network: SAN for resource (devices) sharing and NAS for file sharing.

There is a lot more we could say about the technologies behind computer systems and networks. In the above discussion we concentrated on the concepts which have some relevance to e-commerce, and we will return to some of those concepts, as well as address some new ones later on in the chapter. Some additional systems concepts will also be discussed in the next chapter. Further information on these topics is available from the books mentioned in the bibliography (especially Dodd (1998), Norris *et al.* (2000), Rajput (2000) and Stallings (2000)). We will now move on to the discussion of the technical infrastructure required to support e-commerce.

Find out if your university or place of work uses a client/server architecture and if so, how the processing tasks are distributed.

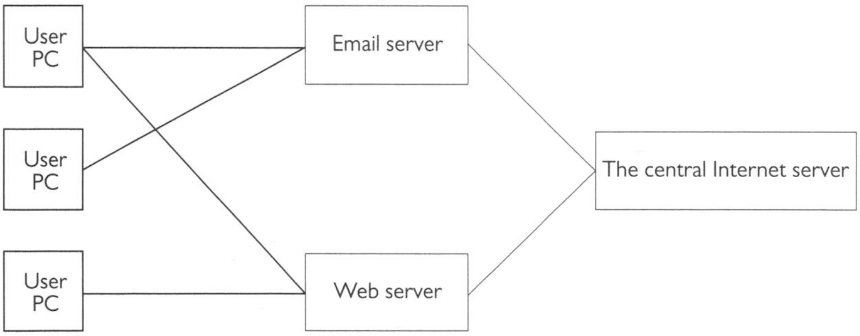

Fig. 5.6 An organisation's internet server

IT STRATEGIES FOR E-COMMERCE SYSTEMS

As discussed in chapters 3 and 4, the contemporary view of organisations within the information society advocates that a company's IT strategies should be formulated within the framework of its overall business needs. It also advocates that e-commerce must not be seen as the application of Internet technologies to run business processes. In order to succeed in the knowledge economy, a company attempting to adopt e-commerce must turn itself into an e-business in which electronic technology both defines and manages the business. Thus, according to this philosophy, a company's success in today's environment depends on its ability to employ technology to build business processes that support the challenges of the knowledge economy and take full advantage of it by using the available IT capabilities. By doing this, it not only gains a competitive advantage in a fast-changing corporate world and in the face of increasing customer demand, it also equips itself to understand the complexities of new technologies and their roles in supporting the business needs of an organisation.

Building an e-commerce initiative demands the establishment of a technical infrastructure capable of supporting a complicated array of technical and business systems. It involves making decisions on a wide variety of issues such as:

- Which business processes are directly affected and which IT systems are required to serve these processes; for example, an on-line sales system would require a number of databases such as order processing, customer records, stock control and so on.
- How the existing technical infrastructure fits in with the proposed changes.
- How the company should address the challenges of data communications requirements.
- Which new applications are required and how the company should acquire them.
- The characteristics and development of the user interfaces such as portals.
- The integration of backend information systems (the information systems supporting company's existing services) in order to fully automate all aspects of on-line trade.
- The involvement of external agencies for some of the services such as the Internet service providers (ISPs) and domain name suppliers.
- New internal systems and services to be facilitated by the initiatives such as the use of intranets.
- Links with business partners in order to support the supply chain, for example the development of an extranet.
- The infrastructure for security and reliability of the system.
- The connectivity with customers and business partners.

Introducing e-commerce affects existing information systems, networked applications, internal and external communications. An organisation must introduce strategies for handling the challenges presented by the proposed changes.

A company attempting to formulate its IT strategies in the wake of e-commerce initiatives must evaluate its goals and business models, and select the technology solutions which are most appropriate to its business directions. In order to do this, the organisation must have a clear understanding of the technical as well as the procedural infrastructure that supports e-commerce. In this and the next chapter we will discuss the hardware and software technologies; we will come back to the question of business procedures in the last chapter of this section. The implementation of these technologies and processes and their consequences will be discussed in the consequences section of the book.

THE PRINCIPLES BEHIND TECHNOLOGY INFRASTRUCTURE

Addressing the issues mentioned above requires widespread electronic links capable of transferring data securely and efficiently across national and international boundaries. The aim of a company's IT infrastructure should be to provide facilities for the integration of its systems in a way that enables it to build a platform for sharing its knowledge resources fully. The introduction of an e-commerce system not only entails making decisions about development and operational details of the system, but also how they relate to the organisation's existing infrastructure and processes. Thus, the principles behind the technical infrastructure underpinning e-commerce can be summarised as:

- Integration with the legacy systems supporting the company's existing IT provision, for example, centralised inventory records run on a mainframe.
- The incorporation of distributed information systems supporting the organisation's knowledge infrastructure, for example, a customer database on a client server system providing information required for customer relationship management.
- Integration with current hardware resources such as PCs, laptops, mobile phones and local area networks.
- The accessibility between systems and networks within the organisations and over the Internet in order to achieve secure communication between systems, employees, customers and trading partners.
- The provision of user-friendly and innovative on-line services involving the transmission of data of various formats such as text, graphics, audio and video.
- The flexibility and scalability of the system in order to suit the varied needs of users worldwide.
- The maintenance of security and speed of transactions at all levels.

A communications infrastructure for e-commerce is expected to resolve issues surrounding the reliable data transfer between the components (machines, back and front end information systems, trading partners, customers, employees etc.) of an e-commerce system.

The continual development in communications and information technologies (CIT) in the last two decades has presented organisations with numerous choices of technologies to support their infrastructure. Before we can discuss specific choices, we must understand the nature of the communication-related issues that underpin e-commerce.

What would be the consequences for an organisation of introducing e-commerce without an understanding of the infrastructure for electronic communication?

COMMUNICATIONS TECHNOLOGIES – AN OVERVIEW

Innovations in communications technologies in recent years have enabled companies of all sizes to join the global market. They can now use the infrastructure provided by the Internet to perform business transactions, employ the services of the providers of e-commerce applications to implement a business interface with little in-house expertise, and take advantage of the mobile telephony to join the e-commerce phenomenon without the need for large investments in capital. In today's world, technology advances at a rapid and sometimes confusing rate. Organisations faced with such enormous possibilities must understand the following underlying trends in order to make an intelligent choice:

- The options in telecommunications. Many networking options offering a wide variety of speed and versatility of communication are now available to organisations involved in e-commerce. For example, a country's telephone network provides stable and efficient communication of mainly voice. On the other hand an integrated services digital network (ISDN) is capable of transferring multiple data types (audio, video, music etc.) at a high speed. More recently, innovations in wireless technologies have given organisations the option to use mobile phones, notebook computers or a pager to connect to the Internet. They enable companies to make a choice of one or a combination of services in order to achieve convenient and high speed communication tailored to their needs.
- Access to the Internet. The telecommunications options mentioned above offer a wide range of speed and functionality. Access to the Internet can be made via such technologies using the services of one of a large number of ISPs available. They offer varying degrees of services and have different characteristics. Internet domain name service (DNS) is another initiative which enables a user to connect to an Internet site by using an address allocated to it by the DNS. There are other initiatives, for example that taken by UCAID, a project supported by a group of universities and telecommunications companies, designed to improve the communication of high bandwidth data, and the .net project started by Microsoft which intends to make communication between different applications and appliances transparent to the user.
- The technologies of security. Security of data can be put into two broad categories: the transmission of data through the network without the risk of loss or corruption, and the confidentiality of the transmitted data without interruption by unauthorised users. Security is one of the most crucial and least understood issues associated with Internet communication.
- The infrastructure for visibility. Visibility in cyberspace is crucial for companies attempting to use it as a business environment. This is facilitated by concepts such as directory services and middleware. Directory services (DS) are designed to enable users to find websites and other network resources on the Internet. DNS, mentioned above, is a DS which identifies an organisation on the Internet and gives users easy access to cyberspace. This in turn, increases the visibility of an organisation trying to attract visitors to its website. Middleware harmonises a company's backend information systems with the services and applications running on the Internet to enable the company to provide a customer service based on integrated systems. OMG (the Object Management Group) and Microsoft are the two major organisations involved in the development of standards for middleware services. Different types of middleware are available to handle communication between different types of applications. For example, transaction processing middleware supports a company's systems associated with transactions such as accounts or stock control; database middleware integrates databases by different vendors, enabling a company's business partners to access each other's databases. An e-commerce company must understand some of the concepts behind these services in order to find the options suitable for them.
- The importance of customer user interface. In addition to the hardware infrastructure, a company needs to build a frontend system that gives value to its customers. This requires a graphical user interface – the website or the portal that is the company's gateway to cyberspace – with features that lead a

user to the information and services required. The speed and efficiency with which the website manages to do this depends on the content of the interface. Extraordinary advances have been made in the last 10 years in the technologies of content development. Programming languages such as Java, HTML and its extensions and various standards and techniques have been designed to provide the means to create, maintain and run websites with multimedia displays and communication links between an organisation and its users. Organisations attempting to gain a competitive advantage in the fast-moving world of e-commerce are required to stay abreast of these developments in order to make the most of what technology can offer.

- The infrastructure for information systems. Information systems provide the basis for the applications and services of an organisation engaged in Internet-based transactions. A wide variety of technologies, design concepts and methodologies exist to support the development and implementation of these systems. The standard of e-commerce provision depends critically on these issues and the choices made by an organisation seriously affect its competitive positioning in the market.
- An operational infrastructure for e-commerce. An operational infrastructure is necessary to provide support for the business processes which form the basis of e-commerce applications. This includes a wide variety of tasks ranging between management of the content of the website, establishing management procedures which would support the system, introducing the payment infrastructure for on-line business, through to the monitoring of networked traffic. Some of these tasks are performed within the organisation, and a large number of tools are available to facilitate those. On the other hand, in the last few years many external service providers have entered the market and organisations are increasingly using them to contract out (outsource) some of their operational management functions. The choice of which solution to opt for depends on how the available technology fits in with an organisation's goals and resources, and how the business leaders are able to utilise them for a competitive advantage.

A technical infrastructure defines a framework for decisions on:

- network connections
- methods of access to the Internet
- visibility in cyberspace
- user interface
- security measures
- information systems
- operational procedures.

With an appreciation of the issues concerned, organisations must evaluate the technologies available and make decisions which provide the infrastructure appropriate to their needs. This calls for an understanding of the technologies which support communications infrastructure. In the following section, we will discuss the choices available to an organisation in terms of the technologies of networking, Internet access and security. We will discuss the other issues mentioned above in chapters related to information management systems supporting e-commerce, and operational infrastructure required for making it work.

COMMUNICATIONS TECHNOLOGIES – THE CHOICES

In describing the choices we will address the issues mentioned above and discuss the technologies which provide the infrastructural basis for effective communication in each of those areas.

Networking options

There are many networking options for e-commerce providers and users to choose from. They differ from each other in their use of technologies, standards and techniques, although the distinction is somewhat blurred. Additionally, some of the technologies involve end-to-end connection (the wired technologies), and some are wireless.

Wired connections

In the early days of EDI, the only option for companies intending to send data over a large distance was to connect to the country's telephone network. Known as the *Public Switched Telephone Network* (PSTN), this utilises a telephone line to make a connection by dialling a number. The user is charged according to the distance and time covered. The number is received by the nearest switching centre (exchange) and the connection is made with the destination address via a network of exchanges covering the country (and beyond). Once connected this way, the sender and the receiver stay 'on-line' until the message is completed. This is known as *circuit switching* as the route connecting the two parties remain dedicated (switched) to each other for the duration of the call. This is inefficient because unused (idle) times during the transmission could be utilised by other data traffic. This makes the service wasteful, slow and expensive. However, as the oldest communications technology, usually serviced by large and established companies, PSTN has a reputation for reliability and stability. It was designed to carry analogue data but can be used to carry digital data by connecting to a modem. In the event of communication between a PC and the Internet, the maximum speed attainable by this technology is about 56 Kb/s (1 kilobit = 1024 bits)for downstream data (from the ISP to the PC), but upstream data travels at a slower speed (about 33.6 Kb/s). This is because data from the sender reaches the local exchange via an analogue line whereas the data from the ISP to the local exchange[4] is digital.

A switched connection involves using a switching centre (an exchange) to make a connection. Circuit switching keeps the sender and receiver connected until the transmission is over. Packet switched data travels in separate packets which are re-assembled at the receiving end.

Improvement in efficiency was achieved by the introduction of *packet switching* in the early 1970s. In this mode, a message is broken up into equal-sized 'packets' and the address of the recipient is attached with each packet together with some data for protection against errors, plus a link (an identifying data) to the next packet of the message. The packets are sent separately and sometimes via separate routes. They are collected at the receiving end as and when they arrive through the network and reassembled in the right order using the links. Although more expensive, this method is efficient because the best possible routes are found for packets and waiting times are normally very small.

The problems of data type and speed were both solved by the introduction of the *Integrated Services Digital Network* (ISDN) in the early 1990s (initiatives started in the mid-1980s). This used both circuit and packet switched services and facilitated the transmission of both analogue and digital data. It is a service based on the concept of a number of channels in one cable: B channels to carry data at 64 Kb/sec via circuit switched, packet switch, and dedicated (semi-permanent/leased) lines; and D channels to carry control signals[5] and some data. at 16 Kb/s. In the UK and Europe, ISDN lines come in one of two forms: ISDN2 (called basic rate access), normally used by home users and small companies, comprise two B channels and one D channel, and ISDN30 (primary rate access) designed for large businesses with 30 B (23 in the USA) and one D channel. Techniques are available which allow users to combine numbers of B and D channels to achieve transmission at the speeds required. It also allows users to connect a number of devices to the same ISDN line such as an alarm system, a PC, a telephone etc. The cables used are the same as those used by digital telephone exchanges (most of BT's exchanges

ISDN carries both analogue and digital data. B channels carry data and D channels carry signals. A number of B channels can be used together to increase the speed of communication.

[4] Most modern exchanges are digital supported by a computer system that converts data into a digital format.

[5] Control signals co-ordinate the communication process.

in the UK are digital), which enables a telecommunications company to introduce ISDN lines quickly. However, the user has to be within the range serviced by the exchange (normally about 3 miles), and a multiplexer has to be installed at the user's premises to enable telephone and digital data channels to be joined together to be sent via the telephone line; another multiplexer at the receiving end separates the data. The digital data terminals must also be ISDN compatible; if not, an adapter can be used with the terminal to make the necessary conversion. In spite of the extra cost and equipment required, it is envisaged that ISDN will eventually replace PSTN as the public telecommunications network. High-end ISDN is capable of servicing large companies and Internet servers (large computer systems running programs which support the Internet), while lower end products are suitable for small and medium size enterprises and home users. Improvements in the services and standards for ISDN are in progress; for example, broadband ISDN facilitated by a transmission technology called asynchronous transfer mode (ATM) should support transmission at 622 Mb/s (megabit per second).

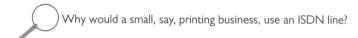

Why would a small, say, printing business, use an ISDN line?

Introduced in the early 1990s, *asynchronous transfer mode* or ATM uses packet switched technology by sending data in separate equal-sized packets. However, unlike packet switched networks (PSN), the packets, called cells in this case, are small – only 53 bytes each. Out of these, 5 bytes are reserved for control information: data-type, destination, links to the other cells, and error-checking. This section (called the header) is bigger for PSN because it uses more security information; ATM relies on the security provided by the transmission systems and protocols. Also unlike PSN, the routes of ATM cells are determined by hardware (ATM switches) before their journey starts on the basis of the information on data-type included in the header. All ATM cells for one message travel via the same route, creating a permanent connection between the sender and the receiver during the transmission. This is referred to as a permanent virtual circuit. Due to this, and the reduced size of the cells, the time involved in reassembling ATM cells is lower, making it much faster than narrowband ISDN. ATM is highly scalable; it can accept data from different devices at different speeds. Thus it can take telephone data at 56 Kb/s as well as high speed video and multimedia data reaching up to about 622 Mb/s. As the route is decided before the data transfer starts, data can be transmitted at different speeds; the router may send a telephone message at a lower speed than that from a video device. It is also possible to upgrade routers to ATM switches. However, ATM is generally expensive and is used mainly by telephone companies, large enterprises such as certain finance houses, and some Internet service providers.

ATM involves sending small, equal-sized packets (called cells) with limited amount of control information via a pre-determined route.

ATM has been in existence for a long time. Find out why the technology has not become cheaper and more widespread.

In 1992 a service called *Frame Relay* was introduced by prominent network service providers (NSPs): large telecommunications suppliers facilitating communication between a company's LANs in different locations nationally or internationally. A client company leases a circuit from the NSP for each of its LANs; this gives it access to the larger network via a router called the frame relay router. The client uses the NSP's communications infrastructure to connect to its LANs via leased lines, achieving a 'virtual' private network. A message from a LAN is sent to the router which converts it into variable length 'frames' with only a small amount of error-checking information and sends it to the leased network; the necessary error checking is performed by the customer organisation themselves. This has the advantage of reducing the size of the frames as well as the amount of work involved in security checks, both of which contribute to speed of delivery. Some control information is attached to the messages for addressing and billing purposes. The B channels of an ISDN line primarily use frame relay technology. Frame relay offers data transmission at the speed supported by the NSPs which can range between 64 Kb/s, through 1.54 Mb/s for T1 (explained below) lines (which combine 24 channels of 64 Kb/s), to 44 Mb/s using T3 with 672 such channels.

Used by the B channel of ISDN, frame relay works by sending variable length frames of data between two LANs by using leased lines from an NSP which connects it to the Internet.

The problem associated with the use of a slow local telephone line to connect to the Internet as done by ISDN is solved by a *digital subscriber line* (DSL). First introduced in 1989, this is a technology which uses the telephone line to carry analogue data from a user while digital data is transmitted separately from the voice data in packets via a parallel line. At the local exchange, the digital data is routed directly to the Internet. This is different from ordinary digital data travelling via a telephone line, which is converted by a modem into analogue and transmitted together with voice, thus making it slower. The separation of data also serves to reduce traffic on the voice lines.

Different types of DSL technology offer different speeds of delivery and support variable lengths of cabling between the user and the local exchange. These are: A(asynchronous)DSL, H(high bit-rate)DSL, V(very high-bit-rate)DSL, RA(rate adaptive DSL, and I(integrated)DSL commonly grouped as xDSL.

DSL uses a telephone line to carry analogue data and a parallel line to carry digital data in packets. Versions of DSL, collectively referred to as xDSL, exist offering different speeds and modes of delivery.

- ADSL is so called because the data from the user to the Internet line, the 'upstream' traffic, is slower (16 to 640 Kb/s) as it normally contains smaller files; the 'downstream' data in the other direction often contains video files and is sent at a higher speed (1.54 to 9 Mb/s). It supports a distance of between 3.7 to 5.5 km around a local exchange, and is suitable for users requiring high speed Internet access.
- HDSL is a symmetric technology with speed between 1.544 or 2 Mb/s and a cable length of 3.7 km. It requires two pairs of twisted cable wires (a telephone line is made up of one twisted pair cable), supports a smaller range than ADSL, and does not carry voice. Thus, it is not suitable for residential users; the main users are private data networks, Internet servers or PBXs (private branch exchange) – a company's data exchange technology (switchboard) with a processor to transfer data from telephones, printers, faxes and so on.
- VDSL is another asymmetric system with an upstream speed of 1.5 to 2.3 Mb/s and a downstream speed of 13 to 52 Mb/s, and supporting a distance of up to 1.4 km but requires fibre optic cabling for the longer distances. This is seen as the ideal candidate for applications such as high-definition television channels.
- RADSL is a variation of ADSL which adjusts itself automatically according to varying conditions and lengths of copper cabling, thus offering more flexibility. It also allows manual adjustment of speed for longer distances.
- IDSL is a ISDN-based DSL. It works on the same customer equipment as ISDN for a fixed monthly charge and supports a speed of 128 Kb/s in both directions. At the moment the use of DSL is limited due to the cost and the complication of installation, and requires the support of both the local exchange (referred to as the local loop, often under the control of a country's main telecommunications company, such as BT in the UK) and an ISP for

Lucent Technologies

Founded in early 1996 as a result of AT&T's division into three parts, Lucent Technologies (LT) was engaged in communications technology and the networking market in the USA. Optical networking was one of the responsibilities of LT; Bell Labs supported the research and development for the company. In 1997, under the leadership of Bill Gartner, the Vice President of Product Realisation, LT decided to create a new product by focusing on three areas: number of wavelengths per fibre, capacity (bit rate per wavelength), and span (how far the system could carry data). LT was already developing optical fibre carrying 8 wavelengths based on the Dense Wavelength Division Multiplexing (DWDM) technology; it wanted to increase it to 100. An R&D team was given the responsibility to come up with a plan to release the product in 14 months.

The R&D team proposed a product called Wavestar 400G, capable of carrying 80 channels, each at 2.5 Gb/s, or 40 channels each at 10 Gb/s, thus delivering data at 400 Gb/s (hence the name). There were many risks: invention would be required in several areas of the project, there was tremendous uncertainty about their expertise in several technologies, the technology required to support signal processing at 10 Gb/s was not available, no budget was allocated, and there were not enough staff to support it.

Nevertheless, the team embarked on the project. However, it set itself an unusual goal; it prioritised performance over reliability and functionality. The size of the R&D team was increased from 30 to 135 in three years comprising people from a wide variety of disciplines, working closely with customers, suppliers and partners. The potential customers included local exchange carriers and backbone builders around the globe.

The strategy adopted by LT appeared successful. The end result was a fully featured version (2.0) delivered faster than old development models would take. However, this would be preceded by earlier, relatively feature-poor versions. This approach was expected to lead to higher product performance, earlier sales, a broader variety of customers and, ultimately, more features and greater reliability by the final version (3.0).

(Source: Iansiti and Feinberg, 1999. Copyright © 1995 by the President and Fellows of Harvard College. Harvard Business School Case 9-600-053. November 12, 1999.)

This case was prepared by Marco Iansiti and Barbara Feinberg as the basis for class discussion rather than to illustrate either effective or ineffective handling of an administrative situation. Reprinted by permission from Harvard Business School.

Questions

1 With the help of further reading on the subject, explain how the increase of channels in a fibre aids speed.
2 We discuss time and frequency division multiplexing later on in the chapter. Find out how DWDM works.
3 In what ways would Wavestar improve communications infrastructure?
4 Using examples of similar product development strategies used by other companies, discuss the pros and cons of prioritising performance over reliability and functionality (using prototypes). We will discuss development strategies later on in the book.

Internet access. Telecommunications standards organisations in both the USA and Europe are working towards the establishment of a commercial xDSL service.

Find examples of some companies using xDSL at the moment. What are the reasons behind their choice and how do they feel about it now? What can you infer from their experiences?

Another networking option, suitable mainly for homes, schools, libraries and so on, is a cable modem. This appeared in the market in the mid-1990s. Often bundled as a combined TV and telephone service, cable companies offer high speed access via copper coaxial cables (the type used in TV aerials) or a combination of coaxial and fibre optic cables. They build exchanges (called headends) around the country to receive TV signals from satellites via a dish, transmitting them through a backbone of cable lines to the serviced areas. The streets in these areas have underground cable connections to which each subscriber is joined by a short line. At the user's end, signals are fed through a modem which separates the signals into audio, video and digital and passes them on to the appropriate device (telephone, TV or computer). Increasingly, cable companies are using optical fibre for the backbone as this supports a high speed of up to 3 Mb/s. The same channel can be used for the traffic in both directions because the upstream data travels at a lower frequency than the downstream and therefore do not get mixed up. At the moment this is mainly suitable for residential customers for inexpensive Internet access and therefore has consequences for business-to-consumer e-commerce. It can also be used for interactive TV services which send HTML files either with the video signals or through an Internet connection to enable users to link to other programs or ask for on-line information.

A modem is used by cable companies together with strategically located exchanges and satellite dishes to provide TV services to home owners. The modem separates signals into audio, video and digital and passes them on to the appropriate device (telephone, TV or computer).

T lines, a technology for the fast transfer of digital data, was introduced in the mid-1980s but became popular in the mid-1990s when prices came down and availability improved due to the entry of competing suppliers. The technology involves multiplexing. T1 lines carry 24–30 channels together (depending on the country) each carrying data at 64 Kb/s, thus giving a total speed of 1.544 Mb/s to 2.048 Mb/s. There are also T2 (with 96–120 channels), T3 (480–672), and T4 (1920–5760) lines, each with successively larger number of channels and speed of transmission. T lines work with all types of medium: twisted pair, coaxial cable, fibre optic, microwave and infrared, and are suitable for all the data needs of large companies, ISPs and telecommunications suppliers. With the growth of e-commerce, organisations of different sizes are choosing from a range of options including partial T1, multiple T1, T3 or T4 circuits to carry a combination of Internet traffic and voice lines which are passed through a PBX which separates them at the receiving end. Table 5.1 summarises the main technological choices available for data communication.

T lines (T1, 2, 3, 4) offer a wide spectrum of speed. They carry a number of channels together, each carrying data at 64 Kb/s.

Another technology worth mentioning here is Ethernet Gigabit: a high speed (10 Gb/s) fibre optic technology for LAN to LAN data transfer suitable for intranets and groupware use. There are other technologies, protocols and services that provide customers with further choices in speed and convenience such as Synchronous Optical Network (SONET), Signalling System 7 (SS7), and Switched Multimegabit Data Service (SMDS). We need not go into the details of these; further information is available from some of the literature (e.g. Rajput, 2000) mentioned in the bibliography.

The availability of advanced technologies has created a demand for streaming audio and video transmission, that is, a constant stream of audio and video data: live, interactive, or on demand. Using one of the high bandwidth services, users can access all forms of data, for example from the entertainment industry, over the Internet via multimedia PCs. Referred to as webcasting, this is the result of the convergence of the media and the Internet, an area which is expected to expand in the near future. For example the UK supermarket Asda has recently launched a service called 'ASDA@t home today' which enables users to 'hop' between the web and telephone to order deliveries. They are expecting to include digital TV in the scheme soon, allowing users to watch TV and use the service intermittently (Field, 2000). Internet telephony, referred to as computer telephone integration (CTI), is another area of growing interest. Using special programs, users can talk to each other either using a PC with a sound card and the Internet. The

CTI is the result of integration between the Internet and the telephone service. CTI and digital TV together are expected to make useful contribution to e-commerce.

Table 5.1 A summary of the choices in wired connections

Technology	Speed	Description
PSTN	33.6 Kb/s–56 KB/s	Supports a country's telephone services; normally reliable and stable; uses twisted pair copper cable; suitable for analogue data; other services use its local loop.
ISDN	B channel – 64 Kb/s D channel – 16 Kb/s	A combination of up to 30 B channels and one D channel used to the access speed required; uses the cabling of telephone lines; can carry both analogue and digital data; service is available only within a limited area surrounding an exchange; expected to replace PSTN.
ATM	56 Kb/s to 622 Mb/s	Highly scalable and fast, but expensive; used by telecommunications companies, ISPs, frame relay networks and large organisations.
Frame Relay	56 Kb/s to 45 Kb/s	Facilitates virtual private networks by leasing circuits connecting the Internet to organisations' LANs; uses T1 and T3 lines.
xDSL	ADSL up to 9 Mb/s VDSL up to 52 Mb/s	Variations of DSLs available; some (ADSL and VDSL) are asymmetric; different versions offer different degrees of service and flexibility; uses a combination of telephone and digital data line; useful for ISPs, large organisations.
Cable Modem	Up to 3 Mb/s	Uses copper co-axial cables or fibre optics, needs cable exchanges; suitable as a combined TV and telephone provider; used in homes, libraries, schools etc.
T Lines	T1: 24–30 channels each carrying 64 Kb/s T2: 96–120; T3: 480–672 T4: 1920–5760	Works with all types of media; useful for medium to large organisations, ISPs, telecommunications providers, backbones to Internet traffic.

conversation can take place PC-to-PC, PC-to-telephone, or telephone-to-telephone; the difference comes from the use of an Internet connection rather than a telephone line during the conversation. Since Internet calls are charged at local rate, this reduces the cost of long distance calls dramatically. Read the books (e.g. Turban *et al.*, 2000) mentioned in the bibliography for more details. The article by Field (2000) discusses the demand of broadband services for on-line customers.

How are CTI and digital TV likely to affect e-commerce technologically, commercially and socially?

Wireless communication

Wireless communication can take many forms such as satellites, radio transmission to fixed locations, mobile radio systems cellular phones via analogue or digital transmission. Mobile technologies enable organisations to communicate speedily with employees and trading partners, thus contributing towards business-to-business e-commerce. Recently introduced WAP-enabled phones have strengthened the business-to-consumer market by providing mobile phone users with the means to get information on-line using the Internet.

Wireless transmission is made possible by microwave towers for transmitting and receiving electromagnetic waves. Satellites moving round the earth's orbit are also used to receive high frequency microwaves from the transmitters, amplify (strengthen) them, and transmit them back to the receiving towers. The transmitters and receivers are normally parabolic dishes (antennas) connected to the users' location. One satellite covers a band of frequencies and therefore several satellites are required to cover all the frequencies at which data is transmitted.

Wireless transmission involves microwave towers transmitting and receiving electromagnetic waves. Satellites receive them from the transmitters, amplify them, relay them to other satellites, and transmit them back to the receiving towers.

Because of the distance the signals have to travel, there is often a short delay between transmission and reception. However, technologies and techniques are available to overcome this. Fast-moving low/medium earth orbit (LEO or MEO) satellites are used to circle the earth close to its surface. No receiver is permanently allocated to a satellite; signals are received from the satellite that is the closest at any time. Because of the large distance satellites can cover, they are ideal for long distance communication between telephone networks, in addition to their well-known applications for TV broadcasting. Organisations with multiple sites can also use antennas to transmit and receive data in between the sites using satellite transmission over large distances in between, thus creating a private data network. Satellites offer low cost and efficient data transmission covering large areas at a speed of about 400 Kb/s.

Wireless communication started with the introduction of car telephones in the 1940s and were used only by certain, affluent people. However, they had to share channels (frequency bands) run over one set of transmitter and receiver in each city. Therefore, the number of simultaneous calls possible was small and the quality of transmission poor. Another form of wireless communication which has been used for a long time is mobile radio. Subscribers to a service share radio channels to talk to each other; communication is only possible in one direction at a time, and only between users sharing the same service. Examples of the use of such services are the police, and drivers with CB radios.

The importance of using mobile communication for data transfer was improved considerably by the introduction of mobile phones in the 1980s. A geographical area is divided into 'cells' (hence the term cellular phone or cellphone) and a number of frequencies are allocated to each cell. The same frequencies are shared by cells which are not adjacent to each other, thus reducing the risk of 'collision'. This is an analogue service designed to carry voice and it works by using frequency division multiple access (FDMA). It works by dividing the available frequencies in a cell into a number of channels, with each user making a call being allocated one channel. Thus, the channel distribution is dynamic (done at the time of the call), a user is not tied to a frequency and can move between cells freely. Each area is serviced by a switching centre (SC) that controls the cells in its range (Fig. 5.7). Communication between switching centres in different areas is achieved by interconnecting them via a base station controller (BSC), which are in turn connected to each other by cables to form the entire network of a mobile service providers. The network is connected to the country's communications system (using PSTN) via a switching office in order to achieve wider connectivity.

A geographical area is divided into cells, each cell being allocated a number of frequencies for transmission. The same frequencies are allocated to other non-adjacent cells, thus increasing usage.

Until nearly the middle of the 1990s, mobile phones could only carry analogue data. Digital transmission was possible by connecting with a cellular modem (a modem which is compatible with the frequencies of a cellular network), but the resulting transmission was prone to error and suffered from disturbance due to the changeover between radio transmission and wired lines. They were also expensive to buy and call charges were high;

the main users were employees of large organisations who needed to keep in touch with head office. The service was also limited by the lack of compatibility between different providers. However, as the technology matured and more mobile phone companies entered the market, prices came down and universal standards such as global system for mobile (GSM) communications was established in the early 1990s; as a result, the popularity of the service increased.

Sharing frequencies with other users made mobile telephony open to 'eavesdropping', that is, other users tapping in to the line by interrupting the frequency. There was also overcrowding due to too many users in the same band creating distortions in transmission. The contribution of mobile phones to e-commerce remained limited due to the analogue nature of the service. In 1995, IBM used a service called *cellular digital packet data* (CDPD) to send short messages such as emails along the unused frequencies of the analogue cellular network. Connecting a CDPD modem compatible with TCP/IP with the handset enables users to access the Internet via a mobile phone. This increased the suitability of mobile phones for e-commerce and initiated further developments in this direction. Digital transmission is also more secure than analogue as bits are scrambled; channels are multiplexed by techniques such as *time division multiple access* (TDMA) and *code division multiple access* (CDMA). TDMA enables three users to use the same frequency on a time-share basis[6] thus reducing overcrowding; CDMA allows users to have access to the entire frequency band, but each user is allocated a unique code by which the network can differentiate the calls. For both these services, voice data is converted into bits before passing on to the multiplexer. TDMA is faster and more secure than CDMA; they both offer low emission transmission thus reducing the possibility of radiation damage to human cells.

Mobile phones can be given access to the Internet by utilising digital services such as CDPD and by using techniques such as TDMA and CDMA.

How can the possibility of mobile data transfer aid communication between:

(a) an organisation and its suppliers, and
(b) an organisation and its customers?

The prospect of mobile e-commerce (sometimes referred to as m-commerce) is further improved by the introduction of two other technologies: *wideband CDMA* (W-CDMA) which uses a wider range of frequencies for wireless communication, and *wireless applications protocol* (WAP) – a protocol that enables cellular network operators to translate the contents of the Internet into a format suitable for mobile phones. WAP also facilitates the display of Internet pages on the screen of the phone and provides search facilities. As a part of the so-called third-generation (3G) mobile wireless initiative, WAP utilises the XML language for web development and governs the necessary rules to ensure that browsers on mobile phones can find information from the Internet.

WAP phones were introduced in the late 1990s amid a lot of hype, expected to revolutionise the extent to which people access the Internet. However, a number of problems stand in the way of making this a reality. Amongst these are: the absence of enough church spires or equivalent to transmit the signals over large distances, the inconvenience of the small screen, the cost of running Universal Mobile Telecommunications System (UMTS), the network which supports WAP, delay in producing handsets and difficulty associated with providing the speed of communication promised. Organisations are also slow in accepting m-commerce as a viable route mainly because

[6] A number of devices in time share mode take control of the network for a fixed chunk of time in rotation. In computing terms the time is so short that the time lag is not felt by users, especially if there is only a small number of users.

of perceived lack of security, speed and performance level. According to the US research firm IDC, currently most enterprises view mobile phones as a vehicle for improving internal communication rather than for achieving business growth or customer relationship management (Nicolle, 2000: 60). However, it is expected that mobile phones will soon be using a technology called general packet radio service (GPRS) which will provide a speed of 115 Kb/s for mobile communication (Bradbury, 2000). The convenience of mobility is likely to drive further innovation in this area. For example, one of the drawbacks of mobiles phones is that the battery runs out fast because each application on a phone requires its own silicon chip, each putting pressure on the battery. Manufacturers are now working towards the development of a chip that can decode incompatible standards and run multiple applications (Tristram, 2001). It has also been suggested that the industry should explore payment options which do not require users to send their credit card number over a wireless service.

While the Western countries have been hesitating over the above issues, Japan has accepted Internet-based, interactive mobile communication as a natural progression from mobile phones. It has introduced a packet-based standard called iMode (sometimes referred to as generation 2.5) rather than using the GSM technologies of the 3G. This allows data to be sent in bursts rather than in continuous stream which allows faster transmission and an 'always-on' service (users do not have to dial up to connect to the Internet). Also, while GSM users pay for the time they are on-line, iMode charges per unit of data transmitted during a message transfer. Additionally, NTT DoCoMo, a global mobile Internet operator which supports the iMode service not only supplies the infrastructure and the billing, but also handsets and accessories thus providing a common standard to its users. Most importantly, it has adopted a policy of open access to unofficial sites which has encouraged more than 600 companies to provide services over the Internet and over 1000 official iMode websites, along with 19,000 independent sites (Nicolle, 2000: 64). Consequently, m-commerce has already taken off in Japan through on-line community building, purchase of cinema and train tickets, access to financial services etc. It is hoped that GPRS will eventually enable the West to overcome the problems and the number of m-commerce users will rise from 1000 in 1999 to

WAP is a protocol that enables mobile phone users to access Internet services. A small screen displays webpages and facilitates the use of Internet-based applications.

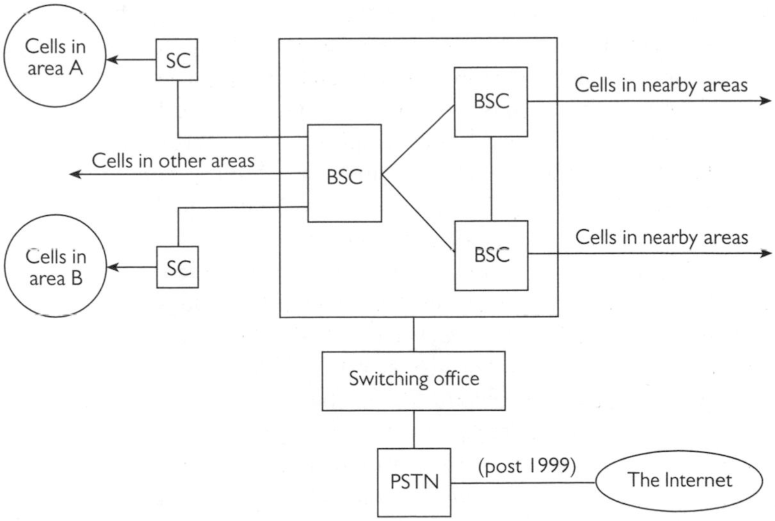

Fig. 5.7 The cellular telecommunications network

29 million by 2004 (according to IDCas quoted in Nicolle, 2000: 60). It has also been predicted that m-commerce in Western Europe will grow from being worth $51.2m in 2000 to $37.7bn in 2004; the sector most likely to benefit is the financial services.

Using examples to support your comments, discuss how mobile phones aid e-commerce.

PCS, pagers and Bluetooth are some other technologies used for mobile communication. Some organisations are now offering packaged networking solutions to help companies to make the right choices out of the wide variety of options available.

There are other wireless services which also have consequences for e-commerce, for example as *personal communication services* (PCS) and pagers. PCS offer a low cost alternative to mobile phones with message display. Frequencies lower than those used by the cellular network are divided into a number of bands and competing companies are allowed to use each band to provide wireless communication services. By promoting competition this way, the prices are kept lower. *Pagers* have been in use since the late 1950s by some professions such as in the medical service (beepers) as a one way tone-only messaging system within a short distance. Pagers have been a cheap and convenient alternative to mobile phones. Now two-way pagers allow users to receive short messages, send back short preset replies, receive specialised Internet pages sent by the network providers, and send a message to a group of users by dialling into a pager modem pool in the network. Pagers can now be used nationwide via the service providers' satellite network, and thus have the potential to enhance a company's on-line communications by facilitating quick message transfer between employees. Another wireless technology called Bluetooth, introduced in the late 1990s, enables detached information appliances equipped with a special device and within a limited area (theoretically up to 100 metres but in most cases, about 10 metres) to exchange data using radio links regardless of the operating systems running them. This enables employees in an organisation working on a project together to share information and facilitates groupware activities.

Companies of all sizes can now take advantage of the above facilities in wired and wireless communication in order to gain a competitive advantage in the e-commerce arena. Increasingly, organisations are able to maintain communication between their global user base and their computer resources – the backend information systems, Internet services, emails, groupware technologies such as electronic diaries and shared applications, varieties of computer devices, mobile terminals and so on. Such connectivity facilitates the fast worldwide communication essential for survival in the e-commerce age. However, it also necessitates the co-ordination of a number of services in order to establish interoperability between different elements associated with e-commerce such as ISPs, telecommunications infrastructure providers, technical infrastructure within the company, users of the systems, regulating bodies and so on. This is a difficult task and the failure to achieve such integration can seriously damage a company's business opportunities. Some organisations are now offering a packaged service designed to provide a total networking solution. One such initiative is the Integrated On-demand Network (ION), which is a digital network based on ATM technology. It offers voice, data and video services at a high speed (1.5 to 45 Mb/s) and guarantees reliable data traffic at a reasonable cost. Wireless Knowledge Services (WKS) is a similar solution for wireless communication; initiated by Microsoft and Qualcomm (a telecommunications company) it enables organisations '. . . to pull the wireless world into mainstream e-commerce-enabled business computing by enabling users to connect to multiple data sources and services through the wireless medium' (Rajput, 2000: 131).

With such a variety of options in networking technologies and services, organisations have a challenging task when it comes to finding the right solution. It involves making choices such as which technologies to use for different parts of the network, whether or

The Sabre Group

SABRE (see chapter 1) started life as an inventory system for seats in American Airlines' flights in the early 1960s. By the mid-1970s, it was a computerised reservation system which took care of AA flight plans, tracked spare parts, scheduled crews, and supported a range of decision support systems. By the 1990s, it became an electronic supermarket linking businesses and customers dealing with almost all aspects of air travel.

In order to expand the business to the arena of mobile communication, IBM and the mobile phone manufacturer Nokia recently started a joint venture called the Sabre Group. It is a WAP service that allows travellers to receive flight information and initiate flight changes if necessary. The new service is designed to allow travellers to alter or make new travel arrangements while on the move.

Using a Nokia 7110 phone, travellers can request flight details, change a flight or search for alternatives. The system can also inform them of any delays to their flight schedule and allow them to make alternative arrangements if necessary.

The Sabre Group has written a Java application to translate its travel-related information into XML. This allows streams of data to be defined and presented as individual objects, such as airlines reservations. IBM provides the Java application development tools as well as the software to translate XML to WML.

To compensate for the 7110's small screen, the display is converted into a series of screens. The user has the option of scrolling through these to access the specific information they need. Nokia has created a microbrowser for mobile screen display.

(Adapted from Campbell, 2000, with permission from Reed Business Information Ltd.)

Questions

1 Discuss how this case study demonstrates the advantage and disadvantage of WAP-based communication.
2 Explain how this venture could expand the scope for e-commerce.
3 In what way does this venture affect the competitive advantage of the companies involved?
4 WML and microbrowser are two new terms used here. Explain what they mean.

not to outsource some or all of the services, which network applications to support, and much more. We will come back to this in the consequences section of the book.

Access to the Internet

As explained in chapter 2, the Internet is supported by a backbone to which the component networks are connected. Users access the Internet by connecting to an Internet service provider (ISP) – a large computer system running applications such as an email service, browsing programs etc. via the local telephone loop. The ISP is connected to a network access point (NAP), an interconnection point that exchanges traffic from a number of ISPs at high speed (a T-1 or a T-3 line) to the Internet backbone (Fig. 5.8). Smaller ISPs connect to the backbone via the larger ISPs.

A website is identified by an IP address, a unique number called the URL (uniform resource locator) by which the IP part of TCP/IP recognises it and verifies the data. The format of the address determines the stages (network points) the data has to go through in order to find the site the same way a telephone number including a country code, and an area code identifies a unique telephone connection. URLs are allocated by the domain name service (DNS) of the Internet, an Internet directory service users have to register with in order to receive an address. The address is written using the dotted decimal notation such as 199.723.12.45 (written in a binary format) in which the decimal number divides the stages of the address. This is simplified for the users by using alphabetic names to signify each stage of the address, for example amazon.co.uk. The address includes the name of the organisation (amazon), the type (domain) of organisation (com or co) – the top level domain for the USA, and the country (uk) – the top level for non-US countries. The URL (amazon.co.uk) is normally preceded by 'http://www' to relate it to the Internet backbone and the hypertext transfer protocol (HTTP). Domain names vary from country to country. Until quite recently there were only a few domain names such as .co (com in the USA), .org, .ac (edu in the USA), .gov etc. This restricted the possibility of separate addresses because, for instance, commercial organisations were only distinguishable from each other by their name.

The DNS has been largely controlled by the US government. During the late 1980s and early 1990s, the responsibilities for allocating domain names and addresses were given to the Internet Assignment Number Authority (IANA). Later on, a company called Network Solutions Inc. (NSI) was funded by the government to handle the registration process for domain names. In 1995, they started charging customers thus becoming a profit-making enterprise with a monopoly. At that time, there were only a few top-level domain names (.com, .org, .net, .edu, .gov, .mil, and .int). In 1997 a number of organisations including IANA, the Internet society (ISOC) and some government authorities advocated self-governance in DNS and managed to establish some more domain names (.firm, .shop, .web, .arts, .rec, .info, and .nom). In 1998, the Internet Corporation for Assigned Names and Numbers (ICANN) was assigned the job of overseeing the process of domain name allocation and address distribution. Its job is to manage the registrars, bodies which look after lower level names, and the registries, the databases of names and addresses. Within national boundaries, a mix of public and private organisations act as the domain name registries. For example, Nominet, a non-profit-making company serves this role in the UK.

Access to the Internet can be obtained via an ISP and NAP. It also requires the services of DNS for the provision of a URL. Until recently only a few domain names were available. This has been changing following the efforts made by ICANN.

At the end of 2000, a new set of domain names were approved (.name, .info, .pro, .aero, .biz, .museum, and .coop) to be available from the middle of 2001. Amongst ICANN's objectives are to encourage competition by allowing additional domain names, and decentralise the process by appointing new registrars, especially in other countries.

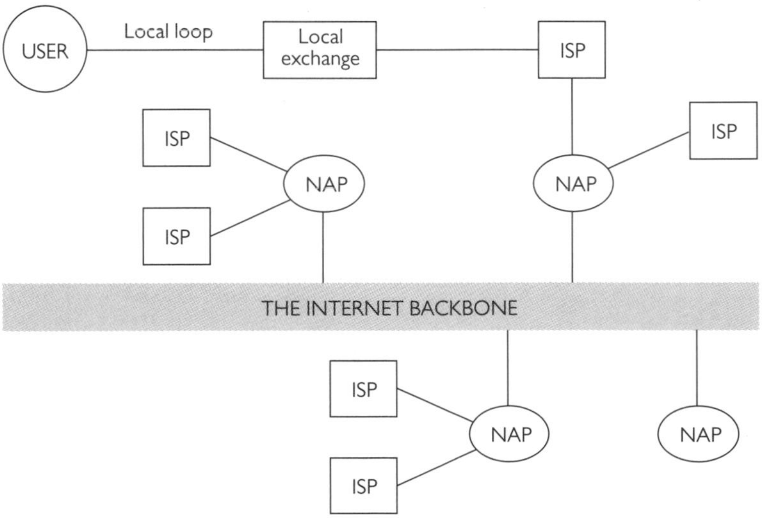

Fig. 5.8 Internet access architecture

What are the dangers of unregulated domain name registration?

In October 1996 a group of academic and networking organisations called the University Corporation for Advanced Internet Development (UCAID) came together in order to improve the quality of Internet access. Their main objective was to provide software to support high-bandwidth applications such as multimedia and virtual reality in order to facilitate services such as on-line laboratories and distance learning centres. Referred to as Internet2, it is designed to enable people in remote locations to work together as if they are in the same office. Telecommunications companies such as Cisco, Nortel and Qwest (together developing a high speed network called the Abilene[7]) as well as some large players in the ICT market such as IBM, Microsoft and AT&T are working together to support the backbone necessary for making Internet 2 a practical possibility. At the time of writing the use of Internet2 is limited to the universities associated with UCAID and some military organisations who can access Abilene and the network provided by the Next Generation Internet (NGI) project. Supported by the US government's Dept. of Defense, Research and Education Network (DREN), NASA's Research and Education Network (NREN) and vBNS, NSF's (see chapter 2) very high performance Backbone Network Services, this is a program working towards the development of high speed networking solutions.

Internet2 is an updated version of the Internet which facilitates the transmission of high-bandwidth multimedia and virtual reality-type data over the Internet.

Access to the Internet must be obtained via computer controlled devices and applications. The most common device to access the Internet is a desktop personal computer (PC) but a large number of other devices such as mobile phones, handheld PCs, pagers and television sets are now also suitable for this purpose. Innovations in hardware as well as software technologies servicing these devices in recent years have increased the possibilities for organisations to use multiple platforms to access the Internet. It is important to integrate these devices in order to achieve total connectivity. In June 2000 Microsoft unveiled a strategy called .net designed to ensure that '. . . all manner of computing devices from mobile phones and handheld computers to desktop and server machines are seamlessly integrated to allow end-users to share information without having to worry about which device to work on' (Saran, 2000). It enables a user searching for information on a subject to enter the request for a search and rely on an intelligent software agent to find the information from all possible sources, collate it, and make it available on any device intended by the user. This is expected to have a profound impact on e-commerce because it would facilitate exchanges of information between different organisations. For example, a medical company investigating the potential for a new drug can communicate with the researchers, who can in turn communicate with the health service in order to create a forum for discussion. However, the service is not expected to be available until 2002.

The technologies of security

There are numerous issues an organisation need to understand in order to enhance the security of its e-commerce systems. The protocols and standards described earlier in the chapter are designed to ensure the safe transfer of data. TCP/IP, the widely used protocol for Internet transmission, has been the basis of the majority of standards used in e-commerce. The organisations which contributed to this effort include Internet

7 This is designed to provide support for universities engaged in the process of developing advanced Internet2 applications.

Engineering Task Force (IETF) and Microsoft. Security has been a difficult issue for organisations because of the intangible nature of some of the risks involved in electronic communication, especially in a global context. We need to have an understanding of the following issues before the technologies of security can be discussed:

- *Confidentiality* – the protection of information from unauthorised access. As an almost unlimited number of users potentially share resources on the Internet, steps must be taken to prevent access to information 'floating around' by unauthorised users. *Encryption* is a method employed to reduce the possibility of information getting into the wrong hands.
- *Authentication* – the steps taken to check the validity of the sender of data, be it a person sending a message or a device trying to access an application.
- *Authorisation* – the next stage of authentication, this refers to the steps taken to check the credentials of a user in order to limit the accessibility by users to particular systems. For example, a person may have the right of access to a university's library but not to its on-line databases containing journals and articles. Both authentication and authorisation can be achieved by the use of password controls.
- *Integrity* – the protection of data against illegal tampering, for example, by hackers. Various controls can be implemented to lower the risks in this area.

On-line commerce needs to maintain:

- confidentiality
- authentication
- authorisation
- integrity
- availability
- non-repudiation.

The security of Internet-based transactions has received a lot of publicity. What are the risks of lax e-commerce security?

In addition to the above there are some other operational issues surrounding the reliability of on-line transactions such as the *availability* of information without delay, and the problem of *non-repudiation* by some users, that is, the denial of commitments made on-line. We will discuss these in chapter 7 while dealing with the operational infrastructure of e-commerce. In this chapter, we will concentrate on the technical measures introduced by organisations involved in improving the security of Internet-based communication.

Encryption

Encryption is the process of crypting (scrambling) data by applying a ciphering algorithm (a mathematical formula which encodes the data). The ciphered text is then passed through the network which, at the receiving end can be deciphered by applying a decrypting algorithm. The crypting and decrypting of data can only be done by a key – a password of a defined length – issued to authorised recipients only. Two basic categories of encryption techniques are available: symmetric key and asymmetric key. There are commercial algorithms for encryption which may be known to many users but the key is kept a secret. In symmetric-key encryption (also known as private key encryption

Encryption is the process of ciphering a message by using an algorithm and using a key to lock it. The same elements are also required to decipher and unlock the message.

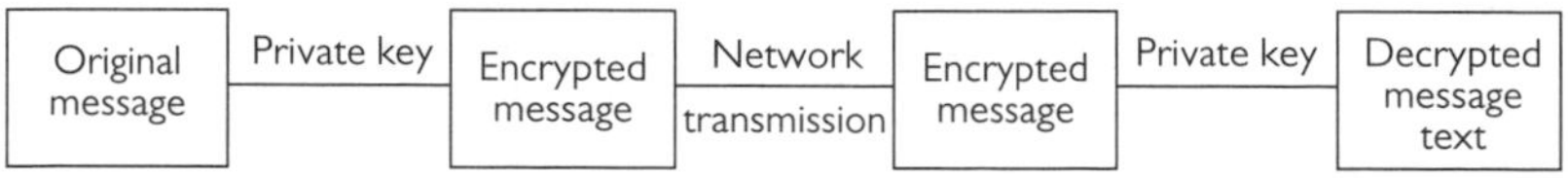

Fig. 5.9 Private-key encryption

– Fig. 5.9) the key is the same at both ends; it works on the basis of the sender and receiver sharing a secret key, agreed upon in advance. Because of the extent of the Internet, providing a key to all intended recipients can be a problem, especially when a sender wants to send a message to a certain group of people not necessarily known to him or her, for example, all users interested in the investigation of extra-terrestrial life forms. Security in this system also relies on the safe keeping of the key by the users. IBM issued a standard called Data Encryption Standard (DES) for private-key encryption; various organisations including IBM have been working together to improve the security of this technique. The smaller the key however, the easier it is to guess (aided by computer programs which can produce a list of all possible numbers within a boundary), thus weakening the security of the system.

A safer option than symmetric-key encryption is to use asymmetric keys – also known as public-key encryption (Fig. 5.10). This is a public–private key pairing system in which a user with a private key can give a pairing public key to anyone s/he wishes. The sender can send a message using a private key with the assurance that only the holders of the pairing public key can open it (and the other way round). In this method there is no need to agree on the keys in advance since the private key holder can place the public key in a register of selected users via encrypted messages. Thus, a user can own a set of public keys provided by those with the corresponding private keys. The standard used with this system is known as RSA, named after the inventors Rivest, Shamir and Alderman. RSA is slower than DES since it involves more complicated processing. Normally DES is used for users to exchange keys while RSA is used for the messages.

Private keys are symmetric, both sender and receiver hold a secret key. Public keys comprise an asymmetric pair, with one public key given to intended receivers by the sender who holds the pairing private key.

One important function of public-key encryption is to implement digital signature – the method used to determine the authenticity of the sender of a message (the same way a signed cheque does). It works the following way: A sends a message to B using A's private key; if B is successful in decrypting it using A's public key, then it confirms A as the sender of the message. The management of public-key encryption and the implementation of digital signature standards requires an infrastructure that ensures that keys are used by legitimate holders, procedures for key management have been established, and so on. Referred to as the public key infrastructure (PKI), this is currently provided by some designated certification authorities (CA) such as Royal Mail Via Code (RMVC) owned by the UK Post Office authority. All legitimate users are required to register with a CA for public-key encryption. The CA creates a digital certificate, an electronic document that keeps a record of the users and their public keys, and also takes charge of all the technical and procedural aspects of data encryption. In the absence of a standard in encryption technologies, PKI provided by private CAs is becoming popular. For example, Anderson-Charnley, a financial planning and portfolio management company, has decided to employ such a company rather than wait for an industry-wide agreement on digital signature (Goodwin, 2000). A new Internet company called UK Smart has teamed up with the Post Office to offer free digital signature software to all customers belonging to RMVC (Dunt, 2000).

Digital signature works the following way: A sends a message to B using A's private key; if B is successful in decrypting it using A's public key, then it confirms A as the sender of the message.

Public-key encryption is also utilised in securing data between applications running on the Internet. Referred to as secure sockets layer (SSL), it is a protocol developed by

Fig. 5.10 Public-key encryption

Netscape which works on the basis of the exchange of digital signature between the client (for example a customer with a PC) and the server (a corporate network) components of a network. The following simplified scenario for the transfer of a message between A and B explains the principle of the method (Fig. 5.11).

At A's end:

- A first requests to see B's digital certificate, which holds B's public key. (1)
- A then generates a secret key, encrypting it with B's public key. (2, 3)
- A puts together the message encrypted with its private key and its own digital certificate, which holds its public key, and encrypts this package using its private key. (4, 5, 6)
- This package and the encrypted secret key are sent to B. (7)

At B's end:

- B decrypts the secret key using its own private key. (8)
- B then uses the secret key to decrypt the package to retrieve the encrypted message and A's digital certificate which also holds A's public key. (9)
- The message is then decrypted using A's public key. (10)
- B also checks that there has not been any distortion to the message by using certain additional techniques (but we will not be going into those).

SSL is used for the transfer of messages between users who are not necessarily known to each other. This has its uses in creating a secure payment infrastructure to support on-line monetary transactions which we will cover in the next chapter.

SSL is a protocol that uses the concept of digital signature by public key encryption to send data between applications securely.

By doing a literature search, find out to what extent SSL is used and how it affects speed of transmission.

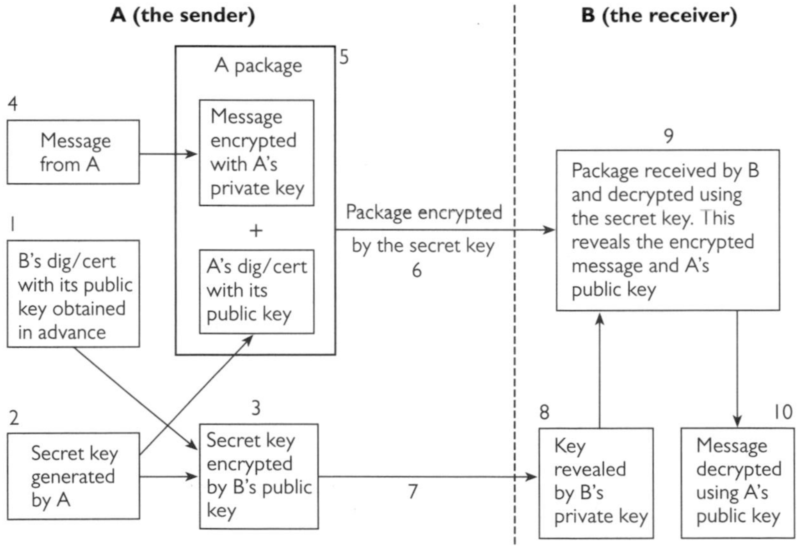

Fig. 5.11 Secure sockets layer protocol

PKI at Anderson-Charnley

Anderson-Charnley is a financial planning and portfolio management company for high earners. Most of its clients are executives in the IT and telecommunications industry. It provides advice on tax planning, tax return and share portfolio management.

The company started developing a web operation a year ago. It is now planning to pioneer the use of public key infrastructure (PKI) technology. Although the jury is still out on PKI, Anderson-Charnley has decided it cannot afford to wait for banks and City firms to agree on technology standards. It plans to persuade large financial institutions that digitally signed documents are far more reliable and secure than paper.

With only 25 employees, Anderson-Charnley lacks a full-scale IT department, but it has been able to develop its technology strategy by working closely with high-tech clients. Their advice was instrumental in the company's plans to launch a website and to adopt digital signature technology.

Digital signatures are critical to Anderson-Charnley's business plan. The company wants to give its time-pressed executives, who currently have to fax or post written instructions, the ability to authorise share deals quickly and securely over the Internet. But the firm has been held back by the lack of progress made by government-backed efforts to introduce digital signatures to the UK. Although the technology has already been recognised by the European Union and Germany, the UK is still working out the practicalities of the system. The company now hopes to force the pace by introducing its own PKI system ahead of the large financial firms. The lack of the UK standard in PKI is a concern for Anderson-Charnley, but the lack of security of transaction for their customers is a bigger concern.

The issues it is keen to deal with are:

- Anderson-Charnley cannot afford to be without its system for even half a day. One lost email could be disastrous. Will the system need time-consuming on-going maintenance?
- Will clients be happier if Anderson-Charnley hosts the system in-house, or should it be outsourced?
- Will PKI slow the system down as the company cannot afford even a 30-second delay.
- Should the PKI system be rolled out gradually or in one go?
- Is it too risky to strike out so early with a digital signature system?

The technology will allow Anderson-Charnley to promote its website as far more than an information source. Clients will be able to look at their tax plans and review their portfolios on-line knowing that their details cannot be viewed or altered by anyone else. In recent months Anderson-Charnley has evaluated PKI products from three IT suppliers and has now decided to opt for a system from US firm Xcert.

(Adopted from Goodwin, 2000, with permission from Reed Business Information Ltd.)

Questions

1. Why is it important for a financial institution to adopt PKI?
2. Why is the lack of a standard on PKI a problem for Anderson-Charnley?
3. Find out what the government is doing about a PKI standard now.
4. In the light of the issues listed above, should the company wait till PKI is more mature? In answering this question, you should do some research to find out if anyone else is using PKI and what their experiences are.

Password control

This is an established method used to control unauthorised access to a network. A user 'logs in' using an ID which often comprises a user name as the first control, followed by a password. A list called access control list (ACL) of acceptable IDs are held in a file in the system in encrypted form; each attempted entry is checked against this file. Passwords are issued on the basis of a user's status in relation to the system. Thus one user may only be able to access information on company products while another is allowed to extract budgetary data. Another method used is to issue layers of passwords in which a user needs to enter a further password to gain access to deeper levels of information.

Various methods have been introduced to safeguard data against fraud. Amongst these are: token-based authentication in which the user needs to use a hardware device (a token) such as a card to be inserted into the system, as well as a password; and biometrics scanning devices fitted to a computer which check a user's face, retina, fingerprint, hand, voice, typing rhythm, signature, etc., against a set of stored data for all legitimate users. Some systems use routers to check an ACL to determine the access rights of users and route data to different parts of the network accordingly.

The security measures described so far are essentially techniques used to control data traffic. There are also some technologies which control the movement of Internet packets by using the Internet protocol (IP). IP has been the foundation of Internet traffic for a considerable length of time but was considered inadequate in terms of address space, the number of bits allowed to write the address of the destination (32 bits in the case of IP version 4, IPv4), security and flexibility. IPv6, introduced in 1996, is an improvement on this. *IP Security* (IPSec) is a standard based on encryption and authenticity control which defines IPv6. Introduced by IETF, it enables two computer systems (hosts) to establish an encryption mechanism and session keys before the transmission starts. This ensures the confidentiality of data. Headers (extra identification data) are added to the data packets (called IP packets) following rules prescribed by the standard, which help to check their authenticity and integrity. All the packets are checked at all levels of networked transmission – routers, applications, firewalls (see below) etc. – thus ensuring maximum possible security. This version of IP offers expanded (128 bit) address space, thus allowing a large number of addresses, and also supports varied data formats. Other standards also exist to govern the movement of Internet data on different platforms, for example point-to-point tunnelling protocol (PPTP) introduced by Microsoft for systems using its server operating system NT4 and remote authentication dial-in user (Radius), which has the support of IETF. Rajput (2000) provides further details on these.

Password control necessitates a user to enter a user ID and a password before access is allowed. Different levels of password use can also allow for different types of access.

Firewall

A firewall is a network component designed to protect an enterprise network from hackers, viruses,[8] data corruption or loss by limiting access to an organisation's network. It restricts external users from accessing a corporate network, and internal users from accessing selective parts of the network. Comprising servers, routers and software, a firewall acts as a filter between a corporate network (or parts of it) and the outside world. It uses a special-purpose server called a bastion-host gateway in between the Internet and a company's internal network. The server contains special programs called proxies (one proxy for each Internet service such as HTTP, FTP etc.); when data packets reach a firewall, the proxies check the packets' sources and destinations, and either accept or reject them on the basis of the rules established by ACLs and security controls. Further security can be added by using a router called a screen-host gateway which screens messages before they can reach the bastion (Fig. 5.12). The degree of screening and therefore the exact methods used for routing are decided by companies on the basis of how much access to their network they wish to give to the outside world. This works at both application level (controlling access to parts of the information systems) and network device level (controlling access to network points). Thus it can be used to check

A firewall acts as a barrier preventing certain users from accessing certain areas of an organisation's system.

[8] A program introduced into a computer system and designed to destroy or damage the system and also attach itself to the hardware devices connected to it. This way it spreads from one system to another destroying every program it comes into contact with.

the authentication and authorisation of an incoming message as well as 'hiding' parts of the network from unauthorised users.

E-commerce systems rely on the ability of users to have access to their network from remote locations regardless of distance and physical connections. Maintaining security and at the same time, providing reliable communication under such conditions is very difficult. One solution that takes advantage of encryption and other technologies in order to create secure communication in cyberspace is the concept of a virtual private network.

Find out to what extent passwords and firewalls have been successful in protecting networks from unlawful access. On the basis of your findings, comment on the effectiveness of these methods.

Virtual private networks (VPN)

The theoretical model of a virtual organisation was discussed in chapter 2, which explained the need for companies to be linked electronically with their partners, buyers, suppliers, and customers to create a network of users unlimited by geographical boundaries. VPN is the result of the creation of a secure network environment for an organisation by 'tunnelling' data over the Internet using leased lines to the local ISP. This involves using encryption, authentication and other security standards to transmit data securely between users situated over an wide area as if they were connected to each other directly by a private network. Referred to as protocol tunnelling, data packets are encrypted, encapsulated into IP packets (data packets validated by IP), and then transmitted over the Internet via a router. The data is decrypted at the receiving end by a router (Fig. 5.13) which also checks the authenticity by using a protocol such as IPv6 or Microsoft's PPTP, thus securing a data tunnel between users. VPN is an inexpensive and secure way to extend a corporate network, for example to enable trading partners to connect to it, thus creating an extranet. A number of hardware manufacturers such as IBM and Intel, together with communications providers such as AOL and AT&T, are providing VPN services for business-to-business e-commerce.

A virtual private network can be created by 'tunnelling' data between two LANs using leased lines to the local ISP and by using security routers at the two ends.

Do a survey to find out which types of organisation are using a VPN. How does it help their business processes?

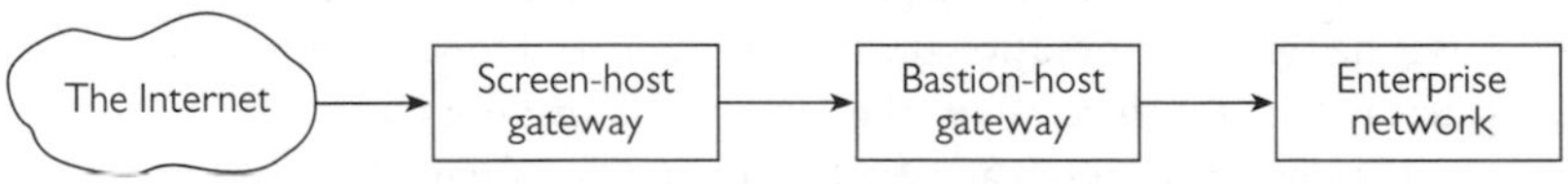

Fig. 5.12 A firewall with screen-host and bastion-host gateway servers

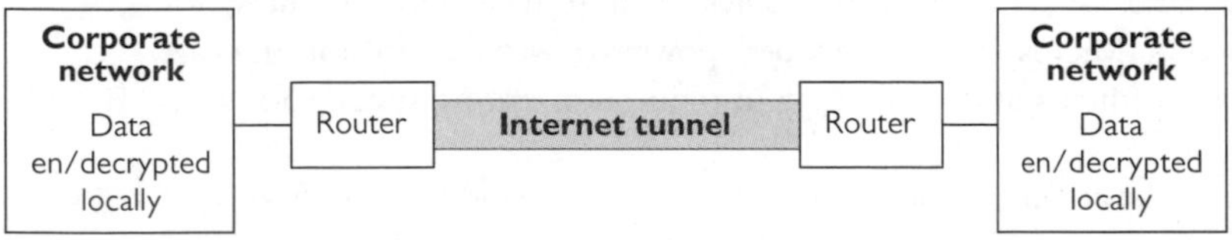

Fig. 5.13 Virtual private network

Friends Provident

Insurance and investment company Friends Provident has decided to implement a global VPN to securely connect the offices for the company's fund management division Friends Ivory & Sime across the UK, New York and Hong Kong. It will connect 300 users across seven offices. The VPN is expected to reduce IT costs and increase staff productivity. Netware 5.1, the LAN operating system, would provide web-enabled applications across the Intranet, Internet access, FTP transfer and news services. The company is hoping that accesssing information through a browser would eliminate the need to maintain multiple applications on the desktop. The company also plans to add pervasive access devices such as PDAs and smart phones later.

Friends Provident is expecting a VPN to provide them with a cost-effective way of managing the needs of multiple office environments. A fixed link could cost the company three times as much; running a VPN instead should provide better performance and reduced cost through the consolidation of systems protocols.

The strategy of Friends Provident is to move towards policy-based management so that it can prioritise traffic and give preferential bandwidth for selected backend applications over the Internet. This gives the company the benefit of a high bandwidth network when it needs it without the infrastructure investment.

(Adapted from Middleton, *Network News*, 4 July, 2000, copyright © VNU Publications 2000. Reproduced with permission.)

Questions

1 How can the VPN help with Friends Provident's business processes?
2 Why is a VPN expected to be cheaper and safer than other alternatives?
3 How could the company plan to maintain the security of its VPN?

SUMMARY

Continual innovations in computer-based technologies moved the computer from large and secluded computer departments to desktops. In the last three decades computers became progressively smaller, faster, more powerful, cheaper, easier to use, more flexible and versatile, and an everyday tool in the office rather than a specialist machine. Hand in hand with these developments, enormous progress was also made in all areas of communications technologies. This included the establishment of wired lines and wireless communications facilities, new developments in network architecture capable of taking advantage of the increasing power of the PCs such as the client server model, the establishment of protocols for secure electronic data interchange such as Open Systems Interconnection (OSI) by the International Standards Organisation, and the development of many hardware devices designed to improve the quality of data transfer such as routers, bridges and gateways. In the meantime, the Internet, introduced in 1986, became increasingly user friendly and widespread, and by the middle of the 1990s was established as an important role in commercial transactions. TCP/IP, the protocol for Internet-based data transfer, was introduced and adopted by all Internet traffic, thus preventing OSI from becoming a standard for e-commerce. Hardware and software manufacturers took advantage of the technologies to introduce new products; for example, IBM and Sun Microsystems developed powerful web-servers for Internet applications, and Linux, Microsoft and Netscape introduced operating systems for such applications.

In the wake of such developments organisations must understand the significance of the technical infrastructure required to facilitate efficient e-commerce. This necessitates an understanding of communications technologies, their relationships with business processes, the role of the backend and frontend applications supporting on-line services, the importance of reliability of service provision and the utility of fixed as well as mobile hardware appliances for access to the Internet. A confusing array of choices is available to organisations in all areas of communication: networking technologies, access to the Internet, infrastructure for visibility in the marketplace, technologies for interface building, methods of ensuring security of data transfer, and so on. Networking technologies include various options for wired and wireless communication offering a wide range of speed. They are categorised as narrowband, providing lower speed than 1.544 Mb/s; wideband, supporting data rate of 1.544 to 45 Mb/s; and broadband, for speed in excess of 45 Mb/s. Transmission media and technologies also range between the public switched telephone network (PSTN), which is also referred to as the plain old telephone system (POTS), integrated services digital network (ISDN); and its successors, asymmetric transfer mode (ATM), frame relay, various forms of digital subscriber lines (xDSL), cable modems, and T lines. Communication over the Internet can use one or a combination of these technologies. Wireless transmission takes advantage of satellites and transmission towers in order to transmit electromagnetic waves over large distances using a combination of services including the PSTN. Now, with the introduction of WAP phones, GPRS, iMode, and other technologies, it is possible to include mobile phones in e-commerce related activities.

Security is one of the most important issues in e-commerce. It is vital for an organisation to ensure that business transactions are based on confidentiality, authentication, authorisation and integrity. A number of techniques are available to ensure security such as: encryption, encoding data with a ciphering algorithm together with a key to lock and unlock it; password and other forms of control to limit access to a system; and firewall, using a filter in a network to hide the system from unauthorised users. With the help of all these techniques it is now possible for an organisation's LANs to gain access to each other via the Internet by leasing a circuit to a local ISP and creating a virtual private network for themselves.

The establishment of a communications infrastructure remains ineffective unless a well-developed infrastructure for the information systems supporting the applications is in place as well. In the following chapter we will discuss the technologies available for doing this.

Revision Questions

1 Describe the basic units of a computer systems and their functions.
2 Describe how the evolution of the PC contributed to the emergence of e-commerce.
3 In what way did the growth of e-commerce fuel the growth of the computer industry?
4 What is the significance for e-commerce of the following: storage devices, amount of memory, processing power of a computer, graphical user interface, programming techniques?
5 Describe how frequency relates to data transfer.
6 Describe briefly the following devices: LAN, WAN, modem, multiplexer, repeater, bridge, router.
7 Discuss clearly the significance of protocols for electronic communication. Why do we need a layered architecture?
8 Describe the TCP/IP model and explain how it works for messages travelling between computer systems.
9 Describe client-server architecture and explain how Internet applications relate to this.

10 Why do we need a communications infrastructure for e-commerce?
11 Which issues should be addressed when developing a communications infrastructure?
12 Describe the networking technologies that support e-commerce for wired communication. What are their relative merits and demerits?
13 Describe the networking technologies that support e-commerce for wireless communication.
14 Prepare a comparative study of existing mobile communications techniques and their uses in e-commerce.
15 In what way have modern appliances contributed to mobile commerce?
16 In what way do the following contribute to Internet access: ISPs, NAPs, URLs, DNS, ICANN?
17 Why is security important for e-commerce?
18 Explain how (a) symmetric and (b) asymmetric encryption work.
19 What is the significance of digital signature? How is this utilised in SSL?
20 What other methods are used to improve the security of Internet-based business? Explain the basic principles behind them.
21 How do organisations utilise the technologies of security to create a VPN?

Discussion Questions

1 Some people have suggested that the future of e-commerce is in the WAP technology; others are more sceptical about its potential. Review the two sides of the argument and make some concluding remarks.
2 With the help of further research, do a critical analysis of the nature of security measures taken by the financial industry and their effectiveness.

Bibliography

Bandyo-padhyay, N., *Computing for Non-specialists*, Addison Wesley, London, 2000.

Bradbury, D., The generation game, *Computer Weekly, e.business review*, October, 2000, p. 54.

Bricknell, D., Jamjars on the highway, *Computer Weekly, e.business review*, October, 2000, p. 22.

Campbell, A., WAP or scrap? *Computer Weekly, e.business review*, December, 2000, p. 66.

Dodd, A. Z., *The Essential Guide to Telecommunications*, Prentice Hall, New Jersey, 1998.

Dunt, R., Post Office venture aims to cut out Internet fraud, *Computer Weekly*, 16 November, 2000.

Enticknap, N. NAS finds a role in big business, *Computer Weekly*, 29 March, 2001, p. 92.

Field, C., Is broadband the e-commerce dinosaur? *Computer Weekly, e.business review*, December, 2000, p. 35.

Goodwin, B., Financial firm blazes a trial to go live with PKI Web solution, *Computer Weekly*, 16 November, 2000, p. 16.

Green, D., The last mile of broadband access, Technical Note; *Harvard Business Review*, 9-800-076, 25 January, 2000.

Huitema, C., *IPV6: The New Internet Protocol*, Prentice Hall, New Jersey, 1998.

Iansiti, M. and Feinberg, B., Lucent Technologies: Optical networking group, *Harvard Business Review*, 9-600-053, 12 November, 1999.

Keyte, C., Learn mobile lessons from Japanese, *Computer Weekly*, 9 August 2001, p. 18.

Langley, N., Rebel with a code, *Computer Weekly*, 25 January, 2001, p. 28.

Middleton, J., Provident connects offices worldwide, *Network News*, 4 July, 2000. Also available from www.vnunet.com/News.

Nicolle, L., M-commerce: the next big thing? *Computer Weekly, e.business review*, December, 2000, p. 60.

Norris, M., West, S. and Gaughan, K., *eBusiness Essentials: Technology and Network Requirements for the Electronic Marketplace*, Wiley, Chichester, England, 2000.

Rajput, W. E., *E-Commerce Systems Architecture and Applications*, Artech House, Boston, 2000.

Rayport, J. F. and Jaworski, B. J., *e-Commerce*, McGraw-Hill, New York, 2001.

Saran, C., Microsoft gets connected, *Computer Weekly, e.business review*, October, 2000, p. 46.

Schatt, S., *Data Communications for Business*, Prentice Hall, New Jersey, 1994.

Stallings, W., *Data and Computer Communications*, Prentice Hall, New Jersey, 2000.

Tristram, C., Chameleon chips, *Technology Review*, February, 2001, p. 31.

Turban, E., Lee, J., King, D. and Chung, H. M., *Electronic Commerce: A Managerial Perspective*, Prentice Hall, New Jersey, 2000.

Whyte, W. S., *Networked Futures: Trends for Communications Systems Development*, Wiley, Chichester, England, 1999.

Information Management Infrastructure for E-Commerce

Chapter Six

Objectives

By the end of this chapter you should have an understanding of:

- The role of an information management infrastructure in e-commerce.
- The systems which underpin information and knowledge management.
- The technologies behind these systems.
- The principles behind the development of these systems.

INTRODUCTION

In chapter 5, we discussed the technologies which support the communication of data required for e-commerce. We explained the processes involved in the transmission of data through different media and described how they contribute to the Internet. We also discussed the hardware devices which contribute to and the appliances which facilitate the processes. These only provide the physical infrastructure for e-commerce; it cannot function without the information management infrastructure that holds the technologies and processes together.

As discussed in chapters 3 and 4, the survival and growth of an organisation in the Internet age depends on its ability to create information, turn it into knowledge, and share it within the organisation and across national and international boundaries. An organisation needs to use its information and knowledge resources to speed up customer services, facilitate customer relationship management by linking a number of systems together, use these systems to improve on-line customer services and provide value-added information, design applications capable of optimising the utilisation of e-commerce related resources, and so on. This requires the development of a number of systems: databases to support management information systems, data mining and warehousing for customer relationship management and an infrastructure for integrating the systems to support enterprise resource planning. It also involves the use of intranets, groupware and extranets for sharing information and knowledge between colleagues and business partners. Additionally, using these systems necessitates the development of user interfaces and the integration of the applications with backend systems. An organisation needs an infrastructure that supports such activities. In this chapter we will discuss these systems: the technologies that support them, the philosophy behind their development and the criteria for their contribution to the success of an information infrastructure.

THE FRAMEWORK FOR AN INFORMATION MANAGEMENT INFRASTRUCTURE

The emergence of the information society and the resulting knowledge economy demands that companies integrate their information resources and business processes in order to create an 'electronic intelligence' capable of responding to challenges quickly, efficiently and easily. Discussing the importance of smooth information flow between different elements of a business, Bill Gates (1999) used the concept of a digital nervous system which facilitates a well-integrated flow of information to the right part of an organisation at the right time. It enables companies to react to their environment, sense competitive challenges and respond to customer needs. A digital nervous system is a combination of hardware and software, clearly distinguishable from a mere network of computers, designed to provide knowledge workers with accuracy, immediacy and richness of information.

This model helps us understand the concept of an information and knowledge management infrastructure by providing a framework to explain the importance of free flow of information between systems in an organisation. As demonstrated by Fig. 6.1:

> A digital nervous system comprises the digital processes that closely link every aspect of a company's thoughts and actions. Basic operations such as finance and production, plus feedback from customers, are electronically available to company's knowledge workers, who use digital tools to quickly adapt and respond. The immediate availability of accurate information changes strategic thinking from a separate, stand-alone activity to an ongoing process integrated with regular business activities.
>
> (Gates, 1999: 16)

The framework described above is built on the principle of integration between organisational systems and procedures – a necessity for companies engaged in Internet-based business. The digital nervous system provides an infrastructure with the following objectives: extend each individual's analytical abilities; create an institutional intelligence and an ability to learn; and facilitate the use of technology to marshal and co-ordinate teams of people quickly and efficiently (Gates, 1999). This involves the implementation of on-line applications, backend systems and software technology capable of transferring information between these systems.

A digital nervous system is a combination of hardware and software, clearly distinguishable from a mere network of computers, designed to provide knowledge workers with accurate, immediate and rich information.

How does the concept of a digital nervous system explain the activities of a supermarket engaged in on-line sale of goods to a particular area?

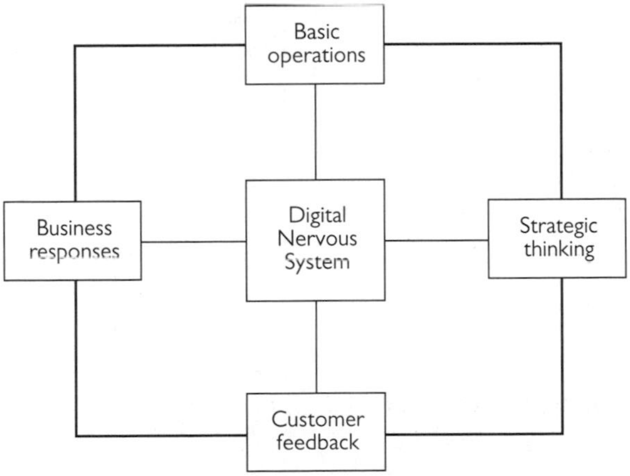

Fig. 6.1 The digital nervous system (Figure 'Digital Nervous System' adapted from figure (p. 16) in *Business @ the Speed of Thought* by Bill Gates with Collins Hemingway (Penguin Books, 1999) copyright © William H. Gates, III, 1999. Reproduced by permission of Penguin Books Ltd.)

The enterprise solutions framework described in chapter 4 (Fig. 6.2) helps us to discover how an information management infrastructure (IMI) creates a digital nervous system. According to this framework, all levels of an organisation need systems to carry information to where it is required. At level 1, individuals use on-line databases, office automation software such as text-based documents and reports, training material and intranets. These help them to find information, gain knowledge and provide an improved service as a result. At level 2, project teams and workgroups use groupware products to communicate, collaborate and create knowledge for the organisation. At level 3, the organisation reaches beyond physical boundaries and uses integrated databases, ERP systems, and on-line communications systems to develop new business processes such as CRM with the help of improved data warehousing. Finally, at level 4, the company uses extranets, Internet-based applications and global on-line transactions, thus joining the business communities in cyberspace.

By combining processes and technologies, an IMI supports the continuous process of transforming data and information into organisational knowledge and distributing it throughout the organisation.

All these applications and interfaces contribute to the widespread availability of information among employees, enabling them to make informed business decisions. By supporting a continuous process of transforming data and information into organisational knowledge and distributing it throughout the organisation, they form the basis of an IMI. By combining technologies and processes an IMI continually advances a company's ability to create, discover, search for and distribute knowledge. It uses tacit as well as explicit knowledge, turns it into organisation-wide knowledge, and then

4. The virtual organisation (extranet, on-line communication and transactions)	On-line transactions	Communication with stakeholders	Ecosystem development	Cybermarket development
3. The intelligent organisation (integrated databases, ERP, CRM products etc.)	Organisational data systems and applications	Organisational communication	Enterprise-wide knowledge management	Improved business processes
2. The organisation with empowered teams (groupware applications)	Workgroup data systems and applications	Workgroup communication	Workgroup collaboration	Improved conduct and control of workflow
1. The organisation with empowered individuals (databases, on-line training materials, text-based documents, reports etc.	Data creation, access and usage	Information access	Training, education and expertise	Integration of knowledge into work processes
	Data (Structured)	Information (Unstructured)	Knowledge (Unstructured)	Work (Structured)

Fig. 6.2 The Enterprise Solutions Framework for knowledge management

facilitates its use at individual as well as at strategic level, in order to influence tacit behaviour (Gates, 1999). Thus an IMI provides the framework for making knowledge available where it is required, thereby supporting the foundation for the management of knowledge and serving as the basis of a knowledge management infrastructure (KMI).[1] An understanding of how to create the infrastructure needs an appreciation of the concepts underpinning these systems, the technologies supporting their development, the philosophy behind their design and the issues surrounding their successful implementation.

Using the examples of the systems mentioned in the enterprise solutions framework, explain how they relate to the model of a digital nervous system as defined by Bill Gates.

CREATING AN INFORMATION MANAGEMENT INFRASTRUCTURE

As discussed in chapter 4, knowledge in an organisation exists in three basic forms: tacit, rule-based (explicit) and background. Tacit knowledge may be reflected through personal exchanges between colleagues in the form of emails, memos, personal notes etc., rule-based knowledge is stored in information systems of various types, whilst the availability of background knowledge depends on the ability of a leader to share it with others. An effective KMI facilitates the sharing of knowledge from all these sources by people at all levels and locations. This requires the integration of organisation-wide knowledge rather than using specific information systems for specific groups. Consequently, this philosophy advocates a move away from the concept of specialised webpages toward web content generated automatically from all business activities. Thus, knowledge of different forms and from different sources must be made available to the whole organisation. This entails *identifying* sources of information and knowledge, *capturing* them in suitable formats and establishing suitable *retrieval* facilities.

A knowledge management infrastructure involves:

- identifying knowledge sources
- capturing knowledge
- establishing a mechanism for knowledge retrieval.

Identification of the sources of information and knowledge

Knowledge is essential for any organisation, but for an e-commerce organisation the situation is complicated by the variety of the type and location of systems. Information on organisational products and processes can be stored in backend information systems, data warehouses, emails, departmental databases, individual documents and reports and so on. Additionally, there are many useful documents on the Internet which could be valuable for the company. An organisation has to perform the challenging but essential task of identifying all these sources before it is able to develop a KMI. This requires leadership from the management, which appreciates '. . . that knowledge is often their main economic resource and that the knowledge worker is their most essential corporate asset. Employees must learn as they work, and it is imperative that the organisation both supports that learning and harvests its value for reuse by others' (Papows, 1999:113).

Capturing information for easy access

The sources mentioned above hold data and information in various formats. For effective knowledge management, the information must be stored in databases with appropriate

[1] IMI and KMI are related and overlapping concepts.

search facilities and query mechanisms in order for users to have easy access. Many different types of systems are used in an organisation to store information such as non-relational databases (often used in older legacy information systems), relational databases, traditional non-database programs and files, unstructured documents and reports and Internet-based information. Access to all this information requires the establishment of a mechanism for extracting appropriate information from each of these sources and creating web-enabled systems which would allow the entire organisation to access information on-line. These systems are essentially databases, reservoirs of data and information organised in a way that enables users to find what they want quickly and efficiently. In order to understand the role of a database in data capture, we must have an understanding of the technical concept behind it.

Databases were introduced commercially in the early 1980s. Until then we had the so-called 'traditional' systems of files and programs tailored to each other. Files are a collection of data organised in a hierarchical order of fields and records, that is, a file comprises a number of records, and each record consists of a number of fields. The concept is the same in computerised as well as in manual files, for example a customer file with one record on each customer with fields such as customer ID, names, addresses etc. (Fig. 6.3). In traditional systems a number of such files would be created for each information system, for example an order processing system would have a customer file, an orders file, a products file, suppliers file and so on. Programs would be designed to 'read' these files, process the data to produce information such as customer invoices for the delivery department and 'items sold' lists for the sales department.

These systems had the following problems:

- The programs were written specifically for the files. If the structure of the files changed, the programs had to be changed accordingly, and vice versa.
- Files were not linked with each other; the same field often had to appear in more than one file. For example, the price of each item was likely to be included in the products file as well as the orders file. This led to two problems: unnecessary duplication of data, and the possibility of incompatibility between files, for example, the price for a product could be updated in one file but not in the other.
- Each system was maintained separately, with its own files and programs. Thus, both the order processing system and accounting system would hold a

Fields

Customer ID	Last Name	First Name	House No.	Street Name	Post Code
94067767	Agbasi	Adele	5	London Road	NW10 5RS
94214524	Collingwood	Gordon	50	Chase Side	N12 2NF
94001934	Farmer	Paula	10	Charter Road	N14 6YY
93539987	Harrison	Gabriele	23A	Gyles Street	W10 5TS
95642201	Kaur	Raj	55	East Side	EC2 1KK
95343321	Parmar	Amrit	90	Highgate Hill	N12 8WE
93898456	Sheikh	Ibrahim	121	Porter's Way	E11 2QJ
94322178	Singh	Eilene	43	High Street	N10 6XE
93446123	Thomas	Sonia	14	Green Lanes	SW10 2BS

Records

Fig. 6.3 A customer file

customer file each. This also led to the problems of duplication and incompatibility, thus lowering the integrity of the system.
- Since systems did not relate to each other, there was no scope for sharing information. Systems were not integrated; a number of systems had to be interrogated separately in order to access the information required.

Databases were introduced in order to eliminate the problems associated with such systems, and to enable organisations to centralise information in order to improve efficiency without loss of security.

A database is a filing system in which files are linked with each other by an identification field called the *primary key*. This has a unique value for each record (such as product code for the products file). A set of programs collectively known as a database management system (DBMS) allows users to create, link and maintain a database. Unlike traditional programs, the files in a database are independent of the DBMS, and because of this, the structure and content of the database can be changed whenever necessary. A DBMS also facilitates the creation of queries by users, which can be used to extract information on an ad hoc basis. A database system therefore attempts to eliminate the aforementioned problems in the following ways:

DBMS is a concept which enables users to create files which are inter-linked, and independent of the programs (held by the DBMS) which manipulate them. This enables users to access information from anywhere on the database by using ad hoc queries.

- Files are linked with each other. Any change in data is automatically propagated through to other related files.
- The integration of files reduces the duplication of data.
- DBMS, the programs which facilitate the creation of database applications and their use, is independent of the applications and therefore their contents can be changed as necessary.
- The centralised management of an organisation's data resources facilitates better control over security and the management of information.
- Users can obtain answers to ad hoc queries and generate reports quickly and easily. This improves an organisation's knowledge-sharing capabilities. A query can be defined by stating the criteria by which it should be answered. Commercial packages present screen formats which allow users to set queries based on a single file or on a combination of linked files. Experienced users can set queries with advanced criteria based on multiple conditions by using a fourth-generation programming language (4GL) called structured query language (SQL) associated with a DBMS.

A database can be used as a centralised repository of data and equipped with menu-driven interfaces to enable users to extract information. Thus they constitute the basic building block for an organisation's IMI.

Using modern database management systems and programming tools, database applications can be created with menus, icons, on-screen prompts and messages, screen layouts and other presentational features. In many organisations, such an application is implemented as a multi-user system with different degrees of access given to users of different categories. For example, a customer management database can be used by the sales staff only to access information on customer orders and availability of products, by the marketing people for retrieving information on products but not on individual customers, and by the senior managers for reports on yearly sales and profit.

Databases provide the basic building blocks for information systems in today's organisations. A customer relationship management system would be built on a number of databases: an order processing database integrating information on customers, accounts, sales, products, suppliers and so on; a customer database holding current and historical information on customers; a marketing database with in-depth information on product description, history etc. These would be supported by software for the integration and analysis of information obtained from these databases and user interfaces for accessing information and responding to customer requests on-line. Thus databases form the core of an information system; other software tools and management processes together with information and communications technologies provide the rest of the ingredients.

There are a number of types of DBMS: hierarchical, network, relational, object-oriented, object-relational and hypermedia. In a hierarchical database, the relationship between records follows a top-down pattern; for example, an organisation may have a record for each department, which in turn may have a record for each project, which could have a record for each employee, and so on. The model is most suitable for situations in which the relationship between data is always downwards. Referred to as a one-to-many relationship, this represents the situation in which each project can have many employees, but one employee cannot join more than one project. This reflects the traditional organisational structure; it is simpler to implement and many legacy systems are built on this model; however, it is not suitable for today's environment. IBM's Information Management System (IMS) is a well-known hierarchical DBMS.

The network database architecture follows the model of cross-functional teams in e-commerce organisations. Known as the many-to-many relationship, this model facilitates relationships for an environment where for example, one employee can belong to many projects and each project can have many employees. One successful network DBMS is the Integrated DBMS (IDMS) by Computer Associates. However, both network and hierarchical architecture necessitates that the relationships are known in advance, thus making the possibility of incorporating new relationships difficult and time consuming.

Relational databases (RDBMS) are the most popular today because they facilitate all types of relationships by organising files in tables and linking the tables rather than records. Although it is slower than other models and is normally used in PC-based or midrange applications, this is more flexible than the previous two because it enables users to set up and change relationships and queries and facilitates easy integration with other applications such as text documents, spreadsheets and HTML files.. Examples of well-known relational DBMSs are Access by Microsoft (for PCs) and DB2 by IBM (for midrange). However, e-commerce applications often involve audio, video and image data which relational databases cannot handle easily. Some software vendors tried to get round this problem by introducing object-relational databases (ORDBMS) which translate complicated data formats into those which are suitable for relational databases, but this affected the speed and performance greatly.

Object-oriented databases (OODBMS) solved the problem of handling complicated data types by using the object-oriented programming (OOP) technique, a programming concept that treats real-world entities such as people, places, things etc. as objects, attaching properties and codes to them, which are called into the program as required.[2] The method provides a database model which is quick to develop due to the re-usability of objects, and efficient because the objects are tried and tested. Also, objects are created in 'classes' in which each class of object has a number of objects within it, which in turn, can have further objects. Objects inherit properties from their parent class but can also have additional properties. This concept of relationships lends itself easily to the database model. Finally, since most e-commerce applications use object-based windows interfaces, OODBMSs can relate to them without the need for translation.

A new approach to database management known as *hypermedia* DBMS uses the concept of linking (cross-referencing) text to each other by hypertext links in the same way pages on the Internet are linked. Documents linked can contain data of any type (text, audio, graphics, video, executable programs etc.); the links are set up by the user and are displayed with special notation on the screen. This is gaining popularity fast because

Types of database:

- Hierarchical: relationship between records is one-to-many. Not practical for today's environment.
- Network: supports many-to-many relationship but is inflexible.
- Relational: supports all types of relationship and allows alteration easily.
- Object-oriented: storing the properties of data and their processing methods as objects; supports integration between systems.
- Hypermedia: uses hyperlinks to relate documents, and is compatible with the Internet.

[2] We will discuss this further later on in the chapter.

of its compatibility with webpages, thus making integration between applications easier.

Knowledge captured in the above ways is held in backend information systems. The basis of the availability of knowledge is the 'web-enability' of these systems, that is, their ability to interact with Internet-based software. This involves using hypertext transfer protocols (HTTP) for backend systems in order to make them compatible with e-commerce applications, creating special interfaces based on languages such as XML or Java between e-commerce applications and backend systems, or using middleware to facilitate integration between the two ends. Intelligent software agents are used to extract information from the applications and information systems, and save them in directories (indexes) categorised into specific topics. Knowledge is also captured and stored in expert systems in which human knowledge is stored in a database (called a knowledge-base) and rule-based logic is used to interrogate the database and extract knowledge from it. Case-based reasoning follows the same technique but works on a database of cases – documented experiences of specialists from previous cases.

Knowledge can be captured in databases, directories, expert systems and case-based reasoning systems. E-commerce applications work by extracting this knowledge and making it available to the web. This necessitates the web-enability of these systems.

Suggest some databases that an organisation such as a bookshop which is a part of a major chain would need for their knowledge capture.

Databases and directories provide the storage of data and a mechanism for extracting information by queries. However, successful use of these resources relies on the facilities established for retrieving the information collected and responding on-line.

Retrieval of knowledge

As explained in chapter 4, knowledge is retrieved from the Internet by search engines – applications software which use intelligent agents to scan cyberspace and find websites with information requested by users. Examples of pioneer companies which have dominated this field include Yahoo!, Lycos, Alta Vista[3] and Inktomi. They use certain techniques to improve search speed and efficiency. For example, Inktomi uses dedicated servers to store copies of frequently searched websites at different storage points along the network. When a keyword submitted by a user matches one on the list, it is delivered from the closest point. Another technique, referred to as the 'push technology', provides users with information tailored to their needs. A browser contains software which prompts users to specify which kinds of information they would like to receive. Using the response as the key, it scans the Internet and sends the relevant webpages to the users with a prompt. The method is also used by corporate intranets and extranets to broadcast company information to the employees.

There are many search engines in the market and some companies, like Yahoo!, started as a search engine but have now turned into a portal. In the face of growing competition users demand the following qualities:

- *Ease of use* – With the help of a user-friendly interface, a search engine should facilitate easy access to information. For example, Yahoo! displays a list of categories of websites; when the user chooses one of those, only the relevant links are searched.
- *Speed* – Traffic on the Internet can be very high, especially at certain times of the day. A search engine must have the tools required to find information quickly.

[3] Yahoo! uses Alta Vista as the search engine for its portal (Cohan, 1999).

Information infrastructure at Frito-Lay, Inc.

In the mid-1980s, the American supermarket chain Frito-Lay began to put an information infrastructure in place. They needed to provide timely and flexible access to information throughout the organisation. Their first step was to introduce hand-held computers (HHC) to its 10,000 mobile sales force in order for them to receive sales reports from different stores as necessary. In April 1988, Charlie Feld, the vice-president of the Frito-Lay's Management Information Systems organisation, and Michael Jordan, CEO, decided to design a more comprehensive information management infrastructure (IMI).

Feld approached IBM and Comshare Inc., the latter a software vendor specialising in management decision support and executive information systems (EIS). The three companies worked out a joint development effort, code-named the Blue Chip Project. As the architecture developed, Banyan Inc. (which specialised in LAN), Scientific Atlanta Inc. (which specialised in very small aperture terminal (VSAT) WAN), and Xcellnet (which specialised in packaging and distributing data over networks) were brought into the partnership.

Like many other companies, Frito-Lay had learnt the hard way that increasing the complexity of the business while trying to decrease cycle times greatly increases the demand for information throughout the firm. When the information processing systems could not supply the information because it was not available, or because the systems were too slow and cumbersome, the organisation became dysfunctional. Management realised that improved information was needed to enable them to transform business processes. They found that different phases of their business operated at different speeds and efficiency. The information technology supporting business operations showed the same varying levels of sophistication and effectiveness. They needed to create management information and decision support systems that would enable them to integrate the strategic perspective of top management with the detailed knowledge of local market dynamics that is present in the field.

The above objectives drew attention to specific aspects of business processes, and the development of a flexible and dynamic information infrastructure. The main elements of this IMI needed to be information management, communications management, and tools that could create, package, deliver, and use information.

Frito-Lay decided to introduce a data warehouse as its information management component. This was constructed as a set of integrated relational databases that received detailed data from both internal and external sources. This data was then filed and stored using a common data format that enabled space-efficient, fast, and flexible access. This had the following advantages:

- A centralised location of data, which improved security and ensured 'orderly access'.
- A single efficient storage and retrieval mechanism was defined to allow many different users to request data without having to know the specifics of how to locate the data.
- Mass updates to data could be accomplished efficiently at one location to prevent redundant and conflicting information.
- In the same way that a physical warehouse keeps frequently needed goods near the loading bay, Frito-Lay's data warehouse kept some of its data packaged together for fast retrieval.

The communications component of the project was built around a client-server approach, in which a set of LANs equipped with workstations, files and database servers formed the foundation of the architecture. The corporate mainframe systems became just one node in the network. The LANs were connected by means of a VSAT WAN, and network management was handled through Xcellnet network services.

The philosophy of the above approach was to perform computing as close to the person or process that required it as possible. This led to an emphasis on the workstation as opposed to the mainframe in the design of applications, which in turn led to end-user rather than programmer control.

The final challenge for the management was to enable managers to gain access to relevant information needed to make decisions and manage the business. A set of software tools were selected to enable the flexible, fast development of end-user applications that would analyse, package and deliver information to all levels within the organisation. The key design criteria were:

- the system must be easy to use for employees without a strong technical background
- it must provide targeted information to users at all levels of the organisation
- it must be easy to create new information reporting systems and maintain the existing ones
- it must augment, rather than replace, management decision making and intelligence.

Comshare's Commander EIS was chosen as the initial tool for designing applications for management decision making and information analysis. The Commander EIS enabled the design, creation, storage and retrieval of graphical information displays. By March 1989, five prototype applications were developed to provide critical information to executives and key decision makers.

(Source: Applegate and Wishart, 1993.
Copyright © 1989 by the President and Fellows of Harvard College.
Harvard Business School Case 9-190-071.
Rev. 24 February, 1993.)

This case was prepared by Lynda M. Applegate and Nicole A. Wishart as the basis for class discussion rather than to illustrate either effective or ineffective handling of an administrative situation. Reprinted by permission from Harvard Business School.

Questions

1 Explain the terms: decision support system, management information system, executive information system.
2 Why is it important 'to integrate the strategic perspective of top management with the detailed knowledge of local market dynamics'?
3 Describe how the features of Frito-Lay's IMI would support: information management, communications management, and tools that could be used to create, package, deliver and use information.
4 What extra features would a similar food chain company today need to incorporate in their systems?

- *Efficiency* – Some searches may require complicated access techniques involving a company's backend systems. The rate of success of a search engine depends on an organisation's ability to integrate its front- and backend systems.
- *Advanced keyword search* – A search engine must have facilities to search by phrases, questions and logical operators. For example, keywords such as 'e-commerce AND e-business' should be able to yield the webpages including both terms.
- *Flexibility* – Users should be able to choose which types of website to include in the search. For example, a user can ask for websites on networking from academic institutions only in order to avoid advertisements or information on specific manufacturers.

Knowledge retrieval is conducted primarily via a web interface comprising a search engine with flexible and user-friendly search facilities.

A KMI based on the above principles and capable of providing a framework for the identification, capture and retrieval of knowledge must be supported by a number of knowledge management systems.

SYSTEMS FOR KNOWLEDGE MANAGEMENT

An organisation needs to build a number of systems which can be used to implement a KMI capable of providing access to knowledge during decision-making processes. We will discuss the following:

- enterprise resource planning (ERP)
- customer relationship management (CRM)
- intranets
- groupware
- extranets.

Enterprise resource planning (ERP)

ERP has been mentioned a number of times before. Deemed one of the essential systems for e-commerce, ERP systems are software packages that attempt to integrate the information flow within a company, solving the problem of incompatibility between systems and operating practices. The German software developer SAP became the fastest growing software company in the world following the introduction of their ERP system in 1992; other companies such as Bann, Oracle and PeopleSoft experienced similar growth (Davenport, 1998).

An ERP system streamlines a company's data flows and provides management with direct access to a wealth of real-time information. This is facilitated by the use of database technologies which link a company's applications together and pass relevant data between them as necessary. Any new information added to one of the systems updates the other systems automatically, thus creating complete integration between them. Directory services and middleware are used in order to connect the applications and provide an infrastructure for users to communicate with each other and connect to the sources of information.

Directory services

Directory services maintain databases on the users, services, hardware and software resources of a network (in the same way that a telephone directory does for business services), and provide on-line search facilities for users to locate information and services. We mentioned directory services in chapter 5 in connection with domain name services (DNS), which hold directories of URLs.

An organisation engaged in e-commerce activities requires the following:

- An email directory of users' addresses and a facility for locating those addresses.
- Directories of passwords and user-IDs to facilitate security checks on users.
- Connectivity to trading partners via intranets and extranets, sometimes via strict firewalls; this requires directories of security credentials.
- The means for customers to connect to some applications, for example an order processing system which enables them to place orders on-line and receive information on the availability of goods. This requires a directory of users of the applications involved and information on the company's data resources which allow the systems to integrate with each other.

Some directory services maintain a catalogue on the location of company files and enable users in different organisations to access information on each other directly without the need for a mediator. Known as peer-to-peer (P2P) transaction, this enables users to send information to their peers while avoiding Internet servers. It provides swift, secure and efficient communication between trading partners. Some P2P service providers hold a directory in a central server while some others disperse it among users. The much publicised case of users swapping MP3 music files via Napster is based on the same concept.

Organisations usually hold different directory services for different applications. This leads to many problems: the lack of inter-operability between systems requires that users must access different services separately, difficulty in finding services; and the need for complicated authentication procedures in order to secure communication between directory services, especially when new applications are implemented. The solution to such problems includes the establishment of standards and the provision of a centralised directory service (DS). A number of DS standards are available for companies to choose from, for example X.500 supported by International Standards Organisation (ISO), and Lightweight Directory Access Protocol (LDAP), a simpler version of X.500 supported by Netscape, Microsoft and Novell. Some companies provide a unified DS which centralises all directories and also follows a suitable standard.

Middleware

Middleware is a system that provides integration between an organisation's frontend applications and its backend systems, thus contributing to enterprise-wide sharing of information. Middleware facilitates interaction between:

- a PC and the backend systems which contain information required by the applications at the frontend
- different applications on a distributed system
- various directory services
- the networking technologies
- different classes of software such as traditional programs and applications built on object-oriented methodologies
- the software supporting systems management functions.

E-commerce becomes dysfunctional without such integration. For example, when a customer wants to place an order s/he accesses the company's website via a PC and connects to the order processing application. Before processing the order, the system has to check if the goods required are available by connecting to the inventory; if it is out of stock, the system accesses the applications dealing with new supplies; it must also check the credentials of the customer in terms of payment history and then respond with the appropriate message. During these activities, communication must take place between the systems software that support these applications, the appliances and services that facilitate message transfer, the communications systems and so on. Middleware attempts to provide the necessary integration between all these services and systems.

B2B e-commerce requires unrestricted sharing at both data and process levels. Systems belonging to trading partners need to communicate instantaneously, in any direction, automatically and in real time. Traditional middleware solutions are often not equipped to deal with such integration. B2B application integration is a term used to describe the special needs of this sector (Linthicum, 2000). It has the following characteristics:

Middleware provides the much needed integration between the backend systems and desktop Internet applications. B2B middleware need to provide seamless, automatic and real-time communication between intra- and inter-organisational systems at both data and process levels.

- Integration takes place at both data and process levels.
- It includes the notion of reuse of data among several linked enterprises.
- It lets users with little understanding of the applications, integrate them.
- It assumes that the integrating systems cannot be alerted, thus the integration is automatic and non-intrusive.

Thus, middleware solution developers must cater for B2B application integration which demands seamless integration of data, information, business rules, processes and methods to ensure that composite applications are available to all interested parties wanting to communicate, collaborate and co-operate from geographically and organisationally dispersed locations.

A number of frameworks have been established for this purpose. The two most well-known ones are Common Object Request Broker Architecture (CORBA), supported by the Object Management Group (OMG), and Microsoft's Component Object Model (COM). Based on object-oriented programming (OOP) technology, these frameworks define the standards (rules) for the development of middleware.

OOP is a relatively new programming method that builds a program as a collection of objects representing real-life entities such as customer, products and payment, rather than lines of instructions defining how to perform a task – as in the traditional programming methods. Objects are defined in hierarchical order: new objects can be created as a 'child' of the existing (parent) ones thus allowing a child to inherit the parent's properties. Objects can be kept in a 'library' and reused in any program.

CORBA defines the middleware specifications for traditional systems as well as for object-oriented programs, thus providing interoperability between the two generations. COM, on the other hand, is a proprietary system for Microsoft (MS) Windows-based applications only. However, because of the ubiquity of MS products at the end-user interface level, it is important for companies to integrate with their products. Additionally, MS has now introduced COM for other operating systems such as AIX (the IBM version of Unix) and Solaris for Sun Microsystems. Based on these frameworks, middleware has been developed for different types of system such as transaction processing middleware to control various aspects of commercial transactions, database middleware designed to make communication with and between different databases transparent; applications middleware to integrate various applications with user interfaces; and communications middleware to facilitate reliable communication by the efficient routing of data and messages between applications.

CORBA and COM are two frameworks based on object-oriented technology. They provide guidelines for the development of middleware. CORBA also supports traditional programming methods. COM is a proprietary system for Microsoft applications.

However, such widespread inter-operability can also create problems for an organisation by pushing it towards integration even when this is not totally desirable. It may also force the organisation away from customised processes towards a generic one (Davenport, 1998). In order to avoid such problems, organisations must form a clear understanding of the implications of ERP and a well thought-out strategy for the implementation of such a system.

Customer relationship management (CRM)

CRM enables an organisation to provide real-time customer service by storing information on individual customers, analysing and then using it to tailor the service to customers' needs. This requires capturing information on customers from on-line transactions and communications, integrating it with other corporate systems in order to get a 'full picture' of each customer and add value to their services. Effective CRM provides improved communication with customers and the scope for targeted marketing by monitoring customer preferences and circumstances. It also facilitates cross-selling, that is, offering a customer an additional product when s/he makes a purchase. For example, AA offers car insurance to its members who sign up for its motor breakdown service. With the help of CRM an enterprise can gain customer loyalty by offering products suited to their specific needs and use the information gathered to perform market analysis and plan expansion.

A CRM system collects information from all possible sources by registering every customer 'event' and uses it to improve customer relationship.

At the most basic level, CRM is a database on customers collected from all contacts such as emails, records of order processing, call centre communications etc. Each interaction between a customer and a website is an 'event' which leaves a 'footprint'. CRM technologies track these footprints and use them in order to guide the customer during

ERP at Cisco

Cisco Systems, Inc., an electronic communications provider, realised its 'Single Enterprise' vision when it integrated its ERP systems with key suppliers. Suppliers use ERP to run their Cisco production lines, allowing them to respond to customer demand in real time. Changes in parts of the supply chain are communicated almost instantaneously. For example, if one supplier is running low on a component, Cisco can instantly analyse the entire supply chain for excess supplies elsewhere. Changes in forecasted demand are also communicated in real time, enabling suppliers to immediately respond to requests for products or materials.

Benefits also accrue in the payment portion of the order-to-payment cycle. Manual processing of an invoice is no longer needed. Payment to suppliers is triggered by a shop-floor transaction in the ERP system indicating that production is complete. The transaction backflushes inventory, figures out the value of components sold by the suppliers and triggers an electronic payment to suppliers, thereby consolidating what were five sequential events into one. Annual benefits from these improvements, and many others, are estimated to run into tens of millions of dollars per year. The ERP solution is also seen to be supporting the rapid growth the company has experienced through its ability to scale and flex with changing business conditions.

(Source: Escalle and Cotteleer, 1999. Copyright © 1999 by the President and Fellows of Harvard College. Harvard Business School Case 9-699-020. 11 February, 1999.

This case was prepared by Cedric X. Escalle and Mark J. Cotteleer as the basis for class discussion rather than to illustrate either effective or ineffective handling of an administrative situation. Reprinted by permission from Harvard Business School.

Questions

1 How does the company benefit from these processes?
2 What information management infrastructure would be required to gain the above benefits?
3 The article by Escalle discusses some problems associated with the ERP. Read the article and discuss how Cisco could be affected by those problems.

subsequent interactions. The information tracked is stored in a data warehouse, analysed (mined), and turned into knowledge on customer behaviour which the company can use to create a profile on each customer.

How can a supermarket use CRM for business benefit?

Data warehousing and mining

A data warehouse (DW) is described as a repository of historical data extracted from all systems in an organisation and made accessible to business users. The data may be obtained from any part of the organisation's e-commerce systems and is usually stored on a specific hardware platform: a PC, a server or even a mainframe. The concept of data warehousing started in the late 1980s as a tool for making business decisions (referred to as a decision support system). Large companies used a DW to collect data from the systems running on a mainframe, checked it for accuracy and stored it on a separate machine in a format suitable for use in decision making. This gave them an integrated and centralised source of information on customers (a single view) and also improved security by enabling companies to control access to the data.

A data warehouse is a repository of historical data extracted from all corporate systems and made accessible to business users.

In the early days of data warehousing, parts of the process of creating a DW had to be done manually. For example someone had to locate the sources of data and develop a system to gather, analyse, process, and store it in its new form on a new platform. Now, software has been developed to monitor on-line transactions and track relevant data from all possible sources and create a DW automatically. This provides a company with 'business intelligence' by turning isolated data into useful information. Dyché described the use of a modern DW as an evolutionary process of decision support (Fig. 6.4); the levels (1–4) represent the increasing depth of analysis and facilitate decision making at increasing levels of complexity. The lowest level (4) of data analysis is the most common and arguably the most useful for an organisation; it answers simple queries about customers, such as providing an account balance or credit record. The next level (3) supports multidimensional queries (queries with a combination of criteria) with more complicated parameters such as the average insurance claims made by customers in a certain area – information which enables users to add value to decisions such as setting the level of insurance premium for an area.

While levels 4 and 3 comprise the majority of the activities of a decision support system; level 2 provides knowledge workers with tools for analysis by answering queries based on historical data. This enables users to categorise (segment) customers into groups and to create a model for customer or product behaviour. For example, the tools can enable users to categorise customers most at risk of mortgage arrears at a time of recession, and aid modelling by answering questions such as what effects will a rise in the mortgage rate have upon customer behaviour? Knowledge discovery (level 1) is a progression from such modelling; only at this level do the data analysis tools provide information without having to be asked. For example, software at the discovery level can identify customer behaviour patterns during a period of time and can volunteer information such as the warning of a drop in house prices. This is the ultimate goal of CRM: the process of understanding customer behaviour in the light of the circumstances surrounding it and making business decisions accordingly.

How may an on-line estate agency tailor its services using the above model? Which factors will impact upon its business, and how will it identify these factors?

DWs can be built at both corporate and functional levels; the difference lies in the extent of coverage and consequently the technology platform it requires. A corporate level DW stores data from all sources on all customers and serves the entire company

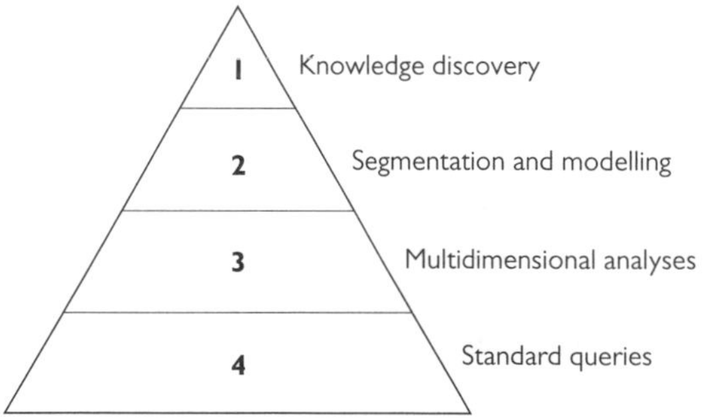

Fig. 6.4 The evolution of decision support by data warehousing (adapted from Dyché, 2000). Copyright 2002, Baseliine Consulting Group. From *e-Data* (Addison-Wesley, 2000), by Jill Dyche.

regardless of the physical location of the offices and workers. Consequently, the hardware used includes large computer systems and widespread networking. DWs at functional level (commonly known as data mart), serve a smaller user base for a particular function, for example providing statistical data on the percentage rise in property prices by area. Functional DWs run on smaller hardware platforms, for example a server; a number of functional DWs can work together to constitute a corporate DW.

Data warehousing facilitates decision support at four levels:

1 Routine queries.
2 More complex queries.
3 Modelling based on historical data.
4 Making prediction voluntarily, based on the models.

There is some misunderstanding about the role of data warehousing in CRM. It must be remembered that:

- Customer 'events' do not necessarily take place on-line. Therefore, the techniques used for tracking data need to include sources such as telephone calls and call centres.
- Data warehousing should be treated as part of a company's knowledge management infrastructure rather than a software tool. Managers must have an understanding of the role of data warehousing and how technology (hardware, software, networking and data) can be used to support CRM.

The term data mining (DM) has sometimes been used interchangeably with warehousing; DM involves mainly the top two levels of Dyché's model (Fig. 6.4) and actually is the process of analysing data to produce models of customer behaviour and make predictions for the future based on market trends. Some authors (Turban *et al.*, 2000) have explained data mining in terms of the process of 'mining' valuable 'ore' by intelligently probing available material. It involves probing data from any sources, for example directly from the Internet, organisational databases, intranet servers or a data warehouse.

The following are some of the tools used for data mining (Turban *et al.*, 2000):

- *Neural computing* – a machine learning approach which uses technology to copy the complicated way that the human brain learns and makes decisions. Neurones work in a very sophisticated way which allows the brain to not only retain a lot of information but also to use experiences to build up a set of rules which allows it to process data even when it is unclear and ambiguous to produce meaningful information.
- *Intelligent agents* – software tools that retrieve information by searching a networked environment by keywords and queries. They can also monitor user movements on the Internet, 'sense' their requirements, and provide assistance by filtering information (see case study on W H Smith later on in the chapter).
- *Association analysis* – also known as market basket analysis, this involves the use of a specialised set of algorithms that can analyse data from a database and produce statement of trends in the market. By studying changes in patterns of behaviour, it can make predictions for the future. This helps an organisation to reach the top level of the model in Fig. 6.4.

Data mining involves the analysis of data stored in a warehouse. The following tools can be used for it:

- neural computing
- intelligent agents
- association analysis.

The purpose of CRM is to understand how customers behave and how their behaviour affects a company. According to Dyché (2000: 53),

> Certain off-the-shelf CRM 'suite' products may turn out to be overkill, while industry-specific or functionally oriented CRM tools might not do enough. Many CRM vendors are naively pushing the technology as an alternative to data warehousing. It should instead be considered the point of integration.

The steps necessary for implementing successful CRM are:

- Creating a centralised DW.
- Developing expertise in the organisation to effect the implementation of the necessary technologies and their use.

- Choosing the CRM products (the hardware, software and operational tools for data warehousing and mining) suitable for the organisation's circumstances.
- Providing the management support necessary to introduce effective CRM processes.
- Utilising the models and predictions made by data warehousing tools to introduce changes in the business processes.
- Building an interface suitable for all personnel involved in gathering customer information.

CRM works on the basis of collecting information on customers. What problems do you think might arise from this practice?

One important element of CRM is an interface which enables customers to access information and services provided by the enterprise, as well as enabling employees to collect information on customers.

Customer interface

A customer interface is the frontend of a company's e-business. It is like the reception desk in an office building, it directs a customer to the right services, or a shopfront which represents the organisation's existence in the market. Just as the behaviour of the reception staff reflects the quality of a company's services and the window and internal layout of a shop reflects a seller's image, the content of the website is the doorway to on-line business and gives valuable information about the company. The design of the interface is therefore of vital importance for success in e-business.

Rayport and Jayworski (2001) used a framework of 7 Cs[4] to represent interface design. These are:

- *Context* – the ethos of the design. For example some organisations opt for a clean, understated and functional interface, while another might prefer a colourful and lively display aimed at young users.
- *Content* – the digital subject matter. This focuses on the features available on-line which includes the use of visual images and sound as well as the services available via the interface. Both of these contribute to a company's success in cyberspace. The objectives behind a well-designed site should be to give customers a pleasant experience while 'shopping' and provide them with value-added on-line services.
- *Community* – as described in chapter 4, users of e-business like to form communities. It is possible to create an interface which facilitates such community building by providing a forum for user-to-user contact. For example, the reviews of books and music sold on-line give readers a platform for exchanging views.
- *Customisation* – a website that can be personalised to customers' needs and preferences. This could be done by features which enable users to tailor a website to fit their own requirements. For example, by entering the details of a payee account once, a customer may be able to pay money into that account with the click of a button rather than having to enter the details every time. Customisation can also be done by the company, for example a website could

[4] Source: J. F. Rayport and B. J. Jaworski, *e-Commerce*, McGraw-Hill, 2001. Copyright © 2001 by Rayport and Jaworski. Reproduced with the permission of The McGraw-Hill Companies, Inc.

collect personal information submitted by a customer automatically and use it to target messages on appropriate products.
- *Communication* – the dialogue that develops between the customer and a site. This could be via targeted emails as described above, or by two-way communication between the user and the customer services. The latter is possible by the use of a call centre which enables a user to click a 'call me' button which links to a telephone number in the customer services or to a chat service which starts a 'live' text-based dialogue.
- *Connection* – a link to other sites. This could be a button that connects the user to a relevant service in another organisation, for example an airlines company providing a link to a hotel accommodation service. Connection to other sites can also come in the form of advertisement, such as a link to Amazon when searching for information on academic subjects.
- *Commerce* – the facility for shopping on-line. This is the most common feature for most dotcom companies and the quality of the interface is crucial for their survival.

The concepts (the Cs) in the above framework are not separate from each other. For example, the content and hence, the context of the website is decided on the basis of the company's philosophy; this in turn determines whether or not they support community building, and so on. Direct Line, the UK's successful telephone-based insurance company introduced jamjar.com, their new car sales business. They received over 500 orders in the first nine months by applying their understanding of customers (and by making the most of customers' brand awareness) into on-line operations. At the root of their success is the hard work they put in to creating the website, refining processes, listening to customers, and getting feedback (Bicknell, 2000). A well-designed interface combines these concepts so that they reinforce each other, and together, they support the business ethos.

The 7Cs concept of user interface design:

- Context: the ethos
- Content: the features
- Community: user-to-user communication
- Customisation: adjustability
- Communication: customer-to-site dialogue
- Connection: link to other sites
- Commerce: business processes.

Discuss the interface elements necessary in the following on-line companies: (a) a bookstore, (b) a luxury clothing vendor, (c) a restaurant booking service.

Technology plays an important part in the success of an interface. For example, a large number of text-based documents and database files supply the content of a website, along with stored images, audio files, streaming live video and audio and so on. Therefore, the interface needs to be integrated with the backend systems and applications and the company's communications infrastructure must support the systems within the company to link effectively with the Internet. Various technologies are in place to facilitate the development of an interface, we will come back to these later on in the chapter.

While CRM supports business processes by providing knowledge on customers, intranets and extranets attempt to support knowledge management by giving the whole organisation access to corporate resources. Their job is to make accurate, up-to-date and well-organised information available on-line to the desktops in a user-friendly format.

Find an example of an on-line company performing CRM successfully and analyse its strategies in relation to the above discussion.

Intranets

As described before, intranets use Internet technologies to present information to users within an organisation. It could be a corporate LAN used by employees within a limited

LIVERPOOL JOHN MOORES UNIVERSITY
LEARNING SERVICES

Mansfield Motors

Mansfield Motors sells Land Rover parts and accessories to customers around the world. By concentrating on creating a customer-friendly environment, Mansfield Motors has built up a successful, global mail order business in less than one year. Their objectives were to:

- Find a low cost method of expanding the business.
- Maintain the high quality, value-for-money service they have always provided.
- Create an informal, club-like manner in customer dealings.

They linked up with an e-commerce consultant who involved the whole sales team in the discussion of the web design. The design was kept small and simple at the beginning and changes were made one step at a time. This enabled Mansfield to measure the benefit of each change before investing further. Attention was also paid to the needs of the international audience; plain English, easy navigation techniques and speedy transaction were given the highest importance.

Mansfield used their website to create a virtual community. By providing a range of features, customers were encouraged to return regularly to the site to keep up to date with the latest Land Rover information. The friendly, approachable atmosphere of the site encourages visitors to participate, provide feedback and suggest content for the site, and to make personal contact with the garage for enquiries and professional advice about sales. Entering into dialogue with visitors helps break down some of the fear associated with purchasing products and services on-line and helps convert them from visitors into customers.

In addition to selling parts and accessories, the site provides a wealth of information about Land Rovers, a discussion board, advice column and classified adds. The feedback from visitors indicates that the club atmosphere is appreciated and the enthusiasm and professionalism of the team shows through. Statistical analysis of the website statistics consistently shows that, after the shop, the 'club' pages are the most popular.

The staff in the garage have struck up email relationships with regular customers, and even Gemma the garage dog receives regular emails from a fan club of visitors.

Email enquiries and Internet orders arrive for Mansfield from about 100 countries. Initially it took two hours to deal with these. The number of Internet enquiries has now grown to 150–200 a week and a new member of staff has been recruited specifically to deal with them. The conversion rate of enquiries to orders has doubled as people have come to trust the Mansfield brand. As the website has introduced international customers, an increasing number of emails and orders are received from non-English speaking countries such as Russia, Portugal and Brazil. In order to make them feel at home, a language expert is used to carry out translations and conduct the initial dialogue via email. Language is therefore no barrier to personalised customer relations. However, although the website offers secure credit card transactions, only around a third of customers pay for purchases over the Internet, which suggests that people are still wary of security on the web.

(Source: Hills, 1999. Copyright KPL E-business. Printed with permission.)

Questions

1. Describe Mansfield's on-line business strategies.
2. Discuss how the features described here fit in with the strategies discussed in this chapter.
3. To what extent does the website conform to the 7 Cs framework, and how do you imagine this affects its CRM processes?
4. How could the company move forward now? What changes can they make to gain further benefits?

geographical area or a WAN to cover larger distances, organised in the model of the Internet. An intranet connects a company's servers, databases, software platforms, backend systems and desktop applications (Fig. 6.5). It uses TCP/IP for secure data transmission and Internet-style browsing and searching tools for access to information. A firewall keeps it separate from the Internet and makes it available to employees of the organisation with the necessary access permission. The firewall can also be used to establish different levels of access to specific parts of the intranet. However, compatibility with the Internet enables an organisation to extend access to its intranet to business partners outside the organisations, thus creating an extranet.

The main objectives of an intranet are to:

- facilitate the widespread sharing of information and computing resources within an organisation
- create an infrastructure for extending the model to include trading partners outside the organisation
- present information on-line following the Internet model, thus making it compatible with e-commerce.

The most common contents of an intranet are corporate documents containing company policies, business procedures, manuals, product catalogues, employee data such as phone numbers, email addresses etc., minutes of meetings, and so on. Employees can use Internet-type browsing and searching facilities to find and download information. It also supports access to databases, interactive training materials, customer records, centralised documents, shared workflow systems such as a transaction processing application and groupware products. Finally, by giving customers access to the order-entry part of an intranet, it can be integrated with a company's e-commerce applications. Thus an intranet supports a virtual organisation in which people can get access to any resource they require from any physical location, and enables the organisation to:

The objectives of an intranet are to provide:

- facilities for sharing resources
- Internet-type interface for the acquisition of information
- communication with trading partners.

- save time by making information readily available regardless of users' locations
- provide quick and efficient customer service
- improve communication and knowledge sharing
- facilitate teamwork by allowing team members to stay in touch and share resources
- improve the speed, security and efficiency of knowledge sharing.

An Intranet plays a catalytic role in moving an organisation into the e-commerce arena.

> Intranets are [. . .] a necessary bridge to the world of external electronic commerce – a web, if you will, to the Web. . . . One great and important role provided by intranets is that the Internet standards they're based on are bound to provide a critical common denominator, enabling truly integrated enterprises around the world to establish compatible information formats.
>
> (Papows, 1999: 70)

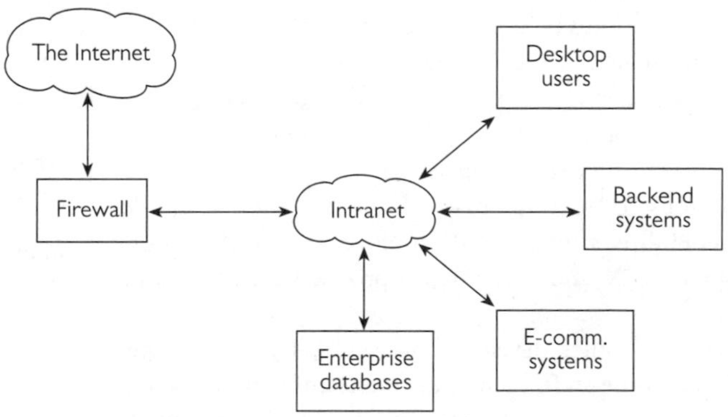

Fig. 6.5 The intranet architecture

A company's experience with an intranet prepares it for the use of an extranet and the Internet globally. Therefore, careful attention must be paid to a number of issues before an intranet is introduced by an organisation. This includes:

- *The usability of applications* – applications and documents available on an intranet must be easy to use and designed to simplify procedures.
- *The communications infrastructure* – this must be capable of handling the traffic created by a large number of employees accessing the network, without diminishing the speed or reliability of transmission.
- *The integration between systems* – an intranet cannot work unless the systems to be accessed are web-enabled and the databases, backend systems and desktop applications are fully integrated.
- *Security* – with increased access to enterprise-wide information, security is a crucial issue for an organisation. Measures in the form of password control and firewalls must be introduced to prevent improper access to the system and ensure that the procedure for selective access works as intended.
- *Employee skill* – an intranet is of little use if employees avoid using it. Lack of use also affects a company's competitive positioning by prohibiting it from making proper use of integrated technology for business purposes. The technical skill of employees and their motivation to use an intranet are important factors management must pay attention to.

An intranet must be:

- usable
- robust
- integrated
- secure
- appreciated by users through skill and motivation.

Find a company which is using an intranet. How does the intranet contribute to the company's knowledge management?

Groupware is one application of intranets that uses the philosophy of knowledge sharing and utilises the power of enterprise-wide networked communication to facilitate live collaboration between people in a virtual workspace.

Groupware

Introduced in 1984, groupware is the technical infrastructure behind the concept of computer supported co-operative work (CSCW). This advocated the use of communications network to enable people working in teams to share information. It utilised the proliferation of desktop PCs, corporate LANs and applications such as emails, electronic diaries and calendars and centralised databases to create a new form of decision support system. Conceptually, groupware appeared long before intranets, with the introduction of Lotus Notes – software which facilitated the collaborative use of a database of documents by a group of users via a LAN developed by the Lotus Corporation in 1984. This was the first step towards the establishment of 'collective intelligence' in an organisation; for the first time people working together, physically or virtually, were able to share information and make decisions collectively on-screen the way they would do sitting round a table. Electronics giant Philips, with 240,000 employees spread over more than 600 locations, has been using Lotus KM and collaborative products for some time (Adshead, 2001).

Groupware is software which provide resources for a team to work interactively, regardless of the physical location of individuals.

The concept of groupware accelerated other developments such as multi-tasking, access to a company network via PCs and the shift from a hierarchical decision-making model to a flatter, networked, cross-functional, and team-based model. Groupware also introduced the concept of on-line workflow management – '. . . the provision of electronic support for business processes previously accomplished by means of laborious manual procedures' (Papows, 1999: 26) – such as the production of a conference schedule to be agreed between a large number of people. Workflow defines the sequence of steps (procedures for checks, approvals etc.) necessary to complete a business process; groupware provides software tools to streamline those steps and perform them electronically. Although groupware worked on corporate LANs initially, Internet technologies have now made it possible to use it via intranets, extranets and VPNs. The following are some of the features available in groupware with special relevance to e-commerce:

- E-mails. Electronic messages are written using a client application such as Microsoft Outlook; the message is first sent to a mail server which transmits it via the network to the destination mail server. From here the message is sent to the mailbox of the receiver who can access it via a client server at that end. Emails are the oldest and most common vehicle for groupwork. A considerable amount of knowledge exchange has been done for a long time by the exchange of emails between colleagues. They are also an important tool for e-commerce as they create a forum for discussions and the exchange of information on customers and products, and they also function as a repository of knowledge when stored in a universal messaging platform (UPM). UPM is a technology that facilitates the storage of messages received in any format (telephone, email, pager etc.) in one mailbox and can be read using an email application. For example, a product called Unified MailCall by PhoneSoft allows the storage of voice mails in a Lotus Notes mailbox; users can retrieve messages by using either a telephone or a computer (Rajput, 2000). A standard known as Telephony Application Programming Interface (TAPI) allows the conversion between circuit switched voice (telephone) and IP packets (Internet data), thus facilitating unification.
- Web collaboration. This refers to the sharing of information over the web. Documents on the web can be passed on to others over the Internet or intranet and the two parties can discuss the documents together by displaying it on the screen. This can be used by sales people to demonstrate products to customers and documents such as product profiles and market statistics can be used within an organisation to discuss business plans.
- Notice boards. Electronic notice boards can be used to post messages for everyone on a system to view. This provides a convenient forum for the distribution of information and for the initiation of discussion by those interested. A version of this known as a whiteboard is used for sharing diagrams.
- Workflow management. Advanced software tools are included in groupware to illustrate workflow sequencing on-line and to enable collaboration on workflow arrangement. By using a company's communications links, they also allow the inclusion of external partners in the process. These methods can be used to implement applications such as a supply-chain management system for orders and deliveries, or to formalise the procedure for handling customer complaints, by integrating groupware with the company's backend systems.

Some groupware applications for knowledge sharing are:

- emails
- web collaboration
- message passing by notice boards
- workflow management.

How could a high street retail chain available in cities all over the world use groupware? How could this influence its knowledge management?

A knowledge management system that is vital for e-commerce, especially for the B2B arena, is extranet. By facilitating communication among users external as well as internal to the organisation, it provides a wider forum for knowledge sharing, and a bigger scope for groupware-based collaboration.

Extranets

Extranets are an extension of intranets; by connecting to each others' intranets companies can create virtual private networks to include suppliers, customers and related organisations. Using firewalls, the connected intranets can be given full or limited access to each other as appropriate. The connection may be made by tunnelling through the Internet thus creating a VPN between the organisations, or by using permanent leased lines which would improve speed and efficiency but would be expensive (Fig. 6.6).

The most important issues associated with the implementation of an extranet are:

- *Security* – the types of control discussed in connection with communication via the Internet are equally applicable to extranets. This includes measures for confidentiality, authentication, authorisation, integrity, availability and non-repudiation (chapter 5), especially when sensitive information or financial exchanges are carried out. This is done by the implementation of encryption technologies such as public key infrastructure, multi-level authentication, and audit trails capable of tracing the full history of transactions.
- *The choice of technology* – organisations face a number of technical decisions before implementing an extranet such as the choice of technology, their suppliers, the mode of connection etc. Amongst the decisions to be made are: whether to use a VPN or communicate through the Internet via an ISP; if the software necessary to run the system should be bought from a commercial manufacturer or developed in-house by using the web development technologies available; and the level of access control to be used for each user group.
- *Integration with the backend systems* – in order to provide effective communication, an infrastructure must be established to integrate

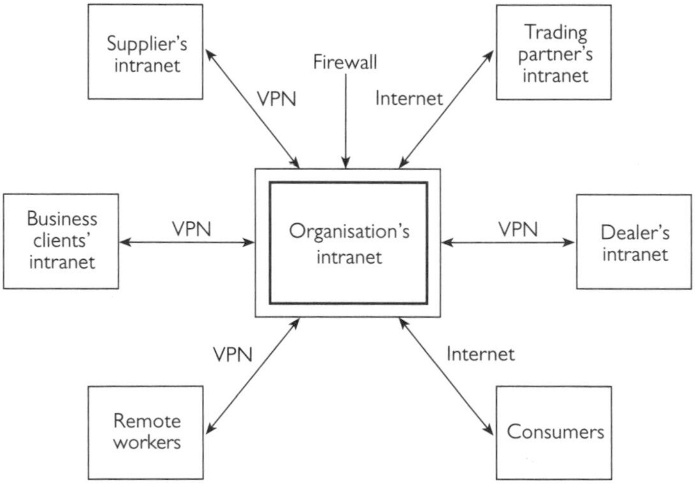

Fig. 6.6 Extranet architecture

applications with the enterprise databases, ERPs and all other backend sources of knowledge.

- *Responsibilities for implementation* – the organisation can use its own technical expertise to make the above decisions or the project can be outsourced. Many companies now offer services varying between interface development to the implementation of a complete service.
- *Management and maintenance* – an extranet is an important route for business transactions in e-commerce; careful attention must be paid to the establishment of an infrastructure for its management and maintenance. Issues such as communication with participating organisations about the services available over the extranet, types of access to different sections of the organisations, user interfaces, legal arrangements between organisations and the methods used to update applications and services must all be discussed at inter- and intra-organisational levels.

Because of its ability to facilitate easy and secure communication between organisations, extranets play a vital role in B2B e-commerce. By enabling business partners to collaborate with each other securely and speedily regardless of their physical location or time zone, extranets offer today's companies a reliable, inexpensive, interactive and global market. Furthermore, these facilities are not restricted to large organisations because small companies can gain the same advantage by connecting to the Internet via a firewall.

An extranet encompasses an organisation's trading partners in its network. Issues important in building an extranet are:

- security
- the choice of technology
- the integration of systems
- development and implementation strategies
- management and maintenance.

What are the advantages and disadvantages of the use of an extranet for knowledge distribution?

Users communicate with the applications and systems described above via websites, portals and applications software. The user interface for these systems provides the point of contact between a company, its employees and its customers. Creating an interface requires an understanding of the technologies behind their development and the philosophy underlying the design of the contents.

INTERFACE DEVELOPMENT FOR KNOWLEDGE MANAGEMENT

A wide variety of technologies is used to facilitate the acquisition and distribution of information from the systems and repositories mentioned above. These are tools which link users to the sources of knowledge. For example, browsers such as Netscape or Microsoft Explorer provide an interface to the Internet, search engines such as Yahoo! and Alta Vista support the search for documents in cyberspace and communications software such as MS Windows MediaPlayer download music and streaming video data. Today's ISPs often provide a portal service which incorporates all these facilities as well as a gateway to the Internet.

The technologies for interface building

The development of an interface is based on standard generalised markup language (SGML), a standard for Web development languages such as HTML and XML introduced by the ISO. Markup is a concept which represents the use of special characters (tags) to define output; for example, the text enclosed within the tags <B> and </B> is to be

A Recipe for Success

A Recipe for Success, a business services consultancy, set up an extranet that would prove vital not only for their own company but other businesses as well. Their primary objective was to use technology to aid collaboration between teams located in up to 12 different locations, all working different hours and to create a virtual area where everyone could trace the progress of a particular project. Created by the small company of 15 already highly IT-literate people – eschewing the need to hire new staff or buy in expertise – the extranet promoted and necessitated collaborative work and knowledge sharing.

The extranet established a system whereby staff, partners and customers could manage and share both general expertise and project-specific knowledge, making it unnecessary to send large file attachments or worry about potential or established clients not receiving vital information. For each project, clients and other users can post informal messages on a discussion board, view designs, monitor the progress being made and access relevant documentation.

A Recipe for Success decided that in order to gauge the success of the project, they must be able to make a statistical analysis of users' activity and glean who is failing to explore the system's features. They could then target those groups or individuals, examine the reasons for their under-use of the system and take appropriate action by providing extra training, more relevant information or clearer site navigation and guidance. This monitoring capability also works to the company's advantage commercially, allowing them to keep track of clients' preferences, habits and needs, thereby providing opportunities for the targeted marketing and advertisement of new products and services.

A primary objective was to create a system capable of satisfying future technological developments. While initial needs were met by the use of an Access database hosted by Vservers.com and accessed from the website using Active Server pages, thus avoiding the burden of managing the web site in-house, this may not always be the case. Given the current set-up, incoming and newly created emails cannot both be saved immediately, creating an information bank which can be accessed in the long term. Instead, they must be saved manually into the shared Vservers server. If A Recipe for Success were to buy their own server they could explore the possibility of intelligent content-based deduction techniques which sorts mail into certain categories: emails to be deleted as soon as they have been read; emails to be kept for the duration of a project; and emails which contain information that will remain valuable in the longer term. However, this process could never be fully automated and would require human assistance and greater effort by users.

Another future plan is to enable key summary information to be accessed via Palm Pilots synchronised with a PC or another network-enabled device, or even via dial-up mobile connections.

(Adopted from Hunter, 2001, with permission from Reed Business Information Ltd.)

Questions

1. Summarise the knowledge management aspects of the system implemented by A Recipe for Success.
2. What business benefits does the system provide the company?
3. Discuss the security needs of such a company and how A Recipe for Success has dealt with it. Is there more they ought to do?
4. Discuss how the system contributes to the company's customer relationship management.
5. Discuss the future potential of a system such as this, especially in the light of a more varied business environment and likely developments in technology.

emboldened. The standards also facilitate searching for documents linked by text the same way files in a database can be linked and searched by a query language. HTML was the first web development language; it was later updated with D(dynamic)HTML which provides improved facilities for layout and varieties of display. X(eXtensible)ML is a further update that supports better search facilities. There are other variations of markup languages such as XSL (extensible style language) to support enhanced styling of an interface, WML (wireless markup language) which conforms to XML and supports wireless browsing, and so on. Developed by Sun Microsystems, Java is an object-oriented language initially introduced to create pages on the Internet, but now it has established its position firmly as a tool for developing all types of application. At the route of its popularity are its ability to run on any computer hardware and software platform and its use of OOP techniques. Because of its portability, today's database applications, which are increasingly dependent on Internet technologies, can utilise Java's special qualities very effectively. Other technologies that support interface design and integration include the file formats for audio and video files to be used with a webpage (GIF, JPEG, MPEG etc.), standards for virtual reality applications on the web (VRML) and so on.

Hypertext markup language (HTML)

An industry body called the World Wide Web Consortium (W3C) is in charge of developing a common standard for HTML. It is run jointly by the MIT (Massachusetts Institute of Technology), Laboratory for Computer Science, the National Institute for Research in Computer Science and Automation in France (on behalf of Europe), and Keio University in Japan (on behalf of Asia) with members from over 150 organisations worldwide (Dodd, 1998). They are responsible for preparing the initial draft, getting feedback from members and producing a final acceptable standard. They are also responsible for standardising any technology related to the WWW, for example managing the HTTP standard and the internationalisation of the HTML standard.

Behind all webpages there is a document written in HTML or one of its extensions with tags which define how the content of the page should be displayed.[5] As the sample page demonstrates (Fig. 6.7), the tags (HEAD, P, H1, BODY etc.) come in pairs to switch (toggle) an action on and off. HTML also defines how the page and the text are to be presented by using attributes such as font size, colour, print enhancement (e.g. <I> . . . </I> to print the text in italics) etc. The sample shows only a few of the large number of attributes available for defining the characteristics of a page; amongst these are: a wide variety of colour, background design, print enhancements, font sizes, alignment of text, heading styles, document style and layout. It is also possible to include tables, lists, files of various formats (pictures, graphics, music etc.), frames to create a number of windows in a document, and so on. Above all, tags can be used to link to other documents (<HREF>) on disk or on the Internet; documents linked can be another page, an image, music, video clip and so on. No matter how ambitious and colourful, every website is a document which defines the characteristics in the same way as shown in Fig. 6.7. However, different versions of HTML have been introduced to improve the scope for creating webpages with richer features and enable users to link them to different types of data format. We will describe a few of those briefly below.

W3C is in charge of creating a standard for HTML. HTML works by defining the attributes for the pages of a document and the links to other documents on the web.

Discuss how HTML changed the concept of information retrieval.

[5] Although technology has moved on from the initial version of HTML, the principle behind web design by content definition is basically the same.

Dynamic HTML (DHTML)

Following the convention of desktop publishing packages, DHTML documents enable users to create a style sheet which defines the layout and presentation of a document. Thus a style sheet may opt for certain background colour, font, headings and subheadings in different sizes and fonts etc. and a document attached to it adopts those specifications. No standard has yet been set for DHTML but W3C has now recommended a set of styles called cascading style sheets for use with web documents.

Virtual reality modelling language (VRML)

A VRML file defines a 3D model using objects which can be linked to a document. For example, a library can be represented by using VRML which uses graphics, animation and navigation through the objects to create an illusion of actually moving along the shelves and handling books. This can be linked to the website of a university to provide a trip through its library in virtual reality.

DHTML and VRML are extensions of HTML. DHTML enables users to create style sheets, while VRML supports the use of virtual reality applications.

XML and XSL

Whereas an HTML document defines how a page should look, XML (eXtensible Markup Language) concerns itself with what is in the document and defines how the information should be organised. In HTML a user uses a set of predetermined tags while in XML the user creates the tags. For example, a tag called <ITEMS> may be created with further tags for each type of product (room, shelf, book); properties can also be defined for each type. Thus, a set of tags can be defined for an organisation's products and parts and they can then be used repeatedly. XSL (eXtensible Style Language) uses a set of rules to display the XML tags, thus acting as the style sheet for the XML document. XSL also enables XML data

```
<HTML>

<HEAD>
<TITLE>E-Commerce</TITLE>
</HEAD>

<BODY BGCOLOR="Blue"TEXT="Black">
<H1>Designing an Interface</H1>
<P>
<FONT SIZE=1>
<I>The development of an interface is based on SGML,
a standard developed by the ISO which outlines the rules
to be followed by the programming languages such as HTML
and XML.</I>
</P>

<P>
<A HREF="http://www.mcgraw-hill.co.uk">The McGRAw-Hill
Companies</A>
<P>

<P>
<IMG SRC="MCG.gif">
<P>

<BODY>

</HTML>
```

Fig. 6.7 A simple HTML document

to be viewed in different formats and by different criteria similar to the way a database query language allows data to be extracted by user-defined criteria.

Because of their compatibility with structures of databases, XML and XSL lend themselves automatically to use with search through documents held in Net servers. The use of tags rather than pages of text also makes the job of search engines easier. This method of web design helps companies to create one repository of XML tags and thus share information between websites, databases and backend systems. Accordingly, different industries are now creating dictionaries of tag definitions specific to their needs in order to share XML tags with other organisations in their sector. For example, PricewaterhouseCoopers has recently proposed FpML, a dictionary to standardise XML tags for foreign currency exchange and other financial transactions (Roche, 2000).

While HTML uses pre-defined tags, XML works by creating the tags itself. XSL provides the style sheet for XML.

The above techniques do not allow interactivity between a website and its users. They provide links which enable a user to move between sites but there are no facilities for the browser to process users' actions. There is also limited scope for interactivity between systems due to limited portability between different hardware and software platforms. The following developments in programming languages and standards attempt to rectify those weaknesses.

Java

Java is an object-oriented programming language suitable for running in any Windows-based environment. Additionally, Java applets, programs written to interact with a web browser, can be used with Internet-based applications. Java is also platform-independent. Most programming languages need to be compiled – translated into machine language – before they can be used. A program for a particular type of machine can only be translated by a compiler tailored to that machine type. This prohibits a program written for one hardware and software platform to be used on another. Java works on a different philosophy; any computer environment installed with a program called Java Virtual Machine (VM) can run Java, thus making it a completely portable language. Normally, a browser holds a Java VM which enables it to execute any applications written in Java.

Java uses object-oriented technology to create program segments called applets. Files holding applets are called by an HTML document.

Java program segments (called applets) can be written and saved; these can then be used in an HTML document using an <APPLET> . . . </APPLET> tag. Applets can be written to create graphics and access a network. They are not included in an HTML document, only references to the files holding the applets are made by the use of tags. When a browser runs the HTML document it downloads the files and runs the applets. Since the VM runs applets rather than allowing Java to interact with a browser, it acts as a screen between applets and network resources. Any interaction with hardware resources is handled by the VM which provides improved security for the system.

However, Java's inability to interact with desktop resources causes inconvenience as it prohibits an applet from printing or from saving interim results of web-based analysis. Also, because of the slowness of the Internet, downloading applets takes a long time, thus limiting its utility for e-commerce. Although theoretically Java is portable, in reality this does not always work because of the differences between the versions of VMs produced by different software vendors. Some of these problems were eliminated by the use of scripting languages.

Scripting languages

Java can access a network and draw graphics but cannot handle a browser. Scripting refers to a programming language that can interact with a browser but cannot access a network or draw graphics. In Netscape's JavaScript (or Microsoft's JScript), program statements are written within an HTML document (rather than entering applet tags as in Java) thus allowing better interactivity with a webpage.

Java and its associated scripting languages do not only facilitate the development of interactive web pages, they also enable software vendors to create desktop applications such as wordprocessing and spreadsheets for web servers, to be used from a browser program. Threatened by the possibility of a consequent disruption in their monopoly in the applications market, Microsoft introduced ActiveX and VBScript (Visual Basic Script) to take the place of Java and JavaScript respectively for their browser called Internet Explorer. These are based on technologies known as Active Server Page (ASP) which can keep track of pages containing scripts and programs on a web server. When included in an HTML document it can access those pages and pass them on to the browser. JSP (Java Server Pages) is a similar technology for programs written in Java. Read the book by Flanagan and Shafer (1998) for further information on developments related to Java. Rajput (2000) also covers all these topics briefly.

Scripting refers to program statements written in an HTML document designed to interact with a browser. They can also be used to create desktop applications.

The above techniques provide static access to the web; links in the form of a URL are inserted via a tag in a document to connect them to other webpages. They can display information added to a document in advance but cannot give access to real-time information. This can be facilitated by the use of a protocol known as common gateway interface (CGI).

Investigate the history of the use of HTTP and object-oriented programming in web development, and compare their contributions in this field.

CGI

CGI is a standard application programming interface (API) – a software tool that provides a way for one form of software to integrate with another. CGI defines a programming method that provides communication between web servers and databases. A user includes a URL for a CGI program designed to access a database in an HTML document. The web server links to the CGI program which, in turn, retrieves the desired data from the database and puts it in the server for the HTML document to access. This way the Internet can be used to make queries on products and services which are constantly updated. CGI programs are also useful for middleware applications because of their ability to search a backend database. However, they are only suitable for small-scale e-commerce applications because they can slow the system down considerably. FastCGI (a faster version of CGI) and some proprietary APIs can be used for improved performance. Another factor that affects speed and performance is the format of files linked by a document. A large variety of file formats is available for data containing graphics, audio, video, animation, streaming video and so on. Different formats offer different choices of features and degrees of performance which must be taken into consideration when using them for access on the Internet. See Rajput (2000) for further details on these topics.

CGI is a standard for writing programs capable of retrieving information from web servers and databases. This makes it possible to access real-time information from the Internet.

Speed and performance of a webpage from a technical point of view must be complemented by the usability of the interface. Interface design is an important aspect of an area of research known as human computer interaction (HCI); it attempts to address the issues that contribute to the level of user experience during on-line transactions. This should be performed as a part of the process of systems analysis and design (SAD), one of the most important responsibilities carried out by those working in business and IT. Although a very important subject, the discussion of SAD is outside the scope of this book; here, we will only concern ourselves with the issues surrounding interface design.

Creating user effective user interfaces requires specialist technical knowledge, design sense and systems development experience. Although some companies have in-house expertise, a large number of organisations opt for commercially developed websites. This may be part of an outsourced project in which all or some elements of the development, implementation and management of e-commerce are contracted out; or a company can hire a web-design house which specialises in the design of interfaces. Which option an organisation chooses depends on their business strategies and circumstances. We will discuss this further in the consequences section of the book.

An effective user interface

A user interface is the most crucial element of making knowledge management systems work together and attracting users to the facilities. The technologies discussed above contribute to the making of efficient interfaces; but the effectiveness of an interface as a tool for knowledge distribution relies on its utilisation.

Expert knowledge in the technologies described in this chapter is naturally an important requirement for creating a good interface. Although it is not easy to build up expertise, in many ways the process is a 'straight foreword' one. Yet, a knowledge management system (KMS) that is not used fully is a failed system; no matter how technically efficient, if it is not accepted by its intended users then it fails to contribute to a competitive advantage. This is not only true for KMS but for any system implemented in an organisation. Therefore the contribution of users in the development process is crucial for a KMS which endeavours to enable its users to participate in the communication of knowledge in the organisation.

The following approaches to interface development have been suggested by those involved in the research of human computer interaction (HCI) (Sutcliffe, 1995):

- *User participative design* users should be actively involved in the process of design and decision making. This intends to narrow the gap between computer specialists and users.
- *User-centred design* – the design should be driven by the needs of the users and not by the functional requirements or the technical resources of the company.
- *Iterative design* – the interface should be designed in stages by developing prototypes and refining them in cycles; feedback from users at each stage can be used to make improvements.

A KM interface, like all other IT systems, must be acceptable to its users. This necessitates user participation in the design and implementation of the system.

The above approaches are not mutually exclusive; any one or a combination of them can be used to create an interface which suits the organisation and fulfils its role as a medium for knowledge management. Together they contribute to the general philosophy of user-centred systems development.

The characteristics of an effective interface for knowledge management are (Quinn *et al.*, 1997):

- Complete integration between databases, search engines, on-line operations and business processes. This is achieved by proper use of links between the interacting elements in a way that achieves a fast and efficient transfer of information. A well-integrated system should be capable of extracting knowledge from all sources anywhere in cyberspace by upstreaming and downstreaming information between knowledge bases.
- Transparency. The technical complexity of the interface should be hidden from its users by means of user-friendly prompts and graphical representations.

- Customisation of learning for individual users. Rather than bombarding users with an enormous array of information, properly programmed KM architecture manages to access information from the decentralised systems, learn from it, and make this knowledge available to users in a way that is useful to them.
- Quality of information. Information must be secure, relevant and quickly accessible.

An interface suited to knowledge management is:

- integrated
- transparent
- customised
- reliable.

In May 1999, W3C released the initial version of a document called Web Content Accessibility Guidelines (see www.w3.org/WAI) which made recommendations for the design of effective web interfaces.

We discussed the criteria for an effective customer interface earlier on in the chapter, and those for knowledge distribution in this section. What special qualities do each of them need in order to serve their respective user base?

One of the methods recommended by some authors as a vehicle for effective knowledge management is the use of an enterprise portal. It provides a focal point for accessing and managing all sources of information and knowledge in an organisation. Organisations can use a portal as the interface for applications accessible via their extranets. These can be customised to provide buttons and links to services specific to certain user groups, for example there may be a special link to the marketing department. Portals can also be used within an organisation to support groupware, an intranet or an ERP system. '. . . the enterprise portal is doing for knowledge management and information access what the Web-browser has done for the user interface in providing a standard model for the industry to work around' (Hunter, 2001: 60).

Enterprise portals provide an all-encompassing interface for knowledge distribution. They must be:

- personalised
- well managed
- useful to individuals as well as groups.

However, although sound as a concept, a portal fails to deliver unless it provides access to the right information resources, which in turn are kept up to date, and are used as a tool for knowledge acquisition. The characteristics of a good enterprise portal are (Hunter, 2000):

- *Personalisation* – this can be achieved by giving users a unique homepage with links to information they need. In order to do so, the portal should also be able to monitor user actions so as to deliver relevant information that users may not have asked for. This requires a knowledge management infrastructure that is capable of matching user activities with information resources, which in turn relies on its regular use.
- *Content management* – it is vital that information available via a portal is useful. This involves connecting all information sources to the portal, updating them and ensuring that the information provided is complete. This requires that users are involved both as consumers and maintainers of enterprise portals.
- *Workgroup support* – users must be able to use their own portal to reach their workgroup or project portal in order to share information. Smaller organisations can use the facilities of personalisation provided by public portals such as Yahoo! to create a homepage and work in groups. Larger organisations must build the features themselves that would give each user a personal homepage but also enable them to group websites together, if necessary.

In 1998, the UK digital TV company OnDigital (now known as ITV Digital) set up a portal to support the helpdesk staff. It gives the staff fast access to customer records thus allowing them to deal with customer calls quickly. The portal also gives customers access to selective areas so that they can browse databases of known faults and solutions and download upgrades themselves.

Like all other e-commerce applications, the development of an enterprise portal can also be outsourced. Alternatively, the ASP (application service provider) model can be used to 'buy' a solution; some ASP providers also supply consultancy and training services.

It is obvious that organisations benefit enormously from a knowledge management infrastructure; however, such systems have not yet had a transformative effect. The technical and strategic discussions in this and the previous chapter give some idea of the complexity involved in building an infrastructure. Papows (1999) listed the following reasons for the failure of organisations to implement an effective KMI:

- *Company size* – large organisations need a KMI more than the smaller ones. However, the size of an organisation also makes the job of making knowledge available to all its users difficult.
- *Volume of information* – if a system is overloaded with information it loses its value and puts users off. Some companies use software tools such as moderators, editors or filters to address the problem.
- *Lack of incentive* – the tendency of some people to hoard knowledge can disrupt a company's efforts to capture and distribute knowledge. Strong leadership and a commitment to cultural change is required to improve incentives for the sharing of knowledge.
- *Lack of criteria for the measurement of benefits* – measuring the value of knowledge management is difficult. Often the benefit is long term and, in a culture of measuring benefits of investment in IT on a tangible, short-term basis, justifying the use of resources in knowledge management can be difficult.
- *Lack of expertise* – the knowledge and experience required to perform the activities associated with knowledge management can be a serious barrier to the process.
- *Rapid obsolescence* – Knowledge bases can become obsolete very quickly and need to be updated continually.

A KMI often fails because of:

- company size
- information overload
- hoarding of knowledge
- intangibility of benefits
- lack of expertise
- obsolescence of information.

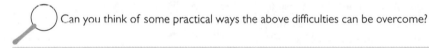

Can you think of some practical ways the above difficulties can be overcome?

Companies need to handle these difficulties in the same way that they address all other e-business challenges: by linking knowledge management with their strategic business activities. They must address knowledge management issues as a part of their overall business decision-making process, and utilise technical, human and organisational resources to meet the challenges.

SUMMARY

An information management infrastructure supports the continuous process of transforming data and information into organisational knowledge and distributing it throughout the organisation. It provides a company with a digital nervous system: a combination of hardware and software, clearly distinguishable from a network of computers, designed to provide knowledge workers with accurate, immediate and rich information, and thus the ability to survive in e-commerce. Building an IMI involves

Net Angel at W H Smith

The 'Net Angel' feature that forms part of W H Smith's on-line unit has been created by UK Software company Meltingpoint. On the W H Smith website, this software application – called Mirazo – tracks users' Internet sessions and, if users should access competitors' sites, strategically places messages there promoting W H Smith's superior pricing and product schemes. Normally, customers search around for websites; here a website moves around its customers.

To take advantage of Mirazo software, visitors to www.whsmith.co.uk must register and, after providing basic demographic details, can download the 500k Net Angel application, which 'sleeps' unobtrusively in the background whenever they go on-line. If a user then accesses a website that had been targeted by W H Smith – usually the site of a competitor in the retail market – the application monitors the pages being read and Meltingpoint's server instigates a rules-based system to assess whether Net Angel should respond. If a page contains information about a product which W H Smith is selling at a lower price, the application might pop up a floating window to alert the user of this, inviting them to go to the relevant W H Smith sales page. When Net Angel is activated, a Dynamic HTML window no bigger than a business card floats in front of the Web browser on the screen. The window contains text, links and images and can be quickly turned off if the message is irrelevant or unwelcome.

At the back end, the Net Angel client – an ActiveX control – intercepts the URL requests entered by the user in real time and sends them to the host NT server cluster at Meltingpoint's offices. The URL is checked against a database of 30 competitor sites programmed in by W H Smith. If the URL is among these sites, the software springs into action at the server end. Meltingpoint sends Mirazo to the page the user is reading and grabs the content from the page. Having already analysed and stored the HTML structure of the pages of all the targeted sites in a configuration file, Mirazo can consult the file and discover which pieces of the user's page contain which type of content. Configuration files are also updated.

For example, if the user is viewing information about the book *Lord of the Flies* on Amazon's web site, Meltingpoint will know which individual sections of the page feature the price of the book, information on availability and book reviews.

Meltingpoint then places relevant 'answering' information into a W H Smith-designed template which could feature a message alerting the user to the fact that the same book can be bought more cheaply on the W H Smith site, suggestions of other books by the same author and hyperlinks to relevant reviews of them on the W H Smith website, or information about how to buy the video of the book. This completed template then pops up on the user's screen. The whole process should only take a few seconds.

(Adapted from Harvey, 2000 with permission from Reed Business Information Ltd.)

Questions

1 Summarise the technical features supporting Net Angel.
2 How does this case study demonstrate the importance of dynamic data capture?
3 With the help of further research, explain the role of an intelligent agent.
4 Discuss the implication of such a system for customers. Would you like to encourage similar developments as a user?
5 How does the above system affect other organisations' business environment and how could they respond to it?

the use of a number of systems which transfer data into information, to work, and eventually to action. This must function for all four levels of a market-facing organisation: individual, team, enterprise and cyberspace. Creating such an infrastructure requires identifying information sources, capturing knowledge and establishing a retrieval mechanism. The main method used to capture knowledge is to create a database: an integrated filing system capable of providing query-based interrogation by users. The information systems commonly used for knowledge management are enterprise resource management (ERP), customer relationship management (CRM), intranets, extranets and groupware. These technologies facilitate access to the Internet for users and the visibility in cyberspace for organisations with the help of directory services, data warehousing (DW), data mining, middleware, effective user interfaces and so on.

Middleware is an essential software to ensure seamless integration between systems within an organisation and between trading partners. B2B e-commerce requires real-time applications integration at data and process levels. CORBA supported by the Object Management Group, and Microsoft's Component Object Model (COM) are two well-known middleware products.

CRM is particularly important for e-commerce because it is designed to collect information from all possible sources by registering every customer 'event' and use it to improve customer relationship. It does this with the support of a DW which is a repository of historical data extracted from all corporate systems and made accessible to business users. A DW supports decision making through an evolutionary process of standard queries, multidimensional analyses, segmentation and modelling and knowledge discovery. Data mines help the modelling and knowledge discovery parts of the process by analysing the data captured in a DW. Implementing CRM requires careful planning at technical as well as managerial levels of an organisation.

Intranets, groupware and extranets provide users in an organisation with interfaces for acquiring, distributing and sharing knowledge and then collaborating with business partners on the basis of what they have learnt regardless of their physical locations. These systems can make a major contribution to a company's information and knowledge infrastructure; their development and implementation require careful attention to details such as the availability of technical skill, maintenance procedures, the establishment of a communications infrastructure, and so on.

At the forefront of a knowledge distribution system is the web interface; it should be built following the framework of 7 Cs: context, content, community, customisation, communication, connection and commerce. It should create an interface that gives an efficient, flexible, personalised and integrated customer service and which also conveys the company's business philosophy. It is the doorway to a company's knowledge distribution mechanism. A number of techniques are available for interface development including various markup languages and object-oriented programming methods. They range from HTML, the oldest technology for the development of hyperlinked documents, through XML, an extension of the former technology with added flexibility, to Java, using object-oriented programming technologies and providing machine independence and better interaction with Internet-based application, and to CGI for support with dynamic data access. Building an interface is part of the process of systems analysis and design and should therefore follow the trend of user-centred design in systems development. An effective interface for knowledge management needs to be supported by full integration between systems and should be integrated, transparent, customised and reliable. Enterprise portals are an effective vehicle for knowledge sharing.

Managers attempting to build an information and knowledge management infrastructure face a number of challenges according to the size of the company, the amount of information to be managed, a lack of understanding by users and managers, opposing culture and the lack of expertise. We will discuss the operational infrastructure required to resolve such problems and to support e-commerce in the following chapter.

Revision Questions

1 Explain what is meant by an information management infrastructure.
2 Using examples of business activities, explain clearly the concept of a digital nervous system.
3 What are the main activities involved in creating an information management infrastructure? How does each of them facilitate information management processes?
4 What are the differences between traditional computer systems and database systems? How can a database contribute to improved knowledge acquisition and sharing?
5 Discuss the contribution of a database to a company's information systems in today's environment.
6 Describe different types of DBMSs and their relative strengths and weaknesses.
7 Discuss the function of ERP in knowledge management.
8 How does CRM relate to knowledge management?
9 Describe the concept of a data warehouse. How does it contribute to CRM?
10 Describe the four levels of decision support by data warehousing and their inter-relationship.
11 Explain the function of a data mine and its relationship with CRM. How does this relate to the model in Fig. 6.4?
12 Discuss the importance of (a) directory services, and (b) middleware in enhancing a company's e-commerce services.
13 What special qualities are required for B2B middleware solutions?
14 Discuss the role of an intranet in knowledge management. What qualities should an intranet have for it to be a useful tool for knowledge management?
15 How do groupware applications contribute to knowledge management?
16 How does an extranet enrich knowledge management?
17 Why is a user interface important for e-commerce?
18 How does the 7 Cs framework describe the ethos of interface design? Explain using examples of real-life websites.
19 Describe the main features of: HTML, DHTML, VRML, XML, XSL and Java. Explain the differences between the ways they contribute to the development of a webpage.
20 Explain the differences between Java and a scripting language.
21 Explain the importance of dynamic information retrieval for knowledge management.
22 Why is user participation important for building an information and knowledge management infrastructure?
23 Discuss how (a) an enterprise portal, and (b) an industry portal help knowledge management.
24 Discuss the problems associated with building an information and knowledge management infrastructure.

Discussion Questions

1 Customer relationship management is one of the most important activities for businesses in cyberspace. Discuss the respective contribution of different technological concepts supporting CRM. Which issues do managers need to address in each case in order to achieve the maximum benefit?
2 Discuss how an organisation should deal with the needs of its customers as well as its employees in the way it plans its information management infrastructure?

Bibliography

Adshead, A., Lotus completes KM jigsaw, *Computer Weekly*, 25 January, 2001.

Applegate, L. and Wishart, N. A., *Frito-Lay, Inc.: A Strategic Transition*, Harvard Business School, 9-190-071, 24 February, 1993.

Beynon-Davies, P., *Information Systems Development: An Introduction to Information Systems Development*, Macmillan Press Ltd, Basingstoke, 2000.

Bicknell, D., jamjars on the highway, *Computer Weekly, e-business review*, October, 2000, p. 22.

Bradbury, D., Win business with Web content, *Computer Weekly*, 7 December, 2000, p. 92.

Cohan, P. S., *Net Profit: How to Invest and Compete in the Real World of Internet Business*, Jossey-Bass, San Francisco, 1999.

Davenport, T. H., Putting the enterprise into the enterprise system, *Harvard Business Review*, Reprint 98401, July–August, 1998, pp. 121–131.

Dodd, A. Z., *The Essential Guide to Telecommunications*, Prentice Hall, New Jersey, 1998.

Dyché, J., *e-Data: Turning Data into Information with Data Warehousing*, Addison-Wesley, Reading, Massachusetts, 2000.

Escalle, C. X. and Cotteleer, M. J., *Enterprise Resource Planning*, Harvard Business School, 9-699-020, 11 February, 1999.

Flanagan, D. and Shafer, D., *JavaScript: The Definitive Guide*, O'Reilley, Sebastopol, California, 1998.

Gates, B., *Business @ the Speed of Thought: Succeeding in the Digital Economy*, Penguin Books, London, 1999.

Harvey, F., Angel guides the customers, *Computer Weekly*, 14 December, 2000.

Hills, T., *A Recipe for Success: Mansfield Motors; E-business – Best practice for SMEs and PLCs*, Published by KPL in association with e-centre^{UK}, 1999, p. 49.

Hunter, P., Doing the knowledge, *Computer Weekly*, 26 October, 2000, p. 58.

Hunter, P., Knowledge-sharing to tickle those tastebuds, *Computer Weekly*, 1 March, 2001.

Laudon, K. C. and Laudon, J. P., *Management Information Systems: Organisations and Technology in the Networked Enterprise*, Prentice Hall, New Jersey, 2000.

Linthicum, D. S., Application integration for real-time B2B, *e-Business Advisor*, September, 2000, p. 20.

Papows, J., *Enterprise.com: Market Leadership in the Information Age*, Nicholas Brealey, London, 1999.

Quinn, J. B., Baruch, J. J. and Zien, K. A., *Innovation Explosion: Using Intellect and Software to Revolutionize Growth Strategies*, The Free Press, New York, 1997.

Rajput, W. E., *E-Commerce Systems Architecture and Applications*, Artech House, Boston, 2000.

Rayport, J. F. and Jaworski, B. J., *e-Commerce*, McGraw-Hill, New York, 2001.

Roche, E., *Explaining XML*, Harvard Business School, F00403, 2000.

Sutcliffe, A. G., *Human–Computer Interaction*, Macmillan, Basingstoke, 1995.

Turban, E., Lee, J., King, D. and Chung, H. M., *Electronic Commerce: A Managerial Perspective*, Prentice Hall, New Jersey, 2000.

Operational Infrastructure for E-Commerce

Chapter Seven

Objectives

By the end of this chapter you should have an understanding of:

- Business processes in the digital economy.
- The components of an operational infrastructure for e-commerce.
- The management challenges of the implementation of e-commerce.

INTRODUCTION

The introduction of e-commerce involves the use of Internet technologies to develop an infrastructure enabling a company to share its information resources with business partners and customers locally and globally, provide improved services and, in turn, achieve a competitive advantage. This requires an architecture comprising three main components: a communications infrastructure to support the reliable transfer of data; an information infrastructure to facilitate the sharing of organisational knowledge; and an operational infrastructure to underpin the processes appropriate for today's virtual, global, and dynamic business environment. In the previous two chapters we covered the first two elements of this model and we introduced the concept of an operational infrastructure; here we will discuss its nature and explore how it contributes to an overall business model.

The survival of an enterprise in the digital economy depends on its ability to take advantage of the opportunities offered by the Internet as well as to withstand the threats coming from customers and companies empowered by the advances in electronic technologies. An organisation needs to build an efficient framework capable of supporting the business activities that contribute to its strategic goals and the successful delivery of its promises to customers. In this chapter we will describe these activities and their relevance to on-line businesses.

CHALLENGES FOR ORGANISATIONS IN THE GLOBAL MARKET

Porter's competitive advantage model (chapter 4) demonstrates the uncertainty and competitive nature of the environment within which organisations in the Internet age have to function. On the one hand the environment presents them with new opportunities opened by a global marketplace in which all companies can operate at an almost equal level regardless of size and location; on the other, these opportunities pose a threat as new, smaller companies with no history in the off-line world enter into competition by providing alternative services and products.

The electronic age forces businesses to re-examine their strategies in order to (a) take advantage of the communications infrastructure provided by the Internet, and (b) cope with the uncertainty created by a global marketplace. In order to participate in e-commerce, companies are reviewing their goals, re-inventing business processes and introducing new methodologies in the light of the opportunities and challenges presented to them. This involves creating an operational infrastructure that is capable of supporting the activities associated with their new venture.

The activities most affected by e-commerce are:

- supply-chain management
- procurement
- the payment infrastructure
- delivery and logistics
- the legal framework for global distribution
- marketing.

Hoque (2000) described a company's transformation in the Internet age as an evolutionary process of four phases: brochureware, e-commerce, e-business, and finally, e-enterprise. The brochureware stage started in the middle of the 1990s (Fig. 7.1) when a large number of companies introduced a website which was no more than an electronic catalogue (see chapter 1). In the last five years some companies have moved up the scale while some others stayed stuck at the initial phase. The establishment of an operational infrastructure creates the framework for a company's journey through this phase.

Hoque described the e-commerce era as the beginning of the dotcom period and the B2C business models. This stage was marked by the proliferation of 'start-ups' such as amazon.com and priceline.com which entered the on-line business world selling goods and services directly to consumers. Many bricks and mortar companies such as Tesco also joined them by establishing an on-line presence in parallel. The emphasis at this stage was to create a web presence and provide value-added services in order to promote and sell on-line and maintain a healthy customer base. By 1998, a large number of companies moved on to this stage.

In the last five years businesses moved to different degrees through an evolutionary process of:

- brochureware
- e-commerce
- e-business
- e-enterprise.

CommerceNet, the industry consortium of companies which use, promote and build e-commerce solutions on the Internet defines e-commerce as the use of the Internet to transform business relationships which goes far beyond buying and selling on-line. Here, information is shared within and across organisational boundaries and new relationships are developed between businesses, as well as between businesses and customers.

By 1999, a large number of firms began to see the potential of the Internet for B2B applications. This started the e-business era with a drive towards the use of technology to strengthen core business processes. Organisations began to see information as a major

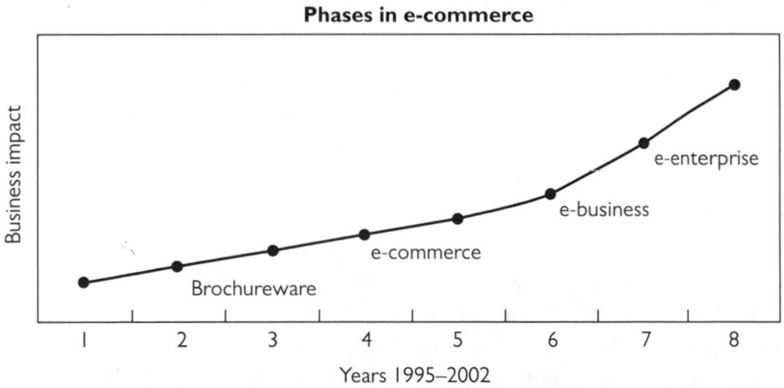

Fig. 7.1 The four phases of e-commerce (Source: Hoque, F., *e-Enterprise: Business Models, Architecture, and Components*, Cambridge University Press, New York, 2000, Adapted with permission.)

business resource and its management as one of the most important business functions. They learnt to focus on information and knowledge management as an essential element of their overall business objectives; developments in information and communications technologies kept pace in order to support this new era.

At this stage, many companies began to apply the philosophy of e-business to build a business model necessary to support both B2B and B2C applications. CommerceNet called this stage the e-enterprise phase, in which a company combines traditional business processes with the efficiency of the electronic medium; it uses Internet technologies to perform B2B activities necessary to support their core competencies as well as to provide on-line customer services typical of B2C e-commerce. By the end of the twentieth century, many large companies such as banks entered this era. With the increasing maturity of technology and business models, this phase is expected to bring about rapid changes in the business environment. On the one hand B2B companies will increasingly adapt their established infrastructure in the bricks and mortar world to embrace a B2C model; on the other, B2C companies will expand their philosophy of customer-centred business model to encompass B2B activities.[1]

Trace the origins of a non-chain, independent, specialist chocolate-making shop through all stages of the evolutionary process.

In the preceding chapters, we discussed the emergence of the information society and the resulting knowledge economy. We also introduced the concept of a digital nervous system (DNS) as a combination of hardware and software, designed to provide knowledge workers with accuracy, immediacy and richness of information, thus helping an organisation develop an 'institutional electronic intelligence'. Companies which are able to do this stand to benefit most from the digital economy in which organisations of all sizes are attempting to move through the phases of evolution. The degree of their success depends on their ability to create an appropriate business model that equips them to participate in this economy.

In what way can the development of a DNS allow, say, a medium-sized car-selling company to move from e-commerce to the e-enterprise stage?

BUSINESS MODELS IN THE DIGITAL ECONOMY

As we established already, the business model adopted by companies in this age must be built on three elements: a communications infrastructure to support the electronic communication of information between an organisation and its stakeholders; an information infrastructure that underpins its knowledge management activities; an operational infrastructure that is built on the above and is designed to provide the foundation for the establishment of business processes capable of delivering the 'products and services' to the 'customers'. Referred to as the delivery system by some authors (Rayport and Jaworski, 2001), it creates the configuration of processes that produces the final market and financial results and fulfils a company's 'business goals' (Fig. 7.2).

An operational infrastructure provides the foundation for the delivery of products and services to customers, and creates the environment for a company to meet its strategic goals.

In the uncertain environment of e-commerce, a business model can never be final and definitive. Talking about companies attempting to launch a new business model in order

[1] We will remember the distinction between the four stages, but generally speaking continue to refer to the whole phenomenon as e-commerce.

to move into the next phase of the evolutionary e-commerce process, Hoque (2000) refers to the 'launch and learn' strategy: businesses use a short cycle time to launch a new model, then hone their practices by an iterative process of learning and launching. Whether creating a new model or extending an existing infrastructure to accommodate new processes, there must always be the scope for reviews and improvements based on feedback from customers.

THE OPERATIONAL INFRASTRUCTURE

The objectives of an operational infrastructure for e-commerce are to:

- Create the capabilities required by a company to supply on-line products and services.
- Form the basis for the business activities associated with e-commerce.
- Provide a framework for managing a complex technology-based system.
- Support the business ecosystem.[2]
- Establish a procedure for improving an organisation's overall performance.

The components of an operational infrastructure as listed in Fig. 7.2 must be equipped to deliver the above objectives. In the following section we will describe these activities. We will come back to the subject of how they contribute to the fulfilment of the objectives later on in the chapter.

Supply-chain management

Supply chain is an established entity in the bricks and mortar sector of business. Developing and maintaining relationships with trading partners has always been a

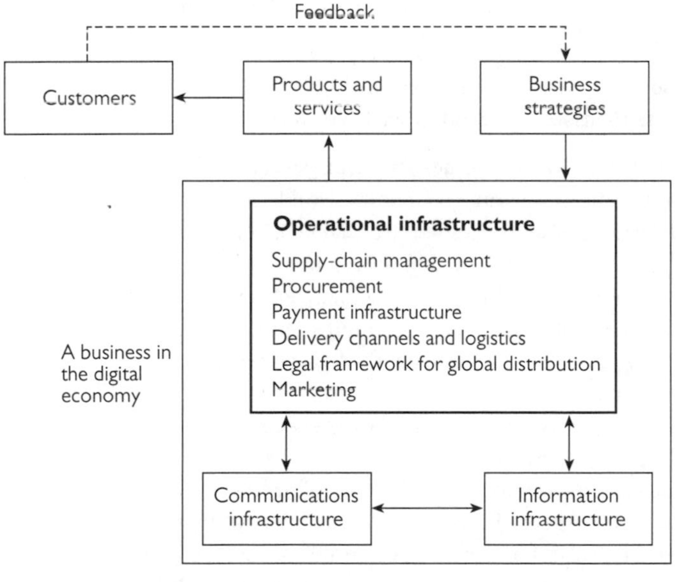

Fig. 7.2 Operational infrastructure for e-commerce

[2] An environment comprising a set of sub-systems which complement each other and contribute to the survival of the whole.

crucial part of organisational activities; companies would usually have a mature infrastructure for this. However, e-commerce changes the pattern of the relationship between buyers and sellers and the logistics involved in the delivery of goods changes due to the complications associated with business in a global market.

A supply chain connects a number of physical entities such as manufacturing plants, distribution centres, retail outlets, warehouses, delivery channels etc., together with other non-physical elements such as information, regulations and procedures. It is also concerned with people (customers and sellers), constraints due to geographical and cultural barriers and business philosophies. In managing the supply chain, a company attempts to build an infrastructure ensuring smooth interaction between these components and create an extended value chain[3] from the source of the products through to consumption. This requires sharing information with suppliers, buyers and other business partners in order to plan procurement, production and distribution of the final goods and services.

A supply chain connects manufacturing plants, distribution centres, warehouses, retail outlets etc. with information, regulation and procedures.

Supply chain management was done in B2C by telephone calls, faxes and physical means until e-commerce came onto the scene. Cyberspace introduced electronic supply-chain management and brought about the following changes:

- Companies do not need to keep a large amount of stock in one place as customers do not see the products and deliveries can be made from any location.
- The supply-chain mechanism for e-commerce is very different from its physical counterpart. Companies are required to deliver goods at short notice to addresses ranging over wide geographical areas; the goods delivered must fit specifications submitted by customers who have not seen them.
- An electronic supply chain relies on the ability of all parties in the chain to fulfil their obligations equally well; any mistake at any stage affects the B2C company, which has to face the customers.
- It is a high competition area as customers can switch easily to other companies if they are not satisfied. Wrong deliveries and broken promises can have expensive consequences.

Because of the high stakes associated with deliveries, companies search for a supply mechanism which would minimise the risks. The models available are:[4]

- Stocking the products in-house. For companies with a physical as well as an on-line presence this would mean the same warehouse. Problems can arise due to differences in the nature of deliveries required. The UK ceramics producer Wedgwood has coped with this by centralising its warehouse; using a warehouse management system called PkMS by Manhattan Associates, it processes all orders from one centre (Samuels and Phillips, 2000). For purely on-line companies, it can work to their advantage if they have the facilities as deliveries can be more reliable.
- Outsource warehousing. This involves the use of logistics specialists such as FedEx to store and deliver the goods. The success of this model depends on the ability of the contracted company to handle the type of orders received. The UK food retailer Iceland merged with Brooker, a distributor of frozen and chilled food; this will enable Iceland to use Brooker's warehousing facilities as a collection point for its home delivery service (Samuels and Phillips, 2000).

[3] Stages of business processes which add value to a product or a service at each stage.

[4] Source: J. F. Rayport and B. J. Jaworski, *e-Commerce*, McGraw-Hill, 2001. Copyright © 2001 by Rayport and Jaworski. Reproduced with the permission of The McGraw-Hill Companies, Inc.

- Drop shipping. In this model, an e-commerce company leaves it to its suppliers and distributors to pack and deliver orders. Established mail order companies are often used as the intermediary; they use their warehouse for storing goods and deliver them directly to customers when orders are received via the e-tailer. Watford Electronics, a PC supplier in London, reduced its stockholding by more than half by getting orders shipped directly from the supplier to customers, and is hoping to reduce it to nil in the near future (see case study at the end of the chapter).
- Fulfilment intermediaries. In this model the entire order processing side of the business is outsourced, leaving the e-tailer to concentrate on managing the business. A number of companies (the intermediaries) now offer such a service, for example Ingram Micra, originally a PC distributor, now provides inventory management and fulfilment services to vendors and resellers (Alfreds, 1999).

Four models used for the supply mechanism in B2C are:

- Stocking products in house.
- Outsourcing the warehouse.
- Drop shipping.
- Using fulfilment intermediaries.

In the B2B e-commerce arena, supply-chain management historically involved the use of EDI or a proprietary network which clearly favoured large businesses, for example Ford's use of Fordnet (chapter 1). It gave them the power to control their supply chain cheaply, securely and reliably knowing that their smaller trading partners could not afford to switch to other companies. Advances in information and communications technologies have changed the situation in a number of ways:

- It has provided the technology required to build cheaper and more convenient platforms for communication. Companies can use VPNs, extranets or simply the Internet to share information. Software tools are now available to facilitate this, for example IBM's QCS.net provides catalogue and transaction services along with workflow templates to help retailers negotiate with suppliers (Laudon and Laudon, 2000).
- It has given both buyers and suppliers extended 'reach', thus radically changing the power balance. Smaller partners in a supply chain are now in a position to 'shop around' for better price and service.
- The use of web-development technologies such as XML and Java enables business partners to integrate their information resources and ERP systems and therefore to accelerate the decision-making and supply-chain management processes.
- The establishment of communication standards, improved security and an international information infrastructure have provided a platform for fast and reliable communication between trading partners regardless of physical boundaries.

These factors have enabled smaller companies to venture out and try different options; they have also encouraged larger companies to experiment with Internet-based models for supply-chain management. The following are some of the benefits of electronic supply-chain management:

- Just-in-time (JIT) delivery. By using a system of procuring goods only at the time they are required, a company can reduce the need for holding a large stock. Both Sainsbury's and Woolworths (a subsidiary of Kingfisher) are now using a web-based planning and information-sharing software called Eqos to build a collaborative system. It enables them to plan promotions and track sales data in order to deploy stock where needed (Samuels and Phillips, 2000; Mathieson, December, 2000).

- Faster delivery. The automation of processes and the use of integrated filing systems reduce delays due to the time taken at intermediate stages, thus enabling a company to provide faster and more reliable delivery.
- Accountability. Having an electronic watchdog tracking activities at each stage of a supply chain means a company can identify weak links in the chain. This results in better control and financial savings.
- All round improvement. The above benefits of electronic supply-chain management are mirrored on a smaller scale for all the links: the deliverers, manufacturers, marketers and customers.

Some benefits of electronic supply-chain management:

- just-in-time delivery
- speed
- better control and cost saving
- efficiency.

A manufacturer of margarine which supplies supermarkets all over the country is considering converting to electronic supply-chain management. How will it benefit from the process and what will it learn that it could not otherwise know?

Procurement

Companies are increasingly using electronic means to manage the processes associated with the purchase of non-strategic goods and services. They are using web technologies to adopt a purchasing strategy that enables them to select a preferred supplier – a company that is able to provide an end-to-end service. This can be done in one of two main ways. The first involves the use of emails and on-line catalogues to co-ordinate the buying and selling of goods which we have already discussed. The second, more elaborate method is the use of electronic marketplaces (exchanges) which are geared towards searching and negotiating for suppliers and prices. We introduced the concept of an exchange in chapter 2 as a provider of on-line auctions; however, their main role is to facilitate collaboration between buyers and sellers in the B2B community.

Marketplaces can be classified in two main ways (Duschinsky, 2000a, b): vertical or horizontal. Vertical marketplaces support a particular industry (for example, the automobile industry); they offer suppliers increased visibility and buyers an improved opportunity for negotiation and pre-contractual collaboration with a wide range of suppliers. Horizontal marketplaces do the same but for a specific community of users (for example, the government) or a class of goods and services (for example, educational material for universities). Marketplaces can also be classed as public – open to any organisation (subject to some entry rules) – and exist to provide a forum for buyers and sellers to find each other; or they can be privately owned by a major purchaser who creates a medium to bring a group of buyers and sellers together. MarketSite is a B2B e-marketplace introduced by the software company Commerce One (see case study on Schlumberger). It is also possible to use a hybrid model in which companies find suitable trading partners through a public marketplace and then create a private area to work with them on a specific project.

Procurement is the process of the purchase of non-strategic goods and services. Electronic procurement can be done at three strategic levels by using standard on-line activities or with the help of a marketplace.

Electronic procurement (e-procurement) can be used at three strategic levels:

- *Transactions* – to facilitate the simple process of buying and selling of goods and services over the Internet. Most e-commerce projects concentrate on this at the beginning and progress to the higher levels in time.
- *Strategic sourcing* – to use strategically obtained information from the company's knowledge base to create a smarter purchase mechanism. Organisations in this category build a procurement platform capable of reducing its labour and administrative costs as well as finding the best prices and terms of purchase.

Supply chain management at Wedgwood

Founded in 1759 and now a part of the Irish-owned Waterford Wedgwood group, Wedgwood is one of the world's leading manufacturer of quality ceramics. By the mid-1990s, the company realised that it needed to improve its customer service and order processing systems. It identified three problem areas: lack of order fulfilment and the resulting customer relationship damage; the manufacturing schedule; and new product introduction. In 1996, it embarked on an ambitious overhaul of its supply-chain processes with a view to:

- reducing inventory
- cutting the supply cycle time
- improving customer relations
- cutting cost if possible.

Wedgwood decided that it needed to move from its push model driven by a centrally generated monthly forecast of expected sales to a pull model driven by demand from customers. They changed their forecasting model to tailor it separately for each market, determined on the basis of the opinions of the sales people. Products were only manufactured when stock levels triggered an order for refill, thus tying production tightly to sales.

This method was cascaded down to the suppliers of raw materials, packaging and lithographic transfers (for producing the patterns on the pottery). The majority of the transfers come from one supplier, which has now adopted a form of vendor-managed supply in which a low stock level automatically triggers a new order.

Wedgwood opted for a planning tool called Mimi, developed by Aspen Technology. Although a new product in the market, Wedgwood was reassured by a visit to see Mimi in action at tobacco giant Philip Morris in North Carolina. It also moved the responsibility of the planning from central control to the people closely involved with sales and the market in each area.

At the same time, Wedgwood replaced half a dozen traditional warehouses with a new outsourced dispatch centre which makes use of the latest warehouse technologies. Staff were transferred to the outsourcer's operation; they had to adapt to a pack-to-order goods model from their previous roles where goods were dispatched from the factory already packed. Finally, to ensure the company remains focused on the goal of improved customer service, it introduced a number of key performance indicators.

As with most major changes, the transition has not been easy but the company has been rewarded with spectacular improvements in its supply-chain operations. The major benefits have been:

- a dramatic reduction in replenishment lead time (time taken to top up stock)
- minimum stock-out
- reduced back orders (orders delayed due to lack of supply)
- reduction of staffing involved in supply-chain management by 20–25 per cent.

(Source: Warren, March, 2001. Printed with permission from Reed Business Information Ltd.)

Questions

1 Discuss how the steps taken would contribute to an improvement in the system.
2 How do customers benefit from the changes?
3 With the help of further research, discuss the push and the pull models and their effects on businesses.

- *Market transparency* – to create an infrastructure capable of harnessing the supply chain of the entire company and facilitate collaboration between all facets of the chain. Enterprise-wide integration of information and knowledge sources is essential for this purpose.

Traditionally, companies maintained a department responsible for performing all purchases and purchase-related information. Although the expertise provided by such a set-up was enormously useful, the cost of maintaining the service counterbalanced a large proportion of any savings made by cost negotiations. E-procurement can offer a number of benefits to businesses:

- *Lower cost* – cost savings can be made at different levels. With the help of an integrated inventory for the entire organisation, the best prices and suppliers can be found for each product. The company also saves money due to a shorter buying cycle (the time it takes between putting a tender out and the final stage of having the product delivered in the physical world), reduced warehousing arrangements, lower inventory management needs, and a reduction in the staffing required for order processing. Many companies who adopted e-procurement early such as Reuters, Cisco and Philips claim savings on their indirect spend of between 8 per cent and 15 per cent and returns on investment in less than 12 months (Duschinsky, 2000b).
- *Better co-ordination between different parties* – e-procurement involves collaboration between different departments in an organisation together with buyers and suppliers with whom they have to build a long-term relationship. This provides the company with a buying environment based on improved communication, which benefits the enterprise in general.
- *Optimise purchasing* – enterprise-wide procurement and resource management enable a company to monitor and analyse purchasing data in order to optimise quantities, suppliers and prices. By using collaborative buying techniques, multiple departments or even multiple enterprises can work together to meet sourcing needs or negotiate pricing (Hoque, 2000).

Benefits of e-procurement are:

- lower cost
- better co-ordination
- optimised purchasing.

E-procurement is on the agenda for most medium and large companies but many of them are not taking full advantage of it, mainly due to concerns related to security. Managers are still worried about the absence of standards or a well-established payment infrastructure suitable for electronic transactions.

Payment infrastructure

Financial transactions over the Internet have grown enormously in recent years and new forms of electronic money, such as Mondex, Digicash, smart cards, have been introduced. Forrester Research has predicted that for B2B e-commerce, global Internet revenues will be about $1.3 trillion by 2003 (Everett, 2000). This necessitates a secure, fast and reliable payment infrastructure, although there is still a great deal of mistrust amongst consumers over the safety of the medium for electronic transfer of money. Customers are required to enter their card details on-line, which raises the fear of 'eavesdropping' by unscrupulous users. Creating a reliable environment for the transfer of money over the Internet has been a major concern for organisations. In the following discussion we will describe how the concept of electronic money works and how the two main e-commerce sectors use them for on-line payments.

Most readers of this book are likely to be acquainted with credit cards. They are part of a loan system in which the issuer (e.g. Visa, Mastercard) of each card makes payments to the sellers on behalf of the cardholders. The holder is required to settle the amount when they receive an invoice, either in full each time for no extra payment, or in part, in which case they have to pay interest for the outstanding amount. Each card has a unique number which is used for identification and an expiry date which confirms the validity of the card. Another type of card is debit card, which often also serves as a bank guarantee and cashpoint card. This is not a loan system but a form of electronic cash; the amount due is debited from the card holder's bank account at the time of purchase and sent to the payee a few days later.

E-Procurement at Schlumberger

Schlumberger is the world's largest oil service company, trading in 100 countries. Recently, it introduced a web-based procurement system in its largest division, Oilfield Services. The company replaced its old paper-based as well as EDI system with a single desktop solution. The system has two parts, both developed by Commerce One. The first is a procurement software called BuySite which runs on its intranet and allows employees to shop on-line using a browser on their desktop PCs. The system incorporates a simple-to-use catalogue of office supplies, technical equipment, specialist items, furniture etc. Once an employee selects the items, the system automatically issues a requisition, routes it electronically to the proper people for approval and turns it into a purchase order.

The second part is MarketSite, an electronic marketplace for B2B transactions which lets employees connect to hundreds of suppliers using a single, open system. Each buyer can customise the catalogue of products and prices according to the products they require and the prices they negotiated with the vendors. Eventually they expect to be able to negotiate prices in real time.

The system has produced both cost and process benefits by reducing the amount of time people spend ordering supplies, freeing them to do their real jobs. It is also cheaper to operate than the EDI links it replaces. Additionally, the suppliers benefit due to increased efficiency which they will pass on to buyers in the form of lower prices. Having a corporate-wide single system saves time and money otherwise required in staff training. It also enables the company to track its overall purchasing activity from a desktop and access information which it can use to further improve its procurement efficiency.

(Reprinted by permission of *Harvard Business Review*. From 'E-Procurement at Schlumberger' by Andrea Ovans, May–June 2000. Copyright © 2000 by the Harvard Business School Publishing Corporation; all rights reserved.)

Questions

1 Discuss how this case study demonstrates the points made in the text about e-procurement in terms of (a) its methods and (b) its benefits.
2 Which issues should the management address in order to get the most benefit out of the system?

At the moment, card users are asked by companies selling on the Internet to enter their personal and card details on an on-line form. This form is protected by the secure sockets layer (SSL) protocol (see chapter 5): information travelling in cyberspace is encrypted using a combination of public and private key systems. The card details are also checked by a verification authority before they are accepted. However, even though SSL promises to deliver security in terms of the integrity of data entered by the users and the validity of a transaction, payment by card suffers from the following weaknesses:

- Data is not protected from individuals in the companies receiving card details; this may lead to fraudulent activities by insiders.
- Although card details can be verified and protected, there is no mechanism for ensuring that the user is actually the card holder. This can lead to non-repudiation.
- Export regulations place a limit of 40 bit encryption keys for exported messages; this reduces the amount of control information the key can hold and weakens the level of security of SSL.

Another security measure used to protect credit card payments is the secure electronic transactions (SET) protocol. This offers an increased level of security to customers and non-repudiation for businesses (referred to as 'merchants' in protocol terminology) by demanding that all parties involved in a transaction use SET certified products.

SET was introduced by Visa and Mastercard in 1997, but has been joined by the Japanese giant JCB and American Express since then. Jointly, they have established a company called SETCo. SETCo tests the software used for payment to the SET standard, ensures retailers' compliance and own the SET cryptographic master key. The company provides a certificate to all its users; this comprises: the holder's public key, identification details and card number, the certificate authority's digital signature and signing algorithm and the expiry date of the certificate. The protocol also addresses country-specific issues in order to enable international electronic fund transfer.

Credit and debit cards are frequently used for payment in e-commerce. Security is implemented by the use of two protocols: secure sockets layer (SSL) and secure electronic transaction (SET).

In order to use SET, the customer's computer must have software known as an electronic (or digital) wallet which holds a SET certificate (this can be obtained after SETCo checks the interoperability between the user's system and merchants' software). The certificate can also be stored on a smartcard to be read at the merchant's premises during off-line electronic payment. All parties involved in a transaction – the customer, merchant, card-issuing financial institutions and payment gateway (the hardware interface which connects the Internet and the financial network and is used to get authorisation for payment and clearing) – must make their digital certificates available to the payment system. Before information is passed on from one entity to another, SET checks the certificate of both sides. The system of authentication follows steps 1–9 as described in Fig. 7.3.

SET is based on digital certificates and encryption. It is more secure than SSL because it gives the merchant only the order information. The payment information is sent to a payment gateway for authorisation before money changes hands.

At the end of the processes, the merchant delivers the order and receives payment from the card issuer following authorisation by SET.

The advantage of SET over SSL is that the merchants do not receive any payment details, thus eliminating the possibility of internal fraud. Also, the customer cannot retain their anonymity as the certification authority checks personal details before issuing

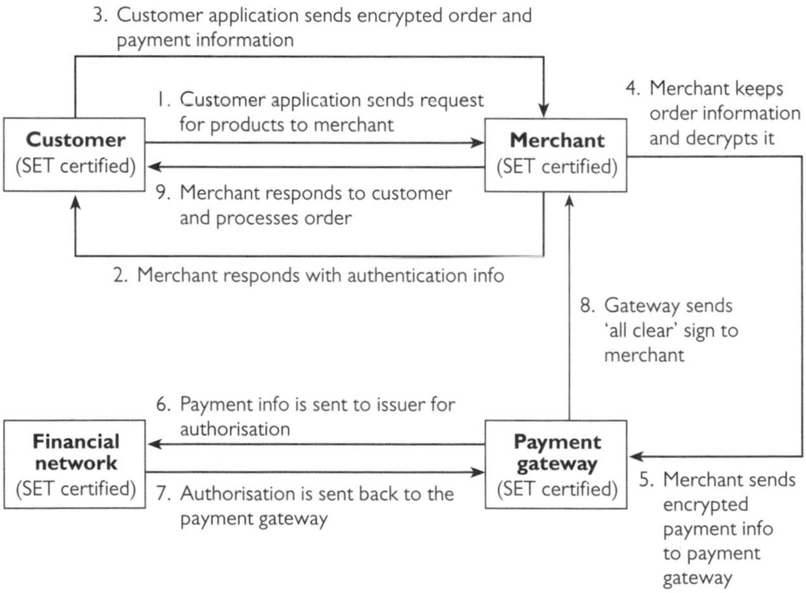
3. Customer application sends encrypted order and payment information
1. Customer application sends request for products to merchant
Customer (SET certified)
Merchant (SET certified)
4. Merchant keeps order information and decrypts it
9. Merchant responds to customer and processes order
2. Merchant responds with authentication info
8. Gateway sends 'all clear' sign to merchant
6. Payment info is sent to issuer for authorisation
Financial network (SET certified)
Payment gateway (SET certified)
7. Authorisation is sent back to the payment gateway
5. Merchant sends encrypted payment info to payment gateway

Fig. 7.3 Secure electronic transaction (SET)

authentication, thus reducing the risk of non-repudiation. However, SET demands interoperability between various systems, it is complex to implement and certificates are not available easily.

Security is one crucial element of electronic payment systems; another is an infrastructure that facilitates the smooth circulation of funds between banks. The central bank of a country, for example the Federal Reserve System (FDS) in the USA and the Bank of England in the UK play that role. They devise policies regarding financial transactions between banks and countries within the framework of government regulations. In the UK a service called the bankers automated clearing services (BACS)[5] is provided by a conglomerate of the Bank of England and other financial institutions, to facilitate the electronic transfer of relatively small amounts between member banks. For example, when a customer instructs his or her bank to pay a company by direct debit, the transaction between the two banks is handled by BACS. A clearing house facilitates electronic fund transfer (EFT) between banks and their corporate customers. EFT has been in existence before the days of the Internet when companies used a financial value added network (VAN[6]). In the UK a same-day payment service is provided by the clearing house automated payment system (CHAPS)[7] supported by BACS.

In the UK, the circulation of funds between banks is controlled by BACS, a conglomerate of the Bank of England and other financial institutions. Other countries have a similar set-up.

The security of Internet-based payments can be improved by the use of electronic cheques. Cheques have been in use as a payment method for a very long time. The transfer of money took a long time due to the physical stages involved in the movement of the cheque from one bank to the other via the clearing house. Although the use of magnetic ink character reading (see chapter 5) enables cheques to be read and sorted by computerised devices, their handling can be time consuming. Security is also a problem due to the possibility of forgery. Used more commonly in the B2B sector than the B2C, electronic cheques are basically an on-line version of a real cheque; using encryption and a digital signature, a cheque is sent via the Internet and processed within minutes rather than days. The identification details (PIN code, account number etc.), together with the private key of the payer, are stored on a smart card which is read by a hardware interface; the key is used for digital signature. Further security required for the transfer of large sums between large companies in the B2B sector can be established by the use of SET technologies because they are capable of providing interoperability and facilitating the exchange of digital certification between the trading partners.

Another secure method of electronic payment, particularly suitable for small amounts, is the use of e-cash. Based on smart card technology, which stores customer details on a card with a silicon chip, e-cash uses the concept of loading a PC or a smart card with a certain sum of money from a bank. In principle, the bank generates an electronic coin, which is basically a number representing an amount, digitally signed by the bank. The money can then be used for payments in the same way cash has always been. At present, only a bank counter or a cashpoint machine can charge a card but in future, especially with the proliferation of Internet banking, users will be able to do this via their personal computers. Two well-known e-cash systems are Digicash and Mondex. In 1994, Digicash introduced this concept by using the Internet to store electronic money on a user's PC and facilitating anonymous payment over the Internet. However, due to the complications involved in ensuring audit trails and other security measures, the system was too expensive and never became popular; it has now ceased to exist (Rajput, 2000). Known also as a storecard, Mondex was introduced in the early 1990s. A smartcard is stored with

5 In the USA this is called an automated clearing house (ACH).

6 Networks set up and managed by private companies or a combination of private channels and national data networks which users can connect to for a price. A VAN often services a specialised user group such as financial institutions.

7 The equivalent in the USA is called the clearing house interbank payments system (CHIPS).

a predetermined sum of money which can then be used in any transactions (compatible with the technology) independent of the banking network, or even for transferring money from one card to another.

Another system, introduced by a company called First Virtual, uses a combination of on- and off-line data transfer to facilitate e-commerce for its customers. The company provides all its customers, both buyers and sellers, with a PIN which it stores in its own computer, together with their credit card details. Users buying over the Internet send orders together with their PIN to the sellers, who send both PINs (theirs and the buyers) to First Virtual, who processes the financial transaction independent of the Internet. Various other initiatives are now in the pipeline, aimed at improving the convenience and security of payment in e-commerce. For example Mondex is trying to introduce a system in which GSM mobile phones will enable a user to insert an e-cash card on the phone in order to connect to their bank and load their cards with money. Similar technologies can also be used to facilitate the transfer of money between a buyer and a seller over the Internet. This has great potential for electronic bill payment (EBP).

EBP is becoming increasingly popular in the B2C sector. An EBP service provider (EBPSP) facilitates bill payment over the Internet by acting as a web interface between customers and businesses. Customers send details of their accounts and identification data to the EBPSP they register with. Billers registered to the system send customer bills to the EBPSP; a customer logged onto the service provider's website can access his or her bills on-line and make payments. The EBPSP processes the bills using the payment infrastructure available. They use SSL or SET protocol for security and a financial network such as a clearing house for the transfer of money. The advantage of such a system is that customers can keep track of all bill payments via the service provider's website. Cybercash, Netbanx and Wordplay provide such a service.

Some other methods used in electronic payment are:

- electronic cheque
- electronic cash
- First Virtual payment system
- electronic bill payment service providers.

In an alternative model, sellers avoid the use of a service provider by providing payment facilities from their own website. They create a webpage for customer bills which can be viewed by users logged onto the website. Some companies are using this model as it provides them with a better mechanism for controlling their order processing, for example amazon.com takes customers' account details and deals with the financial transaction with the bank itself. However, it is inconvenient for customers as they have to log onto separate company sites to monitor the status of all their bills. It also has a security risk as some individuals in the seller company can view customer account details.

Although our discussion of payment technologies has been mainly geared towards the B2C sector, they are equally suitable for B2B. However, the amount of money transferred in this case can be large; companies need an integrated system that supports their entire supply chain, including procurement and distribution. Organisations connect to a country's financial networks by using a payment gateway supported by a major technology provider; Ariba, Commerce One and I2 Technologies are some examples of such companies (Duschinsky, 2000b). Some technology providers are also moving towards EBP services by developing a partnership with public key infrastructure (PKI – see chapter 5) providers; together they offer a secure bill payment infrastructure. Companies using B2B e-commerce are required to invest in creating an integrated backend system that provides a framework for secure and seamless data transfer between their procurement, billing, order processing and other supply-chain management systems.

B2B e-commerce frequently involves the transfer of bills and payments over national boundaries. This can pose a problem because companies have to depend on a country's regional banking networks for clearing funds in the absence of a global network. The only global network available is the one for credit card payments but it is expensive, charging a fee of 2–4 per cent of each transaction. At present there are 14 clearing houses in Europe (Ward, 2001); there needs to be a cross-border clearing house to support all international transactions.

The differences in the regulatory framework between countries can affect the delivery of goods, billing, tax arrangements and so on. Companies must establish clear procedures for the delivery of their products within and across national boundaries. This involves two areas: the mechanism established for the distribution of goods and the legal framework for national and international business activities.

The B2B sector uses a payment gateway service provider by major technology companies. It also has partnership with PKI service providers; together they support a secure electronic bill payment service.

Find out what measures are in place to ensure the security of financial transactions between a seller in the UK and a customer in the USA.

Distribution channels and logistics

We mentioned distribution models during our discussion of supply-chain management and its use of warehousing. Here, we will concentrate on the principles behind the establishment of effective logistics – the procedure for the distribution and receipt of raw materials and finished products in a supply chain.

Delivering goods reliably to customers or business partners in a supply chain is the ultimate obligation an organisation has to fulfil. Sometimes referred to as 'fulfilment', this has been a vital part of established bricks and mortar companies. Their systems are capable of generating the information required to provide the correct data for packaging and shipping. However, they can also be inflexible which leads to inefficient distribution systems when the time comes to convert to e-commerce. New companies without any experience are able to create an integrated system with web-enabled technologies suitable for meeting the demands of the new market. But their views of the importance of end-to-end logistics are often limited, thus leading to inadequate support for delivery channels.

According to a survey done by Forrester Research, on-line businesses are expected to grow 750 per cent in just 18 months, yet 85 per cent of firms cannot fill international orders because of complexities of shipping. Of the 15 per cent who can handle global orders, they are doing so only for deliveries in Europe and Asia where local warehouses can provide the services (Bicknell, 2000). According to the survey, the new so-called 'dot-coms' supporting the B2C market are the most vulnerable.

In the uncertain environment of e-commerce, providing quick and reliable delivery of goods is a challenging task. There are a number of actions companies can take in order to enhance their logistics capability. Leed (2001) quoted the examples of two companies in this context: DHL, a worldwide courier service which handles shipping and delivery for a large number of businesses, recommends that the logistics companies should be involved from the planning stage; and Ryder, a Fortune 500 logistics and supply-chain provider, facilitates synchronised information flow between business processes and delivery channels by integrating its warehouse management, transportation systems, backend information systems, e-commerce standards, communication protocols, technology infrastructures and application formats. This gives them an infrastructure for the development of a distribution system capable of supplying goods fast and without complication; it also enables them to track the progress of delivery and respond to customer queries effectively. Organisations providing their own distribution system can follow the same route for improved e-fulfilment solutions.

Logistics provides an infrastructure for a distribution system which is capable of supplying goods fast and without complication. It also enables a company to track the progress of delivery and respond to customer queries quickly.

Business process re-engineering focused upon the following four areas can have a major impact on logistics (with permission from Chaston, 2001):

- *Dematerialisation* – the introduction of a system which reduces the need for stock holding and warehousing. This can be done by linking order processing and manufacturing systems in order to establish just-in-time (JIT) delivery as done by Dell Computers (see chapter 2).
- *Disintermediation* – the establishment of on-line processes and information systems to eliminate some of the steps in the supply chain. This would reduce the need for the delivery of goods between trading partners, resulting in improved logistics. Ingram Macro, originally a supplier of PCs, took this route (chapter 2).
- *Deverticalisation* – the process by which one organisation performs more than one function in a supply chain. Industry-wide service in some aspects of delivery can be provided by these companies, thus improving logistics for all participating firms. For example, one company could manage both order processing and distribution for the food retailers in a region.
- *Service development* – the Internet enables companies to provide new services which they can also offer to their business partners. For example, it may be possible for an enterprise to develop innovative services such as an effective complaints procedure and a procedure for returned goods.

The areas which need to be reviewed in order to improve logistics are:

- the amount of stock holding by a company
- the number of intermediaries used
- supply-chain activities performed by one company
- new service development in supply chain.

The PC company Dell is often mentioned in relation to its e-commerce strategies. Find out how it manages the logistics required to see its strategies through to their goal.

If it wishes to distribute goods internationally an organisation must abide by the legal framework for business transactions in the participating countries. In the following section we will address the issues associated with the legal aspects of Internet-based business activities. However, this is a vast and specialised area mostly outside the scope of this book. Here, we take a generalist rather than a specialist view of the subject and focus on the concerns which have surfaced in the context of e-commerce. It does not attempt to address precise legal complications but to draw readers' attention to the issues which the providers and consumers of e-commerce should be aware of.[8] We will come back to the topic briefly again during our discussion of the consequences of e-commerce for consumers in the last section of the book.

LEGAL ASPECTS OF E-COMMERCE

Laws are generally introduced for use within a country. The Internet is a global system and while sales over the physical medium can be controlled by customs, duties and charges, the information-based nature of the Internet makes it a difficult medium to control. Once information is 'released' into the WWW, it becomes available to authorised as well as some unauthorised users and therefore very difficult to limit access to. The areas which raise concerns are:

- *Trademarks* (TM) – a trademark distinguishes the goods or services offered by one company from those of the others. This could be a name or a logo or even a sound, something that serves as a distinct indicator of an organisation's identity. Protecting a TM on the Internet is complicated by the fact that a user

[8] You should read the book by Ian Lloyds (2000) for further information on this subject.

Hanson Construction

Hanson Quarry Products Europe is part of the international buildings materials company Hanson. It has improved the service it offers to customers while cutting its own costs by developing an e-billing solution. The system, which was piloted in October 2000 with a small number of users, allows customers to view their invoices, statements, proof-of-delivery notes and credit notes over a secure extranet.

A lot of information on the company's databases has a use and value to its customers. It needed to find a way to make it more accessible to customers.

The e-billing system arose from a deal between Pioneer International – a building materials company acquired by Hanson early in 2000 – and document management specialist Microgen. Pioneer outsourced its printing and document management to Microgen. Initially, staff at Pioneer accessed copies of customer-requested documents through a dial-up link to Microgen, then gave selected customers direct access to the dial-up service. However, this was laborious and not user friendly; thus, Pioneer Online was born. Initially it offered on-line retrieval and proof-of-delivery notes for all of Pioneer's customers. It currently handles 6000 requests each month.

The company tested the system by establishing test areas that allow one customer in without giving access to other people. It believed that the best way to introduce a web-based system was to learn how to do things with two or three customers at a time rather than launch internationally from the start. The first users reported time and cost savings as a result of being able to access documents on-line. For Hanson, having made the initial decision to outsource its document management to Microgen, the cost of offering customers the significant benefits of on-line access has been relatively small.

(Source: Warren, October 2000. Printed with permission from Reed Business Information Ltd.)

Questions

1 How does the above system improve the business processes between the partners involved in this B2B scenario?
2 Which factors should Hanson pay attention to, in order to make its e-billing system work properly in the global marketplace?
3 How does Pioneer Online affect Hanson's image to customers?

in one country with a legitimate TM cannot rely on its uniqueness because a user in another country is free to adopt it, thus giving rise to confusion. It leads to the obvious problem of businesses losing their customers as users can easily be diverted to the hijacker. Once lost, recovering one's unique TM or domain name can be extremely difficult and expensive. Companies in cyberspace often register their domain names as a TM in order to prevent cybersquatting, a term used to describe the theft of a domain name; for example, amazon.com is a registered TM in the USA (Lloyds, 2000).

- *Taxation* – tax laws are difficult to apply to Internet-based sales. On the one hand, the sale can go unmonitored thus making no contribution to a country's revenue; on the other, the customer may end up being taxed in both countries. Applying tax regulations to knowledge-based e-commerce companies is also complicated by the difficulty associated with measuring the cost of information or the share price of knowledge.

Differences in taxation in different countries can affect businesses because in some cases it is cheaper to buy a product from a foreign country. EU customers often have to pay less or no tax when they buy from a non-EU country. Due to widespread liberalisation of telecommunications regulations

Legal issues we must address are:

- protection of trademarks
- protection of domain name
- clarification of tax laws
- customers' rights to full and correct information.

Contd. . . .

in many countries, a company can offer telecommunications services without necessarily having to reside in that country. Until the law was tightened in July 1997, this enabled Internet service providers (ISP) such as Compuserve and America Online (AOL) to operate in non-EU countries without charging VAT thus gaining substantial competitive advantage over their EU rivals (Lloyds, 2000). Recently the Organisation for Economic Co-operation and Development (OECD) and the EU have started to address these issues. A recent proposal suggests that like the goods sold in the physical market, non-EU companies would have to register in every country they operate in and charge EU customers VAT for digital deliveries at the same rate as that paid by local shoppers in those countries (Ody, 2001). The companies would then be required to return the tax collected to the relevant countries. However, while OECD wants the same rule to apply to EU companies selling to non-EU customers, the EU does not want that. Until there is global agreement on the above issues and a technology-based solution, these problems will continue to affect the progress of e-commerce.

- *Sales information* – in the world of bricks and mortar, the seller is expected to provide its customers with full and correct information on the products sold. The Sale of Goods Act of 1979 requires that goods should comply with any description attached to them, be of satisfactory quality and reasonably fit for the purpose for which they are supplied. These terms are implied in a sales contract; seller and buyer are not required to say anything specifically. However, implications may not always be sufficient, especially when trade between two different countries is concerned. There is a lot of confusion and ignorance in the virtual world about consumers' rights to sales information. Findings from a survey carried out by the Office of Fair Trading (OFT) showed that, out of 637 consumer sites reviewed, 52 per cent did not provide easily accessible information about refunds or exchange policies (Ward, 15 March, 2001). It has also been suggested that for businesses trading internationally, calculating a final cost which covers taxes and tariffs is a long and complicated task (Ward, 22 March, 2001).
- *Contracts* – in the physical world, a business contract is made when the sale of goods or services is agreed between two parties willing to enter into a legal relationship; a sale follows only when agreement has been reached on the correct price. The contract serves to provide documentation that all the essential elements of the bargain have been agreed by both parties. If anything goes wrong during the sale or if either party fails to fulfil its obligations satisfactorily, it is covered by law. Such agreements are difficult to establish in e-commerce as the concepts of sales agreements or acceptance of terms are rather obscure in cyberspace. In this medium, a sale is made by exchanges of emails and by the use of a website. Because of the non-real-time nature of the environment, it is possible to place an order on the basis of an out-of-date price list; when the seller fails to fulfil the order, the customer may interpret this as a breach of a contract. In e-commerce, different jurisdictions may interpret the contract in different ways. When and where a contract is made determines which courts have jurisdiction and which laws apply, unless the parties have specified. The fact that different countries adopt different approaches causes problems in establishing a common ground in international trade. The EU is trying to address this issue through a new proposition in its Electronic Commerce Directive (ECD) introduced on 31 October 2000 which aims to give consumers the basic level of protection

in e-commerce. In the light of these directives, on-line businesses may be forced to review their websites, advertising methods and ordering procedures. It also advocates that the consumer buying on-line be provided with specific information regarding the seller, the goods and the prices prior to the conclusion of a contract, and that this information is confirmed by a separate medium such as an email or a fax. The directive would require member states to lay down in their legislation that in cases when a buyer accepts an offer of a service by technological means (such as clicking an icon), a contract is concluded only when s/he receives an acknowledgement of the acceptance from the seller electronically (Lloyds, 2000). However, there are oppositions to this proposal, especially from the UK, on grounds of complication and applicability, and the discussion is continuing.

A contract serves to safeguard a company as well. Internet-based services can be disrupted by many factors such as disturbances in a country's communications infrastructure, a virus attack due to weak security controls and suspended services due to software problems. On those occasions, a contract provides the seller with a safety net; it also gives customers an assurance that the company has taken all possible measures (such as the use of encryption techniques) to avoid such occurrences and limit the damage done by such disruption.

- *Financial services* – in addition to security concerns, financial services suffer because of the added pressure of the responsibility to create public confidence in on-line banking and share dealing. There have been cases of undue inflation in share prices by hoax notices sent to financial newsgroups, or by bulk buying of shares by one person in order to artificially inflate the price and then selling them to make a profit. This problem is not unique to on-line trading, but there must be some guidance on how to deal with it in this sector. The legal framework provided by the Data Protection Act (DPA) and Computer Misuse Act offers some safeguards in this area. The DPA is discussed in chapter 9. Introduced in 1989/90, the Computer Misuse Act (CMA) makes it an offence for a person to perform any function that can be interpreted as unauthorised access to data, information or program from any type of computer (including bank cashpoints). The CMA covers access to information for illegitimate purposes even when a legal password is used as a measure to prevent employees of an organisation from misusing data.
- *Spam* – this is a term used to describe unsolicited emails. This is at best a source of irritation and at worst a barrier to e-commerce as it can slow a system down and thus cost businesses heavily. Spam also raises the issue of privacy of individuals. The European Distance Selling Directive introduced in the early 1990s requires that telephone and fax messages (emails were not common at the time) may not be sent to customers who have expressed a clear preference against them. The Electronic Commerce Directive (ECD) introduced in October 2000 clarified the case of electronic communication by the statement that an unsolicited email must be clearly and unequivocally identifiable as soon as it is received by the recipient. This enables the latter to choose whether or not to read it. The directive also suggests that service providers should regularly consult an opt-out register in which people not wanting unsolicited emails can register themselves. Additionally, in an attempt to eliminate any loopholes, it recommends a further opt-in scheme for those willing to receive such emails to register. The EU countries are divided in their opinion in the effectiveness of such regulations. A major difficulty stems from

. . . Contd.

Legal issues we must address are:

- clarify the concepts of a contract for electronic sale
- establish reliability of financial services
- provide a framework for consumers to avoid unsolicited emails (spam).

Contd. . . .

the fact that a large number of emails originate outside the EU and until an international agreement is reached, the situation cannot improve significantly.

- *Copyright* – the copyright law gives the owner of an intellectual property an exclusive right to copy or to authorise the making of copies of a protected work. The law applies to physical transactions of all written material regardless of its country of origin. This prohibits anyone except for the owner of the property to make copies of the material in any format (printed or electronic). Due to the difficulty in enforcing the law in some countries, the issue has also been addressed in international trade negotiations. This resulted in the introduction of a protocol on Trade Related Aspects of Intellectual Property Services (TRIPS) which obliges countries to abide by the copyright law. The law applies equally to digital products such as computer programs and covers documents published on the Internet. The law is not clear on the linking of documents to a website but it is advisable to request the permission of the author before doing so. However, deep-linking, that is linking directly to the pages of a website while bypassing the homepage, may also be copyright infringement (Booth-West, 2000). Databases are also protected by copyright laws, provided they are original and substantial in the quality and quantity of information stored. Recently the British Horseracing Board (BHB) brought an action against the UK bookmaker William Hill because it used the BHB database for its Internet service even though it only had permission to use the information for its telephone service (Booth, April, 2001).

  However, enforcing the laws in cyberspace can be difficult because of the ease and anonymity with which information in digital format can be downloaded, sent to others or printed. There are also those who argue that protection of digital information is moving too far in favour of the owners and a balance is required in order to maintain enforceability of the law. Napster, the company that introduced the practice of swapping MP3 files (digital music compressed to a tenth of its size) by peer-to-peer transmission (see chapter 5) has been entangled in a legal battle with the music industry on this issue.
- *Discrimination* – the application of discrimination laws is another area e-commerce companies need to pay attention to. For example, at the end of 1999, the National Foundation of the Blind brought an action against the Internet service provider AOL claiming its software is not compatible with the screen-access software used by the blind (Booth, 2001).
- *Libel* – libel in cyberspace can be a problem the same way it can be in the physical publishing medium. However, it is difficult to trace the originator of an offending email or a publication of malicious information by a newsgroup. The requirement by the ECD to make all emails identifiable by sender may be helpful in this respect. Regulation about libel is unclear, especially in the UK. This has resulted in a number of actions brought against the Internet service providers (ISPs) who displayed such material. Following the cases of some ISPs such as Compuserve and Demon (*Computer Weekly, e.business review*, 2000) being sued for contents in websites they host (of which they have little knowledge or control) on grounds of libel and the infringement of copyright laws, the EU and the USA have been working towards the introduction of a directive which would make ISPs only liable for material of which they have knowledge.

. . . Contd.

Legal issues we must address are:

- copyright of material published on a website
- discriminatory behaviour in electronic publishing
- the concept of libellous activities
- protection for consumers during on-line sales.

- *Security of trading* – we already discussed the security risks in e-commerce in detail. Buyers are increasingly worried by the lack of security of the medium. On the one hand, they are worried about sensitive information such as their personal or financial details transmitting over the Internet. On the other, people are seriously concerned about buying through a medium in which anyone with a website is potentially able to advertise and sell goods. Once money changes hands, consumers have little protection, especially when the business operates in another country. Sellers are equally worried as this is standing in the way of consumer trust and therefore their acceptance of e-commerce. Protecting electronically saved or transmitted data against loss, theft or misuse is vital in e-commerce. This has been a topic of much debate since the early days of computing and a legal infrastructure (the Data Protection Directive) has been established in order to provide consumers with some safeguard against invasion of privacy. We will discuss this in detail in chapter 9.

  While privacy laws enable organisations to gain consumer trust, they can also prohibit them from making the most of some technological innovations. For example, the technology now exists to locate individual mobile phone users and send marketing information in that locality directly to the phones. However, such activities contravene the current Data Protection Act (the law is expected to change soon). Although the law has sound basis in protecting an individual's privacy, it can have a negative effect on businesses.

The governments in a number of countries have proposed the use of digital signatures to establish a legal framework for e-commerce. However, the major problem in regulating such electronic authentication process is the lack of understanding between technologists and lawyers: neither of the two professions has any knowledge of the other. 'The result is laws which are either questionable or over-regulatory' (Kuner, 1999). As a result, increasingly companies are using their own procedures within the confines of intranets and dedicated financial networks which do not need to abide by government regulations. Governments in different countries are making attempts to deal with the situation in different ways and provide a system of authentication without restricting the course of business.[9] The European parliament has formed a European Directive on digital signatures that requires all countries in Europe to pass national legislation and create a voluntary licensing system for trusted third parties offering digital signature and encryption services. With the aim of limiting the obligation for companies trading internationally to comply with multiple jurisdiction, the EU directive on digital signature proposes that a company adheres to its Internet service provider's national regulations. In the UK, the government has introduced the Regulation of Investigatory Powers (RIP) Act, which allows it to intercept on-line communications. The act gives security services such as MI5 the right to monitor Internet traffic; if criminal activity is suspected, they can request a Home Office warrant to intercept and decode the content. If the message is encrypted, the Act would force the sender to submit the keys. The Bill has attracted considerable opposition and is still being debated.

The law in this area is very different in different countries. The US government was the first to start legislative procedures in an attempt to enable nominated third parties (escrow agencies) to hold a key. In 1993, the Clinton Administration introduced the concept of the Clipper chip, a high-security silicon chip inserted in all digital devices. Every Clipper chip would have a serial number; a universal key held by the FBI would give

[9] See the following websites for more details on the initiatives taken by some countries: http://cwis.kub.ni/~frw/people/hof/DS-lawsu.htm and http://www.ilpf.org/digsig/survey.htm.

them access to a serial number on the chip. The key that would decrypt the message would be kept in two pieces by two different government agencies (trusted third parties); using a court order and by presenting the serial number, the FBI could ask the two agencies to supply their half of the key and use them together to decrypt the message. The initiative generated enormous controversies and public protest. There were debates over the effectiveness of the system, the resulting cost of the equipment and the compatibility of devices with a Clipper chip and without. But the protest about the ethical consequences of the system was the most vociferous as a result of which the plan had to be dropped.

France has relaxed regulations for domestic encryption; Germany is opposed to restrictions on the use of encryption; Russia, Singapore and Malaysia have passed laws similar to RIP (Guardian Unlimited, 2001). We will come back to the consequences of such an Act as part of our discussion of privacy in cyberspace in the next section of the book.

In order for e-commerce to benefit both buyers and sellers we need the following:

- A legal framework which encourages rather than dampens the growth of e-commerce.
- Clarity and uniformity of the laws.
- A balanced view of the rights of businesses, users and consumers.
- Laws which are enforceable.

Regulations which have been introduced or are being proposed are:

- Distance Selling Directive
- tax laws for transactions between EU and non-EU countries
- use of digital signature
- use of escrow agencies for the interception of encrypted messages.

According to the US analyst Aberdeen Group, even large organisations have been guilty of violations of import and export laws. Since 1995, 200 'high tech' companies have incurred a civil or criminal penalty in the USA. Most of this is due to administrative errors rather than wilful negligence (Ward, 22 March, 2001). Non-compliance with international trade laws can result in penalties ranging between hefty fines, a revocation of export privileges and even a prison sentence. Internet technologies are growing at an amazing pace and regulators have the almost impossible task of keeping up. However, attempts are continually being made to address these issues. For example, Interpol (the International Police Co-operation) wants to create an international intelligence network to deal with cybercrime (Mathieson, December, 2000) by co-ordinating the efforts of the police forces in different countries and acting as an early warning system. However, this has been discouraged by experts for a number of reasons one of which is the problem of identifying illegal activities since the concept of legality varies between countries. We will come back to this topic in the last chapter of the book.

The regulatory framework for e-commerce must ensure that:

- some agreement is reached internationally
- the law is balanced, enforceable, clear and uniform
- there is a legal infrastructure that encourages rather than dampens the growth of e-commerce.

Conduct a survey of e-commerce related tax laws for international deliveries. How could these laws affect ordinary consumers?

Marketing

The goal of a company's marketing and promotional activity is to maintain a healthy and growing customer base for its products. Marketing has always been an important part of business. Although most bricks and mortar companies have substantial experience in this area, the increased competition, higher customer demand and changing patterns of buying brought on by the on-line revolution created additional push factors for organisations wishing to establish a closer relationship with their customers. According to Moon, (2000: 2), each connection in the global network of the Internet '. . . creates the possibility of a relationship, whether it be between firms and customers, firms and other firms, customers and other customers, or customers and machines. Consequently, it is important to recognise that network technology can not only be used to manage *information*, but can also be used to manage *relationships*'. Thus, while e-commerce requires that companies establish stronger relationships with customers, it also actively facilitates this process by providing the technologies required to reach the customers. The mechanism used to achieve this includes:

- market research
- promotional activities such as advertising and publicity
- brand establishment
- building relationships with customers
- assessment of customer behaviour.

Market research

These are corporate research projects designed to find the market potential of a product being considered for development. It involves establishing a research question, deciding on the specific objectives, performing a study of historical backgrounds and models, collecting data, analysing it and finally proposing an answer to the question. The finding of the research can then be used to formulate a relationship between potential buyers, the proposed product, the enterprise and the strategic goals of the company.

Market research (MR) is an old and established business method for the bricks and mortar sector. We are all acquainted with telephone surveys, marketing questionnaires distributed by post and other means and interviews conducted by MR personnel in public places or at our doorsteps. These methods have obvious problems such as public resistance to such intrusion, the cost of such surveys in terms of time and money required to collect and analyse the vast amount of data and the unreliability of data if unwilling participants provide false information. E-commerce companies have an advantage in that technology enables them to interrogate a large sample of people who can provide information while remaining anonymous. Users can choose whether or not they want to participate without any direct pressure (although indirect pressure is applied by companies in the form of offer of gifts and benefits) and the system can be interactive, quick and inexpensive for the company. However, there are problems in this method also, for example, all customers targeted by a firm for its proposed product may not be Internet-savvy or have the right technology yet. Security and privacy may also be the concern of some users. For these reasons e-commerce companies often need to rely on some off-line MR methods.

Electronic market research.

Benefits:

- large sample
- anonymity of sample
- user's discretion in participation
- interactivity
- speed
- cost saving.

Problems:

- dependence on technology
- security
- privacy.

The following techniques used by CRM systems (as discussed in chapter 6) can also collect MR data:

- Information on customers obtained by the use of software agents that track each customer event.
- Data collected from call centres, chat rooms and user communities.
- Customer histories taken from logs of user access.

As well as serving to improve CRM, the information collected from these sources can be fed into the market research project. Additionally, an enterprise can use MR companies which specialise in this field.

Advertising

The Internet is a powerful medium for advertising as it offers a company reach for its promotional activities and richness for its material. Advertising in e-commerce can be pursued *on-line* by using either a generalised approach such as mass email or a personalised approach such as messages to targeted customers with the help of data collected by tracking users' browsing habits. Advertising can also be done *off-line* via the mass media such as television and magazines or by direct mailing.

Several techniques can be used to perform on-line advertising. Amongst these are the following:

- *Banner* – a graphical image placed in websites and portals a click on which takes a user to the advertiser's website. A banner can also appear as a result of keyword search in which case surfers view advertisements on products they are interested in. Sometimes companies form associations with each other for banner display (see below); there are also ad-server companies such as DoubleClick which can serve messages simultaneously to multiple websites, measure results, create reports on the campaign and so on (Moon, 2000).
- *Emails* – referred to as spam, this is the on-line version of junk mail. Emails can also be targeted, that is, a group or community of users chosen on the basis of their buying habits are sent a mail. For example, a music e-tailer may send an email about new releases to all those who bought pop music in the last six months. Random emails are those sent to all users of a website, for example an ISP sending information about its new facilities to all its registered clients.
- *Viral marketing* – involves advertising via the Internet using customers' contacts to spread a message. All recipients of messages via Hotmail are presented with an offer for its free email service. 'Hotmail grew a subscriber base more rapidly than any new on-line, Internet, or print publication ever. This method utilises customer contacts in a way that makes an advertisement more acceptable to its receivers' (Moon, 2000). Many websites have a facility whereby a user can send a webpage to likely interested parties by simply entering their addresses. This is facilitated by companies to encourage one user to send an advertisement to his or her acquaintances.
- *Partnership between organisations* – a pact between companies who display each other's banners. This can be done by firms which are related to each other, for example a holiday company that incorporates links to hoteliers and tour guides. This method can also be used by companies not directly relevant to each other by the formation of a linked group, that is, by creating a chain in which a link from one company leads to the next relevant one and so on. Such partnerships can be formed on the basis of exchange of favour, or by contracts such as payments based on how many clicks or sales result from a banner display. Amazon.com uses this technique and pays its associates a referral commission every time they make a sale resulting from such a link.
- *Splash display* – a message flashed on the screen when a user is on-line. Such messages stay on display for a few seconds and provide information on a product, a button to access the webpage etc. often using colourful multimedia presentation tools.

Methods used in e-advertising:

- banner on websites
- emails – random or targeted
- viral marketing – using users' contacts to advertise
- partnership with other companies
- splash display.

As a consumer, how do you rate the above methods of advertising for their effectiveness?

On-line advertisements may also be personalised. This is done by acquiring information on customers and using it to differentiate and thereby target them for advertisements customised to suit a specific lifestyle. This is referred to as relationship marketing; we will come back to this later on in the chapter.

Off-line advertising is traditionally deployed via the mass media such as national newspapers, television, radio etc. or by the use of a direct (individualised) approach such as mail shots and telemarketing. While on-line marketing relies on its customers to use the Internet and take the initiative to click on a banner or reply an email, its off-line counterpart has the advantage of imparting its message without much customer involvement. This is especially true for the mass media as advertisements appear in front of users as a part of their daily routine of watching TV or reading a paper. This form of marketing can also have an entertainment value and therefore a good chance of success; direct advertising, on the other hand, can be a source of annoyance and is often ignored. According to research by Forrester, consumers, even younger people, trust traditional media more than they trust advertising on the web (Cap Gemini Ernst & Young, 2000).

Advertising strategies can take one of two main forms, which are both applicable to on-line and off-line businesses: pull or push. The pull model employs techniques which make advertising features available to consumers but wait for them to access them. For example, a banner for a company on the website of a search engine allows a user to decide whether or not to click on it. In the push model, a splash display will force a user to view the information presented by the message.

The pull technique of advertising make its features available to consumers but waits for them to access; the push technique forces a user to view the information presented.

Branding

A brand is a company's identity in the eye of its customers. It can be defined as 'a name or a word that conveys a promise to deliver on a value proposition' (CGEY, 2000: 30). In other words, it creates an expectation that the company can fulfil a promise to its customers that is meaningful and valued. Success in e-commerce depends on a number of intangible factors such as a company's brand profile, its attitude to building and maintaining customer relationships, the innovativeness of its products and presentation and so on. A company needs to utilise its resources as much as possible in order to enhance these areas; effective branding is a part of this philosophy. 'In the absence of a physical product or service, a brand can create an emotional relationship between the provider and the customer' (Nicolle, 2001: 53). One way for on-line companies to differentiate themselves from others is to use their brand to create communities of interest and thus strengthen their attraction, familiarity and therefore, market position to customers. Branding can be an effective advertising strategy for an enterprise because it helps it to give the appearance of developing a relationship of trust and loyalty with its customers. For example, Charles Schwab, the discount brokerage firm established in 1975, continued to attract a large customer base when it entered e-commerce. Although it does not execute on-line trades at the lowest cost, its customers trust it to continually innovate and provide value-rich and effective services such as asset allocation and free research software (CGEY, 2000). However a survey done by the advertising company Young & Rubicam in 1997 (as quoted in the CGEY report) using a very large sample of companies and brands in 32 countries showed that brand awareness is now much less important than relevance to the marketplace and differentiation from competitors. Thus when a brand's value proposition is successfully imitated by a competitor, it loses its differentiation, and therefore its standing.

Branding is the establishment of a company identity by creating:

- communities of interest
- familiarity
- attraction
- a relationship of trust and loyalty.

Branding in e-commerce is complicated by the visibility factor of the Internet. On-line businesses belong to a different genre, with different criteria for customer attraction. Although there is evidence that customers trust the established brands of the bricks and mortar companies and are likely to switch to their on-line counterpart, organisations cannot always rely on this. They must give careful thought to their strategies for going on-line. The report by CGEY lists three strategies used by such enterprises:

Urbia.co.uk

Urbia.co.uk is a pan-European family portal which went live in the UK in May 2000. Hugely successful in Germany where it was first launched, the site now also has a following in France. Urbia is aimed at families and provides everything from discussion forums to on-line clubs for people with shared interests.

The managing director of Urbia believes that the most important thing for a dotcom is to keep its brand values uppermost in its mind and to ensure that these are not lost in its marketing, advertising and PR campaigns. He uses the example of Boo.com to explain how easy it is to fall into the trap of creating strong brand awareness without truly communicating what it is a company does. Very few people associate Boo.com with fashion because companies like this plough too much money into expensive and 'clever' advertising which does nothing to communicate the real value of brand.

Urbia's approach has been to use advertising to create awareness and rely on PR to convert this awareness into real understanding. Its top priority has been to communicate its key message that 'Urbia is family' so people have no doubt what the company does.

According to the MD, logos should not be extravagant or complicated but simple and easy to remember. Urbia's logo is two-dimensional and can easily be recognised whether replicated in colour or black and white. That is not to say there is no room for fun and innovative ideas in the dotcom world, but clarity and simplicity in branding must be carried through to the logo.

(Source: Nicolle, 2001.
Printed with permission from
Reed Business Information Ltd.)

Questions

1. What principles has Urbia followed in its branding process?
2. With the help of more information on the company, find out how it conducted its other marketing activities.
3. Go to Urbia's website. Having established that Urbia is a family website, how may it develop its site features to keep its current users for 5 years or more?

- *The purposeful approach* – using the same brand name for both sectors, as done by Charles Schwab.
- *The Darwinian approach* – creating a new brand. Wingspan is an American bank operating independently of its parent company Bank One.
- *A combination of the above* – creating a new brand closely associated with its physical counterpart. Egg.com, which belongs to the insurance company Prudential, created an identity for itself under the umbrella of its parent.

As for advertising, branding can also be personalised. Sometimes referred to as rational branding, the ethos behind personalisation concentrates on solving customer problems and creating better experiences by offering help during shopping. Some companies founded their business by utilising this philosophy; US-based e-Loan and Mortgage.com help consumers looking for loans find better terms and rates. However, the world of brands is volatile. Historically large names such as Coca-Cola and Marks & Spencer (a UK retailing giant) have now got a much reduced customer loyalty. In the uncertain environment of e-commerce, the situation is much more sensitive; the only way to survive is to maintain relevance and differentiation. When amazon.com entered the booktrade, despite its completely unknown brand name, it managed to shake the foundation of the established physical marketplace. However, the same company has had to re-invent itself continually by introducing new products and services in order to remain relevant and differentiated. An organisation must develop a clear understanding of its customers as well as its own core competency and identify the target audience for its brand on the basis of this. It must

Brand loyalty is volatile and depends on its relevance and differentiation. Physical companies entering e-commerce can use the purposeful, Darwinian or mixed approach to create an on-line brand.

also review its performance continually by soliciting feedback from customers and by monitoring its competitors in order to remain competitive in the branding war.

Boo.com entered e-commerce with a high profile but the business failed soon afterwards. Find out what the reasons are.

Building customer relationships

Building a relationship with customers is arguably the most important part of marketing for e-commerce. 'Mindshare' or 'share of customer loyalty' and the resulting 'customer retention rate' are the key criteria for success for an enterprise (Moon, 2000). The Internet creates the perfect opportunity for companies to achieve this by providing an interface suitable for developing a relationship on-line. As it is about five to eight times more expensive to gain a new customer than it is to retain an existing one, companies must invest in acquiring information on customers, anticipate their needs, and attempt to develop a one-to-one relationship with each of them as if s/he is a market segment (customer group) of one, (Fingar *et al.*, 2000). Thus the basis of relationship building is the establishment of an interactive dialogue between customers, market specialists and business leaders. The introduction of a new product or a service must be a collaborative process in which users are allowed to take an active role. This is true for off-line as well as on-line enterprises, but the latter have an advantage because of their direct link with customers.

According to Moon (2000), building customer relationships involves an iterative cycle of knowledge acquisition, customer differentiation (differentiating customers on the basis of their needs and value to the firm) and customisation of marketing strategies (Fig. 7.4). An efficient customer relationship management (CRM) system discussed in previous chapters enables an enterprise to perform the first two functions. By using interactive technologies, today's firms gain knowledge of their customers and personalise their marketing strategies. The process of customisation provides the company with further knowledge of its present and potential customers, which it can utilise to enrich its knowledge base.

Relationship building is the establishment of an interactive dialogue between customers, market specialists and business leaders. It involves an iterative cycle of learning about customers, differentiating between them and customising marketing strategies accordingly.

Customising relationships can be performed by customising the following: products and services, communications techniques, distribution channels, and prices. We discussed

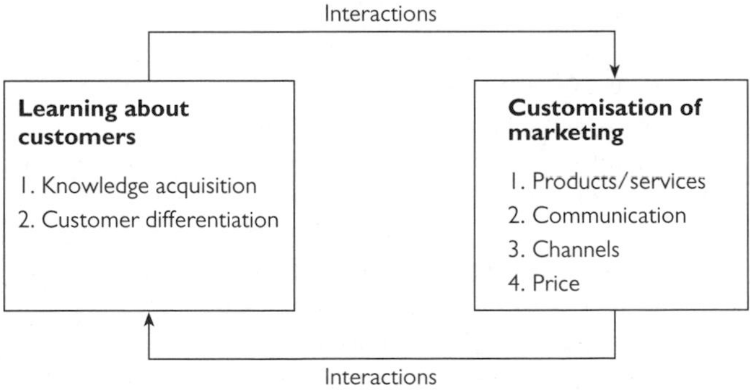

Fig. 7.4 Building a customer relationship (Source: Y. Moon, *Network Technology and the Role of Intermediaries*, 9-599-102. Boston: Harvard Business School, 2000. Copyright © by the President and Fellows of Harvard College. Reprinted with permission)

how customisation (or personalisation) is performed in this and previous chapters; the processes involved in doing this strengthens a firm's relationship with its customer. The company learns about customer preferences; remembering them and incorporating them into *products and services* contribute towards relationship building. For example, when buying on-line, a customer should not have to enter his or her bank details every time (see the example of Changeslive.com below) provided stringent security checks are built into the system. Anticipation of customer preference goes one step further in leveraging the firm's knowledge of its entire customer base and connecting it to individual preferences. For example, on-line booksellers can utilise one customer's preferences in book selection, compare it against its knowledge of other users with similar preferences, and recommend new selections to the original customer on the basis of the books bought by those users. Such marketing strategies enhance a firm's relationship with customers which, in turn, ties a customer to the enterprise.

Relationships with customers can be customised at four levels: products and services, communications techniques, distribution channels, and prices. A well-established knowledge base on customers helps to achieve this.

Moon has suggested four areas in which *customised communication* can be used: banners, emails, viral marketing, and experimentation. We discussed how personalisation can be applied to the first three areas in our discussion of advertising; experimentation involves the creation of a simulated environment in which customers are made to feel like they are part of some larger experience. For example Calvin Klein has developed an interactive on-line campaign to promote its unisex fragrance CK One. Users are invited to send emails to (and receive replies from) the characters (fictional on-screen images) of an advertisement of the product (Moon, 2000). Such techniques also contribute to community building, an important vehicle for advertising. On-line communities are the electronic version of 'word of mouth'; customers form relationships with each other and therefore with the enterprise that supports the community. By providing applications such as chat rooms, bulletin boards and newsgroups, organisations can enable customers to interact with each other during shopping, a practice not common in the physical world. In this way, companies can build communities around products and give consumers the sensation that they are participating in a lifestyle shared by others. Forrester Research calculates that people who participate in on-line communities are 36 per cent more likely to buy products on-line, 38 per cent more likely to read product reviews, 48 per cent more likely to request service for their products, and 17 per cent more likely to take part in market research on purchases than those who do not (Harvey, 2001: 53). However, the forum provided by a company for community building can also be used by unsatisfied customers for negative publicity; some organisations implement facilities for monitoring and managing (and censoring) these systems. For example, Changeslive.com, a company which sells health and beauty products has created chat room message boards and other community features. Customers can post questions on bulletin boards to be answered by experts on site, and they can hang around, and chat, and take part in community events on-line. However, the site retains fundamental controls such as a site monitor and a filter which takes out offensive content (Harvey, 2001). Any form of customised marketing must also allow users to 'opt out' if they so wish, otherwise the effort can be useless as well as irritating to individuals.

Electronic communities are a valuable technique for building a relationship with customers. Chat rooms, bulletin boards, newsgroups etc. help to build user communities and also creates a relationship of trust and familiarity with the enterprise and a shared lifestyle.

Customising *distribution channels* involves the use of multiple outlets for customer contact. For example, American Airlines regularly sends emails directly to certain customers. *Customised pricing* has been widely used by airline companies to attract travellers of different categories. In the e-commerce world, this model has been utilised uniquely by priceline.com (see chapter 1). As well as allowing customers to choose a price, some organisations allow them to choose a version of a product that suits them, a method which is most suitable for software products. However, the differentiated price model often used in the past by businesses to take advantage of customer ignorance can be difficult to implement in e-commerce. The Internet is a great leveller in customer power because it provides every user with an easy access to information, which enables them to choose the company that offers the best price.

In the global market of e-commerce, building trust is an important aspect of customer relationships. Enterprises are constantly seeking to enter new territories and attempting to communicate with societies of different cultures. A vital part of marketing in this situation is to create an image of trustworthiness for themselves in the new arena. A company which manages to build a relationship with its customers and learns to understand the pattern of their behaviour has an advantage in cyberspace.

In what ways could a website selling high-end stereo equipment build a relationship with its users while also benefiting from the relationship in market research terms?

Understanding customer behaviour

An understanding of customer behaviour is essential for all companies, physical and virtual. It helps an organisation form a relationship with customers and plan its future development. In order to do this, an enterprise needs to monitor customer actions throughout the buying process. The main stages that the company must be aware of are:

- A customer's acknowledgement of the need for a product and the beginning of a search. A customer considers buying a product or a service and starts a search. The decision to search does not come until the customer is certain that s/he needs it. Established bricks and mortar companies can use data from their surveys to understand consumer trends and desires before they start the buying process. On-line companies can only monitor information after the customer has established the need and started a search. It is therefore useful for them to use traditional market research in order to understand the behaviour of potential customers.
- The decision-making process. Once the on-line search starts, the tracking methods mentioned above can be used to monitor customer actions and deduce the searching pattern. A knowledge of this pattern enables a company to understand customer preferences. By combining this with the background of the user, the company can build a customer profile for its products. This can give them an understanding of customer behaviour by age, gender, ethnic background, economic and educational status and so on. A knowledge of the search process – how long a user spends at it, whether or not s/he comes back or proceeds to the next stage etc. – also gives the company feedback on the acceptability of its website to its users.
- The purchase. Monitoring this process enables an enterprise to obtain further information on customer behaviour. The methods used to select a product, pay for it, choose the delivery option and other actions all strengthen the model of customer profiles built up so far.
- The return visit. This step can confirm the information collected during the previous processes and acts as useful feedback on the products and services offered by the firm. Empowered customers of the Internet age are in a position to switch suppliers if they are not satisfied; their on-line behaviour enables an organisation to recognise any shift in the pattern of customer loyalty and act accordingly.

The pattern of customer behaviour can be understood by monitoring the processes of:

- acknowledging the need and starting a search
- decision making
- purchasing
- returning to the website.

By continually monitoring customer behaviour, businesses can evaluate a market and feed the information gathered into its business strategies. Thus, marketing not only contributes to a company's sales figure, but is also a major process that provides a valuable tool for an organisation to design its strategic mission.

Monitor your own (or another user's) behaviour when you buy on-line. Discuss what conclusions a company might make from the above processes and how those can help the company's marketing.

Although the examples used in the above discussion of marketing apply mainly to B2C, the B2B sector also undergoes similar processes, with additional formal procedures associated with each activity. The main difference between the marketing methods used by the two sectors is that for B2B, the buyers also happen to be businesses with their own rules, methodologies and bureaucracies. Therefore the processes must be accompanied with documentation and supported by a formal legislative framework. For example, understanding buyer behaviour in this sector would be based on a written request for product information, the presentation of quotes, sales figures, target product demographic and so on.

The development of an operational infrastructure that supports the above activities equips an organisation to utilise its knowledge- and technology-based resources to deliver the products and services in a way that fulfils its strategic goals. The infrastructure provides an enterprise with the framework it requires to develop its business processes and implement the systems described above. The extent to which it succeeds depends on the ability of the company to address the management issues associated with the implementation.

Critically review the processes of on-line and off-line marketing from a customer's point of view.

MANAGEMENT ISSUES

At the beginning of the chapter we listed the objectives of an operational infrastructure. Business leaders aiming to meet those objectives must be capable of providing a framework for the management of the business processes described above. They must make strategic decisions based on the findings of the marketing and promotional processes, and address the issues surrounding the implementation of the systems which would support them. They must also develop a technology infrastructure that these systems need and create an environment in which the technical, informational and operational activities complement each other. In order to improve a company's overall performance, management must review its strategies and business processes and re-design where necessary. This involves leadership on the following issues:

- *The management of IT* – this requires decisions on how to develop and implement the IT systems. This includes hardware, applications and user interfaces; careful attention must be paid to ensure that they fulfil their full potential.
- *Implementation of the business systems* – implementing the systems described in this chapter necessitates decisions on how to develop and introduce the systems, whether or not to outsource, and so on.

- *Risk management and recovery procedures* – a framework must be established to ensure that there are guidelines for the continual review of business processes, risk management procedures and a recovery plan. In the uncertain world of e-commerce, an absence of such a framework can be the reason behind a company's bankruptcy.
- *Resource management* – an organisation must have established procedures for managing all its resources such as technology, labour, capital, management expertise and user skills.
- *Business process re-engineering* – BPR involves the re-thinking and if necessary, the re-designing of business processes in the light of new innovations and the introduction of a dramatically different business concept to gain advantage in the market (Hamel, 2000). E-commerce was introduced as a result of BPR in the 1980s and 1990s; the practice should continue in order to make it a success.

Implementation of an operational infrastructure requires:

- management of IT
- development and implementation of business systems
- risk management and recovery procedures
- resource management
- business process re-engineering.

These issues are addressed as a part of the implementation of e-commerce and will be discussed in the consequences section of the book.

SUMMARY

In the last 10 years, organisations in cyberspace used the Internet to move through the stages of: brochureware, e-commerce which saw the rise of B2C companies, e-business which started the B2B era, and finally the e-enterprise era marked by the attempts by some bricks and mortar companies to combine B2B and B2C. At present, different businesses are at different stages in this evolution; the success rate in this process depends on the ability of the organisations to build an operational infrastructure that takes advantage of their communications and information infrastructure in order to facilitate business processes such as supply-chain management, procurement, payment infrastructure, logistics, regulatory framework and marketing.

Supply-chain management is the process of communication between business partners in order to organise the supply of material between businesses, the production of final goods and services and their essential distribution. Different models can be used to perform these activities and advances in technology provide the means for doing so cheaply, quickly and reliably. Electronic procurement can be achieved by the use of standard on-line activities or by the use of a marketplace. It can be applied at different strategic levels of increasing enterprise-wide involvement; it facilitates cost saving, better co-ordination between partners and the optimisation of purchasing procedures.

A payment infrastructure is essential for providing a secure platform for financial transactions. Protocols such as secure sockets layer (SSL) and secure electronic transactions (SET) are used to deliver the platform. Other services used are the bank clearing systems in different countries, electronic cheques, smartcard-based technologies and a combination of on-line and off-line activities introduced by First Virtual. For the transaction of larger amounts typical to the B2B sector, it is possible to use countries' financial networks as well as the electronic bill payment (EBP) systems supported by major technology companies. Logistics is another area that an operational infrastructure needs to support. Using a number of established strategies, it provides the basis for an efficient distribution system.

One important aspect of e-commerce which needs to have a clear infrastructure is that of national and international regulations guiding on-line business transactions. This concerns areas such as tax, trademarks, sales information and contracts, customs restrictions, copyright, use of unsolicited mails, the concepts of libel, discrimination, security

Watford Electronics

Watford Electronics started life in 1972 in the bedroom of its managing director (MD) as a mail order supplier of electronic components. From selling home computers in the 1980s, it moved on to Wintel PCs in the 1990s, and finally to manufacturing and selling its own brand plus 7000 items of hardware, software and peripherals. It utilised its knowledge of IT to adapt to the Internet early. In 1997, Watford Electronics developed a website to display product information and take orders. Today, the site receives about six million hits and provides a channel for 3500 orders a month, worth £500,000. It is now using the communications facilities of the Internet to turn itself into a virtual operation. Its motto has been to streamline operations and turn itself into an e-business not only to survive but to become successful in an increasingly competitive global economy. According to the MD, the company can sell goods at very low prices because it does not have the usual overheads such as warehouse space, stock forecasting, obsolescence issues, booking and despatching stock, staff training and so on.

However, Watford has had its fair share of problems. Its attempts to create a virtual company with seamless links to its suppliers' systems have been frustrated by organisational issues with its trading partners. While some people have been very keen to liaise at top level about their supply-chain management, some, even major, suppliers have been much less interested. Its first website, developed for very high fees by an external consultancy, failed to deliver a versatile and user-friendly interface.

Following a hard search for a suitable web developer at the right price, the company decided to do it in-house. It recognised that the risk of this route was that the techies in the company might take over and not deliver what was required. Therefore it maintained top-level commitment and continual involvement from the board with the aim of ensuring that the project delivered real e-business benefits. Improvements were made to the site in four stages in order to provide additional facilities and usability. Now the website has express checkout facilities for repeat customers so they just have to enter their customer numbers and click on the order; the system will remember the rest.

The IT team and management hold regular meetings to evaluate the performance of the website. The company monitors customers' reactions to the site, soliciting feedback by thanking people who make comments with a small gift.

At the root of the efficiency of the website is its integration with the back-office enterprise resource planning system. Microsoft's Data Transformation Services is used to synchronise front- and back-office databases every five minutes and Masterpack, running on IBM RS/6000, is used to get data in and out of the ERP system. Such integration allows Watford to keep customers posted on the progress of their orders. Seamless links with suppliers' systems allow the company to forward the confirmation of orders and delivery dates by email. EDI messages from suppliers update Watford's system, so customers can access a summary of orders and find the status of the items in their order. They can even link to couriers' sites to find out whether their parcel is in the delivery van or when it was signed for.

Links with couriers also allow Watford to wait until delivery has been confirmed until it debits customers' credit cards. This increases customers' confidence in the company. Watford uses sophisticated anti-fraud measures at the start of the ordering process, including a card authorisation solution from a company called Checkline which can authorise a card in just four seconds. If there is a query, the details are automatically directed to a human operator. Customers are also protected through a series of security solutions based on SSL. Digital certificates are used for encrypting sensitive data, while a firewall screens all traffic.

Watford relies heavily on return customers and delivering excellent customer service is the prime objective of the website. If customers are unhappy with a product, the site enables them to access information about manufacturer warranties and Watford's own return policies. It also allows them to arrange a refund or exchange. The concept of customer self-service has been extended to other areas also. Customers can access detailed product specifications on-line, check prices even when they are on another site for comparison, and a build-to-order PC configuration tool which would display a running total as the customers select components.

Customers are increasingly using email to send queries rather than use the call centre. Watford has now restructured its customer services team and introduced systems to automatically distribute email queries to agents. The receiving agent sends a reply within an average of 10 minutes. The company has also changed its promotional tactics; it has reduced the size of the off-line catalogue that it sends to about half a dozen specialist magazines from 64 pages to just 16. Savings have also been made due to a dramatic reduction in number of breakages and obsolescent stock. The purchasing team, now called the supply management team, is now able to spend more time sourcing new products.

(Source: Warren, February 2001. Printed with permission from Reed Business Publishing Ltd.)

Questions

1. What were Watford's main objectives?
2. Discuss how the company's supply management system was changed and what benefits it provided.
3. Discuss Watford's strategies for customer relationship management and the benefits they brought.
4. Discuss the steps the company took to create and utilise customer communities for business benefits.
5. To what extent does this case study address regulatory issues? What else does a similar company need to consider in this area?
6. What are the main management issues for the company and to what extent did it deal with those?
7. Discuss the case study in terms of the evolutionary model of an e-enterprise.

and privacy in trading etc. A regulatory framework must be established to ensure that a company follows the guidelines established by the law governing bodies. There is a debate going on in Europe and the USA (some other countries are beginning to take part) about the use of PKI-based digital signature and the appropriateness of enabling a government-nominated third party to intercept electronic messages. Government initiatives taken so far have met with public protest and have not been successful. However, it is important to ensure that the law is clear, balanced, uniform, enforceable and beneficial to the industry.

Marketing is a major business activity. It includes market research, advertising, branding, relationship building and the assessment of customer behaviour. Both on-line and off-line procedures, aimed at the general public as well as individuals, are performed to facilitate these activities. Market research can use communities, chat rooms etc. to gather information on customer preferences; advertisers can use banners, emails, and viral marketing techniques to promote their products; branding with relevance and differentiation must be used to build trust between a company and its customers. The acquisition, remembrance and anticipation of information on buyers and customising marketing procedures on the basis of these allows companies to build relationships with customers. Understanding customer behaviour is also very important for e-commerce; this is done by observing the actions customers take during the processes of searching, decision making, purchasing and re-visiting a website.

The processes described above apply directly to B2C companies but can also serve the B2B community when formalised, accompanied by documentation and supported by legislative framework. The development of these processes requires that company leaders address a number of issues that we will discuss in the consequences section of the book. We will explore how businesses can approach the implementation of e-commerce systems and how these processes can affect individuals, businesses and communities. We will also consider what can be done to avoid any negative consequences of Internet-based businesses and attempt to assess the future of e-commerce.

Revision Questions

1. Explain the concept of an operational infrastructure. Why do we need it?
2. Describe the four phases of evolution of electronic commerce.
3. List the business processes contributing to an operational infrastructure and explain the basic principles behind each of them.
4. How does supply-chain management in cyberspace differ from the bricks and mortar companies?
5. Describe the models used by e-commerce in order to accomplish an efficient supply-chain.
6. How has electronic supply-chain management changed the balance of power between large and small businesses?
7. Describe the three strategic levels at which electronic procurement can be used. Discuss the benefits of such systems.
8. Describe secure electronic transaction (SET) protocol for e-commerce payment.
9. Compare the contributions of SET and SSL in the development of a payment infrastructure for e-commerce.
10. Describe the contribution of credit card companies in the establishment of a payment infrastructure.
11. Discuss the suitability of the payment technologies described in this chapter for the B2C and the B2B sector.
12. Discuss the concept of electronic cash and how it contributes to a secure payment system.
13. Describe how First Virtual combined on- and off-line activities to ensure security of payment.
14. Describe an electronic bill payment (EBP) system
15. Discuss the importance of an efficient framework for logistics for e-commerce.
16. Describe the four logistics used in e-commerce which are expected to improve distribution channels.
17. Which areas of e-commerce require a legal infrastructure?
18. Discuss the national and international regulatory framework designed to provide the above.
19. What are the main activities in marketing in the e-commerce sector? Describe each of them briefly.
20. Discuss the relative merits and demerits of on-line and off-line marketing.
21. Discuss the relative merits and demerits of individualised and generalised marketing.
22. Distinguish between marketing strategies for the B2C and the B2B sector.
23. What are the main methods used to perform market research in e-commerce?
24. Which methods are used for advertising in e-commerce? Describe each of them.
25. How can off-line brands go on-line with equal success?
26. Why is it important for e-commerce companies to build customer relationship? How can this be achieved?
27. How can an electronic community contribute to market research and brand development?
28. Why is it important to understand customer behaviour in e-commerce? Describe the methods used to do this.
29. Which issues should management address in the establishment of an operational infrastructure and why?

Discussion Questions

1 Discuss the roles played by different processes involved in building an operational infrastructure. In what ways can an enterprise gain most from these processes?
2 What are the problems associated with e-commerce from a) the buyer's and b) the seller's point of view? How can those be minimised?

Bibliography

Alfreds, L., Ingram woes pinned on mismanagement, *PC Dealer*, 29 October, 1999.

Bicknell, D., Delivering the goods, *Computer Weekly, e.business review*, May, 2000, p. 16.

Booth, E., Think before you link, *Computer Weekly, e.business review*, March, 2001, p. 87.

Booth, E.; Calculating data costs, *Computer Weekly, e.business review*, April, 2001, p. 94.

Booth-West, E., Untangling the legal web, *Computer Weekly, e.business review*, December, 2000, p. 101.

Cap Gemini Ernst & Young LLC, *Electronic Commerce: A Need to Change Perspective*, Special Report on the Financial Services Industry, 2000.

Chaston, I., *e-Marketing Strategy*, McGraw-Hill, Maidenhead, UK, 2001.

Computer Weekly, e.business review, May, 2000, p. 7.

Duschinsky, P.; Can you afford not to buy into e-procurement? *Computer Weekly*, 24 August, 2000a, p. 28.

Duschinsky, P., Get sold on e-procurement, *Computer Weekly*, 7 December, 2000b, p. 38.

Everett, D. B., Cashless society? *Computer Weekly, e.business review*, July/August, 2000, p. 52.

Fell, J., Regulation and the future of virtual financial services, *Global Electronic Commerce, UK*, Issue 6, 2000, p. 5.

Fingar, P., Kumar, H. and Sharma, T., *Enterprise E-Commerce: The Software Components Breakthrough for Business-to-Business Commerce*, Florida, 2000.

Gates, B., *Business @ the Speed of Thought: Succeeding in the Digital Economy*, Penguin Books, London, 1999.

Glennie, R. and Macpherson, S., Electronic commerce: Key legal issues, *Global Electronic Commerce, UK*, Issue 4, 1999, p. 32.

Guardian Unlimited Website, www.guardianunlimited.co.uk

Hamel, G., *Leading the Revolution*, Harvard Business School Press, 2000.

Harvey, F., Want to be in my gang?, *Computer Weekly, e.business review*, April, 2001, p. 52.

Hoque, F., *e-Enterprise: Business Models, Architecture, and Components*, Cambridge University Press, New York, 2000.

Kuner, C., National legislation on electronic authentication: An answer without a question, *Global Electronic Commerce*, Issue 4, 1999, p. 30.

Laudon, K. C. and Laudon, J. P., *Management Information Systems: Organisations and Technology in the Networked Enterprise*, Prentice Hall, New Jersey, 2000.

Leed, H., Messaging: The missing link in logistics, *e-Business Adviser*, January, 2001, p. 14.

Lloyds, I., *Legal Aspects of the Information Society*, Butterworths, London, 2000.

Marsh, D. J., Legal infrastructure in electronic business, *E-business – Best Practice for ESMs and PLCs*, e centre^{UK}, 1999, p. 106.

Mathieson, S., Coalface: Advanced supply-chain management means Woolworths is avoiding seasonal blunders, *Computing*, 14 December, 2000, p. 18.

Mathieson, S., Will Net police ever patrol a global beat? *Computing*, 26 October, 2000, p. 18.

Moon, Y., *Interactive Technologies and Relationship Marketing Strategies*, Harvard Business School, 9-599-101, 19 January, 2000.

Nicolle, L., 'Bricks' lead brand backlash, *Computer Weekly*, 22 March, 2001, p. 53.

Ody, P., Codifying the tax collectors, *Computer Weekly, e.business review*, April, 2001, p. 33.

Ovans, A., E-Procurement at Schlumberger: A conversation with Alan-Michael Diamant-Berger, Harvard Business Review, F00302, 2000.

Rajput, W. E., *E-Commerce Systems Architecture and Applications*, Artech House, Boston, 2000.

Rayport, J. F. and Jaworski, B. J., *e-Commerce*, McGraw-Hill, New York, 2001.

Samuels, M. and Phillips, T., Retail goes e-tail – and more besides, *Computer Weekly*, 26 October, 2000, p. 37.

Turban, E., Lee, J., King, D. and Chung, H. M., *Electronic Commerce: A Managerial Perspective*, Prentice Hall, New Jersey, 2000.

Ward, H., Most sites breach fair trading law, *Computer Weekly*, 15 March, 2001, p. 3.

Ward, H., Reuters spearheads call for global bank network, *Computer Weekly*, 15 March, 2001, p. 3.

Ward, H., Taxing times for global sales, *Computer Weekly*, 22 March, 2001, p. 18.

Warren, L., Electronic makeover, *Computer Weekly*, 8 February, 2001, p. 27.

Warren, L., Handle with care; *Computer Weekly*, 8 March, 2001, p. 8.

Warren, L., Turning e-dash into e-cash, *Computer Weekly*, 26 October, 2000, p. 62.

Consequences

Part Three

Strategic Implementation of E-Commerce

Chapter Eight

Objectives

By the end of this chapter you should have an understanding of:

- Some of the debates on strategy formulation in the Internet era.
- The importance of a strategic model for businesses in cyberspace.
- The steps involved in the development and implementation of e-commerce systems.
- The principles behind the management of e-commerce.

INTRODUCTION

In the concepts section of the book, we explored the importance of a set of infrastructures in ensuring that e-commerce functions properly, and discussed the characteristics of the technical, informational and operational systems which underpin these infrastructures. In this section, we will explore how those systems should be implemented and what effects they have on businesses and customers.

An enterprise must have a mission and certain business goals based on that mission. Leaders of an organisation formulate strategies to fulfil those goals and guide the development and implementation of the business systems capable of completing its mission. A number of strategic models for businesses in the Internet era have been suggested by scholars; organisations thriving to become e-businesses must adopt the strategies that suit their needs and develop e-commerce systems accordingly. In this chapter, we will discuss how an organisation can establish its e-commerce strategies, the steps involved in the development and implementation of e-commerce applications and the challenges faced by management regarding both the on-line and off-line aspects of the implementation process.

DEFINING BUSINESS STRATEGY IN THE INTERNET ERA

Michael Porter (1996) describes competitive strategy as being different from others. He stresses that many companies fail to distinguish between this and the principles of operational effectiveness (OE), which is the use of management tools and techniques to perform better than competitors. Japanese firms reaped enormous advantages in the 1970s and 1980s by following the principle of OE; the introduction of the philosophy of just-in-time (JIT) deliveries gave Japanese manufacturers major advantages over their Western counterparts during that period. However, operational techniques are easy to imitate and so the advantages of OE are short-lived. Strategic positioning attempts to achieve sustainable advantage by performing different activities from rivals or performing similar activities in different ways. Thus, creating a strategic agenda is about defining a unique position and maintaining it with discipline and continuity. A major part of a successful strategy is to continually improve a firm's OE by making relentless efforts to achieve the best results. Thus, while both OE and strategy are essential for market advantage, OE is the tool a company uses to fulfil its strategic goals.

In a paper written in March 2001 on the strategic importance of the Internet, Porter argues that contrary to common perception, the Internet is not necessarily a blessing for businesses because 'It tends to alter industry structures in ways that dampen overall profitability, and it has a levelling effect on business practices, reducing the ability of any company to establish an operational advantage that can be sustained' (p. 64). He recommends that the Internet should be used as a spur to the traditional sphere of competition because 'Far from making strategy less important, as some have argued, the Internet actually makes strategy more essential than ever'. In order to create economic value – the gap between price and cost of business – enterprises must shift their focus from the technology of the Internet to its strategic benefits.

According to Michael Porter (2001), a combination of operational effectiveness and strategic positioning is required to gain a sustainable competitive advantage.

Mintzberg[1] defined strategy in terms of the 5 Ps: plan, ploy, pattern, position and perspective.

- *Plan* – Strategy as a plan is the process of formulating a plan before any action takes place consciously, purposefully and sometimes stated explicitly in formal documents, such as a plan of war drawn by the military. Thus, plan is a route to follow, the practical steps to take in order to complete a mission.
- *Ploy* – A ploy can be seen as a specific 'manoeuvre' designed to 'outwit rivals', as performed by a chess player.
- *Pattern* – While plan and ploy may be intended but not necessarily executed, pattern represents a series of of actions taken consistently with or without a plan. Thus, pattern may comprise tactics which may or may not have risen from strategy, for example, Ford's decision to produce only black vehicles in the 1920s. However, Mintzberg argues that the distinction between strategy and tactics can be arbitrary and misleading and suggests that the word tactics should be dropped and issues should be referred to as more or less strategic because 'There are times when it pays to manage the details and let the strategies emerge for themselves'.
- *Position* – Position refers to the 'niche' or the 'domain' an organisation occupies and dedicates its resources to, and the rules it follows to cope in this environment. A position can be taken against one competitor or a number of them; it can be established by the assumption of a niche to avoid competition; it can also be done collectively by joint ventures and mergers. A number of dotcom companies such as the on-line auction firm eBay succeeded by finding a niche.
- *Perspective* – Perspective refers to the 'character' of an organisation, the collective ideology and the driving force of an enterprise. For example, Virgin Atlantic, the airline company created by Richard Branson, follows the same 'lifestyle' perspective that drives his other companies and employees.

Mintzberg defines strategy as: plan, ploy, pattern, position or perspective. An enterprise uses the one that suits its purpose to find a winning path.

Mintzberg (1998) suggests a company needs strategies for a number of reasons: to set a direction which would outsmart competitors and enable the company to manoeuvre through threatening behaviour; to focus the effort required to co-ordinate activities; and to provide consistency and efficiency by reducing uncertainty and aiding knowledge creation. Strategies require that resources are invested in order to design a 'winning' path; however, Mintzberg also warns business leaders of the danger of an organisation becoming blinded by outdated strategies and losing peripheral vision. Therefore, strategy formulation must be focused on achieving company stability as well as development.

[1] Mintzberg, H., The strategy concept II: Another look at why organisations need strategies. In H. Costin (ed.), *Readings in Strategy and Strategic Planning*, The Dryden Press, Orlando, 1998. © Thomson Learning Corporation.

According to Gary Hamel (2000), in the new economy of the Internet, wealth does not come from innovation in technology or in a product, but through business concept innovation (BCI) which involves building a business model that is unlike anything that has come before. A company must first differentiate existing business concepts, then define new ways to create wealth and finally, put them into practice by building a suitable business model. Thus, like Michael Porter, Hamel also puts the emphasis on differentiation (being different) but argues that BCI is not strictly about competitive advantage because it is not a way of positioning against competitors, but of going around them to find dramatic new ways to create new wealth. We will come back to this concept later on in the chapter.

Gary Hamel emphasises the need for business concept innovation to create a competitive advantage for a company's products through a process of differentiating existing business concepts, defining new ways to create wealth and then building a business model to introduce the changes.

Szulanski and Amin (2000) describe strategy making as an art, especially in an uncertain environment such as that created by the Internet. Coping in this environment often requires the creative imagination of a visionary who is capable of formulating powerful new strategies which break with the past and create new values. However, they warn that such imagination may reflect only one person's perspective and can lead to impractical ideas. On the other hand, if strategy formulation is left to the disciplined approach of a professional planner then problems may arise due to too much emphasis on operational effectiveness based on business process re-engineering or total quality management (the measurement of quality of products and services). Those who believe in this approach have gone as far as to say that we do not need strategy (Byrne, 1996 as quoted in Szulanski and Amin). According to them, by sticking with tried and tested paths of analysis rather than synthesis and by preparing the selection of processes rather than the generation of new ideas, strategy prohibits original insights and creative alternatives. Others (Weick, 1989, as quoted in Szulanski and Amin) recommended the use of *disciplined imagination* – a different kind of discipline that allows diversity and imagination rather like musical improvisation. 'Strategy making can be an art, but in situations of uncertainty, strategy making *must* be an art. . . . The rapidly changing reality of emerging technologies strains established approaches to strategy' (Szulanski and Amin, 2000: 204).

Some see strategy as art, disciplined imagination, generation of new ideas and improvisation. Others see it as an accumulation of simple rules.

Eisenhardt and Sull (2001) also support a non-traditional approach to viewing strategy in the new economy. In their paper on 'strategy as simple rules', they advocate the value of taking advantage of the confusion of a chaotic market and probing for opportunities by a process of constantly evolving strategies. 'Rather than avoiding uncertainty, they should jump in', is the advice of the authors. However, they do not recommend the absence of a strategy, rather a few key strategic processes and some simple rules to guide a firm through chaos. This is the kind of opportunistic strategic approach often taken by entrepreneurs in fast-moving markets such as that of e-commerce. They capture unanticipated, fleeting opportunities in order to win against established competitors (as done by amazon.com). This is true for small as well as large companies; while traditional means of strategy development based on a company's market position or resources are appropriate for slowly or moderately changing well-structured markets, the logic of simple rules is suitable for the rapidly changing, ambiguous market of e-commerce. Yahoo! started with very limited resources as a catalogue of websites in a market which was highly competitive, had a very low entry barrier and demanding customers. Although some people at that time suggested that Yahoo! had no strategy, in reality, it followed key strategic processes based on simple rules such as capturing a new market and creating a customer-friendly interface.

Discuss, using the example of a bank, in what ways it can use the above definitions of strategy in launching a new service.

With the above debates in mind, we must now explore the specific strategic needs of businesses and examine the recommendations made by scholars analysing the importance of strategy making in the turbulent world of e-commerce.

APPROACHES TO STRATEGY FORMULATION

Strategy formulation is the development of long-term, risk-aware and target-meeting plans for establishing the well-being and strength of an enterprise relative to its competitors. It involves examining and redefining the firm's mission, reviewing it in the light of the project in hand, analysing the company's strengths and weaknesses, specifying achievable objectives for the project, establishing strategies for development and setting guidelines for implementation. A number of approaches to strategy formulation and advice on how to gain a competitive advantage have been offered by scholars working in this area.

Boisot (1995) suggested a strategic model comprising four approaches to suit organisations with different needs:

- *Strategic planning* – based on the traditional philosophy of working hard at collecting and managing data. In this approach data is collected at regular intervals and a top-down approach is taken in using the data to break down strategies into operational plans. It assumes that data changes slowly and that any short-term changes are reflections of predictable and long-term trends. The strategy depends on hard work and hierarchical management control.
- *Emergent strategy* – follows Mintzberg's idea that strategy formulation must be focused on stability as well as change in order to respond to the unpredictability of the environment. In this approach, those at an operational level are allowed to take action in response to unforeseen circumstances; this might involve the use of a plan and then move on to a ploy and even further, if necessary, in the 5 Ps model.
- *Intrapreneurship* – this assumes that the rate of change in the Internet age is so high that the best an organisation can do is to respond to changes as they occur. Based on the same principle as that advocated by Eisenhardt and Sull (2001), firms tackle challenges at local levels in the organisation rather than activating for a comprehensive corporate strategy. There must be a high level of initiative and trust in the organisation for this strategy to work.
- *Strategic intent* – a long-term strategic vision often formally expressed in the form of a mission statement. This approach depends on collective initiative and focused unity in order to cope with a rapidly changing environment. This strategy lends itself well to the decentralised model of e-commerce businesses and the philosophy of an entrepreneurial vision as described by Szulanski and Amin (2000).

Boisot's approach to strategy formulation:

- Use data to turn strategies into plans.
- Allow those at operational level to take action.
- Tackle challenge at local level.
- Use collective initiative to create a mission to reflect long-term strategy.

Organisations must opt for an approach that suits their circumstances. Businesses facing rapid changes would opt for intrapreneurship or strategic intent, an established organisation in a stable market environment would probably opt for strategic planning, while a company attempting to expand from a physical market to cyberspace might find the emergent strategy more appropriate.

As explained before, Porter (2001) recommends that businesses move away from a focus on operational effectiveness (OE) and reconnect with strategy. He suggests the following actions:

- Create unique activities and find new positions in the market. This can be done by: selling a unique product or service (e.g. priceline.com); serving a unique group of customers such as providing on-line financial services to only those with large savings; or using a unique criterion for accessing customers, such as providing estate agency for rural areas. Here, the strategy is to find a suitable market.

- Acknowledge the need for trade-offs by making choices between activities on the basis of changing needs. This involves limiting what a company offers and deciding what not to do. The strategy used in this case is to make a choice between incompatible activities.
- Find a fit between activities in a way that interlocks them and makes it hard for competitors to imitate any of them. For example, Southwest Airlines in the USA introduced no-frill flights with no meals, seat arrangements or baggage transfers. This enabled it to use airports and routes which are not popular and therefore not congested. Its choice of types and length of routes allowed it to use only one type of aircraft, a Boeing 737. The strategy used here is creating a chain of activities which reinforce each other and save cost collectively thus giving the company a sustainable advantage.
- *Rediscover strategy*. Lured by new technologies, managers often lose sight of strategy and concentrate on the immediate and tangible results of OE. Porter advises companies to reconnect with strategy, re-examine the company's original vision and historical positioning and decide if a renewal of the strategies that gave them uniqueness and competitive advantage in the past can be remodelled in the light of modern technologies. This requires a focus on the following:
  - Find/select the distinct products in the company.
  - Select the most profitable products, customers, channels and purchase occasions.
  - Select the most different and effective activities in the value chain.

Porter recommended:

- Creating unique activities.
- Making choices between what to do and what not to.
- Creating activities that interlock (fit).
- Reconnecting with strategy by finding distinct and profitable products, and different activities.

In discussing misunderstandings about the role of the Internet in businesses, Porter (2001) has warned companies against the low switching cost for customers and the low entry barrier for new entrants. He stressed the need for maintaining uniqueness in this environment by concentrating on real economic value rather than artificially created short-term share prices.

Writing about the importance of business concepts innovation, Hamel (2000) recommended that firms ask themselves a number of questions in relation to their business model, the major components of which are (Fig. 8.1): core strategy, strategic resources, customer interface and value network. Each component comprises a number of elements; a firm must analyse these elements and ask itself how innovation can be created in those areas in order to achieve distinction and economic value. Hamel also describes the role of configuration, customer benefits and company boundaries as the elements that link different components of a business model and thus provide support for the strategies chosen for innovation.[2]

- *Core strategy* – the way a firm competes in the marketplace. This involves making decisions on a number of things:
  - The company's mission – its overall business objectives. Business leaders must revisit their goals and decide strategically if they need to be updated or extended to challenge competitors. For example, Dell Computers used its method of direct selling[3] as the cornerstone of its mission (Michael Dell

[2] The framework for much of the discussion in this section comes from Hamel (2000).

[3] Sales based on direct orders from customers.

started his business life selling stamps by mail order) and decided to introduce build-to-order PCs as soon as technologies equipped to handle it were available.
  - Market scope – the market the company wants to capture in terms of customers, locations and products. The firm must find innovative ways to capture a unique market and extend its services to maintain its position. For example, many supermarket chains (e.g. Tesco) have capitalised on their large customer base to offer financial services.
  - Differentiation – how the company can differentiate itself from the rest of the market. eBay's success in the auction business (unlike most other dotcom companies, it is profitable (Moody, 2000)) was due to its realisation that on-line auction is bound to attract enough curiosity to get noticed.
- *Strategic resources* – focusing on the resource base of the firm and finding ways to utilise it and improve on it for bringing long-term gain. It involves paying attention to the following areas:
  - Core competencies – unique skills and capabilities within the company. Innovation based on existing skills can provide a company with an opportunity to create advantage for itself. A Recipe for Success (chapter 6) utilised the high level of literacy in technology among its staff to create a forum for knowledge sharing and collaboration between project teams as well as customers.

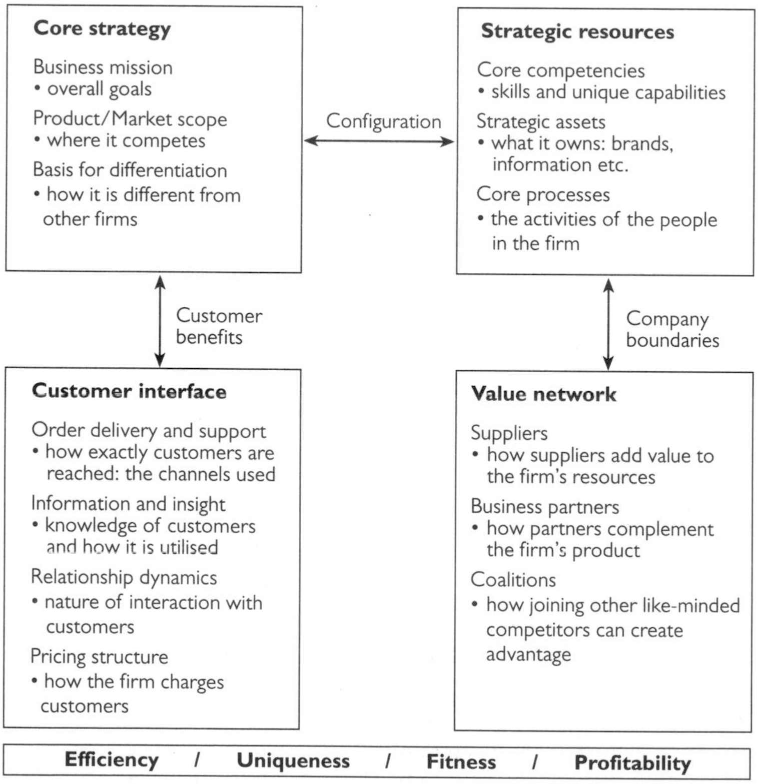

Fig. 8.1 The components of the business model (Reprinted by permission of Harvard Business School Press. From *Leading the Revolution* by G. Hamel. Boston, MA, 2000, pp. 70–98. Copyright © 2000 by The Harvard Business School Publishing Corporation, all rights reserved.)

  - Strategic assets – the strategic strength of the firm in terms of information, infrastructure, brand loyalty, patents etc. Using these, a company can formulate new strategies for expansion and differentiation. Direct Line, the UK's established on-line (initially telephone-based) insurance company used its brand awareness to start a highly successful on-line car selling company called jamjar.com.
  - Core process – the main activities of the company. Reviewing these activities and improving them where necessary can have long-term business benefits. This requires leveraging activities which create most value for an organisation; Dell did this by focusing on its experience of direct selling.
- *Customer interface* – a firm's interaction with its customers is a crucial element of e-commerce. Reviewing the processes involved in serving customers and assessing how customers perceive services provides information which can be used to introduce new ideas. This involves an evaluation of the strategies used for the development and utilisation of a customer relationship management system, especially in the following areas:
  - Order delivery and support – companies must find ways to improve these services. OnDigital's virtual helpdesk (chapter 6) was introduced as a strategy to attract new customers.
  - Information and insight – a company's knowledge of its customers and how it is used. As discussed in previous chapters, information can be collected from on-line sessions and used to improve services in various ways.
  - Relationship dynamics – the nature of the relationship between a business and its customers has a profound influence on a company's market position. The example of Charles Schwab discussed in chapter 7 demonstrates this point.
  - Pricing structure – the way customers are charged should be re-examined with a view to making improvements where appropriate, such as offering long-term customers some price advantages.
- *Value network* – the suppliers, business partners and coalitions which, together, create value for the firm. Coalition involves the alliance between companies prepared to share resources to run business activities together. This is a strategy used often by two (or more) companies with strengths in different areas in order for them to gain from each other's resources. For example, American Express, Concert (a multinational that provides global communications services to businesses) and British Telecom formed an alliance to offer an e-procurement and payment solution for their customers. They used the complementary expertise of the participants to develop a team which could offer a complete solution to their customers. As discussed before, organisations use various ways to communicate and co-operate with suppliers and partners: extranet and groupware for collaboration and knowledge sharing, outsourced service arrangements for better supply chain management and so on. Companies must review the potential of these relationships continually in search of the scope for creative new ideas.

Strategy of business concept innovation requires a review of:

- Core strategy – the method the firm uses to compete.
- Strategic resources – how it utilises its resources.
- Customer interface – how it interacts with customers.
- Value network – its coalition with partners and competitors.

In creating an improved business model by reviewing its strategies using the above approach, an enterprise builds bridges between its business components. By strengthening the core strategies and customer interface, it provides improved *customer benefits* (Fig. 8.1); the utilisation of strategic resources to redefine core strategies result in

Through BCI, a company achieves improved customer benefit, a configuration that can support its mission and a clear boundary between what can be done internally and what should be outsourced.

Edmunds.com

In 1966, Edmund's began publishing its *Automobile Buyer's Guide* and over the next 24 years, built a powerful brand name in the USA. Its mission statement was 'to empower automotive consumers by providing complete, clear, timely, accurate and unbiased information needed to make informed purchase and ownership decisions'. Positioned as an independent and objective resource for new and used car buyers, the guide found a large audience among customers who wanted technical information in addition to vehicle pricing information. In 1994, the company began experimenting with the Internet as a method of distribution and put the entire textual content of the Edmund's guides on-line. Computer-savvy shoppers could download desired portions of the guide via a gopher service.

In the spring of 1995, the company launched its website and within a year, officially announced a corporate identity change from Edmund's Publication Corporation to Edmunds.com. Initially the website offered the same information as the print publication but in a web-based, interactive form. Users could select the car model and year that they wanted to review and pull up pricing information, extensive reviews, consumer information and safety updates. As the website developed, additional web-specific features were added to make the user experience richer, such as the Edmunds.com marketplace, a website providing buyers with a single, complete resource for all their car buying needs; Edmund's Town Hall, an on-line discussion forum for car buyers; Edmund's Custom Workbooks, a website which enabled customers to buy a workbook for a specific car for $9.95; Edmunds2Go, a mobile version of Edmunds.com; and EdmundsLIVE – an interactive live auto show.

Whereas Edmund's printed publication was paid for by people buying the information, its web business was driven by the information being given away and Edmund's receiving a finder's fee for each customer it sent to seek out a product or service provided by either a referral service or a retailer. One such strategic partner was Autobytel, a company which locates the best deal available for the customer on price, financing, delivery and so on. On Edmunds.com, a serious buyer could fill out an Autobytel form stating car make and model, options, description of trade-in, lease or buy and need for financing. Edmund's captured this information and sent it to Autobytel. In turn, Autobytel contacted the dealer nearest the customer who had the relevant inventory of cars who called and began the sales process. The customer and the dealer negotiated directly with each other. Autobytel made its money by selling 'subscriptions' to the dealers for the service. On the other hand, every time a customer filled in a full Autobytel form on Edmunds.com, the latter got a 'finders fee' of several dollars regardless of whether or not the deal was consummated.

A similar relationship existed with GEICO, a company which sold auto insurance and had a logo on the Edmund.com website. In 1999, Edmunds.com began greatly expanding its partnership; by August 2000, the company had six new car partners (Autobytel, CarsDirect, Microsoft CarPoint, Driveoff, Honda, GM), one used car partner (i-motors), one warranty partner (1Source Auto), one finance partner (PeopleFirst.com), two insurance partners (Esurance and GEICO Auto Insurance), one vehicle identification partner (Carfax) and one aftermarket partner (JC Whitney).

(Source: Akers, 2000. Copyright © 2000 by the President and Fellows of Harvard College. Harvard Business School Case 9-701-025. Rev. 26 September, 2000.)

This case was prepared by Research Associate Christine Akers under the supervision of Professor Stephen P. Bradley as the basis for class discussion rather than to illustrate either effective or ineffective handling of an administrative situation. Reprinted by permission from Harvard Business School.

Questions

1 What strategies did Edmund.com use to obtain a competitive advantage?
2 How would the partnerships help the company to create a business concept innovation?
3 What strategies can Edmunds.com apply in order to stay ahead in a market where many other companies (e.g. Microsoft CarPoint) also provide similar services?

a *configuration* (an infrastructure) capable of supporting the firm's mission; and a review of the resources available within the company and support required from its value network determine the *boundary* between what can be done internally and what needs to be outsourced. By using the above methods to implement an improved business model, an enterprise develops a firm basis of efficiency, uniqueness, fit (the way different elements fit together to reinforce each other) and profitability (Fig. 8.1) upon which to build its business.

The strategy of co-operation as opposed to competition has also been addressed by Dyer and Singh (2000). This is the process of working with some traditional rivals for selective segments of the market. Managing the co-existence of competition and collaboration (sometimes referred to as co-opetition) is a challenging task. In co-operative mode, skilled leaders use joint resources in order to gain a joint competitive advantage, while in a competitive mode, they manage to maximise the company's individual advantage by utilising as much as possible of the partner's resources while protecting their own.

Gather some information on the strategies a successful company such as Microsoft, Dell or Cisco used and discuss them in the light of the above model of strategy formulation. To what extent do they fit in with the above discussion?

Ghosh (1998) stresses the value of a firm's ability to steal certain business advantages from other companies by entering their territory while adding a little digital value of its own at a time. When Amazon started its business selling books on-line no one expected it to have much influence on the market (the same way mail order books remained in the periphery). However, by slowly adding value to its services and by expanding to far more products than just books, it became a household name. Customers keep coming back to the company out of loyalty, a sense of community and its all round service for books, reviews, discussion groups and so on. Enterprises can use this strategy to pirate their industry's value-chain and become a powerful new force – the so-called magnets for customer attention. 'Ultimately, the risk for established businesses is not from digital tornadoes but from digital termites' (Ghosh, 1998: 132). Ghosh suggested that over time, a strategy of becoming a customer magnet through a process of taking small steps could have enormous influence on the shape of their industry.

A report produced by Cap Gemini Ernst & Young puts the emphasis back on tactics as the 'rule of the day' for the uncertain and highly competitive world of e-commerce, in which customer service is one of the most important criteria for success. It recommends an iterative plan of short-term moves to tide a company over while constantly looking for a long-term '. . . transactionally sound and technologically secure environment' (Cap Gemini Ernst & Young, 2000: 15).[4] It suggests that businesses must achieve three basic competencies: making products or services and taking risks; marketing and selling those products and services; and providing an infrastructure to support transaction processing and back-office activities. The report argues that no one company needs to achieve all three competencies and presents six general business models. There may be sub-models and variations to these and organisations can use one or a combination of them:

[4] Source: Cap Gemini Ernst & Young, 2000. Special Report on the Financial Services Industry. Reprinted with permission. This report is written for mainly financial services but has strong relevance to all businesses in the Internet age.

- *Commodity provider* – providing reliable products and services at low cost. These are companies which operate with narrow margins and make their profit through the volume of sale. A bank's basic services of savings accounts and mortgages fall into this category.
- *Infrastructure provider* – supports the infrastructure for completed transactions, for example the clearing services discussed in chapter 7.
- *Market maker* – provides a marketplace (virtual or physical) for customers to interact. We have already discussed the increasingly popular role of virtual marketplaces (exchanges): auction houses such as eBay.com is another example of a market maker.
- *Superior performer* – companies which make a profit by providing better products and services than their competitors. Firms which follow this model often gain considerable advantage at the beginning but find it hard to sustain it as others soon copy and often better their services. Many dotcom companies experience this and only those which can continually innovate survive.
- *Innovator* – develops unique products, services, processes or technology. Firms following this model are in the same situation as the superior performers. Virgin started a new concept in lending by opening its VirginOne account which enabled customers to put their savings and loans (mortgage etc.) into one account which allowed the balance of the loans to benefit from the savings. However, other banks quickly copied the concept.
- *Relationship manager* – concentrates on customer services. Suitable for businesses dependent on customer services, for example financial planners and insurance brokers.

A CGEY report suggested that businesses need to take risks to create new products, market and sell them and provide an infrastructure by becoming a commodity provider, infrastructure provider, market maker, superior performer, innovator or a relationship manager.

Using a few finance companies as examples, perform an analysis of which company belongs to which of the above categories and how they can benefit from this position.

In his paper on the strategic potential of business process re-engineering in the network era, Nolan (1995) points out the difficulty of assessing the value of IT and using this knowledge to make strategic decisions because of the uniqueness of its characteristics. Firstly, as IT gets continually cheaper, what seems uneconomic now can become economic next year. Secondly, innovations in IT have a 'creative destruction' impact on older technology, that is, new developments can easily make existing systems obsolete. Thirdly, progress in technology constantly presents an organisation with new possibilities in customer services by providing real-time information on customers. To generate strategic opportunity in this environment, an organisation often requires radical changes in its business processes. Nolan defines radical change as that which results in an economic benefit such as '. . . doubling the quality while halving the cost. Radical change is like achieving benefits more like 10 times the investment as opposed to 10%' (1995: 7). To achieve such benefit requires the re-engineering of business processes and using the power of technology to implement them. Nolan recommends a continual process of strategic re-engineering by constantly negotiating new ways to make improvements in efficiency by utilising emerging technologies.

All e-commerce firms exist in an uncertain and multinational environment. In his article on international business strategies, Becker (1998) stresses the need for a company's ability to cope with uncertainty. He suggests three approaches to planning strategy:

- The conventional 'predict and prepare' approach. Although this appears to be cautious, it is exposed to the danger of 'uncatered for' situations which

Constant evolution at Charles Schwab

Demonstrating a pattern of continuous growth, Schwab's market value ballooned from $152 million in 1991 to $41.6 billion in 2000. Such success is due to consistent aggressive visioning and revisioning and an appetite for change. So far, Schwab has been wise enough to be lulled by success, visionary enough to keep exploring the demand of future customers and nimble enough to change its value proposition and its operating model every few years – well ahead of the crowd.

First business model: the value-added discounter

When the company entered the discount brokerage business in 1975, the market was new and very competitive. Setting fees higher than other discount brokers but substantially lower than the full-service firms, Schwab positioned the new firm as the value discounter. It invested in a limited branch network, computer technology and brand building. Customers trusted Charles Schwab, favouring its fast, reliable trades, basic investment function, physical presence, and advertising that featured its 'friendly face'.

Second business model: partnering with independent financial planners

As the number of small investors began to expand in the early 1980s, so did the number of independent investment advisors. Schwab developed services for these small planners, offering them inexpensive transaction processing and gaining a sales force that actually paid a small fee to develop new customers.

Third business model: the financial supermarket

In the late 1980s, as the mutual fund market exploded, Schwab noticed that investors faced a confusion of fund options, high fees and other financial burdens, and too many different statements. OneSource, Schwab's mutual fund marketplace, changed the entire mutual fund industry – saving customers money while saving the company's marketing costs. At the same time, Schwab, hard-hit by the 1987 market crash, now added recurring fees to its transaction-based revenue stream and took ownership of the customer relationship.

Fourth business model: Schwab.com

Quick to seize the opportunities presented by e-commerce, Schwab led the pack by introducing what was then called e-schwab in mid-1996, revolutionising its culture and investing heavily in the requisite technologies. Schwab has maintained its leading market share ever since, despite the barrage of competition from deep discounters on one side and traditional brokers on the other. At each critical juncture, Schwab has been daring enough to bet its future on e-commerce.

Schwab has taken steps to woo both day traders and wealthy investors. For the day traders, Schwab modified its price structure for heavy traders and acquired CyBerCorp, an Internet brokerage with state-of-the-art trading technology. At the same time, Schwab positioned itself to serve wealthy investors by acquiring U.S.Trust.

(Source: Cap Gemini Ernst & Young, 2000. Special Report on the Financial Services Industry. Reprinted with permission.)

Questions

1 Which of the operating models described by the Cap Gemini Ernst & Young report (pages 213–214) fit in with the path Schwab took?
2 How does Schwab's strategies relate to the other approaches to strategy formulation discussed in this chapter?
3 How did Schwab's strategies provide it with the 'basic competencies'?

management are not always equipped to deal with within the context of the local region.

- The power approach of attempting to dominate or eliminate uncertainty. This involves an attempt to control the environment. This could be by using political or financial influence to limit the effect of change, using a country's legal framework to control competitive forces and so on. This can be implemented to gain an advantage or to compete against a powerful opponent. For example, in 1977, IBM was asked to leave India when it refused to allow majority ownership (greater than 50%) to Indian companies (Singhal and Rogers, 1989).

- The structural approach of building an internal capacity for flexible response and adaptation. This is a method of absorbing uncertainty and of being prepared without relying on predictions. Firms can do this by broadening their product and market scope or by creating local strategic alliances to an extent that enables them to cope with the diversities of different countries. The transnational rather than multinational view of a business (chapter 4) is useful in this context.

In the international arena one of three approaches can be used:

- Predict and prepare – the cautious route.
- Use power to limit damage.
- Build internal capacity by broadening scope.

Which of the above strategies a company adopts depends on its resources, differential advantages, competitors and the environment of the countries it does business with.

In his discussion of the evolutionary process of Internet-based businesses Hoque (2000) discusses the importance of a 'launch and learn' approach (chapter 7). He argues that for a bricks and mortar company, the creation of an e-enterprise means marrying its existing capabilities with the Net model and, for dotcom companies, acquiring some traditional-style strengths and resources in order to face competition from the traditional sector. He suggests the following steps as the 'ultimate source of agility' in a world where an enterprise has to respond to customer demand in real time:

- Define an e-enterprise vision that brings the company's existing real-world and virtual-world strengths together.
- Create a business architecture comprising a business model, processes and applications based on the above vision.
- Build the technology infrastructure that facilitates the implementation of the business model and processes.
- Recycle every piece of learning, review the business model continually and refine the business and technology architecture by reusing existing components.

To build an e-enterprise, a company must first create a vision by bringing the firm's physical and virtual strengths together, then build business and technology architectures based on that vision which it should review, refine and recycle continually.

Find out what strategies Dell Computers used when they extended its business to the virtual world.

So far we discussed strategy options for mainly business processes; knowledge management and information systems must also be given similar considerations. Talking about the importance of the seamless integration of information between applications in an organisation, Davenport (1998) raises the question of the strategic implication of the implementation of enterprise systems. On the one hand the Internet encourages the democratisation of an organisation by facilitating a flatter management structure (chapter 2) with real-time access to information at all levels; on the other, an enterprise system provides the means for the centralisation of information and therefore the possibility of a standardisation of processes and management control. There are also debates over whether or not uniformity of information in different regions or countries is desirable. A federalist model raises the most difficult challenge for organisations: determining what should be common throughout the organisation and what should be allowed to vary. Davenport suggests that difficult questions need to be answered before major information systems are implemented: How important is it to process orders the same way world-wide? Does the term 'customer' mean the same thing in every business unit? and so on.

Hansen *et al.* (1999) compare the respective roles of a focus on technology and people in the management of knowledge. They suggest a codification approach if the product or service sold by the company is standardised and a personalisation approach if the business relies on the knowledge and know-how of individuals. Codification is the technology-based solution, the organisation of data in databases for employees and customers to access. On the other hand, personalisation is based on direct personal communication between people. Companies (e.g., McKinsey & Company) following this option develop electronic document systems the same way other companies do; managers use these systems to acquire information but share knowledge and information with other managers at a personal level. Firms do not have to make an absolute choice between the two options but effective knowledge management is normally achieved by focusing on one strategy and using the other in a supporting role.

There are different approaches to strategy development for knowledge management:

- Democratisation vs. centralisation of information

and

- Technology-based vs. human-based knowledge management.

In an article on strategies for e-business, Lipsitz (2000) puts an emphasis on the importance of full involvement of the IT director in the process. A good corporate strategy must first be established and then followed up by the IT strategy that is equipped to support it. If the IT department identifies the need to address the strategic implications of the Internet (which is often the case), then sponsorship must be obtained from business executives. Other steps to be taken before strategy formulation can take place are: a decision on whether to use in-house expertise or bring in an external e-strategy consultant; the establishment of a project team which would take ownership and implement the project as soon as decisions on strategy have been finalised; and the allocation of appropriate resources that involves assembling the members of strategy teams which should include representatives from different areas of the business in order to reflect the views of all stakeholders, gathering existing documentation, and drawing up a list of people to be interviewed.

The distinct steps[5] a strategy formulation team can take are (fig. 8.2):

1 Declare the company's overall vision in the form of documented mission statement. This is the long-term purpose of the organisation.
2 Determine strategic objectives for e-business. At this stage, an enterprise must establish its specific aims for the business or the project in hand. A company's basic vision remains the same; the objectives change according to the environment.
3 Gather information on current situations in the firm and in the environment and analyse it. A number of questions must be asked in order to analyse the environment of strengths, weaknesses, opportunities and threats (SWOT analysis) before the company can proceed to create its e-business strategies. We will discuss this further in the following section.
4 Develop strategies for coping with unpredictable events such as future threats and opportunities. These strategies should be based on the financial and managerial risks the enterprise can withstand, whether it wants to act in an offensive or defensive manner to competition and the firm's ability to implement the strategy in terms of its resources. These form a part of its preparation before embarking in e-business.

Based on an approach that suits a company, a set of distinct steps should be taken to formulate strategies. Following the processes as shown in Fig. 8.2, the output of the steps should be a list of e-commerce initiatives.

[5] Experts vary in their opinion about the number and order of these steps (e.g. Ward and Griffiths, 1996; Lipsitz, 2000). For example, some would argue that the current situation should be analysed before objectives are set; some would not differentiate between mission statement and objectives. The above list reflects the steps taken commonly; firms set their objectives on the basis of their vision and amend them at a later stage if necessary.

5 The project team can now produce a list of initiatives or a plan for e-commerce projects with phasing and timing schedules for each. This should include the allocation of resources, the development of project teams, the formulation of criteria for the measurement of performance and a review of the objectives.

Following the establishment of the overall objectives based on a corporate vision, steps 3 and 4 of the above list are designed to provide an organisation with knowledge of the potential of e-commerce for the firm. Out of many approaches to strategy formulation, the one an enterprise adopts depends on the environment of strengths, weaknesses, opportunities and threats (SWOT) within which it operates. Business leaders must attempt to understand customers and their needs; they must ask themselves a number of questions on customers, market opportunities for their products and their competitive positioning in the environment in order to develop a strategy for the business. The answers to these questions provide them with an analytical tool to assess the potential of e-commerce in the competitive environment. They also enable an enterprise to develop the strategies for its e-business. The last stage of producing a list of initiatives will come after the organisation has assessed its strategic potential and established its policies for the future.

THE STRATEGIC POTENTIAL OF E-COMMERCE

A number of tools are available for the analysis of the strategic potential of e-commerce; here we will discuss the methods based on the analysis of SWOT, value chain, critical success factors and return of investment.

SWOT analysis

This involves management asking itself a set of questions (Lipsitz, 2000, Ward and Griffiths, 1996) and analysing the answers. This is done in two phases; the first concentrates within the organisation and assesses its strengths and weaknesses by analysing the following:

- What are the company's distinctive internal competencies?
- What resources are available internally in terms of products, services, skills, experience, motivation, relationships, culture, attitudes and operational effectiveness?
- How ready is the company for change?
- How strong is the company's research and development (R&D) portfolio? Is it researching new products and markets? What is its history of success in such research?
- What is the state of the company's current communications infrastructure?
- What is the state of the company's current knowledge management infrastructure?

The internal component of SWOT analysis attempts to assess a firm's competencies, readiness and strength to face the new market, legislative issues and customer needs.

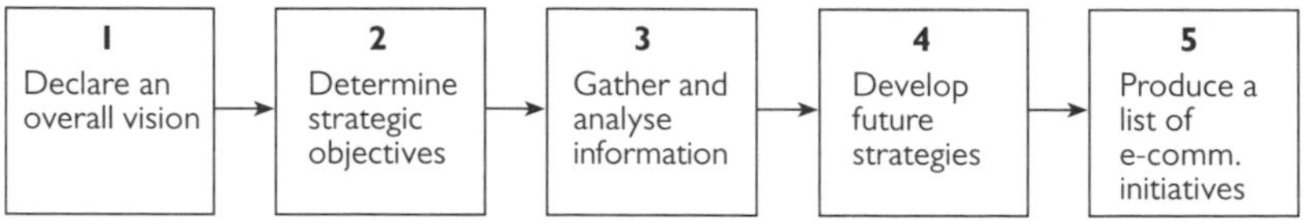

Fig. 8.2 Steps in strategy formulation

- What is the state of the infrastructure for the rest of the value chain (suppliers, partners etc.)?
- Are there legislative issues to consider?
- What are customers' current and latent needs?
- What is the state of the company's relationship with its customers?

The second phase focuses on the external factors and performs an analysis of the threats coming from the environment and opportunities available to the firm as a result of changes in the environment:

- What are traditional and new competitors doing?
- What are the strengths and weaknesses of current and potential competitors in the way of products, services, marketing, finance and expertise?
- What are the specific industry and general new economy trends?
- Is there a scope for increasing the share of the market or of increasing the total market size (the number of customers who buy the product offered)?
- Is there a scope for the company to extend the life cycle of the products of strategic importance with the help of R&D?
- What is the best practice in analogous industry?
- What are the possibilities of substitute products and services entering the market?
- What are the possibilities of improving relationships with existing customers and creating new relationships with potential customers?

The external element of SWOT assesses the position of the competitors, market trends and scope for extension, risk of substitute products and the possibility of new relationships with customers.

Information gathered from the above analysis together with the company's agreed business mission for e-commerce (e-vision) should provide the strategy management team with the tools required to create a definite strategic direction. The management team must use its leadership and entrepreneurial skills to establish a plan of action by which to exploit its strengths and opportunities and to overcome its weaknesses and the threats from the environment.

The value chain

Value-chain analysis, suggested by Michael Porter in a paper in 1985 (discussed in chapter 4), involves an assessment of the value added at each stage of a chain and an estimation of how e-commerce would influence it. The questions to ask for this purpose are (Turban *et al.*, 2000):

- Is there any gain for the company in taking over parts of the value chain, for example, the order delivery service?
- Is there any competitive disadvantage if another company does the above?
- Will the customers benefit from a reduction in the number of entities they have to deal with, for example in the order processing stage?
- Does the company have the skills necessary to take over some parts of the value chain?
- Can the company offer additional value-adding services to its customers?
- Can the company create a new customer segment for its products, for example, can it attract customers traditionally belonging to a different market (such as attracting younger customers to an insurance service)?
- Is there the scope for increasing the customer base by advertising or by supplying additional products?

Value-chain analysis assesses how e-commerce can influence the value added at each stage of the chain and how the company can improve it by taking over some of the tasks.

- Will the business be at a competitive disadvantage if another company takes over a part of the value offering services?

Answers to the above questions enable a strategy team to assess if/how it would gain from investing in e-commerce and if a competitor can take some of their market advantage away by embarking on e-commerce.

Critical success factors (CSFs)

CSFs are the aspects of an organisation's activities which are crucial to its business; success in those areas are directly related to the overall performance of the organisation. The analysis of CSFs is a powerful technique used by businesses to interpret the most vital aspects of the business processes, technology and management skills which need attention in order to meet the objectives of an enterprise. It attempts to assess the strengths and weaknesses of existing systems and estimate the information needs of those systems, thus relating a company's business needs with its information systems needs. CSFs can be determined at the following hierarchical levels (Ward and Griffiths, 1996) with each level having an influence on the ones below it:

- Industry level: all firms in an industry have similar CSFs. For example, if there is a problem with the supply of certain raw material, all companies which need it are affected.
- Organisational level: a company's overall business goals are dependent on the success of its overall CSFs. For example, an adequate communications infrastructure is a CSF for the entire enterprise and the lack of it reduces a company's ability to meet its e-business vision.
- Business unit (divisions or departments within an organisation): this is where concrete, practical strategies are determined. CSFs at this level could be the marketing techniques used by the marketing department or security controls used by the IT department.
- Management level: the success of an enterprise is directly related to the leadership qualities of its business unit managers.

CSFs are the critical aspects of business processes, technology and management skill. They can operate at many levels: industry-wide, organisation-wide, within a business unit and at management level.

CSFs should be determined when the objectives of a business or a project have been established. The CSFs for each objective should first be formulated (these should take into consideration the industry CSFs) and then consolidated for the overall project. CSFs for organisational objectives should then be used to derive those at business unit and management levels. A SWOT analysis of the existing systems must be done in order to assess the current status of the CSFs. For example, if an agreed CSF is the level of interactivity of a website, a SWOT analysis of the website would indicate how it rates at the moment. Examples of typical CSFs for e-business include:

- The commitment of the top management levels.
- The relationship with customers.
- The quality of the website.
- The competition in the market.
- The integration of corporate backend information systems with e-commerce applications.
- The communications infrastructure.
- The security controls.

The result of CSF analysis can be used to develop plans for the implementation of e-commerce.

Return on investment (ROI)

ROI is the ratio of the cost of financial investment made on a project to the benefit generated. In order to assess the profitability of e-commerce initiatives, the ROI figure should be used in conjunction with a consideration of the other, more intangible benefits of long-term strategic gains. The measurement tools used must count the cost of resources such as hardware, software, personnel, implementation of procedures etc. against overall profit. However, although intangible benefits such as customer satisfaction, improved partner interaction, faster supply chain etc. are difficult to measure, they have important financial implications and must be included in the analysis. One method used to measure ROI is the balanced scorecard (so called because it balances the tangible financial and the intangible non-financial perspectives) approach introduced by Kaplan and Norton (1996) which advocates the assessment of benefits in the following four areas:

- *Financial* – the measurement of growth in revenue, productivity and assets.
- *Customer* – includes market share, customer retention and acquisition, extension of customer satisfaction, selection of customer segments and so on.
- *Internal process* – internal activities such as innovation in products and services, operational efficiency, better value chain management etc.
- *Learning and growth* – these issues are related to gains in human and cultural aspects of the organisation such as improvement in corporate knowledge, level of job satisfaction, employees' personal growth and satisfaction etc.

ROI is the cost : benefit ratio which can be measured by using the balanced scorecard method to ascertain growth in revenue, customer retention and acquisition rate, the quality of internal activities and cultural aspects such as the growth in learning of employees.

Measurements in these areas must be made by gathering feedback on performance continually, and using the information for the purpose of formulating or updating e-business strategies. In measuring benefits, managers must include the perspectives of customers and other stakeholders (trading partners). They must also include the competitive environment for the products and services offered. Read the article by Dudman (2001) for further information on the above methods of analysis.

What challenges would organisations face while attempting to undertake the above analytical tools?

The tools for analysis described here enable managers to refine their objectives and strategies and then develop a plan for the implementation of e-commerce projects. However, before moving on to implementation, management must establish some guidelines (rules) based on the company's strategies for creating maximum opportunities for success. It must evaluate its existing business policies in the light of its e-commerce strategies as a preparation for delivering the e-commerce promise.

PREPARING FOR E-COMMERCE

An emerging e-commerce company must establish certain rules and policies to guide its activities. This can be done by following the simple rules model (Eisenhardt and Sull, 2001) introduced earlier:

- *How to rule* – how the firm should execute its processes in order to make them unique. For example, Dell has a policy of rapid re-organisation of processes based on the needs of targeted customer segments. Rules must be established in all areas of activities such as customer relationship management, dealings with trading partners, web-development criteria and so on.

Lloyds TSB Commercial Finance (LTSF)

A recent survey by on-line marketing specialist E-marketing revealed that only two in five companies have implemented ROI measurements such as the cost of recruiting customers through on-line marketing, measuring any change in turnover after implementing B2B strategies, or even monitoring any increases in customer traffic on the website. Chris Morgan, computer services manager at LTSF, has recently implemented Redwood Software's Report2Web package to distribute reports on-line, rather than on paper. The company has a normal rule that there must be payback from a project within two years. Morgan drew up a business case for the new system by looking at direct, quantifiable savings, including things like printer maintenance, staff time, the cost of consumables such as paper and ribbon, and even floor space and electricity. According to his calculations, the company should save £100,000 a year and achieve payback within 12 months. He is more cautious about intangibles and does not trust the method used by Redwoood which includes lots of intangibles. Morgan believes that when the objective is to gain competitive edge or enhance the company's brand in a market, the firm has to be able to put together an effective business case even though it may be a complicated process. This is a difficult area in which gut responses may play an important part.

(Adapted from Dudman, 2001 with permission from Reed Business Information Ltd.)

Questions

1 Discuss how this case study demonstrates the need for the measurement of success.
2 How can the company proceed to measure ROI on the intangibles?
3 What other methods of analysis can the company use and how?

- *Boundary rules* – rules regarding which opportunities can be pursued and which should be rejected. For example, Lego, the maker of children's toys (and now, clothes), uses a checklist of rules such as: Does the product have the Lego look? Is it educational? Will parents approve? etc. before the product is given the approval for manufacture. This is a part of the company's strategy for maintaining its central vision and philosophy.
- *Priority rules* – the criteria by which priorities are allocated to activities. For example, Intel decided to give priority to manufacturing processors rather than memory chips because of the high profit margin of the former.
- *Timing rules* – guidance on how to set deadlines for the completion of tasks and projects. For example, the telecommunications company Nortel has a rule that product development time must be within 18 months.
- *Exit rules* – rules that dictate when to abandon a project. For example, Oticon, a Danish hearing-aid company stops a project if a key team member leaves for another project.

The firm should establish rules on how to be unique, select opportunities, prioritise activities, set deadlines and terminate a project.

It is crucial that the rules are precise (not just overall principles), appropriate for the competitive environment, clear and optimal. Too many or totally inflexible rules paralyse a company's activities and discourage people from following them. The rules must also be reviewed regularly in order to ensure they fit well with the on-going business environment.

As a part of its preparation for e-commerce, an organisation must also establish policies in a number of areas on the basis of its strategic vision. Some of the areas in which policies are necessary are the following:

Simple rules in Autodesk

In the mid-1990s, Autodesk, the global leader in software for design professionals, dominated the mature design market. As a result, growth slowed to single-digit rates. CEO Carol Bartz was sure that her most promising opportunities lay in making use of those Autodesk technologies – in areas such as wireless communications, the Internet, imaging, and global positioning – that hadn't yet been exploited. But she wasn't sure which new technologies and related products would be big winners. So she refocused the strategy on the product innovation process and introduced a simple, radical rule: the new product development schedule would be shortened from a leisurely 18 to 24 months, in some cases, to 3 months. That changed the pace, scale, and strategic logic with which Autodesk tackled technology opportunities.

While a strategy of accelerating product innovation helped identify opportunities more quickly, Bartz lacked the cash to commercialise all of Autodesk's promising technologies. So she added a significant new strategy: spinouts. The first spinout, Buzzsaw.com, debuted in 1999. It allowed engineers to purchase construction materials using B2B exchange technology. Buzzsaw.com attracted significant venture capital and benefited from Autodesk's powerful brand and its customer relationships. Autodesk has since created a second spinout, RedSpark, and has developed simple rules for the new key process of spinning off companies.

(Reprinted by permission of *Harvard Business Review*. From 'Strategy as Simple Rules' by M. Eisenhardt and Donald N. Sull, January 2001. Copyright © by the Harvard Business School Publishing Corporation; all rights reserved.)

Questions

1. Itemise the problems and respective solutions faced by Autodesk in the mid-1990s.
2. How does the framework of 'simple rules' discussed in this chapter relate to Autodesk?
3. Could Autodesk use any other model described in this chapter?
4. In what ways is Autodesk's success due to e-commerce?
5. In what ways has Autodesk utilised both its off-line status and on-line expertise (combined) to ensure its success?

- *Technology* – An organisation must establish clear guidelines for the introduction and utilisation of its technology infrastructure. We listed the issues which need to be addressed in chapter 5 under 'IT strategies for e-commerce systems'.
- *Security and privacy* – As discussed in chapter 5, security is a critical factor for business on the Internet and a wide variety of techniques and technologies are available to ensure it. A secure system should also be equipped to safeguard the privacy of data on users. An organisation must have policies to ensure that personal information is protected. Formal policies should dictate decisions such as to what extent information flow should be restricted, which technologies to use for security, how to deal with security breaches and so on. We will come back to this in the next chapter.
- *Customer relationship* – We already discussed the importance of customer relationship management for e-commerce. The following questions enable an organisation to determine its e-commerce initiatives:
  - How can we select our most profitable customers?
  - How can we extend the loyalty of our customers?
  - How can we utilise our customers in a more profitable way?
  - How can we retain our customer base?

A firm should have policies on how to deal with:

- technology infrastructure
- security and privacy
- maintaining a healthy customer base
- unforeseen problems
- human resources problems
- the assessment of its effectiveness.

  - How can we acquire new customers?
  - How can we gain most effectively from our new customers?
- *Risk management* – In spite of very careful plans, businesses always run the risk of failure due to sudden changes in the environment. Factors such as a low entry barrier for new companies, low switching cost for customers, high customer demand, rapid technological innovation etc. are responsible for such changes. A company must use the analytical methods described above (SWOT, ROI, CSF etc.) to establish guidelines for dealing with uncertainties and unforeseen problems.
- *Human resources* – Policies regarding expertise in the company, the allocation of management responsibilities, access to knowledge etc. are essential for the survival of businesses in cyberspace.
- *Measuring business performance* – Finally, there must be clear guidelines for the measurement of performance enabling an enterprise to monitor its health. Using a tool such as a balanced score card, an organisation can assess the effectiveness of its business and technology systems, level of customer satisfaction, financial achievement and rate of learning.

You are an independent bookshop selling specialised art/architecture books. You wish to expand into e-commerce. Outline three different strategies by which you could achieve this goal.

Having assessed the potential for e-commerce and made the appropriate preparation, an organisation is finally equipped to move on to the final stage (step 5, Fig. 8.2) of strategy formulation. The project team produces a list of initiatives for e-commerce projects; this is taken on by the project development teams in charge of implementing e-commerce.

IMPLEMENTATION OF E-COMMERCE

An essential characteristic of e-businesses is its on-line and real-time interaction with other enterprises and external entities such as customers and suppliers. As Fig. 8.3 shows, there are three basic elements which constitute the foundation of the architecture for e-commerce: business processes and information systems which form the physical basis of the organisation's activities; customer-facing e-commerce applications at the external end which constitute the output; and a value chain that utilises existing processes and systems in order to create the final product to be delivered to customers. A value chain involves communication between a company's trading partners and its internal systems and processes. The technology and human resources elements (Fig. 8.3) support this communication and, together, they provide the complete architecture for e-business.

E-commerce architecture comprises backend IT and business processes, customer-facing systems and the value chain relating to these. It needs technology and people to complete the picture and it responds to the ecosystem of other businesses.

The above model can be applied to both B2B and B2C sectors. For the former, the customers are other businesses and the value chain extends into a network comprising many other organisations. Thus, the architecture functions within an ecosystem of similar architectures of other organisations. For the B2C sector, although customers may be individuals, the value chain extends to other organisations (suppliers, fulfilment companies etc.) and therefore the interaction of a company and the ecosystem also needs to be supported by the architecture. Thus all e-commerce systems are inter-enterprise in nature; organisations must therefore develop an architecture capable of crossing corporate boundaries.

An enterprise develops its architecture on the basis of its strategic vision and the result of the analyses described above. However, the inter-enterprise nature of an e-commerce project demands that implementation of the customer-facing applications must take place in stages. Each stage must be thoroughly tested and proven internally before it is released to the ecosystem. Figure 8.4 shows the key processes involved in implementing an inter-enterprise system. At the initial stage of project development, an initial architecture should be developed on the basis of the organisation's *strategic vision*.

A part of creating the *initial architecture* is the process of allocating management responsibilities for the projects associated with implementing e-commerce. The list of initiatives produced at the last stage of strategy development (Fig. 8.2) would often perform this function as a part of evaluating the level of expertise available in the enterprise. Management skill is required to oversee the development of the business process, backend information systems, communications infrastructure, frontend applications and a web interface. A number of projects, each with a *project manager*, would be set up with a view to building the different facets of e-commerce initiatives.

Projects must be started based on an initial architecture. The development of e-commerce initiatives should be performed and implemented, initially internally, in stages, by following a process of step-wise refinement. External implementation should also follow the same pattern.

These processes should be implemented as pilot projects internally to activate only a limited number of initiatives. The projects must be refined and extended in steps as feedback from initial implementations are received. In a continual process of step-wise refinement, an increasing number of e-commerce initiatives should be implemented. When a satisfactory result is obtained from internal processes, further improvements should be made to the inter-enterprise architecture following the same pattern of step-wise refinement, involving additional initiatives at each stage. The principle of continuous review and improvement should carry on even when e-commerce is fully functional.

Infrastructure building

Building an infrastructure involves the following processes (Fig. 8.3):

- The development of the customer-facing processes. Customers of e-commerce want on-line applications which provide a transparent and all-encompassing

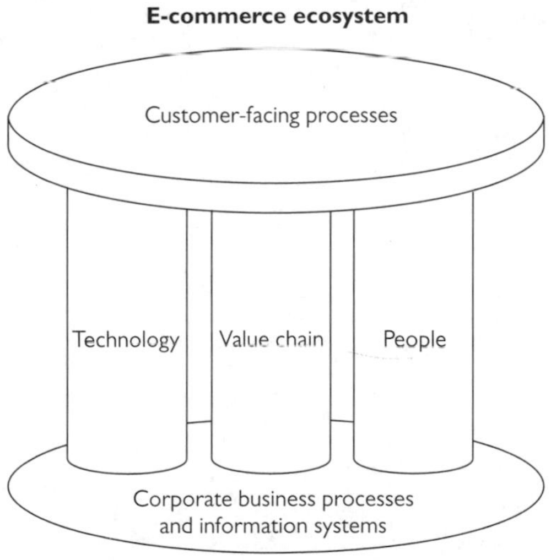

Fig. 8.3 Inter-enterprise e-commerce architecture (Source: Fingar, P., Kumar, H. and Sharma, T., *Enterprise E-Commerce: The Software Components Breakthrough for Business-to-Business Commerce*, Meghan-Kiffer Press, Tampa, Florida, 2000. Adapted with permission.)

service that meets all their on-line needs. For example, when a customer places an order, s/he wants to know if the product is available, when it can be delivered, how the payment can be made etc. in real time without having to log into different websites or perform complicated access procedures. Customer relationship management prepares a firm for these functions and also provides the requirement specifications for the applications which need to be developed at this end. The development of customer-facing processes also determines the demands of the value chain.

- Value-chain development. This involves integrating the processes of enterprise-based systems with those of its trading partners in order to provide the seamless integration that the customer-facing applications require. We have discussed the technologies, standards and techniques available for this purpose; the project team of an enterprise must manage the development process in a way that makes the most of those tools.
- Building business processes and information systems. Using the method chosen by the management (build, outsource or use components),[6] the project team must develop the information and the operational infrastructure (chapters 6 and 7) for e-commerce. This would include building the databases and information systems necessary, developing the ERP system, building and integrating the frontend and backend applications, developing the associated business activities and so on. However, the systems built are to be operated by people in the company who may not have technical knowledge. Similar to the needs of the customers of an enterprise, users of e-commerce systems also want transparent information systems with easy-to-use interfaces.

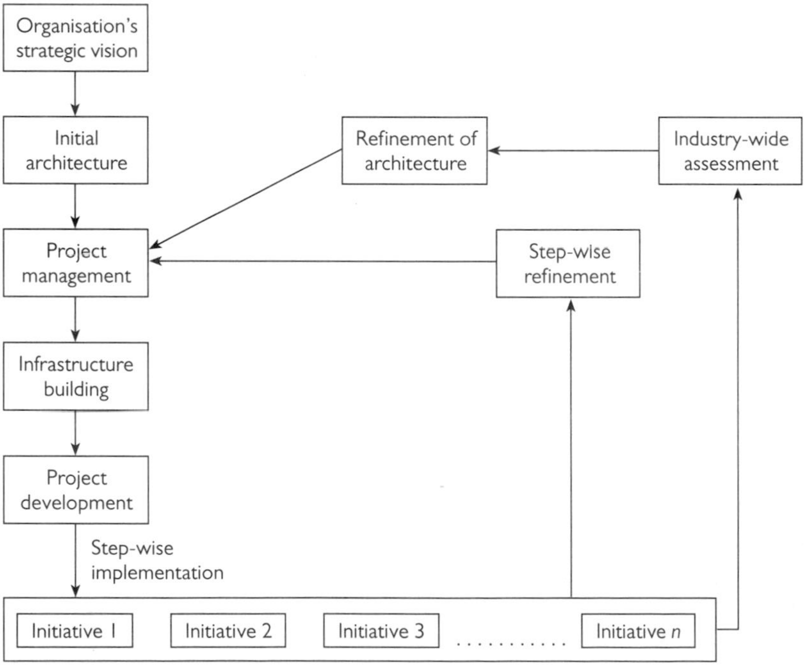

Fig. 8.4 Implementation of e-commerce

[6] Explained in the next section.

- Building the technical infrastructure. The systems described above can only work when an efficient technical infrastructure supports the way they relate to each other. We discussed this in chapters 5 and 6. An e-commerce project development entails the management of the processes involved in bringing the technologies together and facilitating the implementation of the infrastructure. In addition to developing the communications infrastructure and ensuring integration between various inter- and intra-organisational systems, this must also facilitate storage management solutions. E-commerce applications have created 50 to 100 per cent annual growth in storage requirement with some businesses quoting an increase of 500 per cent (Langley, 2001). A technical infrastructure must cater for such challenges and establish arrangements such as the outsourcing of storage management or the development of storage area networks.
- Providing human resources. This involves building the human support system required to run e-commerce. At this stage of the project, the management and operational responsibilities for e-commerce initiatives must be allocated. Project managers must ensure that there is an enterprise-wide skills base and that the information and operational infrastructure established is capable of supporting the day-to-day activities of its users. This requires that the systems and processes built are acceptable to and usable by its operators, otherwise they become failed systems. Systems developers and project managers must be aware of the concepts of human computer interaction (HCI),[7] an important area in information systems development, involving the study of the quality of experience users get as a result of their interaction with a computer system. A well designed system enables its users to attend to the task in hand rather than the machine. The principles are the same as those behind creating suitable customer interfaces (Bandyo-padhyay, 2000): the ultimate goal should be to empower users by making the machine respond to their needs rather than the other way round. This requires an understanding of the way humans acquire knowledge, memorise and perceive information, communicate, apply reasoning and so on. The discipline which dominates the study of these issues is cognitive psychology. It enables us to create a mental model of users in an attempt to conceptualise the strengths and weaknesses of human perception. For example, an appreciation of how human visual system works enables us to understand how the patterns and colour of screen display work for users. This necessitates the combined efforts of technologists, cognitive scientists, business executives and most importantly, users at the development stage of business and information systems (and thus should be done in conjunction with this stage). The outcome of such collaboration also enables the management to assess the need for skills development within the enterprise and plan the necessary training schedule.

An effective architecture provides:

- An all-encompassing service for customers.
- An integrated value chain.
- Integrated backend information systems and business processes.
- An infrastructure to support widespread communication.
- An effective human support system for employees.

As is evident from the above discussion, the stages are neither isolated nor specific. There are many overlaps between them and activities mentioned under one category here may be performed as a part of another one in some organisations.

At the end of the above functions, an enterprise moves on to implement the infrastructure, initially internally and eventually in cyberspace (Fig. 8.4).

[7] We will not go into the details of the concepts here.

Developing e-commerce initiatives

The development of initiatives can be pursued in a number of ways: building all components of the system in-house, using the experience of servicing companies or taking a component-based assembly approach:

- Building in-house requires considerable technical expertise. Integrating an organisation's legacy systems with its e-commerce applications, creating a platform which is compatible with its trading partners' e-commerce activities etc. are difficult and time-consuming tasks. On the other hand, if successful, this method can fulfil the exact needs of an enterprise and provide major value.
- Commonly referred to as outsourcing, using external expertise is a popular option. There may be different levels of external services: appointing a company to develop the entire system, buying prepackaged solutions, outsourcing the front-end applications to an ASP (applications service provider) but performing the other functions in-house, hiring an applications management service which would provide on-site management service for all e-commerce applications, outsourcing data storage, or just using an ISP for connecting to the Internet. Outsourcing has many advantages: the availability of expertise, reduced risk of failure, savings in terms of time and cost, etc. However, problems may arise due to a conflict of management responsibilities, loss of control within the company, a poor relationship between the vendor and the supplier and so on. Management must also establish the necessary agreement with the providers of outsourced services (service level agreement) in order to ensure that high quality provision is maintained.
- Component-based assembly is an approach modelled on the philosophy of object-oriented systems development. Applications are developed as software modules (objects), each providing one or more business services. For example, one business object may support routing of data, while another provides hierarchical access control for security management. Objects may be available for functions within an application, for communicating between different applications and for relating different systems between organisations within a particular industry such as retail. The components can be reused as necessary to build an e-commerce system, the same way objects are reused in building object-oriented programs. This approach enables an enterprise to integrate its systems within the company and with its trading partners, take advantage of the software tools available (e.g. CORBA COM etc.) in order to build standard and flexible systems without the need for exceptional technical expertise and maintain control of applications management in-house.

- In-house development requires time and expertise but produces tailor-made systems.
- Outsourcing has many advantages but can cause conflicts of control.
- Component-based development using object-oriented software tools can be used to build standardised systems without the need for exceptional technical skills.

As mentioned already, each of the above approaches has benefits and drawbacks; organisations can choose one or a combination of approaches to suit their needs. The decision should be made on the basis of the technology policies adopted by the company at the preparation stage. Whichever approach is used, an organisation must follow a methodology for the development of its e-commerce initiatives, guiding its progress from the initial stage of establishing the requirements for the system to the final stage of implementation. A number of methodologies based on different philosophies of systems development are in existence. Traditionally, computer systems were developed by following the hard systems methodology, so called because of its formal approach to development: a team of experts started with a formal request from users, then went through a series of stages to design, develop, test and implement the system. The process did not encourage much involvement of users and, due to the absence of step-wise refinement, enabled very little flexibility. It did not make allowances for indecision, 'fuzzy' statement of needs or errors in judgement. Following a number of IT systems failures which were blamed on (a) poor usability of the systems and (b) the absence of adequate testing with real users, researchers have presented us with a number of alternative methodologies. Referred to collectively as the philosophy of 'soft' systems design, it lays a strong emphasis on user involvement with two main aspects: an iterative approach to design and implementation, and user involvement at all stages of development. A systems team following the iterative approach develops a basic model and improves it incrementally by collecting user feedback at each stage. Systems designed by end users themselves are also becoming increasingly popular. All in all soft systems design has been collecting momentum for a while, although it has not been easy to persuade some of the technical staff to accept the new philosophy. Although a very important part of the study information systems, detailed discussion of this is outside the scope of this book.

Traditionally firms followed the hard and formal approach to systems development which did not allow much user involvement or 'fuzzy' specifications. Contemporary, 'soft' systems design rectifies this.

On the basis of the choices made about the mode of development and the methodology used for incorporating user involvement, the project development team proceeds to build e-commerce initiatives.

Step-wise implementation

Following the philosophy of iterative design and implementation advocated by the soft systems methodology, infrastructure building and implementation should take place in stages. Initially, only a limited number of applications for e-commerce should be built and implemented as a pilot initiative. For the next initiative, improvements based on user feedback should be made to these applications and further applications should be built. This method of incremental delivery helps the enterprise improve the integrity of its systems and also raises the entry barrier for its competitors.

The process should carry on internally until all the initiatives function satisfactorily. They are then opened up to the outside world for an industry-wide assessment. The philosophy of step-wise refinement should carry on at this stage also, thus testing the system in phases by introducing only a limited number of initiatives to customers and trading partners at each phase, and making improvements and extensions before the following phase.

The success of an enterprise's e-commerce initiatives depends as much on its ability to develop and implement efficient systems as on the degree to which the executive management is able to provide the leadership required to maintain high quality services for its customers. It must evaluate its policies, establish an excellent relationship with its trading partners and monitor customer reactions to its products and services. Thus the tasks of strategy development, infrastructure building and the implementation of new initiatives should carry on through an evolutionary process of continual review and update.

Discuss how the principles of step-wise refinement would work for a B2B company such as Intel. What difficulties might they face?

Implementing a new system or re-engineering existing processes often requires dramatic changes in corporate culture and practices. Unless handled with care, such changes often result in the failure of new initiatives. During a period of rapid growth and widespread innovation, it is vital for an organisation to manage the process of change and

E-procurement at NSPCC

Brendan Major, the head of information services at NSPCC, stresses the importance of extensive user involvement. The NSPCC piloted an e-procurement application from Get Real Systems in the early 2001. Rather than just working with users, Major, together with the charity's heads of procurement, finance and internal audit as well as representatives of Get Real, mounted a roadshow to sell the idea to every one of the system's potential users.

These meetings were a two-way process. Certain issues were not up for discussion; for example, the system would run on the organisation's intranet and end users needed to accept the suppliers chosen by the management. But within those parameters, the management was keen to know what users wanted their system to do.

Major admitted that without the consultative processes they would remain unaware of many organisation-specific details – for example that some suppliers have donated things such as toys to the organisation to benefit its work. However, even though users play a key part in the project, it was actually initiated by the department of information systems (IS). The business wanted software but was thinking more in terms of reporting and analysing current procurement activities. Major's team believed that if IS function is not allowed to be proactive and is just expected to deliver whatever the business thinks it needs, the organisation is likely to be a generation late in taking advantage of e-business ideas. The team was able to point out a way of optimising the process using the infrastructure that was already in place.

The implementation of the project involved technicians from several organisations. While Get Real supplied and configured its software, NSPCC staff retained responsibility for infrastructure. Thus, there was a three-way collaboration between the charity's IS people, the supplier of the financial package CA Masterpiece and Get Real. NSPCC did not have to recruit any extra staff; web skills and security know-how acquired by the team while maintaining the society's intranet and public website proved transferable to the e-procurement project.

(Adapted from Classe, 2001 with permission from Reed Business Information Ltd.)

Questions

1 In what ways has the NSPCC incorporated the principle of user involvement in its e-commerce strategies? In what ways does this approach augment the process outlined in this chapter?
2 How does the membership of the project team fit in with the organisation's objectives?
3 Discuss the role of the department of IS in the project.
4 What problems could the project team face in the above process?

build a climate of trust and integrity within the enterprise. This is particularly true for e-commerce as people often work in dispersed locations, sometimes involving workers in different countries. We will come back to the question of trust in chapter 9; here we will go on to discuss the importance of the management of change.

MANAGING CHANGE

It has been suggested that 70 per cent of all change initiatives fail because 'Managers flounder in an alphabet soup of change methods, drowning in conflicting advice' (Beer and Nohria, 2000: 133). At the time of change, some enterprises try to create economic value quickly by taking the 'hard' approach in which shareholder value is the only legitimate measure of corporate success; some others adopt the 'soft' approach and take time to establish the necessary trust and culture change in the organisation. According to the above research, organisations can use a mixture of the two but often fail to manage the combination appropriately for them to succeed.

Beer and Nohria suggest that a balanced combination of the two approaches is necessary for maintaining a sustainable competitive advantage during a process of change, calling them theory E (for economic value) and theory O (organisational capability), respectively. Managers taking the E route use traditional 'hard' measures such as economic incentives, drastic layoffs, downsizing (reducing the scale of activities and use of resources in selected areas) and restructuring. Those following the O approach to change believe in developing corporate culture and human capability through individual and organisational learning and by an iterative process of making changes, obtaining feedback, reflecting and making further changes and so on. The authors argue that an attempt to combine the two approaches without resolving the inherent tensions between them creates an atmosphere of distrust. They recommend the sequencing of the two strategies and confronting the tensions by encouraging dialogue at all levels of the enterprise. In December 1991, the UK supermarket ASDA (now merged with the USA giant Wal-Mart) went nearly bankrupt; its new CEO managed to reconcile the O and E theories and brought the company back on its feet. The following table (Fig. 8.5) adapted from the paper by Beer and Nohria shows how ASDA used a combination of O and E strategies to support different dimensions of the change process.

Two approaches are used for managing change: E (for economic value) which uses hard measures and O (for organisational capability) based on developing human capability to accept change. The sequencing of the two approaches is recommended.

The above ideology is applicable equally to large enterprises such as Asda and new start-ups such as dotcom companies that need to manage rapid growth. Both types must find ways to combine the qualities of theories E and O. On the one hand, the new economy has presented organisations with opportunities as well as the pressure for growth; on the other, it has created an environment of enormous uncertainty and risk. Whichever route a firm follows, leadership skill is the most important aspect of change management. Some entrepreneurs in start-ups subscribe only to theory E and, with strong leadership qualities, manage to build a powerful market presence. On the other hand, some can be dedicated followers of theory O but get overly wrapped up in idealism and fail to exercise the pragmatism required by the market. A sustained advantage can be obtained by a careful combination of the two approaches: developing the organisation for the long term, at the same time, constantly monitoring shareholder value.

What conflict may arise in an enterprise attempting to balance theories O and E?

SUMMARY

E-commerce affects relationships between areas of an organisation's work internally as well as with trading partners world-wide. An enterprise aspiring to succeed in the Internet age must function with a corporate vision; strategies to support this vision must be developed before implementing e-commerce. There are many debates about the definition and role of strategy. Scholars agree that its main role should be to find a way to be different; however, they vary in their interpretation of the effect of the Internet on businesses and how strategies fit in the circumstances. Michael Porter (2001) argues that the Internet is not necessarily a blessing for firms and extreme care must be taken in making sure that their strategies go beyond the principles of operational effectiveness. Organisations must attempt to find a strategic position in the market that uses technology to complement a traditional way of competing, rather than focusing on the technologies themselves. Gary Hamel (2000) recommends that strategy should be part of creating an innovative business model that links an organisation's mission with its core competencies, customer interfaces, trading networks and strategic resources. Other scholars range between seeing strategy as a series of practical steps based on a company's own situations, as art which should seek to find new ideas and as simple rules devised according to market opportunities. Such debates have given rise to recommendations for different methods of strategy formulation. Some of them present a model suggesting different approaches for different companies, some view it as a set of actions to be followed by all firms, others suggest that strategies should be decided on the basis of the answers to a number of questions in order to assess the needs of organisations attempting to create an innovative business model for the new economy. Different tactics for strategy making have also been suggested: strategy as co-operation with competitors; creating a customer magnet by slowly taking value away from competitors; and making short-term moves while working towards a long-term solution iteratively with the help of a number of available models to choose from. The principle of an iterative approach of launch and learn has been supported by a number of experts, especially those who view e-commerce as an evolutionary process in which the physical world and cyberspace are attempting to merge.

Dimension of change	Theory E	Theory O	How to combine theories E and O	Examples from ASDA
Goals	Maximise shareholder value	Develop organisational capabilities	Confront the paradox between economic value and organisational capability	ASDA's new CEO Archie Norman started by declaring his main objective of securing value for shareholders through a process of building a culture of common ideas coming from the shop-floor upwards
Leadership	Manage change from top down	Enable participation from bottom up	Set direction from the top and engage people from below	Norman started his new pricing strategy and then shifted power to the shop floors. He established a mechanism for direct dialogue between executive management and employees on the shop floor
Focus	Focus on physical structure and systems	Focus on Culture: attitudes, conduct etc.	Focus on both hard and soft sides of the organisation	Norman made hard choices such as freezing all wages and removing top layers of hierarchy. He also spent 75% of his time at the early stage of change as the human resources director trying to win the support of his employees by creating a culture of egalitarianism and transparency
Process to follow	Establish plans and programs	Experiment and evolve	Allow spontaneity	Norman encouraged experimentation by setting up three 'risk free' stores where managers were allowed to experiment without the risk of any penalties in case of failure. A cross-functional team produced significant innovations as a result
Reward system	Financial	Commitment building; payment is used as fair exchange	Use incentives such as payment to reinforce change but not to drive it	ASDA encouraged all employees to participate in changing the store. It rewarded them by providing stock ownership and pay based on corporate and store performance
Use of consultants	Consultants take an active part	Consultants support management	Consultants are used as expert resources to empower employees and to shape solutions	ASDA made limited use of four consulting firms in the early stages of its transformation. They worked alongside management and supported its leadership of change

Fig. 8.5 Management of change at Asda using theories E and O simultaneously (adapted from Beer and Nohria, 2000). Reprinted by permission of *Harvard Business Review*. From 'Cracking the Code of Change' by M. Beer and N. Nohria, May–June 2000. Copyright © 2000 by the Harvard Business School Publishing Corporation, all rights reserved.

In practical terms, strategy formulation can follow a set of distinct steps: the declaration of a corporate vision; the determination of strategic objectives; the collection of information on the competitive market and the assessment of risks and opportunities; the establishment of future strategies; and, finally, the production of a list of e-commerce initiatives with an allocation of project teams and management responsibilities. The analysis enables an organisation to evaluate its strengths, weaknesses, threats and opportunities in the uncertain environment of cyberspace with trading partners and customers potentially all over the world. An enterprise must determine its critical success factors in this environment and attempt to assess the tangible and intangible return on investment. Eisenhardt and Sull (2001) have suggested a set of 'simple rules' an enterprise can follow to establish some boundaries and policies on which to build its e-commerce initiatives.

The business processes and information systems constituting the foundation for e-commerce must be equipped to support the customer-facing processes and the value-chain which extends beyond organisational boundaries. This involves creating an inter-enterprise architecture comprising technology, people and the e-commerce ecosystem; development of e-commerce initiatives must be geared towards creating this architecture and making sure that the challenges presented by all elements of the architecture are addressed. The challenges include relationship building with customers and trading partners, managing human–computer interaction and meeting the needs of the technical, informational and operational infrastructures. The implementation should follow a process of step-wise refinement by developing initiatives in stages and implementing them, initially internally and then to include external partners. A number of alternative approaches can be taken to develop e-commerce projects such as outsourcing, doing it in-house or utilising component-based development. Implementing e-commerce involves an enormous change in the activities and culture of an organisation; an enterprise must be able to manage this change by balancing its needs for economic benefits with developing human capabilities for accepting change.

Revision Questions

1 Discuss Michael Porter's views on the role of strategy for businesses in the Internet era.
2 Explain the 5 Ps concept of strategy. Discuss how an organisation chooses between them.
3 What is the relationship between business concept innovation and strategy?
4 Discuss the ethos of strategy making as an art.
5 Critically discuss the principles of strategy as a set of simple rules.
6 Discuss the four approaches to strategy formulation presented by Boisot. Under what circumstances could a company use each of them?
7 Discuss Porter's approach of reconnecting with strategy by taking a set of actions.
8 Explain the model presented by Gary Hamel for strategy formulation associated with business concept innovation. How does each component in the model support uniqueness and differentiation?
9 Explain how the components in the above model relate to each other to improve the efficiency of an enterprise.
10 Discuss the concept of creating customer magnet by taking small steps.
11 What are the three basic competencies needed by a business? Discuss the six models an enterprise can adopt to achieve these competencies in e-commerce.
12 Why do organisations sometimes need radical changes and what do scholars recommend in that situation?

13 Discuss Becker's approaches to strategies required to cope with the uncertain environment of multinational businesses.
14 Discuss the strategies required for an organisation attempting to enter the e-enterprise stage. Why is this approach useful for all organisations?
15 What are the conflicts between the democratisation of organisations and the central control of ERP systems?
16 What are the conflicts between the strategy of a technology-based solution and an approach based on personalisation for the management of knowledge?
17 Explain the five steps of strategy formulation.
18 Why do companies need to gather and analyse information before they determine the potential of e-commerce for the enterprise?
19 Describe the phases of and the steps involved in SWOT analysis.
20 Why do organisations need to review their value chain? What questions should they ask themselves in doing so?
21 What do we mean by the critical success factors for an organisation? How does an organisation determine its CSFs?
22 How can a company measure its ROI given the mixture of tangible and intangible benefits associated with e-commerce?
23 How should a company proceed to set the rules which it would follow in developing e-commerce projects?
24 What are the areas in which an organisation should establish policies before developing e-commerce?
25 Describe the inter-enterprise architecture an organisation needs in order to implement efficient e-commerce ventures.
26 What processes are involved in the implementation of e-commerce?
27 Why does an organisation need an iterative process of implementation?
28 Describe the process involved in building an e-commerce infrastructure.
29 What are the options available to an organisation for developing its e-commerce initiatives? Discuss their relative merits and demerits.
30 Why does an organisation implementing e-commerce need to understand the principles of human–computer interaction and design methodologies?
31 Why is the effective management of change important for an organisation?
32 Discuss theories E and O of change management.

Discussion Questions

1 Critically review the different views and models of business strategies discussed in this chapter in terms of their relevance to e-commerce, effectiveness and practicality.
2 Various business methods and philosophies have been mentioned in this chapter (SWOT, CSF, ROI, HCI etc.) Discuss their contribution to the implementation of an e-commerce company's business strategies.

Bibliography

Akers, C., *Edmunds.com*, Harvard Business School, 9-701-025, 26 September, 2000.
Bandyo-padhyay, N., *Computing for Non-specialists*, Addison Wesley, London, 2000.
Becker, K., International business strategies and multinational corporations. In H. Costin (ed.), *Readings in Strategy and Strategic Planning*, The Dryden Press, Orlando, 1998.
Beer, M. and Nohria, N., Cracking the code of change, *Harvard Business Review*, Product Number 651X, May–June, 2000, pp. 133–141.

Boisot, M. In B. Garratt (ed.), *Developing Strategic Thought: Rediscovering the Art of Direction Giving*, McGraw-Hill, London, 1995.

Byrne, J. A., Strategic planning is back, *BusinessWeek*, 1996.

Cap Gemini Ernst & Young LLC, *Electronic Commerce: A Need to Change Perspective*, 2000 Special Report on the Financial Services Industry, 2000.

Classe, A., E-skills on the up and up, *ComputerWeekly*, 29 March, 2001, p. 58.

Davenport, T. H., Putting the enterprise into the enterprise system, *Harvard Business Review*, Product Number 98401, July–August, 1998, pp. 122–131.

Dudman, J., A measure for measures, *ComputerWeekly*, 29 March, 2001, p. 62.

Dyer, J. H. and Singh, H., Using alliances to build competitive advantage in emerging technologies. In G. S. Day and P. J. H. Schoemaker, with R. E. Gunther (eds), *Wharton on Managing Emerging Technologies*, Wiley, New York, 2000.

Eisenhardt, M. K. and Sull, D. N., Strategy as simple rules, *Harvard Business Review*, Product Number 5858, January, 2001, pp. 105–116.

Fingar, P., Kumar, H. and Sharma, T., *Enterprise E-Commerce: The Software Components Breakthrough for Business-to-Business Commerce*, Meghan-Kiffer Press, Tampa, Florida, 2000.

Ghosh, S., Making business sense of the Internet, *Harvard Business Review*, Product Number 98205, March–April 1998, pp. 125–135.

Hale, R. and Whitlam, P., Toward the Virtual Organisation, McGraw-Hill, London, 1997.

Hamel, G., *Leading the Revolution*, Harvard Business School Press, 2000.

Hansen M. T., Nohria, N. and Tierney, T., What's your strategy for managing knowledge? *Harvard Business Review*, Product Number 4347, March–April, 1999, pp. 106–116.

Hoque, F., *e-Enterprise: Business Models, Architecture, and Components*, Cambridge University Press, New York, 2000.

Kaplan, R. S. and Norton, D. P., Using the the balanced scorecard as a strategic management system, *Harvard Business Review*, Product Number 4126, 1996.

Langley, N., Taming the tiger, *Computer Storage Magazine, E-business special*, March, 2001, p. 16.

Lipsitz, J., Your game plan for ebusiness, *Computing*, 19 October, 2000, p. 44.

Mintzberg, H., The strategy concept I: Five Ps for strategy. In H. Costin (ed.), *Readings in Strategy and Strategic Planning*, The Dryden Press, Orlando, 1998.

Mintzberg, H., The strategy concept II: Another look at why organisations need strategies. In H. Costin (ed.), *Readings in Strategy and Strategic Planning*, The Dryden Press, Orlando, 1998.

Moody, G., Brand new auctions, *ComputerWeekly, e.business review*, October, 2000, p. 39.

Nolan, R. L., *Reengineering: Competitive Advantage and Strategic Jeopardy*, Harvard Business School, 9-196-019, 7 July, 1995.

Porter. M. E., What is strategy? *Harvard Business Review*, Product Number 4134, November–December, 1996, pp. 59–78.

Porter. M. E., Strategy and the Internet, *Harvard Business Review*, Reprint R01031, March, 2001, pp. 60–78.

Singhal, A. and Rogers, E. M., *India's Information Revolution*, Sage, New Delhi, India, 1989.

Szulanski, G. and Amin, K., Disciplined imagination: Strategy making in uncertain environments. In G. S. Day and P. J. H. Schoemaker with R. E. Gunther (eds), *Wharton on Managing Emerging Technologies*, Wiley, New York, 2000.

Turban, E., Lee, J., King, D. and Chung, H. M., *Electronic Commerce: A Managerial Perspective*, Prentice Hall, New Jersey, 2000.

Ward, J. and Griffiths, P., *Strategic Planning for Information Systems*, Wiley, Chichester, UK, 1996.

Weick, K. E., Theory construction as disciplined imagination, *Academy of Management Review*, 14(4), 1989, pp. 516–531.

Creating Trust in E-Commerce

Chapter Nine

Objectives

By the end of this chapter you should have an understanding of:

- The importance of trust in e-commerce.
- The role of security in building trust.
- The security risks involved in on-line businesses.
- The steps an organisation can take to implement a secure system.
- The potential problems related to privacy and how to address them.

INTRODUCTION

In the last chapter we discussed the importance of a strategic approach in the introduction of e-commerce and the steps necessary to develop and implement e-commerce initiatives. As we know, security is a crucial part of the success of businesses in cyberspace. The growth of e-commerce relies on people's willingness to enter critical information on-line; the lack of an assurance that the information submitted is secure and fully confidential is a major obstacle against the trust that the sector needs in order to encourage consumers to participate. An organisation needs to understand how it can be affected by customer mistrust in e-business, the damage theft and misuse of data can cause to the possibility of creating trust, the level of public concern about loss of privacy and the importance of the existence of a policy equipped to deal with these issues. We approach this topic with the perspective that trust is normally the result of a successful long-term relationship. Organisations in cyberspace must now attempt to minimise the risks involved in business activities as the basis for building such relationships. We discussed the characteristics of a secure system and the technologies available to enhance security in chapters 5 and 7; in this chapter, we will focus on the consequences of loss of security and confidentiality of data, and investigate what steps e-businesses must take in order to implement security and create a relationship of trust with its customers.

THE IMPORTANCE OF TRUST IN CYBERSPACE

Trust between two parties is normally built upon how much confidence each has on the reliability, strength, integrity and honesty of the other. The foundation of successful e-commerce is therefore grounded in a relationship of trust between the buyer and the seller. In the world of bricks and mortar, there is usually a high degree of trust based on the visibility of the seller, its history, experience and the country's legal framework. Building the same level of trust between customers, businesses and the financial institutions in the relatively new and virtual world of e-commerce combined with the speed with which e-commerce entered the arena is a difficult but essential proposition. The models used in the physical world could not always be transferred to e-commerce; for example, a legal framework is difficult to establish in the global context, governments are often reluctant to introduce legislation for fear of obstructing the pace of growth and consumer groups are unable to exert pressure due to the physical unavailability of the firms. In a survey published by PricewaterhouseCoopers (PWC) in July 2000 (Ward, 2000) involving 400 senior B2B companies in the UK, Germany, France and the Netherlands, it was shown that security concerns and a lack of faith in trading partners are the biggest factors holding back the growth of e-procurement. Organisations are increasingly becoming aware of the importance of trust for businesses and are introducing necessary procedures such as displaying warning messages about security risks and using encryption technologies for data transmission. Established bricks and mortar companies are often able to capitalise on their off-line image to establish trust when they move into e-commerce; many of them also acknowledge the special significance of trust on-line and have begun to include security as a part of their e-business strategies.

Trust is a mutual issue: buyers need to have trust in sellers in terms of the quality of products and services as well as the security and confidentiality of data; sellers must have trust in buyers' authenticity, integrity and non-repudiation. Such relationships must also extend to all parties involved in e-commerce world-wide. Although the concerns of consumers buying on-line comes to mind first when we discuss trust, it is as much an issue for B2B transactions as it is for B2C. Over a third of the business leaders interviewed in the PWC survey admitted that security issues are undermining trust between trading partners and affecting the growth of e-business. Decision makers must recognise the significance of the situation and introduce necessary measures in order to support the expansion of e-commerce.

Trust between buyers and sellers in botb B2B and B2C sectors is essential for e-businesses but difficult to establish due to the global and virtual nature of them. Concerns over the lack of security and privacy have kept many consumers away.

We are in an information economy in which knowledge of customers generates significant economic value. Enterprises are increasingly acknowledging the importance of persuading customers to release personal information for commercial uses. This is accentuated by factors such as (Ernst & Young, 2001):

- Gaining trust of customers in foreign markets, jurisdictions and cultures is essential for the survival of businesses operating globally.
- Trust can accelerate transactions and lower costs by eliminating the need for prolonged off-line activities.
- Breach of trust can have a negative effect on a company's reputation, legal cost etc.
- It has been proven that improved trust results in stronger relationships between businesses and their customers, thus leading to better business prospects.
- Established bricks and mortar enterprises are having to work hard at creating the same degree of trust in their on-line counterpart in order to maintain the loyalty of their customers in the off-line sector.

Increasingly, enterprises are joining new trust models formulated on the basis of collective codes of conduct such as those provided by TRUSTe (explained later) and going through a process of re-assessment, redefinition and repositioning of their e-commerce strategies. More and more companies are adopting the public key infrastructure (PKI – chapter 5) and employing certification authorities (CA) to establish trusted on-line identities for themselves. Different types of industry can obtain different levels of certificate according to the sensitivity of the data they handle. For example, a basic class 1 certificate, required normally by individuals using the Internet to send messages, simply binds a user's name with their email address and their public key. A class 2 certificate, used by organisations such as banks, includes the user's customer number. Such a certificate is only issued after a registration authority in the bank has approved the customers' accounts. A class 3 certificate is usually used by the operators of Internet

Many e-businesses are now acknowledging the economic benefit of trust of customers in countries world-wide. Both new and traditional companies are taking steps such as the use of PKI and new business models backed by collective codes of conduct.

Broker selects PKI encryption to secure online share trading
(www.zdnet.co.uk/itweek/casestudy/2001/15/management)

Eduard de Graaff is not a name that is familiar to many in this country. However, the Dutch brokerage profited by £4.1m last year by trading on the instructions of professional investors in shares and convertible bonds, both in the domestic market in Amsterdam and on foreign exchanges. Like many firms trading online, Eduard de Graaff's business depends on having secure systems that customers will trust.

When the company shifted its focus from large corporate customers to individuals, it decided to secure these smaller transactions with authentication from digital certificates. It needed a highly secure system that could be scaled up to meet growing business needs, so the firm decided to use a public key infrastructure (PKI) encryption system. 'We needed a method of authentication that could guarantee our smaller customers the same protection against fraud and other threats that our larger clients enjoy,' says Frank Metz of Eduard de Graaff's IT department. 'Authentication is key for secure transactions, and we needed to make the process easy to deploy and administer.'

The PKI system had to be able to secure a mix of NT and Unix legacy applications, and had to be flexible enough to allow for business growth. After looking at a number of PKI products, including those from Netegrity and VeriSign, Eduard de Graaff decided to proceed with Baltimore Technologies and its Sel-ectAccess product. Metz says that larger clients at Eduard de Graaff were already using Baltimore's UniCert PKI product for user authentication, so it was not a big step for the company to adopt Baltimore's SelectAccess to support its smaller clients. 'There are a number of reasons why we selected Baltimore,' says Metz. 'We had a good feeling about their proposition, and we got a very good service in return.'

A pilot project involving 50 customers was established, and Baltimore trained core members of Eduard de Graaff's staff to use SelectAccess over a two-week period. Seamus Gill, director of business development for Europe, the Middle East and Africa at Baltimore, says, 'It was essential to provide an easy-to-maintain solution for Eduard de Graaff, as it will be managed from the business side of the operation, freeing up the IT department to concentrate on critical tasks.'

Metz says that there were some teething problems regarding the functionality of the Web site, but Baltimore arranged for technicians to fly from Canada to the Netherlands to resolve a configuration problem. Eduard de Graaff said it was generally happy with the service Baltimore delivered.

Recent research from analyst group Forrester has found that the third most-popular content on the Web in Europe is financial in nature. Forty-three percent of Web users conduct financial activity online, such as researching stocks, viewing their accounts or trading online. Eighteen percent of European Internet users, roughly five percent of the adult population, use online banking. Given this growing trend, secure transactions are becoming increasingly relied on. PKI looks set to play a crucial role in the future growth of online finance.

(Source: Lee, C., *IT Week*, 16 April, 2001.
VNU Business Publications 2001.
Reproduced with permission.)

Questions

1 Discuss the technical considerations an organisation needs to address before implementing an encryption system.
2 How can Eduard de Graaff expect the system to improve their customer services? What business issues do they need to address for the success of the system?
3 In what ways does this case study demonstrate the importance of the reliability of the supplier of a PKI product for the success of an authentication system?

servers. It binds the server's URL with the organisation's name and its public key and is issued following rigorous security checks. This is a way to give consumers the assurance of the backing of a validating body (the CA) and increase the level of trust. Sometimes a CA is required to obtain a certificate by a higher level CA, thus creating a hierarchy of trust.

Studies undertaken in 1999 and 2000 in North America, Latin America and Brazil by Cheskin (2000), a commercial surveying company in the USA, reported that customers believe that anarchy rules in the Internet, leading to a lack of privacy and security, and that governments (the 'big brother') and marketers and advertisers (the 'little brothers') monitor and manipulate our activities. The report suggested that some, mainly young, male and Internet savvy customers are prepared to trade privacy for lower prices – this has a negative effect on the overall move toward improving trust in e-commerce. However, some large enterprises, especially in the financial sector, are making significant efforts to establish financial and functional trustworthiness. According to Cheskin's survey, the most trusted website in the Americas is Yahoo! with Hotmail/MSN a close second. In Brazil, banks run the most trusted websites possibly because they often function as the ISPs for their customers. Amazon also ranks high in all three lists (America, Latin America and Brazil).

You are thinking about purchasing rare records over the Internet. What elements or factors in the process would discourage you from doing so?

PROBLEMS WITH TRUST BUILDING

While the unlimited geographical extent of e-businesses and the electronic mode of data transfer make it almost impossible for an organisation to monitor transactions, some monitoring is essential in ensuring that such data is free of the possibility of corruption, theft or misuse because of the relative ease with which it can be intercepted. In a survey conducted by *BusinessWeek* and Harris Poll in the USA, 57 per cent of those Internet users surveyed said that their decision to buy on-line was influenced in favour of those websites which have a guaranteed security policy. 50 per cent of those polled believed that the government should pass laws addressing the issues of the security of personal data (Ferraro, 1998). As discussed in chapter 7, attempts have been made by the governments in some countries to introduce a legal framework for e-commerce, but in most cases B2C e-commerce has relied on self-regulation. *Business Week* examined 100 top websites and discovered that only 43 per cent posted privacy policies. Another survey done in 2001 by the Consumers International – a conglomeration of a number of national consumer organisations – in early 2001 (Warren, 2001) found that while a majority of sites collected personal information on consumers, fewer than two-thirds had a privacy policy. The policies which existed did not provide adequate protection for consumer privacy and could not explain how information on consumers is obtained and utilised. The consequences of such behaviour for the prospects of e-commerce has prompted many previous supporters of self-regulation to start advocating government intervention.

The lack of consumer trust stems from the lack of visible corporate policies on privacy. Enterprises are losing money due to the loss and misuse of data because many of them do not yet understand the risks involved in on-line data transfer.

Another survey done in late 1999 by the FBI and the Computer Security Institute in the USA of Fortune 500 companies found that financial losses from computer crime went up by $360 million between 1997 and 1999 (KPMG, 2000). The figure is likely to be even higher if we take into consideration the fact that companies are normally reluctant to report losses resulting from breaches in security due to the fear of negative publicity.

LIVERPOOL JOHN MOORES UNIVERSITY
LEARNING SERVICES

Innovations in technology are pushing companies to introduce new systems so fast that many organisations neglect to give adequate consideration to security. Unfortunately, innovations that enable companies to introduce e-commerce are also available to criminals waiting to benefit from the easy availability of information. We discussed the available technical and operational infrastructure which help to provide security in chapters 5 and 7; here we will concentrate on the consequences of criminal activities, inadequate controls and the abuse of a position of privilege all of which lead to the loss of security for companies, privacy for individuals and trust between trading partners.

THE NATURE OF THE SECURITY RISKS IN E-COMMERCE

Risks in security can be put into a number of categories:

- An attack on a company's computer system by an outsider – the so called 'hacking' of computer systems has become a common phenomenon on the Internet; in the year 2000, a virus called 'I love you' which was sent as an email to on-line users world-wide managed to paralyse a large number of computer systems. The effect was estimated to have cost businesses and governments more than $10 billion (KPMG, 2000). However, sending a virus by email is just one aspect of hacking prompted by an attitude of vindictiveness and vandalism by individuals; there are many virus detection programs in existence which can safeguard a system against such nuisance. A more serious side of hacking is performed by experienced programmers who, working either for themselves or on contract with firms, use their skill to gain access to a competitor's information resources with an attempt to destroy, damage, block or steal information.
- An attack by a disgruntled or corrupt employee – It has been proven by the UK's Computer Audit Commission report, published in 1994, that only 15 per cent of the total amount of computer abuse comes from external break-ins; the rest are rooted in the organisations themselves. The situation has not changed much since then; about 80 per cent of all security breaches are caused by a company's own staff (Goodwin, 2000). Although external hackers gain more publicity in the media, it is often an insider who uses his right of access to a system to perform unlawful activities. High turnover of IT staff, dishonest IT staff, disgruntled employees who have left the company etc. have been stated as the main factors. Damage could be done out of a sense of revenge, to make personal gain by manipulating information in the attacker's favour or to profit from the sale of information to external bodies. Sometimes employees simply give outsiders the details necessary to gain access to a system, thus causing serious damage with little chance of anyone detecting the intrusion. There have also been many cases of a user introducing a 'Trojan Horse': a program that creates a dummy screen display for logging in; when other users try to use it the procedure results in writing their user ID to a file which is later used by the culprit to gain access. A similar approach can be taken to gain access to a customer's on-line account in order to transfer money or exploit other facilities in e-commerce.
- The vulnerability of a system due to inadequate security measures, leading to the loss or corruption of data – although criminal activities have dominated public discussions on security, a large amount of data and equipment are damaged by accident due to inadequate physical safeguards such as fire, flood

and power failures, incorrect data entry or an undiscovered error in a computer program due to inadequate testing. Such errors are dangerous as they may affect output a long time after a system is operational, creating panic and taking a long time to locate. Traditionally, many organisations depended on the security procedures built into network software and put too much trust on employees with supervisory access rights to the network. Hackers depend on the ignorance and lack of awareness of the users of data; some hackers have been known to collect all the information they need to get into a computer system from the waste paper bins in an office. Even after a number of well-publicised cases of theft and fraud, many companies fail to recognise the seriousness of the problem because (Bandyo-padhyay, 2000):

- Managers are often not directly involved in the handling of data and therefore do not understand the risks.
- Many computer systems are left in the hands of a few technical people, thus giving a limited number of employees too much power over technology.
- The benefits of security measures are not tangible and are therefore difficult to justify – especially to managers with non-technical backgrounds.
- One important feature of e-commerce is partnership and alliance, a relationship that relies on the widespread availability of information between partners. This can increase an enterprise's vulnerability as the situation can be abused by some parties.

- The wrongful utilisation of data collected by a firm from a website – an organisation collects information on users using different means: large amounts of personal data are regularly submitted during the purchase of products on-line; websites often have facilities to 'clickstream' – track the activities of a user through the series of clicks during a web session in order to monitor his/her preferences in products and subjects; use 'cookies' – a file transferred to a user's website at the first log-in which has a program that enables the organisation to collect information on the user's movement in cyberspace. Information can also be registered when a user enters a competition, makes enquiries or even uses a service provider to send personal emails. Sometimes one organisation passes such information to others; for example, a credit card company can share a customer's credit details with insurance companies, banks etc. A firm can use information on individuals to target advertisements, screen customers, assess a customer's suitability for insurance cover, check a job applicant's medical history and much more.
- The use of pervasive computing – intelligent processors are now embedded in most business and personal appliances. Referred to as pervasive computing, this has the potential to create a 'hyper-extended networked world' (Ferraro, 1998) when connected to the Internet, enabling enterprises to collect data for mining and knowledge management. Although such practices contribute to the development of effective e-commerce, it also creates the possibility of a society in which people are continually monitored and are forced to live under the threat of the abuse arising from the misuse of personal information.

Risks in e-commerce:

- External hackers – vandals and serious data thieves.
- Corrupt (ex)employees.
- The vulnerability of a computer system due to lack of physical security and management support, neglect, misuse by external partners etc.
- Inappropriate use of data collected on-line.
- Use of networked mobile equipment.

It must be remembered that risks exist in the physical world of business as well, but it is far easier to trace such events and take steps against them in this world than in cyberspace. Creating public trust in e-commerce depends on the ability of organisations collectively to acknowledge the existing fears and engage in developing an infrastructure for the security and confidentiality of information.

You are an IT manager in a large on-line car dealer. You wish to set up your own dotcom selling motoring insurance on-line. How could you benefit from your old job to establish your own business?

TAKING ACTION TO ENHANCE SECURITY

Security cannot be established in business by simply taking specific actions or introducing particular technologies. It must be treated as a central part of a company's e-commerce strategy. An all-encompassing initiative must be developed which assesses the risks following the company's risk management policies (chapter 8), examines its procedures, reviews the sensitivity levels of e-commerce systems and introduces a defence programme that is an integral part of the business. It must address the behavioural, cultural and political issues relevant to an enterprise whose boundaries go beyond any physical limits to include partners, stakeholders and customers all over the world.

THE DEFENCE PROGRAMME

An integrated defence programme is an on-going and iterative process of activities, as shown in Fig. 9.1. Based upon holistic risk management strategies, the company leaders must first perform a thorough analysis of existing systems and activities. This should involve an examination of the information handled by a system, an evaluation of the importance and sensitivity of the information, assessment of *threats and vulnerabilities*, and a review of the effectiveness of the current safety measures.

A defence programme is an integrated set of processes designed to create an infrastructure for maintaining confidentiality and integrity of data. It involves on-going activities of risk assessment, planning, developing, testing and implementing controls, and awareness raising.

On the basis of the above risk assessment, a *plan of action* must be developed to document a set of guidelines outlining the management, operational and technical controls to be implemented. The plan should include:

- Technical information about the systems under consideration.
- A note of the sensitivity levels of the systems, that is, the degree of availability, integrity and confidentiality required for the information handled by the systems.
- An overview of the security requirements based on the above.
- The controls already in place.

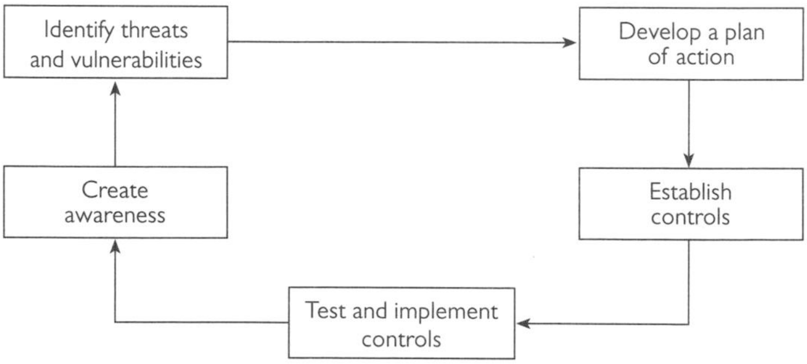

Fig. 9.1 The elements of a defence programme

- The controls to be implemented to fulfil the above requirements.
- The expected behaviour of all individuals in the enterprise – the 'rules of behaviour'.
- Measures taken to protect systems from individual employees.
- Policies to assess the security risks from customers.
- Policies to assess the security risks from trading partners.
- Management and operational responsibilities for implementing and monitoring security plans,
- Response procedures in case of breaches of security.
- Plans for training programmes and awareness-raising activities.

A plan of action is created following a process of studying the operations, checking existing controls and investigating what more needs to be done in terms of employee behaviour, policies on operation and management, recovery plans etc.

The above plan requires the collaboration of business managers and security professionals. The latter should include those with the technical knowledge of implementing e-commerce related security systems, experience in investigating criminal activities and skill in handling legal action from customers and business partners. The plan provides a framework for managing security; it gives management formal and documented guidelines to follow when implementing procedures. On the basis of those guidelines, a set of *controls* must be designed and implemented to protect e-commerce systems against damage and theft and to deal with situations if something goes wrong.

Controls can be put into two categories: operational controls which are measures to be taken by people and technical controls to be implemented using technology. Operational controls address the following issues:

- Personnel security – as mentioned already, the greatest threat to computer systems comes from insiders. The damage inflicted could be intentional or unintentional; it is therefore most important that necessary procedures are established to prevent both. There must be documentation containing details of the methods used to screen individuals, rights of access allowed to individuals and the justification for these, controls to be implemented to deal with the associated risks, steps to be taken if users are found to be exploiting their rights etc.
- Physical controls – this involves the steps taken to ensure that equipment and data are physically safe. For example, entry to computer rooms and storage areas must be restricted to authorised personnel only, precautions must be taken against fire, flood, structural and electrical damage and decay, printed information must be destroyed rather than thrown into a bin and so on. There have been recent cases of laptops and other mobile computer equipment being stolen; procedures must be in place to prevent this and ensure that organisational data on such devices is either inaccessible or unintelligible to strangers.
- Operational procedures – a mechanism must be established to ensure that procedures are in place to maintain security at a high level. This includes things such as: the availability of data protection mandates and sensitivity statements on data items for operators; a limit on the extent to which data handled by operators are readable to them; and the maintenance of audit trails – a mechanism designed to record the sequence of system activities which can be used to trace the 'footprints' of a system, reconstruct events and track down data or applications causing a problem.
- Contingency plans – these are required to permit an organisation to carry on with its normal business even if some interruptions take place. This involves keeping multiple back up copies of information in different locations, introducing disaster recovery procedures detailing how to re-establish an

interrupted operation, which personnel to contact, what training must be provided to prepare employees for such situations etc.

- Validation procedures – validation procedures are security measures used to ensure that data entered into a system is correct and safe against corruption or theft. Although this is managed by technical controls, manual procedures must also be introduced to strengthen them. For example, checks must be performed to confirm that virus programs are installed and are up to date, that data is validated before entry, that logs of user access are checked regularly to detect any signs of intrusion, that one individual is not left in charge of a sensitive system longer than a specified period etc.

The above measures must be supplemented by technical controls which are designed to provide automated protection of applications and data from intentional or accidental damage. This mainly involves procedures for access controls in three specific areas:

- The policy used to allocate rights of access – access to a computer system must be strictly regulated by using passwords, user IDs, firewalls and other technical means. These methods can be used to provide access of varying degrees to users; one way of controlling access is to use a system of 'least privilege', that is, giving users the minimum access they require to perform their duties. There must also be a system of monitoring user log-ins and enforcing compulsory periodic change of passwords. Strict rules must be followed to guide how passwords should be formed, for example how many and what type of characters are allowed, which words are not acceptable as a password and how users should decide on a password (e.g. names or words sounding like names are unsuitable). Some organisations allow biometrics such as user's face, retina, fingerprint, hand, voice, typing rhythm, signature, etc. as user IDs which provide extra security against fraud. If digital signatures are used then the systems must conform to the standard adopted by the organisation and there must be established procedures for the management of encryption keys.
- Who gets access and to what degree – policies must be established to guide the criteria by which access will be allocated to users. The criteria might include the function of the individual in the company, length of service, whether to allow access from anywhere and at any time etc. If the company uses a system of least privilege then special attention must be paid to determine the minimum privileges a user must be given without affecting the level of service s/he can provide.
- How to allocate access to users outside the organisation – one of the main reasons behind the lack of public confidence in e-commerce security is the threat of fraudulent activities by hackers and thieves and the risk of loss of integrity and confidentiality of data due to neglect and inefficiency. It is therefore crucial for trust-building that controls are in place to protect a system and that customers are aware of the measures taken. Amongst them are:
  - The establishment of a proven system of authentication and identification checks for all users. This is difficult to implement as a company relies on widespread availability of a website. However, it is possible to limit the level of usage according to a user's status, thus allowing everyone the right to 'surf' the website but limit the extent to which they can access information at deeper levels with passwords and other security checks. It is

Operational controls on security involves:

- Taking steps to protect a system from corrupt individuals.
- Improving physical security to limit damage and theft.
- Making recovery plans.
- Improving manual procedures to ensure accuracy and safety of data input.

now common for on-line users to be asked to enter security details additional to the password, based on specific information known only to the holder of an account, such as mother's maiden name. Some organisations hold a series of such details and ask for a selection of them at each session.

- The use of digital signatures during the transaction of any financial or personal data.
- The separation of information open to public access from the company's databases.
- The implementation of an efficient audit trail.
- The implementation of a legal infrastructure designed to assure users of the integrity of a website as well as to provide the company with the framework it needs to deal with litigation, illegal activities, the regulatory framework of the countries using the website etc.
- The vetting of service providers and trading partners. The checks to be carried out should include: which organisations and individuals are associated with them, the quality of the companies' security infrastructure and the legal framework of the countries they and their associates are situated in.

Technical controls include:

- Proper management of user access procedures.
- Policies on the distribution of access rights.
- Management of the allocation and maintenance of access to partners and external users.

You run the member website for a major political party. What measures would you establish – both physical and technological – to ensure data security, and why?

The most effective way to ensure the security of a system is to perform thorough *testing* before the controls are implemented. The importance of testing a computer system has been discussed in chapter 8; e-commerce is no exception. Before any security controls are put into practice, their functionality and effectiveness must be checked by following the principles of good systems design. Enterprises rushing into e-commerce sometimes add a website to their traditional systems without checking its effect on the rest of the technical infrastructure. When Halifax, a large British bank, added a new routine to its on-line share dealing site and allowed it to go 'live' without checking the impact of the addition to the existing system, customers found that they could access, and even trade, other customers' share portfolios (Booth, 2000). A defence programme provides value only when the steps taken to secure the operations have been tested and proven to be effective.

An important characteristic of a secure e-business is the *awareness* amongst its employees of the importance of security and a knowledge of how to maintain it. Creating awareness is therefore an important element of a defence programme and should include:

- Training for employees on how to use security features.
- Training on how to deal with breaches of security.
- Awareness-raising sessions to develop a collective sense of the importance of security.
- Training on how to respond to public concerns.

The dilemma for those attempting to find security solutions is that no system is 100 per cent secure. Although innovations in technology provide us with the means to implement new methods of security, they also enable hackers to find new ways of intercepting a system. We are heading towards an era in which computer devices will be embedded into everyday items (WAP is one example of this); new standards and protocols will also emerge to address the issues arising out of increased connectivity. An organisation must therefore undertake a continual process of *monitoring and reviewing* its defence programme. The review may be done by internal or external bodies but must exclude those who are responsible for the systems concerned. Following a set of criteria, the review team must monitor the management, operational, technical and personnel controls implemented and assess their effectiveness within the context of the acceptable level of risk for the systems.

User awareness of the importance of security is crucial for an organisation. Training must be provided to create awareness and the steps to be taken to preserve it through a well-formulated defence programme which is continually reviewed and updated.

One of the main objectives of a defence programme is to uphold the confidentiality of personal information about data subjects (the persons on whom data is stored). Thus, a well-established programme contributes to improved privacy for individuals. However, there are some specific issues surrounding privacy that enterprises must deal with.

What difficulties might business leaders face in implementing an effective defence programme?

PRIVACY IN E-COMMERCE

Privacy is one of the main issues users are concerned with when deciding whether or not to buy on-line. From a survey in the USA the Merchants Association found that only 5 per cent of consumers visiting a website actually makes a purchase, the primary reason being concerns over privacy and security (PWC, 1999). The same publication quoted an earlier survey carried out by Louis Harris and Associates and sponsored by PWC and Privacy & American Business which concluded that:

- A large majority (over 90 per cent) of those buying on the Internet want to see notices posted on a website explaining how the personal information provided by customers buying on-line will be used by the company.
- A large majority of those who do not use the Internet yet said such notices would be very important if they were to go on-line.
- 44 per cent of those who are not likely to use the Internet in the next year said that greater privacy protection would be a major factor to convince them to do so.

At present public confidence in organisations' ability to provide security and privacy in e-commerce is low. There have been many cases of complaints by consumers which forced businesses to amend their ways on a number of occasions. For example, in 1997, a major on-line service provider was sued by customers on charges such as divulging information on individuals' sexual preferences, the navigational habits of customers etc. The service provider had to change its policies within 24 hours of this becoming public (PWC, 1999).

Customers are also suspicious of organisations' reasons for collecting information. Banks and building societies, credit card companies, the Inland Revenue, employers, doctors, the Department of Social Security, the DVLA office (which deals with our car registrations and driving licences) etc. all hold information we supplied them with in order to get the services they provide. The proliferation of on-line businesses has given companies additional excuses to ask for information in these and many other areas of our lives. As we discussed in chapter 6, customer relationship management (CRM), founded on the collection of data on customers (data warehousing and mining), is a major aspect of e-commerce. This has raised concerns over:

- How much of the information collected is really necessary?
- Who is in charge of the information – the data subject, the user/holder (the organisation which stores data), the service provider or the advertisers who use it to send marketing information?
- What are the rights of the above entities?
- On what basis is the information passed on to third parties? Do the data holders have the right to do so?
- Is self-regulation adequate or is government intervention required?[1]
- Can a country's legal framework protect overseas on-line customers?

At the root of consumers' resistance against e-commerce is the uncertainty surrounding how data submitted by them on-line is used and what regulatory framework there is to safeguard it.

Failure to respond to these concerns is likely to seriously affect the growth in e-commerce; 'Privacy issues drive – or drag – the information economy' (PWC, 1999: 9). Also, the absence of some guidelines can cost companies dearly. The PWC report quoted the example of a case in 1998 when a federal jury in the USA awarded a victim $50,000 in actual damages and $4.47 million in punitive damages against a credit-reporting agency (a company providing reports on individuals' credit records to businesses on request) who failed to follow reasonable procedures to maintain accuracy. Businesses and governments must take steps in order to alleviate some of the fears and create public confidence in e-commerce; the following is an account of some of the initiatives taken in this respect.

The moves made to create public confidence in e-commerce

Different countries have addressed the issue of privacy in different ways. In the UK, the Data Protection Act (DPA) specific to computerised data was introduced in 1984 and updated by the European Data Protection Directive in 1998. The revised act, which came into force in March 2000, puts increased responsibility on data users to tell customers how the data collected will be used, how it will be secured and what choices they have in the way it is used. There is also an added emphasis on getting customers to actively 'opt in' to allow data on them to be used for marketing and other purposes rather than to go ahead unless they have opted out.

The DPA works in two ways: it gives individuals certain rights and it compels those who record and use personal information on computers to be open about that use and to follow proper guidelines. The act concerns 'personal data' which is 'automatically processed' and is administered by the information commissioner (called the data protection registrar in the 1984 Act), an independent officer who reports directly to the Parliament, with whom, by law, anyone holding personal data on computers (with a few exceptions) has to register. The commissioner has the power to investigate (a) whether or not a data user is registered and (b) if a charge of misuse of data is brought against a user. The DP register, which is available for inspection by data subjects who make a written request, at no cost, contains data users' names and addresses together with broad descriptions of:

- the data held
- the purposes for which data can be used
- the sources from which information can be obtained
- the people to whom information can be disclosed
- any overseas countries or territories to which data may be transferred.

In the EU the Data Protection Directive of 1998 aims to:

- Give individuals certain rights.
- Compel data users to comply with the law.
- Force data users to inform data subjects of how their personal data will be used.

[1] The European Union follows the EU Data Protection Directive of 1998 while an industry-wide self-regulation is followed in the USA at present.

Centre for Trust Online at Ernst & Young

Recognizing e-businesses' concerns about privacy and security, professional services firm Ernst & Young has launched the Center for Trust Online (CTO) to foster trust and confidence in electronic commerce.

Ernst & Young contracted Technometrica, Inc. to conduct a consumer trust survey of 966 adults and 51 randomly-selected Fortune 500 companies. The results indicate that although one in every two Internet users over the age of 18 made a purchase online, major trust barriers still exist. 'Privacy, security, reliability and the ability to fulfill orders promptly online are just a few of the issues that impact consumer trust on the Net,' said Carolyn Buck Luce, director of Electronic Business for Assurance and Advisory Business Services at Ernst & Young. 'With the CTO we hope to build consensus within the business community and break down the barriers that currently discourage transactions online.'

Building consensus may be easier said than done, according to the results of the Technometrica, Inc. survey. Results showed 66 percent of those who have not made a purchase online are unlikely to do so in the near future because they still believe that the Internet is a risky environment for transactions. Additionally, 63 percent of all Internet users are still uncomfortable providing credit card numbers online, and 49 percent are uncomfortable providing personal information. Not surprisingly, 95 percent of executives polled believe that security is a very important factor in achieving e-commerce success. If the CTO has one mission that may alleviate some of these concerns, it is to educate consumers about the myths and misconceptions associated with online commerce. One such example is the $50 liability limit for most victims of credit card fraud.

Ernst & Young is referring to its new venture as a 'virtual trust community', and in that community spirit is inviting companies to start collaborating online through its Web site. Plans call for online events, forums and chat rooms to address online business experiences, as well as global trust issues such as privacy and security regulations, industry standardization, and responsible handling of consumer information.

CTO's debut appears to be timely because of the onslaught of new e-businesses that are racing to beat their competitors into the new frontier of e-commerce. Forecasts from Forrester Research, Inc. predict that business-to-business transactions could grow to $1.3 trillion over the next four years, up from $43 billion in 1998. Most businesses are seeing the cost-saving benefits of doing business on the Internet, as much as they are seeing the potential of increased revenues. A study from Giga Information Group released in August predicted that corporations around the world will save up to $1.25 trillion by doing business over the Internet by 2002.

Still, until consumers get past their fears of online transactions, companies will likely have a hard time realizing maximum cost savings or profits. The trust issue roadblock is significant, particularly in view of current research which suggests that most businesses will be doing at least some transactions online soon.

Ernst & Young's own research, their 18th Annual Survey of Retail Information Technology, reveals that 74 percent of IT executives surveyed say their top priority over the next 12 months is implementing better solutions for collecting and using key customer and operational data. Within the $5 billion-plus companies, 100 percent of IT execs named this issue as the top priority.

(Source: Greenberg, 1999. Reproduced with permission of the E-Commerce Times and NewsFactor Network © 1999–2001 NewsFactor Network. All rights reserved.)

Questions

1 The above article was written in 1999. Conduct a survey of people's feelings about on-line transactions currently. Has the perception changed from the findings described in the third paragraph above? Comment on your own findings in relation to the above.
2 Is CTO a unique idea of Ernst & Young or are other companies taking similar initiatives?
3 How do businesses benefit from the venture?
4 To what degree does the trust-worthiness of a business depend on the type of initiatives taken by Ernst & Young? Are there other issues which need to be addressed?

The new DPA requires the holders of personal data to:

1. Obtain and process data fairly and lawfully.
2. Collect and use data only for specified, explicitly stated and legitimate purposes, as described in the register entry.
3. Collect only data which is relevant (and not excessive) to the stated purposes, and disclosed only to those people described in the register entry.
4. Ensure that data is accurate and kept up to date.
5. Take reasonable steps to rectify or erase inaccurate data.
6. Keep data in an identifiable form for no longer than is necessary for the registered purposes.
7. Protect the security of data against accidental or unauthorised access or manipulation. However, data must be accessible to the data subjects who, where appropriate, has the right to have information about themselves corrected or erased.
8. Guarantee that safeguards are implemented if data is transferred abroad.

There are eight principles of the DP Directive listing the obligations of the data holders/users. It also spells out the rights of data subjects. However, the Act exempts data users from having to conform to the Act under certain conditions.

The Act also gives data subjects the right to (Warren, 2001):

- Receive notification whenever data is collected.
- Approach collectors or receivers of personal data for a copy of the data collected. This includes data in any form: text, picture, computerised, manual or anything else.
- Have the data corrected.
- Object to certain types of data.

The principles of data protection listed above refer to information about people, not organisations. If data subjects consider that there has been a breach of one of the Principles (or any other provisions of the Act), but is unable to sort the problem out themselves, they can complain to the information commissioner. If the commissioner considers the complaint to be justified and cannot resolve it informally, then s/he may decide to serve an enforcement notice to the data user in question. On the other hand, a data user may appeal to the independent Data Protection Tribunal. If a criminal offence is proven to have been committed, then the commissioner can prosecute the user.

As is obvious from the above list, the principles are very broad and imprecise. It is very difficult to determine how much data is 'relevant' or what constitutes 'reasonable' actions; as a result, proving an offence is very difficult. Additionally, a number of exemptions[2] to the DPA free organisations holding personal data under certain conditions of the obligation to register with the information commissioner. For example, in the 1984 Act information held for 'national security' was totally exempted from the legislation provided a clearance certificate has been obtained from a minister. This allowed MI5 or the police the freedom to handle personal information on data subjects with little regard to the DPA. Following concerns expressed by the data registrar, the 1998 Act made provisions for data subjects to challenge a ministerial certificate in a DP Tribunal. However, this did not make it much easier for ordinary citizens to either understand the law or exercise their rights. As a result, very few cases of misuse of data are reported and much fewer are successful in proving the guilt of an organisation. Another reason for the low rate of prosecution is that although the commissioner has a duty to consider any complaints, s/he has no powers to initiate an investigation of registered data users

[2] Full details of the DPA, 1998 can be obtained from the following websites:

- www.dataprotection.gov.uk
- europa.eu.jnt/comm/internal_market/en/media/dataprot/index.htm

or the ability to enforce payment of compensation to data subjects. However, the law provides a useful framework for organisations to follow and allows individuals in the EU, seriously concerned about privacy, to acquire information and support.

Read more about the DP Act and discuss why (a) so few people are aware of their rights and (b) so few data violation charges are brought against organisations.

However, the international nature of e-commerce makes the implementation of such laws difficult as information given to a company in one country can easily leak out to associated companies in other countries not covered by an agreement. So far, the USA has relied on self-regulation by businesses who have started programmes to provide some guidelines for organisations to follow. However, very few of those are in operation, leading the US Federal Trade Commission (FTC) to demand faster action from the industry towards the creation of policies in the following areas (PWC, 1999):

- Awareness – companies collecting and using personal data must be responsible for creating awareness amongst consumers. They must inform them of the identity of the collector, the intended use of information collected and what consumers can do to limit its disclosure.
- Choice – consumers must be provided with a simple, readily visible and easily available mechanism to exercise choice with respect to what extent their personal information is used by the collector or any third parties.
- Data security – companies collecting information must take reasonable measures to ensure its security and provide an assurance to consumers that sufficient precautions have been taken by them or any third parties to prevent loss, misuse, alteration or destruction of data.
- Data integrity – data stored should be accurate, complete, current and strictly relevant to the nature of the transaction.
- Consumer access – consumers should be allowed reasonable and appropriate access to their personal information and the right to amend it if necessary. Organisations must give serious consideration to the extent to which they can provide such access and what consequences this has to the way they collect and store information.
- Accountability – companies must be held accountable for complying with the above policies.
- Consumer recourse – companies using personal information must offer consumers readily available and affordable means by which their complaints can be resolved.
- Third-party verification – the industry must establish an appropriate (for example, sensitive information may require more stringent verification) and cost-effective mechanism to ensure that the privacy policies organisations claim to have implemented are verified by a third party.

The FTC has put pressure on e-commerce companies to either implement privacy policies or face government intervention. Legislation has already been passed to protect the privacy of children through the 1998 Children's Online Privacy Protection Act because of the failure of companies to provide any safety measures for children. Canada and some countries in Latin America, Asia and the Indian subcontinent are also in the process of establishing a framework for privacy protection.

In the USA, self-regulation has so far been preferred to a government act. But now there is pressure from the FTC for organisations to take action to provide choice and awareness among consumers and establish policies for security, integrity, accountability and verification procedures.

Discuss the relative merits and demerits of government acts and self-regulation for combating the misuse and theft of data.

The absence of an international agreement on privacy laws and its effects on different countries' global e-commerce opportunities has raised concerns, especially in the light of the revised DP Directive of the EU. The eighth principle of the DPA prohibits the transfer of personal data outside the European Economic Area (EEA) unless that country ensures adequate protection for the rights and freedoms of data subjects (Jagessar and Hamilton, 2001). This raises problems due to the difficulty of assessing what is adequate and has prompted the information commissioner to instruct exporting controllers (who control the transfer of data to another country) to check that:

- If data is meant for transfer (and not transit), it can be accessed from a website in the destination country.
- If the destination country is within the EEA then the transfer will not be affected by the eighth principle of the DPA although there may be other acts to follow.
- There are some exceptions to the adequacy clause; for example, an overseas website selling goods on-line can take names and addresses of customers for delivery.
- For the non-EEA countries, the EU publishes a list of countries with 'adequate' level of protection.
- For countries not belonging to the list, the exporting controllers will have to perform some adequacy tests.

The list referred to above has been drawn in collaboration with some countries' governments. The EU and the Department of Commerce in the USA have established the principle of a 'safe harbour', a list of US organisations which volunteer to observe certain privacy principles and, in return, qualify to receive data transferred from the EU. Organisations belonging to the safe harbour must:

- Participate in an industry programme of minimum standards of data protection and privacy
- Be certified to have complied with the above standards.
- Be included on the list published on the website of the US Department of Commerce, regulated by a statutory body.

The EU has created a list of safe countries for data protection based on the 'adequacy' of their data protection levels. The USA and EU have a safe harbour policy which enables US organisations included on such a list to receive data from the EU.

To what extent do you think the safe harbour principle works for consumers?

There have been other global efforts to create confidence in international business transactions. For example, some organisations have joined initiatives such as membership of a regulatory body which provides them with a framework to exhibit their privacy policies. Amongst these are:

- BS 7799 – published in 1999 and backed by the UK Department of Trade and Industry, this is the British Standards Institution's standard for information security. It covers 10 areas of security management including the commercial use of on-line information.
- TrustUK – in July 2000, the Consumers' Association (Which?) and the Alliance for Electronic Business started this non-profit-making venture. Endorsed by the UK government, this is a body which provides a set of codes

of conduct approved by Which?, ABTA (Association of British Travel Agents) and the Direct Marketing Alliance. So far, it has not been taken up by other sectors of the industry because it focuses mainly on the commercial aspects of on-line transactions and also because it has not been given enough publicity.

- Trusted Shops – launched at the end of the year 2000 in the UK and endorsed by the European Commission, this is a commercial scheme that provides on-line businesses belonging to the scheme with a seal of approval.
- UK Smart – this is a new Internet company based in the UK which teamed up with the Post Office in order to create trust between on-line businesses and consumers. It provides free CD-ROMs containing digital signature software to customers cleared by the Post Office's certification authority Royal Mail Via Code. Consumers can use the software to set up their own pin code, which acts as a secure digital signature when they make a purchase. They then receive a digitally signed receipt via an email. This also creates an audit trail which protects businesses against fraud or non-repudiation.
- WebTrust – referred to as the WebTrust™ Principles and Criteria, this is a programme adopted by the accounting profession in the USA and Canada. Companies which match specific principles and criteria on privacy are given a seal of assurance to display on their websites. The seal is developed in conjunction with Verisign, a company specialising in encryption and authentication software (chapter 5), and guarantees the legitimacy of the website which displays it. Consumers can view a practitioner's report on the website by clicking on the seal.
- TRUSTe – this is a programme that enables companies to develop privacy statements detailing their policies on information gathering and dissemination. A seal is awarded to those sites that adhere to TRUSTe's privacy principles, which embody fair information practices approved by the US government. Subscribers can display the seal on their website and users can view their privacy statement by clicking on it. Thus this programme gives consumers some control over their personal information, provides websites with a standardised and cost-effective solution for addressing privacy issues and gives the government some confidence in the ability of the industry to self-regulate.
- P3P – Platform for Privacy Protection is a forum provided by W3C. It enables websites to express their privacy policies and allows users to decide whether or not to accept them. During on-line transactions, a website submits its privacy proposal with statements on its practices regarding the collection, use, distribution etc. An intelligent agent checks the proposal automatically against a user's preferences and takes one of the following actions depending on the consistency between the two: accept it, reject it, refer it back to the user, send the service an alternative proposal or ask the service to send another proposal.

Some companies have joined initiatives facilitated by organisations such as Web Trust, TrustUK and TRUSTe in which they follow a code of conduct in return for a seal of assurance. The display of the seal assures customers of the reliability of a company and also creates a doorway for further information.

Find out more about the above organisations and make comments on how much consumers can rely on them.

A well-established defence programme which ensures both security and privacy is essential for the future of e-commerce. Companies which are able to win public trust are likely to enjoy improved customer relationships and an enhanced image in the marketplace. Mature security and privacy policies also provide a company with a safe environment with reduced risk of expensive and time-consuming litigation cases, battles with government and the business consequences of out-of-date or inaccurate data. However, there are signs that consumers are gaining confidence as on-line transaction becomes more common and organisations increasingly adopt privacy policies designed to assure customers of the measures taken to safeguard information.

An essential element of securing data on the Internet is the use of cryptography. Encrypted data transfer provides consumers with an assurance that personal information travelling in cyberspace is safe from hackers. However, it could also give a criminal the cover he needs to communicate without the risk of getting caught. Governments have been increasingly concerned about such issues and suggested the use of 'trusted' third party key holders. This has given rise to debates over the public's right to privacy and civil liberty against governments' right to intercept and read messages in order to detect criminal activities. We will come back to this topic in the next chapter as a part of our discussion of ethics.

SUMMARY

Trust is an essential element of any business. Traditionally, organisations utilised physical means of relationship building to create trust; this is a difficult proposition for e-commerce because of the virtual and global nature of the business. Enterprises are increasingly becoming aware of the importance of trust and are adopting measures such as the use of PKI and a programme of re-assessing their security infrastructure in order to improve consumers' faith in them. This involves the introduction of a security policy that is capable of providing consumers with the assurance that adequate measures have been taken to eliminate the possibility of the corruption, misuse or theft of data.

Computerised data faces risks from both internal and external elements of an organisation. Amongst these are the possibility of attacks on data by 'hackers', accidental and deliberate misuse of data by the employees of an organisation, loss of information due to inadequate physical security of hardware and software, inadequate technical measures, wrongful utilisation of data collected on a website and so on. An organisation must treat security as a central part of its e-commerce strategies and build an integrated defence programme that establishes a set of on-going and iterative processes designed to guarantee security of transactions. This involves assessing the risks, developing a plan of action that encompasses all aspects of data movement, establishing and implementing controls following thorough testing and creating awareness of the importance of security among employees. The controls introduced must ensure that both operational and technical measures are taken to maximise the physical safety, integrity and confidentiality of data.

One major reason for the lack of trust in e-commerce is public concern over the confidentiality of personal data. A number of moves have been made by organisations and governments to increase the level of consumer confidence in electronically handled data. Amongst these are the EU Data Protection Directive, which prescribes a set of principles data users must comply with and provides a framework for the rights of data subjects to have access to their personal data; government recommended self-regulatory moves in the USA; and the safe harbour principles which allow data from the EU to be transferred to US organisations. A number of joint initiatives by organisations such as Trust UK, WebTrust and TRUSTe also enable businesses to follow a set of principles on privacy and win a seal of assurance which guarantees their integrity in data handling.

OPS at Firefly Network

Firefly, a privately owned company, was founded in March 1995 as Agents Inc. Over the next two years, the company launched its community-based showcase site www.firefly.com that gives personalised recommendations for music and movies. It uses a technique called collaborative filtering which uses information on customers collected from the website and evaluates all users' preferences in order to make recommendations for individuals.

For personalisation by collaborative filtering to be fully efficient, an environment of trust and respect of the end-user's privacy is essential. This is why Firefly has made the development of an industry standard on the exchange of information on the web one of its main focuses. This would specify how on-line businesses collect information from their visitors and use that data to present personalised on-screen offerings.

As one of the major actors in the field of information exchange technology on the Internet, Firefly knows it must promote ways to build trust and protect privacy in order not to jeopardise its core business. One of the most significant moves the company has made in this area is the development and promotion of Open Profiling Standard (OPS). OPS provides end-users with a 'passport' – an electronic ID in which they can store basic personal information such as name, address, credit card number and preferences. The system is designed to provide customers with the convenience of not having to register with every website they visit and at the same time obtain a secure environment protected not only by technology but also by policies that people who use OPS agree upon.

A guiding principle of OPS is that information is controlled by its owner. The OPS allows a user to negotiate with the website on how much information s/he wishes to reveal. Firefly, Microsoft and Netscape have been working together to develop the OPS proposal as a part of the standards review process of the W3C. The proposal has gained the support of at least 60 companies.

According to OPS, individuals will have a personal profile containing information similar to that contained in a Firefly passport. This profile can be stored on the user's PC, or, if the user chooses, in a secure local or global directory. The first time a user visits a website that supports OPS, the website requests information from the personal profile. The site is encouraged to disclose its privacy policies and how it intends to use the profile information to provide specific services. The user has the choice of releasing all, some, or none of the requested information to the website. If the site collects additional information about the individual's preferences, it can, with the user's permission, add that information to the profile for future use. With subsequent visits, the user can authorise the website to retrieve the same personal information without asking permission each time. Thus, Firefly has joined TRUSTe and W3C, both partners of Firefly in OPS, to work simultaneously trying to find ways to improve the environment of trust.

(Source: Charlet, J., *Firefly Network*, Graduate School of Business, Stanford University, S-OTA 22A, March, 1998. Copyright 1998 by the Board of Trustees of the Leland Stanford Junior University. All rights reserved. Used with permission from the Stanford University Graduate School of Business.)

Questions

1 Discuss the advantages and disadvantages for customers of personalisation.
2 Discuss the value of a standard such as OPS.
3 How much trust can customers put on such initiatives?
4 What are the benefits and drawbacks for organisations adopting the system?

Revision Questions

1 Why is trust an important element for e-commerce and how is it different from the world of bricks and mortar?
2 Discuss how the level of security in e-commerce is perceived by consumers at present and why.
3 What are the risks for damage and loss of data in e-business? Discuss each of them briefly.
4 Explain the stages of a defence programme.
5 Describe how operational controls can improve security.
6 Describe how technical controls can improve security.
7 Discuss the importance of testing for security of data.
8 What role does employee awareness play in security and what can an organisation do to improve it?
9 Discuss the significance of privacy in creating trust.
10 Describe the EU Data Protection Directive and explain how it helps to improve the privacy of individuals.
11 Discuss the initiatives taken in the USA to improve privacy.
12 Discuss the principle of a safe harbour in privacy.
13 Discuss the role played by industry bodies such as TrustUK in this country and TRUSTe in the USA to create an environment of trust in e-business.

Discussion Questions

1 To what extent is it possible for e-commerce companies to gain consumer trust?
2 Concerns over the Internet's contribution to the emergence of a 'big brother' state have provoked much debate. Discuss the justification behind such concerns and comment on the effectiveness of the measures described here in alleviating consumer fear.

Bibliography

Bandyo-padhyay, N., *Computing for Non-specialists*, Addison Wesley, London, 2000.

Booth, N., Test now, save later, *Computer Weekly, e.business review*, June, 2000, p. 38.

Charlet, J., *Firefly Network*, Graduate School of Business, Stanford University, S-OTA 22A, March, 1998.

Cheskin Research, *Trust in the Wired Americas*, July 2000, www.cheskin.com/think/studies/trust2.html.

Data Protection – a brief introduction – December 98; www.dataprotection.gov.uk/intro.htm, 1998.

Ernst & Young LLP, *Trust in EC*, a paper from the Center for Trust Online, 2001, www.ey.com/global_trust_online.

Ferraro, A., Electronic commerce: The issues and challenges to creating trust and a positive image in consumer sales on the world wide web, *First Monday*, 1998.

Goodwin, B., Cybercrime: An inside job, *Computer Weekly, e.business review*, October, 2000, p. 56.

Greenberg, P. A., Ernst & Young debuts e-commerce trust community, *E-Commerce Times*, 4 November, 1999.

Jagessar, U. and Hamilton, C., Data transfer across borders, *Computer Weekly*, 1 February, 2001, p. 52.

IBM Multi-National Privacy Survey Consumer Report, October, 1999.

irt.org, E-Commerce on the WWW: A matter of trust, 2001; http://tech.irt.org/articles/js158/index.htm.

KPMG, *E-commerce and Cyber Crime: New Strategies for Managing Risks of Exploitation*, 2000.

Lee, C., *IT Week*, 16 April, 2001.

NIST Special Publication 800-18, *Guide for Developing Security Plans for Information Technology Systems*, December, 1998.

Norris, M., West, S. and Gaughan, K., *eBusiness Essentials: Technology and Network Requirements for the Electronic Marketplace*, Wiley, Chichester, England, 2000.

PricewaterhouseCoopers (PWC), *Privacy . . . A Weak Link in the Cyber-Chain*, E-Business Leaders Series, 1999.

Rappa, M., *Managing the Digital Enterprise: Internet Privacy*, http://digitalenterprise.org/privacy, 2001.

Ward, H., Bosses voice e-procurement fears, *Computer Weekly*, 20 July, 2000, p. 16.

Warren, L., Marketing and online privacy, *Computer Weekly, e.business review*, April, 2001, p. 44.

E-Commerce and Society in the Twenty-first Century

Chapter Ten

Objectives

By the end of this chapter you should have an understanding of:

- How businesses will function in the twenty-first century.
- The resulting tension between different facets and entities in the business environment.
- The pressure on the individuals, communities, enterprises and governments facing these issues.

INTRODUCTION

In the previous chapter we discussed what organisations can do to create the desired environment of trust between buyers and sellers. Trust is just one of a number of issues that need to be addressed in order to secure the position of e-commerce in the twenty-first century. As the business world attempts to survive in the uncertain environment of technological innovations, consumer expectations and revised organisational philosophies, it faces a large number of increasingly complex issues. New patterns are emerging in every aspect of our lives: business activities, regulatory and cultural infrastructures, customer needs and consumer attitudes. The ability of enterprises to deal with these issues and of governments to provide the framework for an effective business infrastructure for a global marketplace will determine the direction for e-commerce in the twenty-first century. In this chapter we will explore the nature of businesses in the new millennium, the changing patterns of relationships between different entities and the options open to individuals, organisations and governments for addressing the emerging issues.

THE FOUR WAVES OF INDUSTRY

We have already discussed how innovations in technology initiated a shift in organisational structure from a hierarchical nature to a team-based and distributed network pattern. The stages of change have been described by scholars (e.g. Maynard and Mehrtens, 1996) as 'new waves'. The first wave, which coincided with the agricultural revolution in the early eighteenth century, saw major improvements in agricultural facilities and subsequent changes in distribution of wealth and social dynamics. During this time, the movement of people was generally restricted; they lived around farms and industries and depended on the craftsmanship of the local population. The industrial revolution in the late eighteenth to the early nineteenth century, referred to as the second wave, was prompted by technological developments and increased the productivity of each worker. There was a shift in emphasis from the farm to the factory where work could be supervised, resources could be centralised and finished products could be transported to other parts of the country. The steam engine was introduced, facilitating the communication of goods, labour and information between different parts of the world.

The farm-based industry structure following the agricultural revolution was the first wave for industry. The second wave started after the industrial revolution. Factories were developed with strict management control and clear division of labour.

The period was also marked by a shift from the community-based cottage industries of the villages to lives in new, rapidly growing towns such as Manchester, Leeds, Liverpool and Birmingham.[1] Organisations in the second wave were marked by materialism, competition, consumption and control. Work in factories was highly organised with strict management control and division of labour, especially following the second industrial revolution of the early twentieth century when electricity, automobiles etc. were commercially available. Organisations during this period were centralised and hierarchical; there was limited scope for integration between people and functions, and senior managers maintained full control from headquarters even in cases of multinational activities. During this period the loyalty of managers resided with shareholders. Monopolies existed in many industries and customers were largely forced to accept what was on offer because they had limited knowledge of alternative products and therefore restricted opportunities for switching to alternative manufacturers or brands. Globalisation was regarded as investment by large companies in foreign countries; parent organisations imposed their own values and methods on the workforce and the customers in the receiving countries. The focus was on making a profit first and satisfying employees and making a good impression on customers second.

The introduction of computers and innovations in information and communications technologies in the late twentieth century started the third wave. This could be termed the information revolution; it saw the emergence of the information society and prompted businesses to recognise the opportunities presented by the possibility of widespread global communication. Centralised control began to give way to the philosophy of shared responsibilities and cross-functional teams, as described in chapter 4. Focus began to shift from making a profit to creating a competitive advantage by providing value for all stakeholders. In this environment, the emphasis changed to building relationships with customers, trading partners and employees locally and globally. In acknowledgement of the increased autonomy of customers, governments and workers all over the world, multinational companies started adopting a collaborative philosophy in which building communities was deemed more beneficial to businesses than management control. As we saw in our discussion of e-commerce, these attitudes were expressed through the development of on-line communities, a customer dictated pricing structure (e.g. priceline.com), customer relationship management, competition through co-operation between firms, transnational rather than multinational companies, groupware for collaboration, equal opportunities for new and small companies and so on.

The third wave started following the information revolution. The central control began to give way to a distributed, team-based structure. The balance of power between businesses and their customers changed, and co-operation between industries world-wide started.

Building on such changes in philosophy, Maynard and Mehrtens (1996) describe the fourth wave as the progression from the third-wave era of connectedness and co-operation to a twenty-first-century philosophy of integration and co-creation. They aspire to see businesses as responsible multipurpose institutions producing moral effects, addressing global issues and turning into serving organisations. They argue that while the third wave focused on meeting the needs of stakeholders, the fourth wave must extend the stakeholder base to include entire countries, ecosystems and natural resources because '. . . the current trend suggests the emergence of an inter-linked economy, played out in a "borderless world" . . . that focuses on the common interests of all people' (1996: 60). In this economy, the survival of an organisation is intertwined with the well-being of the aforementioned parties, and businesses are required to provide leadership in addressing global issues. Although the main focus of the argument put forward by Maynard and Mehrtens is that economic justice and the health of the planet should be the key themes underpinning business activities rather than mere financial gain, the

[1] The industrial revolution started in the UK and did not affect other countries until a later period.

interconnectedness between the entities encourages us to address the social issues in the twenty-first century with a view to advancing the cause of all sides concerned.

To what extent do you think the perception of the fourth wave, as described above, is a desirable one?

The fourth wave is an era of perceived integration and co-creation in which organisations provide the leadership to create a borderless world and in which stakeholders include entire countries, ecosystems and natural resources.

So, what are the needs of the entities concerned? Which issues should organisations address in order to provide the leadership recommended above? Currently, many organisations are still operating in second-wave mode while some have made (or are in the process of making) the transition to the third. For enterprises to thrive and for society to survive in the new environment the following issues must be addressed by all parties involved.

THE EMERGING ISSUES – THE TWO SIDES OF THE COIN

There is some controversy over the effect of e-commerce on society. On the one hand there is widespread scepticism over the effect of Internet-based businesses on security, privacy, employment, social activities, wealth distribution, sensitivity to cultural diversities, democracy and personal attitudes to change. On the other, there is optimism that e-commerce will erase the differences between small and large companies, that the infrastructure of the Internet will enable poorer countries to participate in global marketplaces, that people from all groups in society regardless of gender, race and physical ability will be able to thrive at work and that communities will be built in cyberspace which would allow people to find new social groupings regardless of physical and cultural limitations.

Castells (1998) paints a slightly more pessimistic picture and describes the creation of 'the fourth world'[2] in the late twentieth century as resulting from the exclusion of segments of societies, of areas of cities, of regions and of entire countries. This follows the entrance of some newly developed countries in the global interdependent economy, creating networks of capital, labour, information and markets while excluding those populations and territories not deemed suitable for global capitalism. Castells relates this with the emergence of a criminal economy created by those excluded communities as a desperate attempt to link up with the global economy to escape marginality, satisfy 'forbidden desire' and demand their due from 'affluent societies and individuals'. Where Castells insists that 'The twenty-first century will not be a dark age', he adds, 'nor will it deliver to most people the bounties promised by the most extraordinary technological revolution in history. Rather, it may well be characterized by informed bewilderment' (1998: 358). The following is an attempt to explore the arguments raised about the effect of the new economy on organisations, individuals, groups, societies and countries.

Optimists boast about a global marketplace in which people in all groups of society take part. Pessimists worry about security, privacy, abusive behaviour, social exclusion and criminal activity on-line.

Buyers and sellers

Relationships between buyers and sellers in the information society are very different from how they were before. In the past, buyers adopted a passive role in a business by either buying or not buying a product. The sellers were the active party in the relationship; it was their job to attract customers and keep them happy enough to be able to

[2] Behind the so-called 'third world' which we refer to here as the developing countries.

maintain their market share, contented in the knowledge that unless dramatic changes happened in the market, customer loyalty was relatively stable in business. The focus of an organisation's efforts was how to keep shareholders happy and maintain an overall image that was attractive to the generic market, rather than worrying about individual customers. The Internet changed that; it made organisations increasingly aware of the power of informed customers who are in a position to search for the best value and switch loyalties easily. The Internet created increased pressure on enterprises to understand buyer behaviour and establish an effective strategy for developing an infrastructure for maintaining a relationship of trust and loyalty with customers.

Additionally, while the second wave saw the emergence of technologies that facilitated mass production, the third wave has reversed the trend, erring towards customisation. Buyers are now encouraged to specify their exact requirements and preferred prices. Large warehouses filled with unsold stock have given way to manufacturing by demand (e.g. Dell Computers); even the nature of advertising is changing from mass media promotions to 'reverse advertising' in which buyers advertise their needs and sellers who can match the requirements come forward. On-line marketplaces described before provide a forum for such exchanges. The pricing mechanism is changing from how much a product costs to produce to how much customers are prepared to pay. Due to this, a large number of dotcom companies fail to make a profit and many traditional businesses offer products on-line at a discounted price. E-commerce is also disbanding the concept of a fixed price; companies often offer variable prices for varying degrees of service or even for varying circumstances.

In e-commerce buyers can take an active role. There is a shift of emphasis for businesses from shareholder value to customer satisfaction. This has given rise to the customisation of products and services in all types of commerce.

Are shareholders likely to lose or gain from the shift in loyalty in businesses? How much does it matter to businesses?

Large and small companies

E-commerce creates an environment of equal opportunity for companies of all sizes and background. Customers in cyberspace do not necessarily care about the size of an organisation provided they get value for money. The remarkable success of dotcoms such as amazon.com proved the public's readiness to shift loyalty from large, established companies to a newcomer. The infrastructure of the Internet and the information base of on-line businesses provide an inexpensive method for small organisations to start trading. The ability of these companies to take advantage of their low overheads in order to provide low-cost services and products attracts customers looking for on-line bargains. These companies are also in an advantageous position to serve niche markets, provide personalised services, acquire and dispatch certain types of products internationally (e.g. handicrafts) and sell information-based products widely (e.g. research documents). It has also been suggested (Heeks, 2000) that small enterprises and start-ups are quicker than their counterparts to pick up new trends and have the necessary flexibility to adapt to them more easily.

However, as we know, many new Internet-based companies have failed and the rate of progress made by some others at the beginning of the e-commerce era has been slowing down. This is because large, established enterprises soon catch up with ongoing trends and push smaller companies aside by starting on-line ventures parallel to their physical existence. New businesses also often lack the resources, the know-how and the infrastructure required to survive in the competitive world of e-commerce. Small and new companies need to adopt a strategic approach (as discussed in chapter 8) in order to survive the competition and to maintain a competitive advantage; they must create

E-commerce companies of all sizes can create a global business capable of competing with others at equal levels. However, larger companies enjoy the benefits of experience, stronger foundations and greater resources.

an infrastructure which enables them to combine their strengths (such as flexibility, user-friendliness and personalisation) with broader issues of security, logistics, communications technologies and innovation.

Discuss the qualities of a new and small e-commerce company which would enable it to hold on to customers rather than lose them to its bigger rivals.

Employers and employees

The Internet has opened up the business arena for organisations by enabling them to tap into the talent of workers world-wide. A company with an office in London can advertise on the web, recruit people from anywhere in the world, and people can apply for and even do the job on-line if physical distance or international regulations (such as a visa) pose a barrier. A large number of information workers are now hired regularly by the West from countries such as India and the Philippines on this basis. The web enables enterprises to create project teams with specific skills dynamically by either advertising on-line and giving short-term contracts to appropriate candidates or by gathering employees with appropriate skills from different parts of the company. Such a work model gives employers considerable gain in productivity for the following reasons:

- The labour costs in developing countries are usually much lower than in developed countries.
- A large pool of highly skilled people in some countries can help organisations to overcome the problem of skills shortages.
- Work ethics in some societies are such that people are prepared to work long hours irrespective of pay levels.
- Enterprises can share ideas and benefit from the point of view of a varied workforce.
- New alliances can be created.
- Increased flexibility in work patterns often encourages people to work longer hours previously wasted due to journey times and stress.

Employers in the e-commerce age benefit from global knowledge sharing, new alliances and flexibility in the availability and cost of labour. They are also required to create an environment suitable for this highly dynamic workforce.

E-commerce also places new responsibilities on employers. They must:

- Develop motivation and enthusiasm for e-commerce among employees by introducing a transparent management structure and flexible working arrangements.
- Create an e-business culture that is customer-centric and relationship-driven rather than shareholder-centric and profit-driven.
- Share information with all those involved in a team up and down the hierarchical ladder.
- Maintain security within the new environment of openness.
- Provide training for the new skills required, especially in web development, IT management and operation.
- Find ways to attract new employees and retain existing ones in the face of a trend of high turnover following new opportunities provided by e-commerce.
- Provide an infrastructure for the welfare of 'new' employees.
- Supervise the work done by distance workers.
- Manage the regulatory formalities between the countries involved in off-shore working.

Employees gain from the flexibility and global kinship in employment. However, there is pressure for them to be highly productive at all hours. They must also be aware of the shallowness of some 'new' jobs.

Employees in the new economy are also experiencing changes. The increased emphasis on team work and knowledge sharing enables them to achieve flexibility in work patterns, greater autonomy, more responsibilities, improved kinship with co-workers, valuable experience and therefore enhanced job satisfaction. These achievements also improve their employability and provide opportunities for career growth. The possibility of teleworking enables those who are homebound due to physical disability or family responsibilities a (nearly) equal opportunity to join the workforce. However, as a consequence of these changes increased demands are made on employees: they are now expected to be tied to their company on an 'electronic leash' – permanently available on-line; there is constant pressure for workers to perform at a high level and acquire new skills; and people are also living under the threat of being watched by managers who can monitor their emails and trace their movements through the web.

In the 1970s and 1980s many people lost their jobs due to automation. Widespread debates took place over the effect of IT on jobs and skills. E-commerce helped to alleviate some of the fear by creating new jobs in on-line companies. However, these mainly dotcom companies also created new problems. A large number of mainly young and male workers learnt certain skills quickly and found exciting jobs in start-up companies at inflated salaries. Unfortunately, many of these businesses failed or reduced their operations leaving their employees with no jobs, limited experience and increased expectations. Although those working in dotcoms gain useful skills in providing and maintaining contents for websites, their exposure to technical skills in web development or other transferable skills in corporate activities are often restricted and therefore unsuitable for jobs with equal status in larger companies.

Thus, e-commerce has the potential to benefit those on both sides of the fence while presenting new risks to them as well. The extent to which each aspect takes prominence depends on the strategies adopted by senior management and the effort made by employees. Business leaders who understand the increased power of technology to create business advantages but acknowledge their responsibility to employees can benefit from an empowered, talented and cosmopolitan workforce. Employees who are aware of the pitfalls of the new economy and are prepared to address the new challenges rather than be dazzled by them are in a position to make progress.

Create a profile of an employee who is most likely to benefit from e-commerce. What should s/he look for in a potential employer?

Old and new generations

Like all other aspects of new technologies, older people have largely been excluded from the Internet phenomenon. Many of them do not have a computer at home and often do not have any interest in them. When computers took over jobs in certain sectors in the 1980s and 1990s, it was the older generation who lost their livelihood first because they did not have the skill to use the new technology. This generation grew up in an environment of face-to-face service in business dealings and find the concept of buying in cyberspace alienating. According to a British Household Panel Survey (BHPS) conducted at the end of 1997, 0.8 per cent of people above 60 use the Internet from home (Burrows *et al.*, 2000). However, the situation is likely to get better with time[3] as the next, more computer literate generation, grow into that age bracket. E-commerce

[3] According to a survey done by the National Opinion Poll (NOP), the number of adult users of the Internet from home went up by a factor of three times by the end of 1999 (Burrows *et al.*, 2000).

offers facilities for shopping from home, a large amount of choice on-line, home delivery, the possibility of finding specialised products etc. all of which have advantages for older buyers. However, like many other aspects in life, shopping is a social activity, especially for otherwise housebound citizens. For example, a number of banks have closed some of their high street branches due to an increase in on-line banking; this has affected older people more acutely both socially and organisationally. Unfortunately, in the world of business, the needs of the majority dominate the decision-making process (this is why supermarkets replaced the corner shops in the 1960s and 1970s).

The older generation often does not have the skill or the interest to benefit from e-commerce technology. Although old people may dislike the unsocial environment of e-commerce, they can benefit from home-shopping and delivery, specialised products sold on-line etc.

According to BHPS, those under 20 are the most likely to use the Internet from home. In the USA, the average age of surfers is 35.1 and overall, 21–30-year-olds are the most experienced Internet users (Turban *et al.*, 2000). The young generation grow up with computers in school and at home, and accept it as a natural medium for activities in all aspects of life. E-commerce companies often target young buyers and personalise websites to fit their tastes. The increasing earning power of the younger generation (under 30) is another reason for their dominance in the e-commerce marketplace. The e-commerce phenomenon itself is also generating new wealth for the young; a large majority of dotcom companies were set up by young entrepreneurs such as Jeff Bezos of Amazon.com and Sheila Farrel of LetsButIt.com. The age of new company directors is coming down still; in the UK, a boy of 15 called Benjamin Cohen started JewishNet with £150 and became a millionaire at 17, and a 15-year-old girl in the USA founded Goosehead.com which produces webshows for teenagers and gets 3,000,000 hits a day (Benjamin, 2001).

However, young people have also faced some problems created by the Internet age. According to the BHPS survey, out of all economic groups, students are most likely (by a large margin) to use the Internet from home. The attraction of shopping on-line creates a pressure for young people to buy even when they do not have suitable incomes. Websites often mislead users by displaying reduced prices and special offers. Hidden costs such as transnational shipping charges, tax etc. are not always made clear, neither are the security risks involved in on-line payment. Young (1998) conducted an on-line survey on Internet usage and found that 80 per cent of the respondents fall into the category of being addicted to the Internet. E-commerce is tapping into the weakness of young users to lure them into buying things they perhaps cannot afford, do not need and should not spend time looking for.

E-commerce offers young people who have the skill, interest and even the earning power to enjoy it and start new businesses. However, there is a danger due to over-exposure and lack of security.

Is there a need to draw older people towards e-commerce? Why? In what ways can this be done?

Rich and poor

According to the BHPS, the use of the Internet at home is directly proportional to the household income of a family, with the top 20 per cent using the Net nearly nine times more than the bottom 20 per cent. Economic situation affects one's ability to participate in e-commerce at a number of levels:

- PCs are expensive to buy.
- Using the Internet involves paying high telephone charges and payment to Internet service providers.
- Few people in poor households have the opportunity to acquire computing skills.

- Using the Internet for shopping has little attraction when buying power is limited in the first place.
- Buying on-line requires credit or debit cards which those with low incomes may not possess.
- Poverty creates an environment where people are discouraged from or do not feel they have any role to play in any new phenomenon.
- While many people are starting up dotcoms or finding jobs in e-commerce companies, such opportunities are out of reach of most poor people who do not have the necessary capital, contacts or knowledge.

Such disadvantages have created a society in which poor people are also information-poor due to limited access to information and knowledge. Although such differences existed before the Internet-age, the gap widened as the rich achieved improved access to information provided by technology. The prosperity of a society depends on the ability of its population to take part in the economy. Steps must therefore be taken to raise the above barriers and allow an increasing number of people entry to e-commerce. The UK government has recently pledged to put every citizen on the Internet and create a truly inclusive information society. It has promised to address the problem of those who do not have Internet access at work, cannot afford it at home or are simply unwilling to use computers. In October 2000, the Computers Within Reach Initiatives were set up to provide low-cost recycled PCs costing £60 each to 100,000 low-income families (Ackland, 2001). Other initiatives such as the drive to boost the profile of IT at school, the supply of computers and provision of the Internet in libraries, the use of community-based Internet access (such as that of Newham Online described in chapter 1) are likely to make the Internet familiar to new levels of society and thus encourage better acceptance of e-commerce (see case study on Citizen webpage in Bangalore). As a result of all such initiatives, the number of UK households with Internet access has grown from 13 per cent to 25 per cent in one year (Mason, 2000) and it is hoped that continual action to tackle the digital divide will reduce the problems of information poverty.

High income groups have the means to buy PCs, acquire skills and utilise e-commerce as buyers and providers. Currently initiatives are being devised to include the poorer communities by creating community websites and providing IT facilities at a wider level.

Given that poor people are largely unable to buy on-line, how could e-commerce benefit them in general?

Developed and developing countries

The barriers discussed above are even greater in developing countries (DCs) where the division between rich and poor is far wider. Countries such as India and Brazil have a large technically qualified workforce and the Internet is used as a significant part of business communication. Many websites are in existence and affluent communities in these countries use them almost as much as those in richer countries. However, while the middle classes in DCs enjoy a high standard of living and therefore access to the Internet, for a large majority of the people, day-to-day survival is a major struggle. Using the Internet for buying goods and services by individuals (B2C e-commerce) in the context of these countries is not as profitable, and therefore as important, as creating an infrastructure for efficient communications facilities in order to improve B2B within the country as well as B2C internationally. Heeks (2000) identifies the following opportunities:[4]

[4] Here Southern and Northern mean countries in the Southern and Northern Hemispheres, respectively.

- SB2NC (Southern business to Northern consumer) such as the tourism industry attracting Western customers.
- SB2NB (Southern business to Northern business) such as the software trade between India and the West.
- SB2SB such as business communication between financial institutions within a country.
- SB2SC takes the same form as in the developed world although the number of people who can take advantage of this is much smaller.

There is also the possibility of e-commerce between governments and businesses, and between departments of a government. Governments in DCs are generally slow to adopt technology but they have a crucial role to play in this, especially when new technology can be targeted at projects focused on development.

Heeks warns readers of some of the threats DCs face:

- Barriers to entry in e-commerce are higher for organisations in developing countries than in the developed.
- Countries' communications infrastructure and national policy frameworks are often inadequate. Progress is slowly being made and it is possible that some DCs will be able to leapfrog their current communications difficulties into the era of the third-generation mobile telephony and satellite-based communication in order to benefit from e-commerce.
- E-commerce will not necessarily improve export opportunities; it will also contribute to increasing the trend of import from foreign countries. This means it will replace some SB2SC with NB2SC, thus limiting the possibilities for the Southern companies.
- There is a need to build competency in the production of information and communications technologies (ICTs). At the moment DCs are paying large multinational such as Microsoft, Cisco and SUN heavily for providing the ICTs they require for e-commerce. To benefit from their own achievements, countries must develop local production capacities.

There is a danger that DCs will jump on the bandwagon and invest large sums in starting initiatives without understanding the role of e-commerce in wealth creation. Unless the countries develop an infrastructure for utilising e-commerce for development, powerful interests and market forces in developed countries will reap the benefits. DCs must understand their priorities, assess the potential of e-commerce to meet them, protect their own interests and avoid the creation of new forms of dependency and domination (see case study on Citizen webpage in Bangalore). They need to engage in discussions in global fora such as the World Trade Organisation (WTO) about how to devise a multilateral framework to develop and regulate e-commerce (Bishop and Gay, 2000).

For DCs, national B2C e-commerce is less important than national B2B plus international B2C and B2B. They must overcome the problems of the barriers to entry, poor infrastructure, risk of increased import and low competency in ICTs.

To what extent do developing countries need e-commerce and why?

Global and local

The organisational reach of e-commerce has expanded from local and national communities to a boundariless and global marketplace. But to what extent can we call this globalisation? The Internet has been referred to as the creator of a 'global village' but, as we saw in our discussion of the poor and the rich, what we have really got so far is a 'middle class suburb': '. . . there is a reason to think that the Internet is more likely to increase social fragmentation than it is likely to promote social consensus' (Graham 1999: 83). Globalisation is very different from creating a 'global shopping centre' in which information is treated as proprietary, where central planning, value judgement and control remain in the hands of the big and the powerful; it is about redistributing power on the basis of what is appropriate for the local system and culture while trading with the global community. According to Maynard and Mehrtens (1996), in the third wave, companies shifted their focus from making a profit to serving the needs of the stakeholders with the belief that they in turn, will serve the organisations; the authors hope that in the fourth wave the stakeholder base will be expanded to include the whole world and to create value for the global community. According to a survey done by Forrester Research, users are three times more likely to purchase on the web if addressed in their own language (Classe, 2000). Differences in cultural icons and pictorial representations vary enormously between countries; some gestures seen in a positive light can be offensive to another culture (for example, 'thumbs up' is an offensive sign in some Eastern countries). Creators of e-commerce infrastructures must consider such differences in order to avoid alienation. This requires the adoption of a transnational business model and a philosophy of 'thinking globally and acting locally'; this provides the basis of an organisational culture that respects the attitudes of international customers and creates an environment of trust.

True globalisation involves redistributing power according to local systems and acknowledging differences in tastes and cultural signifiers etc. This follows the concept of being more global yet more local in which locally situated technology is used to run global businesses.

Papows (1999) predicts that the web-based era is going to be both more global and more local. On the one hand, information, ideas and discussion will flow freely; the use of common software will homogenise work patterns and commercial activities will span the world. On the other, the use of the Internet will bring local communities closer together and encourage them to strengthen and reinforce local cultures, languages and customs. He argues that previous technologies such as radios, aeroplanes, telephones, television etc. had the potential to remove national boundaries; while they helped to increase movement between regions, they contributed more to the preservation of the nation-state. He also presents the following, technology-based explanation for his prediction:

- Communications infrastructure has replaced microprocessor speed as the measure of technological strength. However, while the latter was controlled by companies such as Intel and influenced the IT industry in the whole world, developments in communications technologies (bandwidth, satellites, fibre optics, XDSL, WAP etc.) have remained largely localised. Different countries have different degrees of capability and their information infrastructures are also based on national strategies.
- The differences in communications infrastructure will also influence the adoption of end-user devices differently. While some countries will take advantage of their infrastructure to move towards networked computers (NCs)[5] and access applications at a high speed, those with inadequate communications facilities will still use PCs connected to the Internet via a modem.
- The availability of GSM (global system for mobile communications) cellular phones in some countries (mainly Europe) will enable them to utilise mobile telephony for e-commerce while those without it will have to manage with local services.

[5] NCs are low-power, low-speed (dumb) terminals connected to the Internet which use applications software available on the Net rather than storing them on their hard disk.

- While hardware and software industries will become increasingly global with companies such as Microsoft, Compaq (now, a part of Hewlett Packard) and Intel expanding their market continually, communications companies, service providers and creators of the web contents will continue to operate locally or within the boundaries of specific countries.

There are other barriers to globalisation of industries. Government regulations on import and export, tax laws, differences in tastes, trends, languages, currencies, religions and consumer expectations are only some of the factors likely to stand in the way of creating a global culture through e-commerce. Although e-commerce provides the opportunities, for those who are willing, to learn about other cultures and communities via books, films and other products, to create alliances with organisations world-wide and to overcome polarisation between countries and groups, there are opposing forces which will resist globalisation. Geographic boundaries between cultures and nations will blur; however, groups will tend to find new ways to cling together on the basis of religion, history, language and culture. While there will be newly created integration between people in different countries, there will also be groupings and segregation based on specific interests; while some of the groups will be intellectually stimulating (such as academic communities), some others may be based on ideologies such as racism. Dertouzos (1997) suggests (or hopes) that one day nations might be defined by a network of people grouped by emotional and cultural ties rather than by physical location, for example Greece as a Greek network rather than a country. 'A shared cultural veneer arising from the Information Marketplace might offer people a chance to retain their tribal identities while reaching out to share universal experience' (1997: 283).

The concept of cultures may blur, however, new communities based on history, religion and interests may be built. Some of the latter may not be beneficial to humankind.

You run an on-line cookery site which also lists regional recipes, stockists and events. In what way could you run a global business which also respects local cultures?

Isolation and community building

The above discussion exposes the possibility of a conflict between isolation and communication. E-commerce enables us to communicate with colleagues and business associates all over the world, shop, entertain ourselves and even make virtual friends in cyberspace without having to leave home. Thus, while we anticipate the creation of boundaryless nations and global cultures, we are also in danger of isolating ourselves from the physical world. Increasingly, teleworkers are moving away from busy city life to live in the countryside in an environment of relative tranquillity and isolation. Such a trend creates pockets of communities far removed from the realities of modern living and even further from the notion of global cultures. Although we do not need to maintain a physical presence in any particular location in order to become global citizens, the mentality which drives us to such a protected existence often discourages us from participating in anything outside our narrow lifestyle preferences.

Thus, e-commerce has the potential to increase the distance between communities: between knowledge workers and physical workers, between information rich and information poor, between industrialised countries and agrarian societies, between technologists and sociologists and so on. While knowledge workers, industrialists and technologists may feel privileged by their new lifestyle and increased wealth, those on the other side of the fence might find the new economy impersonal and the new business ethos alienating.

Dulux Paints

Dulux Trade, a division of ICI Paints, has created an extranet-based facility to help professional specifiers and decorators choose the right paint for a job without having to refer to the heavy product specification tomes. The system includes a facility that allows a user to see what a particular type of building – a house or a pub, say – would look like if painted in the colour scheme of his/her choice. The technical specifications of the paint are also provided. Once a choice has been made the system puts the customer in touch with a suitable merchant.

The system is based on Rubicon Software's DFinity Web Engine and designed to allow users to maintain content independently of the design of the site itself. Separating the design of a website from its content brings economies in implementing and maintaining a global web presence. It can safeguard the uniformity of the face that a company presents to the outside world by maintaining common design principles while allowing its specific propositions to be adapted to the needs of the local market.

Paint details differ from country to country, with different colours being sold in different markets. The building surfaces on which the paint colours can be tried out may also vary a little between different parts of the world. However, according to the e-business manager of Dulux Trade, the general presentation has to be uniform because the company has global customers who move from country to country. It is important to the company that the website gives such customers a similar feel even though the content is very local.

About a dozen countries have implemented the system and the set-up can typically be rolled out to a new country in just a couple of weeks. The technology allows local content to be maintained in the form of a spreadsheet. The tool is easy to operate so, with some training, a secretary can create and update product details. This means that even though the spreadsheets are usually held locally, they can be updated quickly, for example if any product claim needs to be changed.

(Source: Adapted from Classe, 2000 with permission from Reed Business Information.)

Questions

1 In what ways does the website make it easy for a client, who may not know anything about paint types or specifications, to order paint?
2 To what extent does this case study demonstrate the points discussed in the above section?
3 How important is it in your opinion to maintain a common feel for a website?

However, the ability of the Internet to enable users to communicate virtually also provides a framework for building new communities based on needs. These are communities of self-help and social support referred to as virtual community care by Burrows *et al.* (2000). This may take the form of newsgroups which facilitate discussion between people with similar problems, on-line support systems involving government authorities such as the health service, voluntary groups giving practical help on matters such as domestic violence or disability and a virtual advice centre providing information on matters such as personal finance (see case study at the end of this section). Whilst such communities create a medium for sharing knowledge and ideas, they have a limited power to do things. Concerns have even been expressed over the quality and legitimacy of the advice available through them. However, communities can be instrumental in influencing authorities and persuading organisations and governments to use their e-commerce infrastructure to provide specific, need-based help.

A new type of community is emerging in organisations. Separate from teams and workgroups, these are communities of practice (COP) which serve to complement the formal structures in an enterprise. COPs are groups of people informally bound together by shared expertise and interest. Academic institutions have nurtured COPs for a long time, initially in physical space through conferences and later on by complementing this with virtual communication. People in a COP meet to share experience and knowledge in free-flowing, creative ways that foster new approaches to problems. Such communities can exist in companies as varied as an international bank, a car manufacturer and a US government agency (Wenger and Snyder, 2000). They can be confined to a business unit with a few people, stretch across different units or even include a large number of members from different companies. The members select themselves, are bound together by passion, commitment and common expertise and keep the community alive as long as there is an interest in it. Organisations which increasingly thrive on knowledge must help to develop such COPs and integrate them with the corporate culture. This may sound like a paradox as the origin and purpose of a COP is to create an informal and voluntary forum for self-help, but the enterprise benefits from its existence and therefore must cultivate it so its full power can be leveraged. On-line versions of traditional focus groups are another form of COP (independent from an enterprise but created by it) and are invaluable for gaining an insight into customer preferences.

E-commerce can create isolation by facilitating life from home. However, it can help to create new communities, self-help groups and communities of practice for knowledge sharing. It also provides a forum for immoral and unethical activities in close communities.

On-line communities can also be built to support the philosophy which takes advantage of diversity in a negative way. This is reflected in websites based on racism, anti-Semitism, religious extremism and child pornography. Strictly speaking these are issues surrounding the Internet and not necessarily related to e-commerce as one can argue that the communities are designed to exchange information rather than run a business. However, there are organisations which run rackets for child prostitution and trafficking, materials and instructions for making bombs are sold on the Internet and nationalistic political parties recruit on-line. Therefore such activities have a direct relevance to the future of e-commerce and need to be discussed in this context.

You are the CEO of a large bricks and mortar publishing company for books on art. In what ways could COPs be established in your company? How could the workings, findings or structure of the COPs help you in establishing an e-commerce site for the public?

Control and freedom

One way to limit the damage done by communities formed for dubious purposes is to control the flow of information by passing regulations and finding ways to interrupt a message. However, this raises a conflict between the freedom of individuals and organisations to use the medium and benefit from the information economy and the rights of the regulatory authorities to impose control. The Internet was first created by academics as a channel for the free flow of information and a symbol of the freedom of expression. This feeling is still strong in the minds of many users who see the Internet as belonging to everybody and nobody at the same time and a vehicle for the exchange of ideas and knowledge, while there are others who are disturbed by its misuse; 'Cyberspace is intrinsically a collective space in which interaction with others can become either a place of domination and violence or a place of collective creative intelligence' (Carter, 1997: 140). Such feelings have given rise to widespread debate over whether or not the Internet should be regulated.

We discussed issues such as criminal activities, infringement of privacy etc. in previous chapters. Other factors which give concern are the following:

- Individuals are able to publish anything they wish on the Internet regardless of whether or not it is correct or legal. This can be done by journalists of on-line magazines or individuals with their own websites alike.

The UK Home Repossessions Page

The UK Home Repossessions Page is a website which was set up in 1997 to provide support and information for people who are experiencing mortgage arrears and house repossession. The site is 'expert driven' but also contains comments, questions and answers from people making postings, but with expert commentary on all postings. Users therefore draw upon and share their own experiences. The range of topics covered in the site is evident from the following list on the 'welcome' page: 'stay updated', 'site map', 'voters say', 'interviews', 'homebuying' 'arrears', 'repossession', 'blacklisted? Who helps', 'facts', 'Q&A' and 'links'.

The pages provide factual and legal information about homebuying and repossession. For example, there is much detail on the Dos and Dont's section for people whose homes have been repossessed, and it also offers personalised information for people who 'post' their questions and problems. The site provides a means of collating information from experts as well as from users' experiences. For example, there are profiles of various lenders, extensive information on users' rights and administrative and legal procedures associated with mortgage arrears, repossessions, outstanding debts following repossession etc.

The site includes case histories from users together with the site moderator's response. Other visitors also offer help and advice based on their own experience or knowledge of the field. Feedback from the users of the site indicates that the information was helpful and gave them confidence in dealing with lenders. The site provides both social and practical support for people and also serves as a mechanism to counter the highly individualised nature of the experience, potentially contributing to the formation of a more collective resistance to lending institutions. At present only a tiny minority of those affected by the problem are able to contact the site. However, it reveals the potential of such a site for the use of the Internet for social support and collective civic action. It is a type of informal welfare run on a voluntary basis and functions by the active participation of the users who give and receive help.

(Adapted from Burrows *et al.*, 2000 with permission from the authors.)

Questions

1 Discuss the contributions a website such as the above make to isolated communities.
2 What are the strengths and weaknesses of the venture for mortgage lenders? How can they use it to their advantage?
3 How should a website of this nature be designed to achieve the maximum benefits for providers and the users?
4 'At present only a tiny minority of those affected by the problem are able to contact the site', why? How can this be rectified?

- Organisations can send mass emails (spam) to consumers the same way they send junk mail. While the latter may be annoying but can be ignored, the former wastes receivers' time, often forces them to read it and can take up valuable disk space.
- The Internet is already overloaded with information. For example, some websites, normally belonging to young enthusiasts who use the Internet for amusement, contain little useful information, or anonymous emailers who send chain mails to hundreds of other users. Such activities slow the Internet down and reduce its effectiveness for those using it for business or academic reasons. 'Useless' websites also waste users' time by clogging up search results with unworthy documents.
- It is possible to collect information on an individual by tracing the transactions made on-line and, thus, monitor the activities of a person. Users are increasingly concerned that they are permanently watched in cyberspace;

The suitability of the Internet for publishing unethical material, sending mass emails, creating information overload and collecting information on others and misusing it have given cause for concern.

information on them is constantly being collected, created and recreated for use by others in various ways. Employees might feel that information on them is used by employers to determine their future, trading partners might worry about the possibility of one stealing customers from another, companies joined in an alliance might get involved in a battle over property rights and trade secrets, and citizens of a country might get paranoid about their whereabouts being traced.

The above factors pose formidable problems for organisations involved in e-commerce, employees working for such companies, individuals using the Internet to buy on-line and enterprises attempting to liaise with each other on the information superhighway. This forces governments and law-enforcing authorities to consider the possibility of imposing some regulations in order to create an environment of stability in the medium. The following three models of regulation have been suggested by Spinello (2000):

- Direct state intervention: A country's existing laws covering communications should be extended to regulate the Internet. However, it is very difficult to make this work since the Internet is a global medium and a user can access information and websites from countries not affected by his/her own national regulations.
- Co-ordinated international intervention: A collective, intergovernmental organisation can be set up with international jurisdiction to impose rules and regulations. However, while it is seen as less problematic than the above, it raises questions about the level of authority of such an organisation, the possibility of divisions between countries or factions which might try to push their own agenda etc. Interpol mentioned in chapter 9, falls in this category and has been criticised by experts. A conference held in London in October 2000 by the World Ecommerce Forum voted overwhelmingly against the concept of a single agency to fight cybercrime but called for better ad-hoc co-operation between policing agencies (Mathieson, 2000).
- Self-governance: This model supports a semi-official political structure established by non-profit international groups or organisations for the governance of the Internet. It would follow specific charters for each area of business on the Internet. For example, one charter might set some guidelines to control global e-commerce while another might oversee issues such as intellectual property rights. The role taken by ICANN to regulate the allocation of domain names is one such initiative.

Governments can control and regulate the Internet by direct intervention, by co-ordinating international initiatives or by encouraging self-governance among organisations and international non-profit groups.

Much conflict surrounds the issue of control of the Internet. One school of opinion rejects regulation and wants to leave it as the property of the people to be looked after by them. Others subscribe to the idea of some degree of control but differ about the model to be followed. Governments also vary widely in their opinions in this area. As discussed in chapter 2, some governments exercise strict control over the information that can reach their citizens over the Internet. Attempts have been made and initiatives are in progress in both the UK and the USA to introduce a legal framework for the establishment of key escrow agencies (see chapter 7) in order to maintain some rights to intercept electronic messages. While some governments consider it their duty to impose such controls in order to protect national security, community values and religious and cultural traditions, many citizens all over the world consider such activities an infringement of their personal freedom. They consider any attempt to control the content of the Internet a form of surveillance and therefore anti-democratic.

Those in favour of upholding freedom of speech promote the widespread encryption of messages locked by private keys which are not obtainable by anyone other than the owners of the messages. They want complete anonymity and are against any sanctions or provision for authorities to decode a message. Some authors call them the crypto anarchists (Denning, 1997) and argue that they threaten public safety and social and economic stability by locking the authorities out of computers and communications systems thus making them suitable for criminal activity. Denning uses examples of possibilities such as an employee secretly selling proprietary information to a competitor or the consequences of the loss of corporate data due to lost or corrupted encryption keys to demonstrate the danger of encryption. She also suggests that encryption is by no means a fail-safe method to 'hide' a message since it is possible to intrude a computer system at the level where files and encryption programs are stored which would expose the keys to the intruder.

Those advocating freedom of speech want complete anonymity by the encryption of messages. Others are worried by the creation of safe havens for criminals who can hide behind encryption as well as intrude others' systems by invading the core of a computer system.

Governments and law enforcing authorities are worried that encryption can be used to engage in criminal activities such as fraud, illegal trade and terrorism without the threat of being caught. However, public feeling against any official measures to police the Internet has been strong. The Clipper Chip plan (chapter 7) proposed by the Clinton Administration faced vociferous protests by users complaining about the ethical consequences of the system. They argued that the keys held by the 'trusted' third parties could in fact be used for any purpose and saw the scheme as a massive assault against the freedom and privacy of individuals. As a result of the protest, led by a non-profit organisation called Electronic Frontier Foundation (EFF), the plan was dropped. The US government have been trying to tackle the problem of international criminal activity by imposing import restrictions on encryption programs. However, in the global arena of the Internet, such restrictions are useless since powerful programs can be obtained from other sources. There have since been other initiatives, for example the RIP bill of the UK (chapter 7), and the effort in both the UK and the USA to establish some form of escrow system to enable the government to have access to the data on the Internet. The introduction of certification authorities for PKI and attempts to improve the ability of law enforcement agencies to crack an encryption code are some of the initiatives taken since then.

The issue of unethical activity on the Internet is a serious one and governments need some mechanism by which to control it. When an individual uses his/her rights of free speech to perform activities which hurt others either personally (in the case of child pornography or racial and religious violence) or at a wider scale (for example, through terrorism or international drug trafficking), governments have a duty to take action. The measures proposed so far are presented by governments as a means to impose limited control over encryption, with strict safeguards and guidelines to prevent easy access to a key by unauthenticated agencies. However, the arguments put forward by the freedom lobby are equally strong. Amongst these are:

- The possibility of errors in authentication which might result in a key reaching the hands of inappropriate organisations.
- The risk of abuse of the rights given to authorities by the key escrow policies.
- The possibility of innocent people being harassed.
- The risk of abuse of the system by those involved in the development, implementation and maintenance of the system for personal gain.
- The creation of a 'big brother' society in which people live in the fear of being watched.
- The risk of some countries with strong central control on citizens to use the system against the principles of human rights.

Efforts to control the Internet in the USA and the UK by using key escrow agencies have not succeeded. Concerns were raised about the possible abuse of the system by the key holders, loss of civil liberties and human rights. Also, inconsistencies between the laws of different countries make national regulations unworkable.

- The loss of the freedom of speech which should arguably permit anyone to say anything s/he wishes.

The debate will carry on until a system capable of controlling the security risks without impinging on civil liberties is developed. For example, the RIP bill which permits employers to monitor emails provoked widespread controversy. The employers argue that this is essential in order to avoid being liable for defamatory, offensive or pornographic material distributed through corporate systems. Employees see this as an attempt to control their activities and invade their rights to privacy. An attempt is being made to create a forum for discussion between those responsible for the RIP Act and the Data Protection Act to find a consensus that satisfies both sides and eliminates the lack of trust between them (Kelly, 2001). A major problem in creating an infrastructure for safety in communication is the inconsistency between the attitudes and regulations between countries. As in other areas of e-commerce, we require internationally co-ordinated efforts in this area; Spinello (2000) suggests the formation of a neutral global agency which, working within strict guidelines and an infrastructure designed with respect for the rights of individuals and organisations, will have some authority to control technology.

Conduct a survey of people on the two sides of the above debate and their reasons. What conclusions do you make from the responses?

Women and men

The proliferation of PCs in offices in the 1990s saw an upsurge of women using computers. However, in a large majority of those cases, these were younger female workers who learnt wordprocessing skills in order to create work opportunities for themselves. While women moved on from typewriters to PCs, men were employed to do work defined as more technical and offering higher salaries and career prospects. A survey performed in the USA in 1994 showed that out of a total of 11,790 board seats, only 814 were held by women. By comparison, 64 per cent of help desk workers in computing were women (Bellinger, 1995). Although this improved the level of computer literacy of a large number of women thus making it easier for them to adapt to the Internet when it came onto the scene, the imbalance between men and women (as well as between other underprivileged sectors in society) has remained. According to a survey conducted with British adults in 1997, the Internet was mainly the territory of young, middle class and high earning men (Burrows *et al.*, 2000). Although organisations adopted the Internet fast, this did not change the situation very much as they favoured the above privileged groups. Empirical surveys have shown consistently that even though the situation has improved since the early years of the Internet, women are under-represented as users. The reasons for this are the same as those which keep women in a marginal position in all other professions: economic disadvantage, an image maintained by technology that disassociates women, lack of time, the absence of parental aspirations, social conditioning and a male culture in cyberspace that alienates as well actively discourages women from entering (a tactic known as 'flaming'). Table 10.1 shows a survey done by GVU (Graphics, Visualization and Usability Centre: Georgia Tech University) in 1998 (reproduced in Scott *et al.*, 1999) which demonstrates the slow rise in the number of women, especially in Europe, using the Internet.

The flexibility in work patterns facilitated by the Internet has enabled more women to join the workforce. They can now work from home, in their own time and at a pace that suits them. However, although this could be an opportunity to change the balance in the

Table 10.1 Women as percentage of Internet users (adopted from Scott *et al.*, 1999)[6]

	Europe	USA	World-wide
January 1994			5
October 1994			10
April 1995	7	17	15
October 1995	10	33	29
April 1996	15	34	31
October 1996	20	32	31
April 1997	15	33	31
October 1997	22	40	38
April 1998	16	41	39

workplace, in reality very little change has taken place. The traditional sexual division of labour is reproduced in the new trend known as 'teleworking'; there is a marked gender segregation in the nature of work. While women teleworkers are located in clerical industries, men are more likely to be professionals who are self-employed as consultants or are high-level knowledge workers. While most of the women are young mothers balancing childcare and work within the same space and time, the men set up dedicated offices free of interference by children. Even the few professional women teleworkers cannot separate childcare from their work in a large majority of cases (Adam and Green, 1998).

Women have always been marginalised in technology-related jobs. They are employed at low-level jobs using PCs. However, with this skill they can adapt to the Internet easily and work from home thus balancing family life with some earning power.

The gender division is closely intertwined with the issues of race and poverty. Women in developing countries have been employed for a long time by multinationals in jobs such as assembling the motherboards of PCs (the base which holds the integrated circuits and other hardware components). For educated women in some countries (such as India), the new scenario for women is the software industry which uses female labour to meet the demand of low-level and high-volume coding jobs required for software exported to the richer nations, while men are often given the opportunity to travel abroad as professionals.

The disadvantage faced by women in cyberspace is not a unique problem of the medium. In fact, despite discrimination, women have much to gain from cyberspace. They are now in a position to earn money while taking care of a young family and the work available offers better facilities than the traditional rag trade; employers, increasingly aware of the benefit of the female workforce, are beginning to create a better infrastructure for women teleworkers, cyberspace provides women with a platform where gender (as well as race, physical ability or sexuality) can be disguised in order to gain equal treatment; and it provides a forum for discussion of issues in close cyber-communities. While one school of thought promotes the creation of a women-only cyberspace to provide a 'safe' environment for themselves, others see this as a failure to challenge the critical issues of the Internet and therefore counter-productive. According to the latter, helpless victimisation is not the experience of most women and taking a separatist position is politically paralysing. Scott *et al.* (1999) acknowledge that women are actively discouraged and advocate a 'third way' in which women '. . . must do battle with the prejudices of their contemporaries regarding women's place, women's capabilities, and women's desires. They must struggle to acquire necessary material resources: not a "room of their own" . . . but a computer of their own and the software, education, training, time and space needed to use it' (p. 550).

Some women want to react to marginalisation by creating women-only websites; some others reject this as victim behaviour and want to fight on an equal basis as men. The third way is to battle with prejudice by demanding that women are given the resources to make progress.

[6] Scott, A., Semmens, L. and Willoughby, L., Women and the Internet: The natural history of a research project; Information, *Communication and Society*, 2(4), 1999, pp. 541–565. Reprinted with permission.

Find out how many on-line companies have a woman director. What conclusions do you draw from your findings?

Old and new forms of learning

One of the ways the under-privileged in cyberspace can improve their situation is by the use of new forms of learning. Traditional education, especially at the post-school level, is often unsuitable for the same people who are disadvantaged in society: women, the poor, the disabled, those living in remote areas etc. Distance learning (DL), first started with the introduction of the 'open universities' in the 1970s, is a mode of education in which the teacher and the pupils are situated in dispersed locations. Teaching is carried out by the supply of material produced using non-verbal formats such as books and journals, films, audio tapes etc. and, more recently, disks. The Internet has moved DL to cyberspace by facilitating virtual classrooms as described in chapter 2. This has opened doors for many learners who have had limited opportunities before. People of any age, either sex and any level of physical or mental ability can take advantage of education now. They can learn at any time, any pace, on their own or in collaboration with peers. Their learning can be to gain a qualification, achieve a specific skill, gather knowledge in a subject of interest or as a vehicle for organisations to provide employment-based training. DL is not necessarily an alternative to traditional forms of education; it often complements classroom-based teaching. It can be used as a vehicle for peer learning such as homework groups for students, for experience sharing by small companies and for artistic collaboration such as the Art of Change project initiated by Newham Online (see case study at the end of the section). Many universities currently run courses in which both on-line and face-to-face teaching methods are used in parallel with each other. Providing lecture material on the Internet and using email-based discussion forums is a common phenomenon in most contemporary colleges and universities in the developed world. An extension of this philosophy is the development of DL programs to link universities in different countries in order to serve an international body of students by utilising the technologies and expertise available world-wide. For example, 15 educational and business organisations in Canada are using Virtual-U, an initiative which started as a research project but now offers web-based courses (Martin, 1999).

Traditionally, learning has been for young people and those who missed the opportunity at that stage remained disadvantaged all their life. Information society, the basis of the new knowledge economy, is a society of lifelong learning (LLL). In order to remain employable and increase their career prospects, workers in this economy need to update their knowledge and learn new skills constantly. Traditional education has a respected place in businesses as the provider of rounded individuals with a high degree of basic knowledge, enquiring minds and transferable skills. This must be complemented with continual LLL and organisations, often in association with educational institutions, are increasingly taking the responsibilities to create an infrastructure for it.

Virtual classrooms can help marginalised groups empower themselves. They can complement traditional teaching as well as create a forum for life-long learning thus enabling people to acquire the skills necessary to meet the demands of e-commerce.

How can life-long learning help e-commerce?

Autocracy and democracy

The development of the Internet brought with it the notion of democracy because no one controlled it and users were allowed to publish anything they wanted on it. The

The Art of Change

The Art of Change project, *Infinity Story*, undertaken with staff and children at Goodwin School in Forest Gate, aimed to use the Internet to explore new practices in learning. More than 300 people created a 40,000 word story told and illustrated on a website; a school portrait on one level, an exercise in communal culture making on another and a creative means to break down social exclusion on yet another. As the telling of the story passed from class to class, it branched in many directions, each iteration building on and interpreting what had gone before. Collective as well as individual identities were explored; children had individual ownership of their contributions and evolved mutual ownership through seeing how their ideas were developed by others. Real personal experiences were worked through by children individually and through the imaginations of their peers. The story thus provided a 'safe space' through which they were able to express significant issues relating to actual and perceived life experiences, protected by the story's fundamental humour and their relative anonymity within it. *Infinity Story* was also space in which arts and creative practice could add value to the IT requirements of the national curriculum. The Art of Change has since then been developing further projects with Newham Schools.

Loraine Leeson, the Co-Director of the project made the following comment on the experience: many aspects of the experience *Infinity Story* made possible could be found in drama groups, creative writing sessions, therapeutic work and so on. The convergence of these and the scale of participation, expandability and continuity is new. The interaction of technology and imagination opens doors to new styles and modes of learning. These processes need not be constrained by the same spatial assumptions that the national curriculum both makes and enforces – of group size, age banding, timetable, classroom, etc. This is a tremendous challenge; it is neither obvious nor simple to understand how the practice and management of education will adjust, incrementally, to the learning revolution that ICTs are ushering in. But it is clear that web-based projects may offer a new degree of integrated access to the curriculum, e.g. use of IT skills to undertake arts project which facilitates historical and geographical learning in turn dependent on numeracy skills which assist development of IT skills and so on.

(Adapted with permission from the *Newham Online Report*, 1999)

Questions

1 How would a school with high levels of student truancy, misbehaviour and underperformance benefit from a project of the above nature?
2 How can the pupils in two schools (one in urban New York, USA, and another in rural England) learn about each other through working on the above project?
3 What personal and technological skills could (a) students and (b) teachers learn from the project?
4 How can a similar concept benefit (a) a drug rehabilitation centre, (b) a youth club, (c) a young musicians' organisation?
5 Could such a project lead to greater rather than less inequality?

widespread use of emails in the mid-1990s created a great deal of enthusiasm amongst those who were searching for a quick, easy and inexpensive way to communicate. It started mainly with the academic community who had, for a long time, felt the need for a medium for consultation with colleagues world-wide without the cost of telephone bills and the bureaucracy of writing formal letters. Email was the first medium which facilitated group discussion in a format which did not require participants to receive the messages in real time and also enabled them to store all contents for future references. Commercial organisations caught on to the idea and, with the spread of e-commerce, this mode of communication provided a common forum for teams to work together without the need for the intervention of a department which collected, documented, filed and distributed all correspondence. For the first time, users were able to hold debates and discussions and make decisions via widespread collaboration with little effort, cheaply (rather than paying for an international conference) and without interference from 'above'.

Using the same ethos, organisations of all sizes were able to present themselves to an international audience and compete at an equal level with each other. They could put their views to the mass media regardless of their financial strength; for the first time companies had the opportunity to attract customers on the basis of their vision, business sense and creativity rather than organisational muscle. A website could also be used as a publication to present news, comments etc. by small and niche audience, as well as for the masses. For example, theglobe.com was started as a community website by a few students with a small capital in 1994; by 1998, they had 1.5 million members and were publishing news, stock feeds and even information on car sales (Martin, 1999). Thus, in all spheres of life, workers, individuals and business leaders found a vehicle for co-operating, competing and communicating freely and fairly; this created an image for cyberspace as a democratic medium.

E-commerce can facilitate democracy by enabling users to participate in debates and discussions with peers by email cheaply and easily. Organisations can compete equally on the strength of their vision rather than organisational muscle.

However, any 'euphoria' created by the new medium was dented by the following factors:

- A large majority of the world's population have no access to the Internet. Old-fashioned mediums such as letters and leaflets could reach them more easily than Internet-based communication. Thus, one could argue that the Internet has created a new form of autocracy which excludes the poor, technophobes and the uneducated.
- The uncontrolled nature of the Internet enables groups or individuals to abuse the system by organising violent and immoral activities. This enables the evil and the powerful to use their democratic rights to harm those who have less power such as children, minority groups and the poor.
- There is so much information in cyberspace that it is difficult to differentiate between true and false, worthy and worthless information and good and bad advice. Such lack of integrity is more detrimental to those who are innocent, such as children; inexperienced, such as the young; or unaccustomed, such as new customers. These groups are being bombarded with web-based material which often results in children being exposed to pornography, young consumers ending up in debt and new customers paying for things they do not want.
- On the one hand, the Internet gives us the power to present our views openly and publicly; on the other, it enables those in positions of power to intercept messages, watch our movements and plan actions against us.

The opportunities for democracy presented by the Internet are counter balanced by inequalities such as the lack of universal access, abuse of power and information overload due to frivolous use.

To what extent are on-line businesses a reflection of democracy in cyberspace? Answer this by investigating some business websites such as amazon.com, cnn.com or active.com (a big American sports website).

Thus, while the Internet could be used to hold public debates and iron out differences, it also has the tendency to reinforce common interests and opinions among the like-minded which may or may not be beneficial to society. The government of a country has an important role to play in addressing the above issues. It can use its regulatory powers to steer the course of e-commerce towards profitability and at the same time, it can use its political strength to create an infrastructure for efficient public services that exhibit regards to human values.

Citizen Webpage in Bangalore, India

The citizen's webpage was an initiative designed to make a repository of information about the structure and internal functioning of the Bangalore City Corporation (BCC) and its achievements publicly available for the first time in history. BCC is the focal institution involved in implementing the processes of decentralisation of local governance in Bangalore. The webpage was designed by an enthusiastic ex-Commissioner of the Corporation for the period 1998–1999 and contained the following information:

- An account of general powers vested in the BCC through municipal acts, followed by a listing of obligatory and discretionary functions.
- The constitution of the corporation and its hierarchical structure.
- Details of funds allocated and moneys spent by the Bangalore municipality on the central government-sponsored megacity (a city characterised by its large population, rapid rates of population growth and, the fact that it acts as a hub to global economic activity) projects for infrastructure development.
- A historical background of Bangalore.
- An administrative report of the BCC detailing the names of officers and assistants who have served in particular functions.
- A performance budgetary report showing financial targets and achievements.

While, in principle, the concept of the BCC initiating a webpage for citizens signalled a step towards increased public participation in municipal affairs, the experiment was left incomplete. Once the website was launched on an experimental basis, it came under severe criticism from the Indian press in terms of the page's design, layout and content. The webpage needed to be more explicit about its intended audience – the citizens. If one of the main purposes of the site is to encourage citizen-BCC interaction, then the site either needed to be interactive or to signpost channels of communication to citizens in order to provide feed-back at various stages, for example, by giving email addresses of people to direct comments and suggestions to. Regarding content, a lot of information was deemed irrelevant for citizens such as names of officers and assistants and the textual historical account of Bangalore. The fate of the website is uncertain because of the sudden transfer of the ex-Commissioner of the BCC, who had masterminded the initiative.

(Adapted, with permission, from Madon and Sahay, 2000).

Questions

1 Comment on the role of a citizens' webpage in creating a link between a local government and its citizens.
2 In what ways can the website described here meet its intended objective of the participation between public and municipal affairs?
3 How does this case contribute to the ethos of community-building in cyberspace?
4 How does it contribute to the concept of democracy in cyberspace?
5 Comment on the criticisms made by the Indian press.
6 How can the above initiative help a developing country?
7 How can the concept be applied to rural areas?

THE ROLE OF A GOVERNMENT IN E-COMMERCE

E-commerce plays an important role in the work of a government; countries world-wide have adopted the principles of e-commerce in varying degrees and for various purposes. In an international conference organised by the Italian government and held in Naples in March 2001, participants discussed the implications of e-government[7] for citizens and businesses. They addressed important organisational and social issues such as privacy,

[7] An e-commerce related term that grew out of the trend of adding the prefix 'e' to mean any activity involving the Internet.

electronic document validation and on-line direct democracy (Nuthall, 2001). The objective of the conference was to create citizens' trust in governments in terms of their accessibility and accountability and at the same time find ways to improve governments' contribution to the industry. In the UK, the government has set out a plan of action and pledged to place the country at the forefront of the knowledge economy (Pinder and Hewitt, 2001). According to government reports, 33 per cent of government services in the UK are now available on-line (Simons, 2000).[8] There are more than 1000 websites in the Netherlands providing access to governmental authorities and institutions. Other countries are also working towards creating an e-government with a view to providing support for e-commerce enterprises as well as to create an electronic democracy in which the citizens of a country are able to take part in their government's knowledge management activities. The perceived overall benefits of an e-government for citizens are (according to the Organisation for Economic Co-operation and Development (OECD) who also attended the conference, Nuthall, 2001):

Governments in countries have been taking advantage of e-commerce at different degrees with a view to manage information and create access to advice, information and services provided by the government.

- Better management of information through virtual meetings.
- Better access to advice from experts from sources internal and external to the government.
- Better information service for citizens.
- The availability of a framework for democratic decision making involving both parties (for example, by holding on-line meetings for focus groups).
- The provision of an infrastructure to support public services such as education and health.

The following is an account of some specific activities an e-government could perform and the effects they could have on society:

- Electronic polling and voting – Voting on-line enables the citizens of a country to take part in decision making when physical access to a voting station is difficult. This enables a government to include as many people as possible in decision making. Polling refers to asking people about their opinion in a matter which, in governmental terms, could be to assess the level of public support in issues such as increasing the tax on goods and services. While it could be argued that such a practice provides a forum for public debates and inclusion, it also encourages political parties to put too much emphasis on the popularity of a policy rather than its real significance for the country's prosperity.
- Electronic communication by the police – This has obvious benefits in solving crimes and tracking criminals across international borders. Integrated efforts between the police forces in different countries using the Internet can have valuable effects on drug trafficking, child pornography rings and so on. However, as we discussed already, a great deal of scepticism exists about such use of the medium. Concerns about the infringement of privacy (the police are exempted from the European data protection law), harassment of individuals and wrongful accusation based on erroneous information make this one of the most sensitive areas of the work of e-government.
- The establishment of links with other governments – The ability to liaise with governments electronically strengthens existing links and helps to create new links between countries. Significant areas, especially for underprivileged countries, are tourism, help at the time of national disasters, religious or

[8] Visit the website www.headstar.com/egb to gain access to the UK e-government bulletin.

ethnic conflicts and knowledge transfer on matters such as health education etc. We have already discussed how some developing countries have benefited from global business exchanges. Developed countries can also use electronic links to discuss international politics, trade, and military and intelligence activities. While such links speed up decisions, improve communications and therefore enhance efficiency, people are suspicious of the power it gives governments over ordinary citizens, and of the imbalance between the ability of different countries to participate.

- The co-ordination of international regulations – As we discussed in chapter 7, different regulations on customs, tax etc. in different countries pose a problem for international business activities. E-government has a role to play in co-ordinating efforts to create a global framework in a way that eliminates inconsistencies and ambiguities in these matters. This would provide support for organisations involved in global e-commerce and also protect individuals from illegal activities, unusually high charges and the consequences of the misinterpretation of on-line information.
- The establishment of intellectual property rights – Laws regarding copyright on information available on the Internet are either vague or non-existent. While large corporations have the infrastructure to safeguard themselves, individuals and small dotcom companies need government support to protect their web content from piracy.
- The establishment of an efficient regulatory framework – Government intervention is required in order to create a regulatory framework capable of supporting organisations, customers and the citizens of a country in all aspects of business and society.

An e-government can use e-commerce in electronic polling in order to have access to public opinion, collaborative police work, inter-governmental communication, copyright protection etc.

Due to the global nature of e-commerce, international co-ordination is required to make any effort by government to work. However, a great deal of scepticism exists over the use of the Internet by the government which must be dealt with.

The UK government pledged to make this country the forerunner in e-commerce. Find out what has been done so far.

The solution to these problems can be found if the representatives of governments, industries and civil welfare groups find a common forum to discuss the issues raised. We are only at the preliminary stage of significant transformation sparked by information-driven businesses. How this affects our future depends on our ability to recognise the trends, opportunities and threats presented to us in the twenty-first century and make intelligent choices.

PREDICTIONS FOR THE TWENTY-FIRST CENTURY

Lynn (2001) observes a paradigm shift in the twenty-first century from an organisation-driven societal architecture to an individual-centric one in which people are constantly striving to find an equilibrium between job, family and leisure, referred to by the author as work/life balance. This is the age in which imbalance and uncertainty co-exist with vision, opportunities and innovations. Lynn[9] goes on to predict a neo-renaissance in the near future driven by the following business trends:

- Ubiquitous business – By 2010, businesses will remain permanently open and the boundaries between companies will give way to corporate

[9] Much of the following points come from Lynn, D., *The Neo-Renaissance: Five Business Megatrends That will Transform the Marketspace*, Executive Directions; META Group, 16 February, 2001, File 136. Used with permission.

partnerships, new relationships and widespread interfaces between businesses and customers.

- Techno-convenience – By 2008, people in technologically developed countries will lead a life of automated convenience in shopping, driving, living and working. Homes will be fully Internet-enabled and pervasive computing (chapter 9) will ensure that consumers are totally connected to businesses and permanently available to receive marketing, advertising and CRM messages.
- Virtual workforce – By 2007, virtual collaboration will be the dominant business model and more than 70 per cent of information workers will be free agents who can build their reputation and resumé via a virtual reference network.
- Neo-renaissance lifestyle – By 2015, a neo-renaissance lifestyle will develop in which life and work will become increasingly community-focused and conducted in work centres built around communities. However, this lifestyle will affect fewer than 40 per cent of all information workers since significant co-ordination between employees and enterprises would be required to facilitate such lifestyles.
- Neo-renaissance business culture – In this culture, the focus will shift from the corporate site to virtual offices, collaboration centres and virtual communities. By 2005, this will be a common practice and by 2010, the virtual business manager may manage a global business from home.

Lynn predicts that by 2010, life and work will be fully integrated. People will increasingly adopt community-centric work patterns and total connectivity will enable businesses to stay in permanent contact with employees and consumers. Information workers will become free agents working in and managing global virtual businesses.

It is envisaged that mobile technologies will offer new ways to communicate. Gartner Inc. (2001)[10] makes the following predictions for the technologies of the future:

- Computing and networking devices with audio and video capabilities will be embedded in a wide variety of wearable and/or personal items such as clothes, toys, cars and cameras.
- Devices will become more powerful and versatile, with many devices performing multiple tasks, for example as a phone and camera combined.
- Built-in wireless technology will become pervasive and facilitate personal-area networks (PANs – networks connecting individuals) and wireless LANs.
- Device prices will continue to fall.
- Display technology will become cheaper, more flexible and smaller. For example, retinal projection will allow displays to be built into sunglasses.
- Wireless devices will be locatable by a computer system in its vicinity, thus providing connectivity between a mobile device and a WAN.
- Wireless Internet points will be available in public and private environments such as planes, trains and buildings.

According to the above predictions, by 2010, our mobile phones will detect our location automatically and enable us to find shops which sell products or services we want in that area, negotiate a price, consult with others in real-time and pay for the services using virtual cash., thus providing us with considerable economic advantage and convenience. However, as we saw in our earlier discussion in this chapter, this will only benefit a privileged minority of people in the world. Concerns around privacy and security will also discourage some people from taking advantage of the facilities, and employers will become increasingly weary of their liabilities as personal devices are used for corporate activities. Finally, some bricks and mortar retailers might use

[10] Used with permission from: Gartner, 'The Social Impact of the Connected Society', N. Jones, February 2000.

techniques such as product differentiation, wireless jamming, fast product evolution and the replacement of published prices by personal negotiation in order to maintain their off-line consumer base (Jones, 2001).[11]

With the help of additional information, make your own predictions for the twenty-first century.

The benefit from the success of e-commerce is vast for all those involved. We need the will to utilise the power of technology to benefit the human race as a whole, beyond boundaries and self-interests.

SUMMARY

In the last few centuries, the industrial community went through a series of developments referred to as 'waves'. The first wave was the agricultural revolution which saw improvements in farming facilities and some changes in social dynamics. The second wave came with the industrial revolution of the nineteenth and early twentieth centuries when new factories, towns and organisations were built and centralised control and a strict division of labour were exercised at workplace. An information revolution in the later part of the twentieth century started the third wave as centralisation began to give way to the philosophy of shared responsibilities and cross-functional teams. The main emphasis for organisations began to change from satisfying shareholders to building relationships with all stakeholders such as customers, trading partners and employees. Scholars describe the prospective fourth wave as a phenomenon of the twenty-first century in which the stakeholder base is extended to create a borderless world in which businesses provide the leadership and create an environment for addressing the global issues geared towards the common interests of all people.

Conflicting interests and arguments complicate the process of creating such a society. In the past, sellers had most of the power; in the new wave, buyers are in a position to make demands. Larger companies held monopolies and market strength in the twentieth century; in the knowledge economy of the twenty-first century, new and small companies are able to present a strong opposition. Both employers and employees have a lot to gain from this economy; they can function in a global arena and enjoy new alliances and opportunities by communicating with each other and their peers in cyberspace. However, they both face many new challenges surrounding the issues of security, privacy, skills development and work ethics.

From the beginning of the information revolution, the older generation remained largely ignored because they neither had the skill nor the interest to engage in technology. Young, educated and affluent men are still more likely to embrace the new economy both as consumers and as entrepreneurs. However, they are also in danger of being misled into spending too much time, money and enthusiasm on a business philosophy which is not necessarily beneficial to them in the long term. Like older people, the poor are also neglected by the new phenomenon because they cannot afford the technology and therefore do not have the skill, aspiration or the opportunity to get involved.

Developing countries have been experiencing both the positive and negative effects of e-commerce. While some countries are not in a position to use the Internet in a major way and therefore are left out of the race, those with a pool of technically qualified people and stronger communications infrastructure have been making some attempts to

[11] Read the paper for more detailed information and predictions for the future.

develop e-commerce. There is a risk that these countries might be drawn into following the footsteps of richer nations rather than developing suitable strategies for its use in their own economic development context. Although e-commerce has the potential to create a global business environment, it can easily lead to a situation in which large multinationals create a 'global shopping centre' while keeping power to themselves. Such globalisation is detrimental to society; we must look towards a global infrastructure which respects local culture, language and tastes and also is built on the basis of locally available technologies.

The Internet enables us to conduct lives from the confinement of our homes and thus isolates us from the rest of the community. On the other hand, it facilitates community building on the basis of interests, beliefs, jobs, circumstances and so on, which provide support, opportunities, help and advice. However, the interests shared in such communities may also be immoral or unethical, raising the issue of the control of the Internet. Much debate has taken place regarding whether or not governments should have the power to control the content or the right to intercept a message. There is strong opposition to it from those who believe that controlling the Internet goes against the ethos of personal freedom and that any power given to governments is open to abuse. However, there are others who think some measures are necessary to combat terrorism, religious extremism and other problems in society. The debate continues.

Women teleworkers have benefited from e-commerce as they are able to balance domestic life and work. However, while male teleworkers are normally in powerful knowledge-based occupations, most women are using technology to do low-level jobs while taking care of children in parallel. One of the ways all the under-privileged in cyberspace can improve their situation is by the use of distance learning facilitated by the Internet. It enables us to learn at any age, time or pace and thus update our skills in order to keep up with the demands of e-commerce. Through this and the other advances provided by the Internet, there is scope for the creation of a democratic society in which global communities, enterprises and individuals have the opportunity to communicate, hold public debates and co-operate at all levels. However, this theoretical view has many obstacles in real life. Governments in different countries must co-operate with each other in order to address the challenges of e-commerce. Various initiatives are in progress at governmental level for providing support for enterprises as well as to create an electronic democracy in order to enable everyone to benefit from the new economy. Scholars and business analysts predict that by 2010 we will live in a totally connected global environment; using wearable and portable devices we will be able to integrate our business and living arrangements around communities of our choice. However, this would only affect a minority of global citizens; many others would remain excluded from this phenomenon unless conscious steps are taken to prevent it.

Revision Questions

1 Describe the first three waves of industry and how they relate to organisational structure.
2 Describe the concept of the fourth wave and its potential for creating a global economy in the twenty-first century.
3 Describe how the following pairs of group are affected by the new economy:
   (a) Buyers and sellers.
   (b) Employers and employees.
   (c) Rich and poor.
   (d) Developed and developing countries.
   (e) Women and men.

4 What should governments and organisations do in order to serve the interests of each group?
5 Discuss the nature of the following conflicts
   (a) Control and freedom.
   (b) Isolation and community building.
   (c) Old and new forms of learning.
   (d) Autocracy and democracy.
   (e) Global and local.
6 What should government and organisations do in order to address those conflicts?
7 Discuss the role governments have taken (if any) in creating the global economy recommended by Maynard and Mehrtens.
8 To what extent do you agree with the predictions for the twenty-first century made in this chapter?

Discussion Questions

1 Write an essay describing the consequences of e-commerce for society in the twenty-first century for all areas of life for the whole of humankind.
2 Describe a scenario for life in the twenty-first century based on the technologies available today and the predictions for the future.

Bibliography

Ackland, B., Bridging the digital divide, *Computer Weekly*, 31 May, 2001, p. 36.

Adam, A. and Green, E., Gender, agency, location and the new information society. In B. D. Loader (ed.), *Cyberspace Divide: Equality, Agency and Policy in the Information Society*, Routledge, London, 1998.

Bellinger, R., *Electronic Engineering Times*, 5 June 1995, p. 125.

Benjamin, K., Kindergarten boss? *Computer Weekly, e.business review*, February, 2001, p. 19.

Bishop, S. and Gay, G., E-commerce in an offshore services jurisdiction, *Information Technology for Developing Countries*, Newsletter for IFIP Working Group 9.4 and Commonwealth Network for Information Technology, December, 2000, p. 11.

Burrows, R., Nettleton, S., Pleace, N., Loader, B. and Muncer, S., Virtual community care? Social policy and the emergence of computer mediated social support, *Information, Communication and Society*, 3(1), 2000, pp. 95–121.

Carter, D., 'Digital democracy' or 'information aristocracy'? Economic regeneration and the information economy. In B. D. Loader (ed.); *The Governance of Cyberspace: Politics, Technology and Global Restructuring*, Routledge, London, 1997.

Castells, M., *End of Millennium. The Information Age: Economy, Society and Culture, Volume III*, Blackwell, Malden, USA, 1998.

Classe, A., Tomorrow the world . . . , *Computer Weekly*, 26 October, 2000, p. 80.

Denning, D. E., The future of cryptography. In B. D. Loader (ed.), *The Governance of Cyberspace: Politics, Technology and Global Restructuring*, Routledge, London, 1997.

Dertouzos, M., *What Will Be. How the New World of Information Will Change Our Lives*, Judy Piatkus (Publishers) Ltd. London, 1997.

Gartner, *The Social Impact of the Connected Society*, Gartner Group Research Note, N. Jones, 7 February, 2001, COM-12-9141.

Gentile, M. and Svikola, J. J., *Information Technology in Organizations: Emerging Issues in Ethics and Policy*, Harvard Business School; 9-190-130, 15 February, 1990.

Graham, G., *The Internet: A Philosophical Inquiry*, Routledge, London, 1999.

Heeks, R., Lessons for Development from the 'New Economy', *Information Technology for Developing Countries*, Newsletter for IFIP Working Group 9.4 and Commonwealth Network for Information Technology, December, 2000, p. 7.

Kelly, L., Meeting to set e-mail code, *Computer Weekly*, 17 May, 2001, p. 4.

Lynn, D., *The Neo-Renaissance: Five Business Megatrends That will Transform the Marketspace*, Executive Directions; META Group, 16 February, 2001, File 136.

Madon, S. and Sahay, S., Democracy and information: A case study of new local governance structures in Bangalore, *Information, Communication and Society*, 3(2), 2000, pp. 173–191.

Martin, C., *Net Future: The 7 Cybertrends that will Drive your Business, Create New Wealth, and Define your Future*, McGraw-Hill, New York, 1999.

Mason, P., Impressive words, but will UK Online go far enough? *Computer Weekly*, 21 September, 2000, p. 24.

Mathieson, S., Will Net police ever patrol a global beat? *Computing*, 26 October, 2000, p. 18.

Maynard, H. B. and Mehrtens, S. E., *The Fourth Wave: Business in the 21st Century*, Berret-Koehler, San Francisco, 1996.

news special UK ONLINE, *Computer Weekly*, 21 September, 2000, pp. 26–32.

Nicolle, L., What about the workers? *Computer Weekly*, 29 March, 2001, p. 71.

Nuthall, K., Fostering democracy online, *Computer Weekly*, 29 March, 2001, p. 20.

Papows, J., *Enterprise.com: Market Leadership in the Information Age*, Nicholas Brealey, London, 1999.

Pinder, A. and Hewitt, P., Online strategy is back on schedule, *Computer Weekly*, 29 March, 2001, p. 20.

Scott, A., Semmens, L. and Willoughby, L., Women and the Internet: The natural history of a research project; Information, *Communication and Society*, 2(4), 1999, pp. 541–565.

Simons, M., Delivery pains await labour, *Computer Weekly*, 21 September, 2000, p. 30.

Spinello, R., *CYBERETHICS: Morality and Law in Cyberspace*, Jones and Bartlett, Sudbury, MA, 2000.

The Newham Online Report, 1999.

Turban, E., Lee, J., King, D. and Chung, H. M., *Electronic Commerce: A Managerial Perspective*, Prentice Hall, New Jersey, 2000.

Webster, J., Technological work and women's prospects in the knowledge economy: An agenda for research, *Information, Communication and Society*, 2(2), 1999, pp. 201–221.

Wenger, E. C. and Snyder, W. M., Communities of practice: The organisational frontier, *Harvard Business Review*, Reprint R00100, January–February, 2000, pp. 139–145.

Young, K. S., *Caught in the Net: How to Recognise the Signs of Internet Addiction – and a Winning Strategy for Recovery*, Wiley, New York, 1998.

Glossary

Abilene: an advanced backbone network developed by Nortel, Qwest and Cisco Systems to support the universities involved in developing applications for the Internet2.

Active Server Page: software tool that can keep track of the pages containing scripts and programs on a web server. When included in an HTML document it can access those pages and pass them on to the browser.

ADSL: asymmetric DSL, so called because upstream and downstream traffic travel at different speeds.

Application programming interface (API): a software tool that provides a way for one software to integrate with another.

Applications programs: programs written to perform specific tasks such as those for wordprocessing, creating websites and running games.

Application service provider (ASP): a facility of packaged applications software held and centrally managed by an organisation to be made available on-line to subscribing companies. It enables companies to buy in services they currently cannot access, and also removes the complexity of running these systems themselves.

ARPANET: the network connecting the Advanced Research Project Agency (ARPA), the body co-ordinating the research of different branches of the military in the USA, with the Stanford Research Institute and the University College Los Angeles. Set up in the late 1960s, this was the first step towards the Internet.

Artificial neural network: software mimicking the way the human brain learns and makes decisions.

ATM (asynchronous transfer mode): a packet-switched technique which uses fixed-sized packets called cells and sends data fast because it does not provide error control or flow control mechanisms.

B2B application integration: middleware solution which facilitates seamless integration of: data, information, business rules, processes, methods and portal between systems to ensure that composite applications are available to all interested parties wanting to communicate, collaborate and co-operate from geographically and organisationally dispersed locations.

Backbone network: the 'trunk lines', a country's main communications lines built by the government and its authorised telecommunications companies which support the technical infrastructure. Other, smaller networks, link to the backbone to achieve national connectivity.

Bandwidth: for an analogue service this refers to the difference between the highest and the lowest frequency within which a transmission medium carries traffic, and is measured in hertz (Hz). For digital data, bandwidth refers to the rate at which bits are transmitted and is measured in bits/sec.

Bridge: a device that interconnects two LANs of the same type.

Brochureware: a term informally used to signify a website that serves mainly as a medium of advertisement by displaying an electronic catalogue on the screen, with no facility for the actual purchase of goods and services.

Browsers: software designed to provide a graphical user interface for the world wide web, for example, Netscape and Microsoft Internet Explorer.

Bus topology: a network architecture in which the cable runs at the background (as the route of a bus) with computers connected to it with short cables.

Business process re-engineering (BPR): a business philosophy which involves going back to the basic business activities and inventing a better way to do things. It entails a fundamental rethinking and redesign of business processes in order to achieve dramatic improvements in performance.

Cable modem: a modem used by cable companies together with strategically located exchanges and satellite dishes to provide TV services to home owners. The modem separates signals into audio, video and digital and passes them on to the appropriate device (telephone, TV or computer).

Case-based reasoning system (CBRS): a CBRS consists of a case library and programs designed to solve a problem by retrieving and analysing a similar case.

Cellular digital packet data (CDPD): a service that sends short messages such as emails along the unused frequencies of an analogue cellular network.

Centralised application: software application run and maintained centrally, normally by the IT department with users accessing the processed results via dispersed terminals.

Circuit switching: a network connection techniques in which once connected, the sender and the receiver stay 'on-line' until the message is completed.

Code division multiple access (CDMA): allows users to have access to the entire frequency band, but each user is allocated a unique code by which the network can differentiate the calls.

Common gateway interface (CGI): a standard that defines a programming method for interacting with databases.

Common object request broker architecture (CORBA): defines the middleware specifications for traditional systems as well as for the object-oriented programs, thus providing interoperability between the two generations.

Communications infrastructure: an established set of rules, technologies, procedures and facilities that enables electronic communications to work effectively.

Communications technology: technology that enables the electronic transmission of data.

Competitive advantage: advantage acquired by a company by enhancing its ability to deal with customers, suppliers, substitute products and services, and new entrants to its market.

Component object model (COM): proprietary middleware specifications by Microsoft for Windows-based applications only.

Computer supported co-operative work (CSCW): a philosophy which addresses the issues arising from people working together in physically dispersed locations using technology. It considers how group dynamics, organisational behaviour and communications technologies relate to each other to provide a tool for effective teamwork in today's organisations.

Customer relationship management: this is the use of business intelligence and computer technology to interrogate the vast amount of customer information coming in through every channel of a company's computerised systems, analyse it, and feed it into the decision-making process in order to improve customer services.

D(ynamic)HTML: an extension of HTML which enables users to create a style sheet for a web document.

Data base management system (DBMS): a set of programs which allow users to create, link and maintain a database.

Data mart: a small data warehouse.

Data mining: the automated analysis of large amounts of data in order to locate patterns and trends emerging from data sources.

Data warehousing: the maintenance of a large database which is normally a collection of smaller databases used for the purpose of data mining. While smaller databases are always kept up to date, a data warehouse is normally updated less frequently.

Database: electronic filing system which stores files and links them with each other thus providing an integrated reservoir of data.

Decision support system: software consisting of integrated databases which enable managers to get the information they require for making unstructured decisions interactively.

Digital signature: a security technique based on public key encryption which works the following way: A sends a message to B using A's private key; if B is successful in decrypting it using A's public key, then it confirms A as the sender of the message.

Digital subscriber line (DSL): a technology which uses the telephone line to carry analogue data from a user while digital data is transmitted separately from the voice data in packets via a parallel line.

Directory service: software tools that maintain databases on users, services, hardware and software resources of a network, and provide on-line search facilities for users to locate information and services.

Disk drive: hardware used to hold disks which store programs and files permanently.

Distributed architecture/system: computer system which facilitated the processing of data where it originates. Thus, in this mode, each department of an organisation has its own computer system to serve the department's data needs. These systems are interlinked via a central computer system for the organisation.

Distributed processing: the distribution of jobs in geographically dispersed areas but linked to each other by the infrastructure of an organisation.

Domain Name Service (DNS): an Internet directory service users have to register with in order to receive an address.

Domain name: an address in the form of levels of names (which are translated into numbers by the network) allocated to each Internet site which enables users to connect to find it.

Dynamic disequilibrium: a state in which companies continually dismantle the old order of economic activity (technological, organisational and managerial) and simultaneously invent and build a new one.

EDIFACT: EDI for Administration, Commerce and Transport, the international standard for EDI use.

Electronic bulletin board: an electronic notice board run by special software that enables users to exchange views and ideas.

Electronic data interchange: company-to-company transfer of data using a standardised format via linked computers.

Email: an electronic messaging service which allows the transfer of text messages between computers linked by a network.

Encryption: the process of crypting data by applying a ciphering algorithm and a security key; the ciphered text is then passed through the network which, at the receiving end can be deciphered by applying a decrypting algorithm and a key.

Enterprise resource planning (ERP): an ERP system is software that links together all databases of a company – marketing, production, finance, procurement etc. The purpose of a corporate ERP system is to optimise resources by enterprise-wide information and knowledge sharing.

Ethernet: protocol for the bus topology.

Expert system: computer programs that capture the knowledge of human experts as an electronic database of knowledge (knowledge base) and use it to solve problems by applying reasoning methods based on logical deduction.

eXtensible Markup Language (XML): an updated version of HTML, it is a standard for the development of rules, procedures and systems to integrate applications over distributed systems.

eXtensible Style Language (XSL): acts as a style sheet for XML documents.

Extranet: website shared by a number of trading partners (see below) using a private wide area network.

Field: each type of data in a record is a field representing one aspect of the record such as product ID, product name etc.

File: a collection of data organised in a hierarchical order of fields, records and files. Thus a product file has records on each product.

Firewall: an electronic barrier preventing certain users from accessing certain areas of an organisation's network.

Fourth-generation programming language (4GL): a language which provides a tool for non-programmers to develop software. A code generator converts it into program instructions.

Frame relay: a technique in which a message from a LAN is sent to a router which converts it into variable length 'frames' with only a small amount of error checking information.

Frequency division multiple access (FDMA): works by dividing the available frequencies of transmission in an area into a number of channels, with each user making a call being allocated one channel.

Frequency: the rate at which the signal repeats the pattern; it is measured in hertz.

Gateway: a device that interconnects two LANs of different types.

Giga: a billion.

Gigabit ethernet: a high speed (10 Gb/s) fibre optic technology for LAN to LAN data transfer suitable for intranets and groupware use.

Gigabyte: a million megabytes, a billion bytes.

Graphical user interface: the on-screen display of text, icons and buttons with which users can select and click in order to access the features of applications software. Makes using a computer easier for a non-expert.

Groupware: software designed for a team of workers to share documents and files electronically and work on them interactively the same way they would if they were sitting round a table.

Hardware: physical parts of a computer system such as CPU, disk drives, keyboard etc.

HDSL: a symmetric technology with speed between 1.544 or 2 Mb/s and a cable length of 3.7 km.

Hierarchical DBMS: database in which the relationship between records follows a top down, one-to-many pattern.

Homepage: the interface used as the entry point to a company's website.

Hypermedia DBMS: uses the concept of linking (cross-referencing) text to each other by hypertext links the same way pages on the Internet are linked.

Hypertext Markup Language (HTML): a programming language based on Internet standards used to create webpages with text, graphics etc. plus links to other pages (hyperlinks).

Hypertext Transfer Protocol (HTTP): a protocol that enables a software designer to use HTML to design a webpage with text, graphics, animation etc.

Hz: hertz, the unit for frequency.

Icons: the realistic graphical representation of electronic tasks. For example, the picture of an open folder to represent the zone which, when clicked, facilitates the opening of a file.

IDSL: an ISDN-based DSL. It works on the same customer equipment as ISDN for a fixed monthly charge and supports a speed of 128 Kb/s in both directions.

Infomediaries: intermediaries which sell information.

Information and communications technologies (ICT): computer networks and associated technologies used for electronic communication of information.

Information infrastructure: an effective support system that would enable a user to connect to an information network from anywhere easily, reliably and inexpensively.

Information society: a society in which economic development and therefore the quality of life depend on the exploitation of information and advances in knowledge.

Information superhighway: a digital transmission system that facilitates high-speed and reliable connectivity between all users of an information network.

Information system: a computer application based on database technology which processes business data to provide information to users in a presentable format. An information system uses and integrates technologies to meet the information needs of a company.

Input device: hardware used to put data into a computer, for example, keyboard and mouse.

Intelligent agents: software tools that search a networked environment by keywords and queries, and retrieve information. They can also monitor user movements on the Internet, 'sense' their requirements, and provide assistance by filtering information.

Interface: the software or hardware device connecting two components of a computer system. Graphical user interface is the easy-to-use screen display that separates a user from the intricacies of hardware and software.

Intermediaries: companies involved in the processes a product has to go through between the preliminary state, e.g. the raw materials from the farmer and the finished product – a tin of baked beans in the customer's hands.

Internet: the worldwide network of networks combined with an established infrastructure that enables all users to connect to each other.

Internet Corporation for Assigned Names and Numbers (ICANN): the authority which has been assigned the job of overseeing the process of domain name allocation and address distribution.

Internet2: technology to support high bandwidth applications such as multimedia and virtual reality via the Internet. It is designed to enable people in remote locations to work together as if they are in the same office with applications such as on-line laboratories and distance learning centres.

Internet server: holds software resources which enable the computers in a company to communicate with the Internet.

Internet service provider (ISP): companies which sell Internet services to individuals and businesses by connecting to the country's information backbone.

Intranet: a company network based on the model of the Internet. It uses the Internet technologies (with linked webpages) to communicate information internally, out of bounds to the outsiders.

Ipv6: a standard based on encryption and authenticity control which enables two computer systems to establish an encryption mechanism and session keys before the transmission starts.

ISDN (integrated services digital network): network connection technology that uses both circuit and packet switched services and facilitates the transmission of both analogue and digital data.

Java applet: Java program segments written to interact with a web browser; can be written and saved separately to be used in an HTML document.

Java: an object oriented programming language originally introduced for Internet applications. It is highly portable as it is not created for any specific hardware or operating system. Java can access a network and draw graphics but cannot handle a browser.

Just-in-time: a business process in which a company orders goods only when required rather than holding a large stock.

Keyword search: the search for documents from a database using a word as the key. This method is used widely to find documents on the Internet, for example Yahoo!, Alta Vista etc.

Knowledge management infrastructure: an infrastructure that provides an enterprise with a framework for making knowledge available where it is required, thus providing the foundation for the management of knowledge.

LAN (local area network): a network within a limited geographical area, for example, one building or a campus.

Lightweight directory access protocol (LDAP): a DS standard supported by Netscape, Microsoft and Novell which is a simpler version of X.500.

Links (hyperlinks): the system of linking websites and documents on the Internet to facilitate the movement between related sites.

Linux: an open source and free operating system more recently introduced than Unix, also used mainly by midrange computers.

Mainframe: big and powerful computers used by large organisations for backend legacy systems.

Management information system: a group of general-purpose systems consisting of computer programs, people and procedures integrated with each other in a way that enables it to monitor the operations within the company.

Mega: a million.

Memory: the space inside the computer used by programs and data when the computer is on.

Middleware: harmonises a company's backend information systems with the services and applications running on the Internet.

Minicomputer: as mainframe but smaller in size and capabilities; used mainly by medium sized companies. They are called midrange computers these days.

Modem: a device that connects a computer to a telephone line by converting the digital data to voice-type data acceptable to the telephone network. At the receiver end, the data is converted back by another modem to the digital format before it is accepted by a computer.

Motherboard: the base of a PC which holds the circuit boards with chips and the connections between them.

Multiplexer: a device that interleaves electronic signals coming through a number of channels and sends them via one channel.

Network attached storage (NAS): provides improved file sharing between users, economics of scale, compatibility with existing technology and so on. Initially used by small networks it is now being used more widely.

Network computers (NCs): low-power, low-speed (dumb) terminals connected to the Internet which use applications software available on the Net rather than storing them on their hard disk. This provides low cost and high speed access to software.

Network DBMS: known as the many-to-many relationship, this model facilitates relationships such as one employee can belong to many projects and each project can have many employees.

NSFNET: the backbone to the network connecting the academic communities in the USA in the early 1980s. It was supported by the National Science Foundation (NSF) and was loosely connected to the ARPANET.

Object oriented programming: a programming concept that treats real-world entities such as people, places, things etc. as objects, attaching properties and codes to them. These are called into the program as required.

Object oriented databases (OODBMS): uses the object oriented programming (OOP) technique by storing the properties of data and their processing methods as objects.

Open source operating system: OSs that come with source (program) code which enables users to adapt them to their specific needs.

Operating system: a suite of programs that run a computer system by facilitating communication between hardware and software.

OSI (Open Systems Interconnection): the standard in data communication established by the International Standards Organisation (ISO). It follows a set of protocols with seven layers.

Output device: hardware used to display the results of processed work, for example, printer, VDU.

Packet switching: in this mode, a message is broken up into equal-sized 'packets' which are sent separately and sometimes via separate routes. They are collected at the receiving end and reassembled.

Payment gateway: hardware interface connecting the Internet and a financial network which provides authorisation for clearing of cheques, credit cards etc. and payment.

Primary key: an identifying data in a record with a unique value such as a product code for products file.

Private data network: an electronic communication system belonging to a particular organisation.

Private key encryption: a symmetric-key encryption technique which uses the same key at both ends.

Processor: the central processing unit (CPU) of a computer responsible for running the computer.

Procurement: the process of negotiating quality supplies at an acceptable price and with reliable delivery.

Programming language: the language used to write programs. It moved on from machine code (strings of 0s and 1s), to mnemonic code (abbreviations resembling instructions), to high level (using English words, called the third-generation language), to eventually, a fourth generation of language which provides a programming tool for non-programmers.

Protocols: a set of rules or conventions which govern the way a message is transmitted from the sender to the receiver in a network, quickly and efficiently,

Public key encryption: an asymmetric key encryption technique which works on the basis of public–private key pairing system in which users with a private key can give a pairing public key to anyone they wish.

Public key infrastructure (PKI): provided by some designated certification authorities (CA) it requires all legitimate users to register with a CA. The CA creates a digital certificate, an electronic document that keeps a record of the users and their public keys, and also takes charge of all the technical and procedural aspects of data encryption.

Public switched data network (PSTN): utilises a telephone line and circuit switching technique to make a connection by dialling a number.

RADSL: a variation of ADSL which adjusts itself automatically according to varying conditions and lengths of copper cabling.

RAM (random access memory): a part of memory which is empty when a computer is switched on, and used during processing to hold programs, files and data.

Record: a set of records are repetitions of the same pattern of data on different items in a file. Thus, each record in a product file record has a value for product ID, product name, and so on.

Relational database (RDBMS): the most popular database model because it facilitates all types of relationships by organising files in tables and linking the tables rather than records.

Repeater: sometimes a signal loses its strength during transmission; a repeater in a network boosts the signal.

Ring topology: network architecture in which computer terminals are connected in a ring shape with no hierarchy in the architecture.

ROM (read only memory): a part of memory which holds the programs which starts a computer when switched on. These programs cannot be altered by users.

Router: a device which finds the best route between the sender and the receiver before a message is passed on.

Scripting: refers to a programming language that can interact with the browser but cannot access a network or draw graphics.

Search engine: software designed to facilitate keyword search on the Internet, for example, Yahoo! and AltaVista.

Secure electronic transactions (SET): first introduced by Visa and Mastercard in 1997, it a protocol based on digital certificates and encryption. It is more secure than SSL because it gives the merchant only the order information. The payment information is sent to a payment gateway for authorisation before money changes hands.

Secure sockets layer (SSL): a protocol developed by Netscape which works on the basis of the exchange of digital signatures between the client and the server components of a network.

Silicon chip: a crystal of a chemical element called silicon with special electronic properties.

Software: programs and data for a computer.

Spreadsheet: an electronic worksheet containing rows and columns of data. Calculations involving the data are performed automatically and when data is updated the spreadsheet does the recalculation immediately.

Standard generalised markup language (SGML): a standard developed by the ISO which outlines the rules to be followed by programming languages such as HTML and XML.

Standards: standards in ICT are protocols which are accepted by organisations as the standards to follow.

Star topology: follows the centralised model – a computer in the centre is the processor, with terminals at the end of the spikes.

Storage area network (SAN): a separate network designed to handle storage needs, sometimes used by large systems to create a shared storage facility across a high-speed network. It can include hard disks, magnetic tapes and CD-ROMs, and communication takes place via fibre optic channels.

Structured query language (SQL): a fourth-generation programming language that allows users to set queries for a database.

Supercomputers: large computers containing rows of many small processors. Each instruction to be executed is divided into a number of small ones all processed together in parallel with each other by the processors.

Supply chain: all the bodies involved in a complete business chain ranging between when raw materials are acquired and the products reach the customers.

T lines: a fast data transfer technology involving multiplexing to carry a number of channels together: T1 lines carry: 24–30 channels (each at a speed of 64 Kb/s), T2 carries 96–120 channels, T3 carries 480–672, and T4 carries 1920–5760 channels.

TCP/IP (Transmission Control Protocol/Internet Protocol): the widely followed, five-layered protocols for Internet-based transmission.

Telecommunications infrastructure: the provision of underlying computer network capabilities to support a variety of services based around electronic communication.

Telecommunications: communication by electronic means.

Teletext: a text-based, non-interactive service that provides information from corporate information systems to customers over national TV channels.

Time division multiple access (TDMA): enables three users to use the same frequency on a time-share basis thus reducing overcrowding.

Trading partner: any company that an organisation does business with, for example, dealers, suppliers, customers, banks and so on.

Transborder data flow: international EDI.

University Corporation for Advanced Internet Development (UCAID): a body with the objective to provide software to support for Internet2.

Unix: an open source operating system used mainly by midrange computers.

URL: an address in a specific format that identifies a user on the Internet. This address has to be keyed in a specified location on a website in order to connect to the user's website.

Value added network (VAN): networks set up and managed by private companies or a combination of private channels and national data networks which users can connect to for a price. A VAN often services a specialised user group such as financial institutions.

Value chain: stages of business processes which add value to a product or a service at each stage.

VDSL: a high speed version of ADSL.

Venture capital: the capital provided for a new business undertaken by persons other than the provider.

Videotext: product information held in databases in text and graphics forms made available on TV screens by companies participating in these services via telephone lines. This was an interactive system which enabled customers to place orders for goods and services on-line.

Virtual private network (VPN): the creation of a secure network environment for an organisation by 'tunnelling' data over the Internet using encryption, authentication and other security standards.

Virtual reality modelling language (VRML): defines a 3D model using objects which can be linked to an HTML document in order to create virtual reality applications.

Virus: a program introduced into a computer system and designed to destroy or damage the system and also attach itself to the hardware devices connected to it. This way it spreads from one system to another destroying every program it comes into contact with.

W3C: a consortium in charge of developing a common standard for the WWW.

Webpage: a page on a website on the Internet.

Website: the interface that represents a user's presence on the Internet. Furnished with text, graphics, animation and hyperlinks it enables access to various facilities offered to the user.

Wide area network (WAN): a network which goes beyond the boundaries of a building or company site within a limited area.

WIMP: Windows, Icons, Mouse, Pointers/Pull-down menus; graphical user interface for programs.

Windows: graphical user interface available with PC operating systems such as Microsoft Office 2000 and applications software such as wordprocessors and databases.

Wireless applications protocol (WAP): a protocol that enables cellular network operators to translate the contents of the Internet into a format suitable for mobile phones. It also facilitates the display of Internet pages on the screen of the phone and provides search facilities.

World wide web (WWW): the interconnection of documents linked to each other on the Internet.

X.500: a DS standard supported by the International Standards Organisation.

Index of Case Studies and Examples

1-800-FLOWERS 34

Anderson-Charnley 125
Art of Change 276
Autodesk 223

British Gas 80

Charles Schwab 215
Cisco 145
Citizen Webpage in Bangalore 278

Dulux Paints 268

Edmunds.com 212
Eduard de Graaff 238
Ernst & Young 248

Firefly Network 254
First Direct 32
Ford Motor Company 12
Freeserve 22
Friends Provident 129
Frito-Lay 140

Hanson Construction 183
hmv.com 14
Hyatt Hotels 52

Kao Corporation 58
KPMG 77

Lucent Technologies 112

Mansfield Motors 150
Mercury News 50
Merrill Lynch 65

Nottinghamshire County Cricket Club 15
NSPCC 230

Recipe for Success 156

Sabre Group 119
Sainsbury's 39
Schlumberger 177
Staples 38

UK Repossession Page 270
Unilever 56
Urbia.co.uk 192

W. H. Smith 164
Watford Electronics 198
Wedgwood 175
World Bank 74

Index of Subjects

7 Cs 149

access control list (ACL) 125
Active Server Page (ASP) 160
ADSL 111
Advanced Research Project Agency (ARPA) 18
affiliation 33
Africa 27
AIX 144
allocation of access 244
anarchy 25
analogue signals 99
Apache 97
applet 159
applications programming interface (API) 160
architecture for e-commerce 224
ARPANET 4, 18
ASP (applications service provider) 163
association analysis 147
asymmetric keys 123
asynchronous transfer mode (ATM) 110, 114
authentication 122
  token-based 126
authorisation 122
autocracy 275
automatic teller machines 28
availability of webpages 79

B channels 109
B2B
  communication 81
  e-commerce 8
B2C
  communication 78
  e-commerce 8
back-end systems 94
bandwidth 98
bankers automated clearing services (BACS) 179
base station controller 115
binary digits 93
British Telecom (BT) 26
boundary rules 212
branding 191
bridges 100
brochureware 11
brouter 100
browser 21, 139
BS 7799 251

building
  business processes 226
  customer relationships 193
  information systems 237
  infrastructure, *see* infrastructure
bus topology 103
business concept innovation 57, 207, 209
business intelligence software 78
business process re-engineering (BPR) 35, 57, 182, 197, 214
business processes 34

C2B e-commerce 9
C2C e-commerce 9
Cable & Wireless 26
cable modem 113, 114
cells 115
cellular digital packet data (CDPD) 116
cellular modem 115
central processing unit (CPU) 92
centralised network 103
certification authorities (CA) 123, 237
CGI (common gateway interface) 160
China 27
ciphering algorithm 122
circuit switching 109
clearing house automated payment system (CHAPS) 179
client-server network 103
Clipper chip 187
co-axial cables 99
code division multiple access (CDMA) 116
Common Object Request Broker Architecture (CORBA) 144, 228
communication channels 98
communities 72, 268
communities of practice 268
community building 267
company boundaries 213
competitive advantage 82
component-based assembly 228
Component Object Model (COM) 144, 228
Computer Misuse Act 185
computer supported co-operative work (CSCW) 30, 57
computer system, the concept 92
computer telephone integration (CTI) 113
confidentiality 122
configuration 213

connected decentralised 68
contingency plans 243
contracts 184
control 27, 269
copyright 186
core strategy 209
corporate IQ 67
creating awareness 245
critical success factors (CSF) 220
CSNET 19
customer
  behaviour 195
  benefits 210, 211
  differentiation 193
  interface 107, 149, 211
  magnet 213
customer relationship management (CRM) 66, 71, 144–149
customer-facing processes 225
customising relationships 193, 223
cyberspace 29

D channels 109
Darwinian approach 192
database management system (DBMS) 137
  hierarchical 138
  hypermedia 138
  network 138
  object-oriented 138
  relational 138
data mining 66, 71, 145
  warehousing 66, 145
Data Protection Act 185
Data Protection
  register 247
  registrar 247
  Tribunal 249
databases 135–139
decentralisation 68
decision support system (DSS) 78
dedicated lines 109
defence programme 242
delivery system 170
dematerialisation 182
democracy 275
Department of Defense, Research and Education Network (DREN) 121
developed countries 264
developing countries 27, 265
developing e-commerce 228
deverticalisation 182
DHTML 158
Digicash 179
digital
  certificate 123
  nervous system 133
  signature 123
  subscriber line (DSL) 111
  video disk/display (DVD) 95
directory services 107, 142
discrimination 186
disintermediation 37, 182
distributed processing 96, 103
distribution channels 181
domain name service (DNS) 107, 119, 120
drop shipping 173
dynamic
  co-operation 62
  disequilibrium 67
dynamic network structure 29

EBP service provider (EBPSP) 180
e-business 56, 169
e-cash 179
e-enterprise 169
electronic bill payment (EBP) 180
Electronic Commerce Directive (ECD) 184, 185
electronic
  data interchange (EDI) 4, 10
  fund transfer (EFT) 179
  intelligence 132
  polling 279
  procurement 174
email server 104
emergent strategy 208
employees 261
employers 261
encryption 122
enterprise
  framework model 70
  portal 80, 162
  resource planning (ERP) 71, 81, 142–144
environment 44
environmental scanning 68
escrow agencies 187
ethernet 103
Ethernet Gigabit 113
European Data Protection Directive 247
European Directive on digital signatures 187
European Economic Area (EEA) 251
European Union (EU) 26, 184, 251
exit rules 212
expert systems 139
extended organisation 72
extensible
  markup language (XML) 78, 158
  style language (XSL) 158
extranet 68, 154–155

file transfer protocol (FTP) 20
files 139
firewall 126
First Virtual 180
first wave 257
five forces model 82
Fordnet 10
fourth
  generation language (4GL) 93, 137
  wave 258
  world 259
FpML 159

frame relay 110, 114
freedom 269
frequency division multiple access (FDMA) 115
frequency of signals 98
front-end systems 94
fulfilment 181
  intermediaries 173

gateways 100
gender 274
general packet radio service (GRPS) 117
generalised markup language (SGML) 155
gigabyte (GB) 95
gigahertz (GHz) 95
global
  communities 265
  information infrastructure 25
  Internet exchange 37
  system for module (GSM) 116
Global Information Infrastructure Commission (GIIC) 28
globalisation 265, 267
government 278–280
graphical user interface (GUI) 96
groupware 30, 68, 70, 152–154

hand-held PCs (HPC) 94
hardware 92
HDSL 111
hierarchical organisation 29
high level language 93
human resources 224, 227
hypertext handlers 97
hypertext markup language (HTML) 20, 78, 157
hypertext transfer protocol (HTTP) 20, 139

IDSL 111
iMode 117
implementation of e-commerce 223
infomediaries 38
information and communications technologies (ICT) 23
information
  creation 62
  democracy 54
  infrastructure *see* infrastructure
  management infrastructure 132
  overload 66
  superhighway 22
information systems
  building 226
  infrastructure 108
  quality 79
information society
  cultural definition 49
  economic definition 48
  occupational definition 48
  spatial definition 48
  technological definition 47
infrastructure
  building 225–228
  information 21–25
  operational 108, 171
  technical 106, 227
input devices 94
integrated circuit 93
integrated on-demand network (ION) 118
Integrated Services Digital Network (ISDN) 107, 109, 114
integrity 122
intellectual capital 64
intelligent organisation 64, 67
intelligent agents 79, 139, 147
interface development 155
intermediaries 37
international organisation for standards (ISO) 101
Internet
  access 119
  backbone 23, 118
  business benefits 36
  business environment 31
  connectivity 24
  operability 24
  origin 18
  privacy 24
  revolution 28
  security 24
  server 104
  service provider (ISP) 23, 118
Internet Assignment Number Authority (IANA) 120
Internet Engineering Task Force (IETF) 122
Internet Society (ISOC) 120
inter-organisational network 44
intranet 68, 149–152
intra-organisational communication 82
intrapreneurship 208
IP (Internet protocol) 126
  address 119
  Security (IPSec) 126
isolation 267
IT strategies 55, 105
iterative design 161

Japan 26
java 97, 159
java virtual machine 159
just-in-time (JIT) delivery 173, 205

knowledge
  acquisition 75, 193
  assessment 75
  background 135
  capture 135
  development 75
  distribution 76
  economy 63, 66
  goals 75, 77
  identification 75, 135

knowledge (*cont.*)
management 69
framework 75
infrastructure 69, 78, 135
systems 142, 161
retention 76
retrieval 135, 139
rule-based 135
sharing and distribution 76
tacit 135
utilisation 76

laptops 94
large companies 260
layers of protocols 100
learning 275
learning organisation 64
legal
aspects of e-commerce 182
framework 169
less developed countries (LDC) 27
libel 186
Linux 97
local area network (LAN) 78
local communities 265
logistics 169, 181

machine code 93
mainframe 93
management information system (MIS) 78
managing
change 230
information 53
market research 189
market-facing enterprise 72
marketing 169, 188–196
marketplace 175
marketspace 29
markup 155
measurement of business performance 224
megabyte (Mb) 95
megahertz (MHz) 95
memory 95
men 273
mercury 26
metaphor 49
microprocessor 93
microwave towers 98, 115
middleware 97, 107, 143
minicomputer 93
mnemonic code 93
modem 99
modernist view of an organisation 46
Mondex 179
Mosaic 21
multimedia 94
multiplexer 99
multi-processing 96
multi-programming 96
multi-user system 137

national information infrastructure 22
National Science Foundation (NSF) 19
navigational tools 31
neo-renaissance 281
network
access point (NAP) 119
attached storage (SAN) 104
devices 99
servers 96
service providers (NSP) 110
Network Solutions Inc. (NSI) 120
neural computing 147
notebooks 94

Object Management Group (OMG) 144
object-oriented programming 78, 144
Office of Fair Trading 184
old generation 262
omnidirectional signals 98
open
source movement 97
systems interconnection (OSI) 101
operational
controls 243
effectiveness 205
infrastructure *see* infrastructure
procedures 243
optical fibres 99
organisation
definition
behavioural 44
traditional 44
global 54
understanding 43
Organisation for Economic Co-operation and Development (OECD) 184, 279
output devices 95
outsourced warehousing 172
outsourcing 228

packet switching 109
packets 109
pagers 118
password control 125
payment infrastructure 169, 176
peer-to-peer transaction (P2P) 142
Perl 97
personal communications services (PCS) 118
personal digital assistant (PDA) 94
personnel security 243
perspectives on information 49–53
physical controls 243
planning strategy, approaches to
predict and prepare 214
power 215
structural 216
point-to-point tunnelling protocol (PPTP) 126
police 279
polling 103
poor 263
portal 38

Porter, Michael 82
post-modern view of an organisation 46
predictions 281
primary key 137
priority rules 212
privacy 24, 213, 246–253
private data network (PDN) 78
processor 95
  speed 95
procurement 35, 169, 174
product differentiation 84
protocols 100
public key
  encryption 123
  infrastructure (PKI) 123, 237
Public Switched Telephone Network (PSTN) 109, 114
purposeful approach 192
Python 97

RADSL 111
random access memory 92
rational branding 192
reach 31
read only memory 92
regulating the Internet 71
Regulation of Investigatory Powers (RIP) Act 187
re-intermediators 38
repeater 100
resource management 197
return on investment (ROI) 221
rich 263
richness 32
rights of access 244
ring topology 103
risk management 197, 224
risks in security 240
router 100
rule-based knowledge 69SABRE 10

Sale of Goods Act 184
Samba 97
satellite 115
scripting language 159
search engine 21, 79
second wave 257, 260
secure
  electronic transaction (SET) 178
  sockets layer 123
security 24, 107, 223
  of trading 187
self-renewal 61–63
service development 182
SETCo 178
silicon chip 93
small and medium size enterprises (SME) 93
small companies 260
software 92, 96
spam 185
spreadsheet 97
star topology 103
step-wise implementation 229
storage area network (SAN) 104
storage devices 95
strategic
  intent 208
  planning 208
  positioning 205
  potential 218
  resources 210
strategy
  5 Ps 206
  art 207
  formulation 208, 217
  simple rules 207, 221
streaming
  audio 113
  video 113
structured query language (SQL) 137
supercomputers 94
supply chain 35, 38
  management 169, 171
    B2B 173
    B2C 172
Switched Multimegabit Data Service (SMDS) 113
switching centre 115
SWOT analysis 218, 220
symbolic interpretive view of an organisation 46
symmetric key encryption 122
Synchronous Optical Network (SONET) 113
systems analysis and design 160

T lines 113, 114
tacit
  behaviour 134
  knowledge 135

tags 157
taxation 183
technical controls 244
technical infrastructure *see* infrastructure
techno-convenience 281
teleworking 262
testing 245
theory
  E 231
  O 231
third generation mobile technology (3G) 30
third wave 258, 260
time division multiple access (TDMA) 116
timing rules 212
topology 102
Trade Related Aspects of Intellectual Property Services (TRIPS) 186
trademarks 182
traditional systems 136
transborder data flow (TDF) 4
transmission control protocol/internet protocol (TCP/IP) 5, 101

transnational organisation 73
trust 236
trust building, the problems 239
TRUSTe 237, 252
Trusted Shops 252
TrustUK 251
twenty-first century 280
twisted wires 99

ubiquitous business 280
UK Smart 252
uniform resource locator (URL) 119
Universal Mobile Telecommunications System (UMTS) 116
University Corporation for Advanced Internet Development (UCAID) 107, 123
Unix 97
US Federal Trade Commission (FTC) 250
user participative design 161
user-centred design 161

validation procedures 244
value added network (VAN) 179
value chain 36
  analysis 219
  development 226
value network 211
VDSL 111
video-conferencing 30
virtual
  memory 96
  organisation 29–31
  private network (VPN) 127, 154
visibility in cyberspace 107
vision 62
VRML 158

WAIS 20
waves of industry 257–259
web-enability 79
web server 104
WebTrust 252
wide area network (WAN)
wideband CDMA 116
WIMP 96
winchester disks 95
wired connection 99, 109
wireless
  application protocol (WAP) 30, 116
  communication 114
Wireless Knowledge Services (WKS) 118
women 273
wordprocessing 97
workgroups 70
world wide web (WWW) 4, 20

X.500 143
xDSL 111, 114
XML, *see* extensible markup language
XSL, *see* extensible style language

young generation 262

E-Commerce
Context, Concepts and Consequences

N. Bandyo-padhyay

THE McGRAW-HILL COMPANIES

London · Burr Ridge IL · New York · St Louis · San Francisco
Auckland · Bogotá · Caracas · Lisbon · Madrid · Mexico · Milan
Montreal · New Delhi · Panama · Paris · San Juan · São Paulo
Singapore · Sydney · Tokyo · Toronto

LIVERPOOL JMU LIBRARY
3 1111 01005 2668

Published by McGraw-Hill Education
Shoppenhangers Road
Maidenhead
Berkshire
SL6 2QL
Telephone: 44 (0) 1628 502 500
Fax: 44 (0) 1628 770 224
Website: www.mcgraw-hill.co.uk

Editorial Director	Melissa Rosati
Acquisitions Editor	Julian Partridge
Editorial Assistant	Nicola Wimpory
Senior Marketing Manager	Petra Skytte
Senior Production Manager	Max Elvey
New Media Developer	Doug Greenwood

Produced for McGraw-Hill by Steven Gardiner Ltd
Text design by Steven Gardiner Ltd
Cover design by Leanne Harris, Aricotvert
Printed and bound by Bell and Bain Ltd, Glasgow

McGraw-Hill
*A Division of The **McGraw-Hill** Companies*

Copyright © 2002 McGraw-Hill International (UK) Limited
All rights reserved. No part of this publication may be reproduced, stored in a retrieval system, or transmitted, in any form or by any means, electronic or otherwise without the prior permission of McGraw-Hill International (UK) Limited.

British Library Cataloguing-in-Publication Data
A catalogue record for this book is available from the British Library

Library of Congress Cataloging in Publication Data
The Library of Congress data for this book has been applied for from the Library of Congress

ISBN 0 07 709857 9

Published by McGraw-Hill Education an imprint of The McGraw-Hill Companies, Inc., 1221 Avenue of the Americas, New York, NY 10020. Copyright © 2002 by McGraw-Hill Education. All rights reserved. No part of this publication may be reproduced or distributed in any form or by any means, or stored in a database or retrieval system, without the prior written consent of The McGraw-Hill Companies, Inc., including, but not limited to, in any network or other electronic storage or transmission, or broadcast for distance learning.